VANISHING MOMENTS

TITLES IN THE SERIES:

The Syntax of Class: Writing Inequality in Nineteenth-Century America
Amy Schrager Lang

Vanishing Moments: Class and American Culture
Eric Schocket

Vanishing Moments

Class

AND

American Literature

Eric Schocket

The University of Michigan Press | Ann Arbor

For

Alison, Ben, & Margot

———————————

Copyright © by the University of Michigan 2006
All rights reserved
Published in the United States of America by
The University of Michigan Press
Manufactured in the United States of America
◎ Printed on acid-free paper

2009   2008   2007   2006   4   3   2   1

A CIP catalog record for this book is available from the British Library.

Library of Congress Cataloging-in-Publication Data

Schocket, Eric, 1966–
    Vanishing moments : class and American literature / Eric Schocket.
       p.   cm. — (Class : culture)
    Includes bibliographical references and index.
    ISBN-13: 978-0-472-11569-3 (acid-free paper)
    ISBN-10: 0-472-11569-3 (acid-free paper)
    ISBN-13: 978-0-472-03187-0 (pbk. : acid-free paper)
    ISBN-10: 0-472-03187-2 (pbk. : acid-free paper)
       1. Working class in literature.   2. American literature—19th
century—History and criticism.   3. American literature—20th
century—History and criticism.   I. Title.
    PS217.W66S36   2006
    810.9'355—dc22   2006020163

Editor's Note

Eric Schocket dedicated the last two years of his life to working on this book. He died in September of 2006 of leukemia. He was in the final stages of preparing the book for publication, and appeared to be on the upswing after a year-long battle with his disease.

Yet as with everything he did, *Vanishing Moments* is emblematic of a life and career devoted to the highest standards of both political interrogation and purposeful scholarship. Eric spent most of his career in academia at Hampshire College, where he taught courses in Marxist theory and American literature. He was also active in the Radical Caucus of the Modern Language Association and the Working-Class Studies Association. In 2002, he organized an exceptional roundtable discussion on "Marxism and Working-Class Studies" at the Working-Class Conference in Youngstown, Ohio. It provoked much-needed important debate about the relationship of theory to practice, a topic which burned in Eric's life and scholarship. A transcript of the discussion, cogently and elegantly framed by an introduction by Eric, later appeared in *Rethinking Marxism,* a journal with which he had close ties.

Those who knew Eric as a person knew a stern, incisive, witty, warm, engaged, and engaging man. He thought and cared deeply about his friends, family, and comrades. He was creative and selfless, diligent and meticulous. He was also an early advocate and champion for the Class : Culture book series.

Indeed given his lifelong commitment to the examination of class and social relations, it is both fitting and joyous that *Vanishing Moments* is published as one of the first books in the Class : Culture series. His monograph needs no more honorific than the exceptional life that Eric led, the brilliant work that he did.

Bill Mullen, coeditor, Class : Culture

THE UNITED STATES is "a country where bourgeois society did not develop on the foundation of the feudal system, but developed rather from itself; where this society appears not as the surviving result of a centuries-old movement, but rather as the starting- point of a new movement; where the state, in contrast to all earlier national formations, was from the beginning subordinate to bourgeois society, to its production, and never could make the pretense of being an end-in-itself; where, finally bourgeois society itself, linking up the productive forces of an old world with the enormous national terrain of a new one, has developed to hitherto unheard-of dimensions and with unheard-of freedom of movement, has far outstripped all previous work in the conquest of the forces of nature, and where, finally, even the antitheses of bourgeois society itself appear only as vanishing moments."

—Karl Marx, *The Grundrisse*

Preface

This book project began to take shape in my mind one afternoon in June 1992, during the final day of Youngstown State University's landmark conference on labor culture in the 1930s. After a particularly moving panel, where Tillie Olsen and former activists and organizers shared their memories of that decade, an audience member stood up and made an arresting comment. He asked us to consider whether the conceit of the 1930s still held, whether our sense of nostalgia and eulogistic sentimentality were politically effective. It was one of those remarks that seemed at once stunningly disjunctive and tremendously insightful. An audience full of academics, many of us politically marginalized at our own institutions, had been deeply identifying with the victories and the defeats of the 1930s. What prompted that identification, and what sort of politics adhered in our stance?

That moment stands out for me because it was the first time I understood the complex set of emotions and expectations that readers and writers bring to their study of the working class. Even when these readers and writers are from the working class, their sentiments are multiple and viscerally felt: hope laden with fear, nostalgia weighed down with guilt, anger leavened with remorse. I was particularly struck then, as now, with how many of our own political struggles we displace onto that mythic decade. The passionate arguments over radical politics, working-class identity, and the successes or failures of the Popular Front all seem to me to exceed their historical referents. But these excesses are not incidental, and these passions are not separable from these referents. All are part of the cultural presence of labor in the United States; all must become part of what cultural critics study.

I wrote this book in order to engage the multiple presences of class and labor in American literature. I have tried, in particular, to remain mindful of the multiple emotions I experienced on that June day in

1992—the tremendous sense of solidarity and identification I felt at the panel, as well as the equally forceful perspective I gained afterward. Though class is, I argue here, a relatively specific economic process, its domain of affect is expansive. We inhabit that domain not only as workers but also as readers, writers, and critics. Since class is a process, I do not believe it is an essential aspect of individual subjects (though it effects them significantly). Rather, it adheres in the wide array of relationships between these subjects and their society and within, importantly, the modes of apprehension we employ—either unconsciously or with deep purpose—in our own examinations. Thus this is not really a book about workers and the work they do. This is a book about the image of the working class that we continually confront in U.S. literature from the first appearance of industrial fiction in the 1850s to the rise and fall of proletarian literature in the 1930s. This working-class figure is an icon that takes its place with the noble savage, the angel in the house, and other characters in the pageant of our national imaginary. Yet it is less often critically studied, because its imaginative power registers too deeply with those of us who care enough about class to study it. Our identifications are not, in this sense also, so different from the identifications of the writers who represent workers in their literature. These identifications are concentric circles around a projected center. Together they focalize the intersecting realms of class and culture.

I stress this antiessentialist approach to labor, class, and American culture because class—the key term in this relation—is so often misunderstood, ignored, or repressed. This is due, in part, to a conservative discourse that has always maintained (the facts not withstanding) that class simply does not describe the experience of people in this country, that our lives are mobile, self-fashioned, and free of determinations. But the obfuscation of class is also the product of a liberal discourse that just as insistently attempts to contain class in one or another reification—to discover it (repeatedly) in the shape of poverty, to ennoble it in the stance of resistance, to materialize it in an author, a period, or an identity. Understood in this way, class can, perhaps, inspire efforts toward recovery and recognition. But I want to argue for a different, more Marxist understanding of class, an interpretation that holds out the possibility for radical moves toward anticapitalism and economic egalitarianism. Class is totalizing, but it is simultaneously unstable. It does not describe entities and moments; it describes processes that are open to change.

On a less political note, I argue that an antiessentialist understanding of class also provides a better, more vigorous way of reading classed representations in literature. Modes of reading that treat class as an identity tend to examine representations of workers and the poor for their historical value, to ask what these representations can tell us about the lives of the people they represent. While this question is not without interest, it presumes that mimesis is always the goal, that history lies outside textuality, and that our acts of reading are relatively innocent. An antiessentialist approach to class and representation sees the problem of classed representation as itself historically contingent. The modes through which writers have engaged the working class and the poor reflect an ongoing perceptual struggle that is part of class relations. We should not, in other words, presume identities that are then represented and read. Acts of representation and reading are fundamental to identity formation and, more broadly, to the way class gets materialized in literature. These acts need to be the focus of critical study.

Toward this end, *Vanishing Moments: Class and American Literature* presents a theoretical introductory chapter followed by five historically framed readings of groups of texts that each concern one or more specific problems with the representation of class in the United States. Though these five groups move chronologically from the late antebellum period to the 1930s and early 1940s, they make no pretense of historical or literary coverage. Certain "classics" of labor literature (such as Upton Sinclair's *The Jungle*) go unmentioned, while a number of texts that have never received critical analysis (e.g., the pro-slavery, anti-industrial novels of the antebellum South) are discussed at length. This serves in part to move away from reifying the labor classics, but it also allows this study to focus on politico-discursive problems rather than on aesthetic monuments.

Two structural elements tie these chapters together. First, *Vanishing Moments* demonstrates how various attempts to represent—and, through representation, to remediate—class division have fundamentally shaped the major movements of modern literature. Because of this emphasis, coverage progresses somewhat traditionally, from the heyday of sentimental fiction (1850s), to the flowering of the realist novel (1870s and 1880s), to the influx of naturalism (1890s and 1910s), to the development of high modernism (1910s), and, finally, to the proletarian culture movement (1930s). Second, the progression of chapters shows a fitful, but clear, evolution in the works examined, toward lessening the distance between authors and their characters, the subjects and objects held in tension by the epistemological divide. *Vanishing Moments* appraises various writers' attempts to understand class through racial demarcation (chap. 2), to appropriate the voice of insurrection (chap. 3), to momentarily mimic the class Other through sumptuary signifiers (chap. 4), to manage class by disarticulating it into minute figural forms (chap. 5), and, finally, to embody class by imaginative inhabitations of the revolutionary proletariat (chap. 6). Although this progression is heuristic (since each of these tactics span beyond the specific time frames I analyze), it nevertheless demonstrates the correlation between, on the one hand, capital's successful attempt to exert greater and greater control over the working class and, on the other hand, the ever more proximate relationship experienced in cross-class representations.

Chapter 1, "The Veil and the Vision: Reading Class in American Literature," explores the theoretical and political implications of this argument in greater detail. Focusing particularly on the trope of the veil (and on the consequent action of unveiling), it introduces the book's method through selected short readings and through an extended discussion of the terms *class* and *culture*. Though such an exegesis is not the typical fare in a study such as this, a consideration of these terms' dynamic meanings is necessary in order to grant them the complexity they require. Too often, as chapter 1 argues, very real differences in method and politics are hidden beneath the assumption that we all already know what such compound terms as *working-class culture* really mean.

Once these general lines of inquiry are established, the study moves to consider the first of its five specific case studies. Though each of these studies has broad theoretical and political implications, they work through their problematics at a more microcosmic level. Chapter 2, "'Discovering Some New Race': 'Life in the Iron Mills,' Whiteness, and the Genesis of the American Labor Narrative," looks at the late antebellum era and considers America's earliest labor narratives within the context of slave labor. How did the presence of slavery in the South and the predominance of antislavery in northern reform movements affect the labor narratives of the 1850s and 1860s? What sort of language of class did these circumstances enable or prevent? Reading Herman Melville, Sarah Savage, and Rebecca Harding Davis within the context of antebellum labor papers and against the work of southern pro-slavery anti-industrial novelists reveals the extent to which the problem of slavery and the language of racial determinism inform critiques of class segmentation. Racial tropes and metaphors enable a stinging critique of the physically deformative aspects of industrial labor—but at considerable cost. The sympathy formed between writer, reader, and laborer is more or less explicitly racial. Within a nation increasingly altered by industrialism and immigration, "blackness" becomes a sign of social determination, and "whiteness" emerges as the essence of possibility, a new common property among people who have increasingly less in common.

Chapter 3, "Voices of Insurgency: Strikes, Speech, and Social Realism," looks at strikes and other labor actions in the 1880s as a collective discourse and compares the ways in which novelists responded to and transliterated workers' discursive claims. Working-class actions were predicated on the presumption of the right to free speech, as were, in a sense, the expansively "democratic" realist novels of the period. But by focusing on the Haymarket Riot, the ensuing debate over the legality of "insurrectionary speech," and W. D. Howells's fictional response in *A Hazard of New Fortunes,* chapter 3 explores the very different notions of the limits of political expression.

Chapter 4, "Middle-Class Melancholy and Proletarian Pain: The Writer as Class Transvestite," an analysis of disguised journeys into the working class, is also an exploration of nineteenth-century political culture. Here, however, actual workers are more or less absent—mimed by those sociologists, journalists, and writers who "dressed down" to map the workers' emergent culture. Yet such writers as Stephen Crane, Jack London, and Walter Wyckoff show just how assimilable this "foreign" culture turns out to be. Though working-class culture appears exotic, invigorating, and even radical, the easy trespasses of the "slumming" writer translates that culture into a commodity. Some sixty years before Beat writers would repopularize the activity, working-class culture had already become something one could simply acquire.

In chapter 5, "Modernism and the Aesthetics of Management: T. S. Eliot and Gertrude Stein Write Labor Literature," *Vanishing Moments* moves from the nineteenth-century labor narrative to the inception of high modernism in the 1910s. During this period of Taylorism, labor agitation, and the new aesthetics of the Armory Show, literary modernists joined more populist writers in a fascination with the working class. Focusing in particular on modernism's early attraction to working-class forms of speech, artifacts, and settings, chapter 5 argues for a "labor poetics" in the early work of T. S. Eliot (the "notebook poems") and Gertrude Stein (*Three Lives*). Even though these writers used working-class forms to break out of the strictures of the Victorian lyric and the nineteenth-century portrait, I show that they employed highly developed aesthetic techniques to mediate whatever freedom and energy they found in the working class. Thus modernism exhibits the same set of responses as other, less experimental literary movements: an apprehension of the working class that values its energy and vitality but that seeks to manage it within the domain of literary representation.

Vanishing Moments concludes in chapter 6, "The Fetish of Being Inside: Proletarian Texts and Working-Class Bodies," by turning to the proletarian culture movement of the 1930s. Although a number of recent studies have reinterpreted the literary leftism of this period, none have understood it as the culmination of an ongoing cultural tradition. Whether proletarian literature is understood to emerge from the Communist Party or from the Congress of Industrial Organizations, this largely middle-class movement appears strikingly isolated. By drawing on a number of proletarian novels and reading them alongside the journalism and manifestos of various cultural workers, chapter 6 offers a different, more historically consonant story. Mike Gold's messianic faith in a socialist resolve, like Meridel Le Sueur's fervent desire to enter the working-class "body," echoes and develops nineteenth- and twentieth-century antecedents. Literary modernism gave the labor narrative of the Depression era a new shape and new ways of expressing class tension, but the cultural and political drive of the narrative was, in fact, retrospective. In light of American literature's subsequent move away from depictions of labor and class, we should, I conclude, think of the proletarian culture movement as the end, rather than the beginning, of a cultural era.

ACKNOWLEDGMENTS

My book departs in two ways from previous studies of class and literature. It departs from many of the typical modes of reading these intersecting terms, making different claims for the value and function of culture under capitalism. It also departs from these studies in the same way a child ideally departs from his or her family's home—with a rich collection of facts, history, and hard-won wisdom. I want, in particular, to acknowledge the deep influence of feminist literary critics and radical scholars whose work was published while I was working on this book. I have been influenced, most significantly, by Amy Schrager Lang, Paul Lauter, Laura Hapke, Julian Markel, June Howard, Regenia Gagnier, and Caroline Porter. Rick Wolff has helped me innumerable times with the intricacies of Marx. In addition, my work on modernism and especially the 1930s owes much to the work of Barbara Foley, Alan Wald, Cary Nelson, Bill Mullen, Michael Denning, and Paula Rabinowitz. Though I occasionally take issue with their conclusions, my efforts are only possible because of their groundbreaking studies.

On a more personal note, I thank my family for their unwavering support: my mother, Eve Schocket; my sister, Luanne Schocket; my two children, Ben and Margot; and especially my partner, Alison Greene. Alison has been with me ever since this project began and has commented on every draft and made countless invaluable editorial suggestions. This book would not have been possible without her. At Stanford University, I received help and guidance from Ramón Saldívar, Albert Gelpi, and George Dekker. I thank these gentlemen-scholars for generously sharing their expertise. For support and intellectual provocation, I thank my friends Christine Alfano, Carrie Bramen, Shay Brawn, David Cantrell, Elaine Chang, John Gonzales, Miranda Joseph, Marcia Klotz, Rob Latham, Elizabeth McHenry, Lee Medovoi, Brian Rourke, David Schmidt, Tim Wandling, and Heather Zwicker. From Hampshire College, an institution that has proven to be a fine place to be a leftist critic, I thank my colleagues Aaron Berman, Christoph Cox, Alan Hodder, Norman Holland, Karen Koehler, Brown Kennedy, Michael Lesy, Sura Levine, Linda McDaniel, Bob Meagher, Monique Roelofs, Rachel Rubinstein, Eva Rueschman, Mary Russo, Lise Sanders, Susan Tracy, and Jeff Wallen. At a key moment in my research, I received a fellowship from the American Council of Learned Societies (1999–2000) and a summer stipend from the National Endowment for the Humanities (1999). I thank these institutions for their support. I also thank my editor, LeAnn Fields, and the two anonymous readers for the University of Michigan Press. Hopefully they will find this book better for their efforts. Finally, I would like to acknowledge the support and guidance that Tillie Olsen and other activists and writers of her generation have given me in my path to this book. Truly, all of us who work on American labor culture stand on their shoulders.

Material from chapter 2 previously appeared as " 'Discovering Some New Race': Rebecca Harding Davis's 'Life in the Iron Mills' and the Literary Emergence of Working-Class Whiteness," *PMLA* 115 (January 2000): 46–59. Material from chapter 4 appeared as "Undercover Explorations of the 'Other Half,' or The Writer as Class Transvestite," *Representations* 64 (fall 1998): 109–33. Material from chapter 5 appeared as "Modernism and the Aesthetics of Management, or T. S. Eliot's Labor Literature," in *Left of the Color Line: Race, Radicalism, and Twentieth-Century Literature of the United States,* ed. Bill V. Mullen and James Smethurst (Chapel Hill: University of North Carolina Press, 2003), 13–37 (copyright © 2003 by the University of North Carolina Press; used by permission of the publisher).

Contents

The Veil and the Vision

Reading Class in American Literature

They cannot represent themselves, they must be represented.
—Karl Marx, *The Eighteenth Brumaire of Louis Bonaparte*

Then, again, do not tell me, as a good man did to-day, of my
obligation to put all poor men in good situations. Are they *my*
poor? I tell thee, thou foolish philanthropist, that I grudge the
dollar, the dime, the cent, I give to such men as do not belong to
me and to whom I do not belong.
—Ralph Waldo Emerson, "Self-Reliance"

THE LOOK OF POVERTY

At a climactic moment in *Margret Howth*, Rebecca Harding Davis's
remarkable first novel, Dr. Knowles—mill owner, Fourierite socialist,
and man of science—gives Margret Howth "a glimpse of the under-life of
America."[1] "I want to show you something," he begins, "a bit of hell: out-
skirt. You're in a fit state: it'll do you good. . . . It's time you knew your
work, and forgot your weakness" (149–50). Although Howth proceeds
"indifferently" (149) on this journey, neither Knowles nor the poverty
she comes to "know" under his tutelage will allow her to remain that way.

> He led her up the rickety ladder to the one room, where a flaring tallow-
> dip threw a saffron glare into the darkness. A putrid odour met them at
> the door. She drew back, trembling.
> "Come here!" he said, fiercely, clutching her hand. "Women as fair
> and pure as you have come into dens like this,—and never gone away.

> Does it make your delicate breath faint? And you a follower of the meek
> and lowly Jesus! Look here! and here!"
>
> The room was swarming with human life. Women, idle trampers,
> whiskey-bloated, filthy, lay half-asleep, or smoking, on the floor, and set
> up a chorus of whining begging when they entered. Half-naked children
> crawled about in rags. . . .
>
> He dragged her closer to the women, through the darkness and foul
> smell.
>
> "Look in their faces," he whispered. (150–51)

As contemporary readers will likely know, this "look," this gaze over
the divide at the Other, is an integral part of nineteenth-century narratives of sentiment. Poverty and racial difference divide people (these
novels explain), but the culture of sentiment, with its expressive apparatuses, brings them together and promotes a harmony of interests. The
"look" constitutes a (previously absent) relationship—first ocular and
then emotive—between the viewer and the Other. It sets up between the
viewer, the Other, and the reader a chain of affect that, in the words of
Jane Tompkins, this mode's greatest defender, "succeeds or fails on the
basis of . . . the degree to which it provokes the desired response."[2]
But what, in this case, is the desired response? What is, to echo Tompkins once more, the "cultural work" of such looks at the classed Other?
For the majority of this labor narrative, Davis writes to humanize those
who suffer under the developing industrial regime, to satirize religious
and nationalist dictums that hide or normalize their subjugation, and—
most centrally—to create a fictive world capacious enough to encompass
a divisive society within a discursive "commonplace" (6). The rhetoric of
this particular scene is, however, anything but humanizing. Passive sentences confuse the animate and the inanimate ("The room was swarming"); parataxis blurs character into characterization and caricature
("Women, idle trampers, whiskey-bloated, filthy . . ."); and a gothic
frame denies any substantive verisimilitude. These victims of industrial
capitalism lack the contextual ties to this system of exploitation that
would make their condition comprehensible. They are, in this sense,
both abstract and embodied, emptied of any specific content but
objectified in such a way as to condense and stabilize Davis's signification
of poverty. This does not, importantly, disrupt the chain of affect that
makes this scene of unveiling so essential to the novel and that makes
reiterations of this scene so crucial to cultural representations of labor in
general. On the contrary, affective ties seem often to require just such a

condensation and stabilization. Howth is, for her part, substantially transformed by this "glimpse." A recent victim of proletarianization (her family's decline forces her to work in Knowles's mill), she has been too proud and too shocked to accept her new position as a wage laborer. The revelation of another poverty so extreme and so objectified allows her to recover her equilibrium, to regain her own sense of internal integrity through an act of displacement and sympathy. Like any epic hero, her journey to the underworld proves retrospectively to have initiated a process of ascension. By novel's end, she will be advantageously married, and her family will discover oil on their farm. As the doctor predicted, her "glimpse" of the "under-life" did her good.

In the course of *Vanishing Moments,* I will be tracing a history of cross-class representation in the United States by examining a number of such glimpses, looks, and unveilings—as well as through a more sustained analysis of several cultural moments and movements. While the mechanics of revelation and the consequences of objectification will rarely be as overt as in this passage from *Margret Howth,* I will continue to suggest that enactments of class discovery and attempts to cross the class divide cannot simply be applauded (or dismissed) for their affective power or their evident displays of humanism and concern. We need, rather, to put such displays within a historical context, to understand how they function (as they must) through larger and more complex cultural discourses and generic conventions, and to comprehend the ways in which such discourses and conventions shape the consequences of their authors' intentions.

The American labor narrative—a genre that encompasses many, but not all, of the texts I discuss in this book—is crucially formulated around a set of these conventions that together comprise a cycle of class unveiling and remediation. Though this cycle does not always appear in its entirety in the plot, it nonetheless consistently inheres in the text's component parts—its figural language, characterization, tone, point of view, and dialect. The ninety-year history of the labor novel in the United States is, in other words, a history of formal repetition as much as a history of progression and development. Indeed, during the 1930s (seventy years after the publication of *Margret Howth*), when the labor novel reached its apotheosis, class was still largely apprehended through a moment of surprise, shock, or rupture. If the compulsive reiteration of this gesture has by now inured many readers to whatever force it might optimally convey (as it had, in fact, even by the time Davis wrote *Margret Howth*), this does not lessen the import of the genre or even of this particular rhetorical move. On the contrary, repetition always signals a pressing concern, a repressed trauma that (to continue the Freudian metaphor) has not been adequately worked through. The repetitious nature of the labor narrative—its conventional revelations and resolutions—does not, in this sense, detract from this genre's meaning; it establishes it. More important, it symptomizes a larger and deeply troubled relationship between American writers and the economic structures and processes of class.

To some extent, both this troubled relationship and the repetitious nature of labor narratives emanate from these authors' conflicted desires to denounce and believe in American exceptionalism. As a descriptive term, *American exceptionalism* can be used to denote everything from a broad and unshakable conviction that the United States is free from class (a conservative notion of exceptionalism) to a belief that the differences in U.S. class formation can be explained through analyses of such factors as immigration patterns, the electoral process, and the role of the state in aiding the concentration of capital (a liberal or progressive notion of exceptionalism). There are certainly features that differentiate the United States from European countries (which typically serve as the model), including the simultaneous existence of wage and slave labor in the antebellum era and the early access white male workers had to political representation (two exceptional circumstances that I will discuss in chapters 2 and 3, respectively). Yet despite these differences, American labor writers have typically focused on exceptionalism's broader meaning and have used their acts of unveiling to testify to the presence of class beneath the exceptionalist promise of classlessness. Exceptionalism, in labor literature, becomes another name for the veil itself, "an ideological construction of a fortunate minority in the New World [and] of yearning intellectuals in the Old."[3]

Yet exceptionalism is neither simply a descriptive term that can be disproved by empirical evidence nor an ideological cover that can be peeled away. It is "a way of talking about American history and culture, . . . a form of interpretation with its own language and logic."[4] Part of this logic lies in the prescriptive modality of exceptionalism—its almost metaphysical insistence that whatever the present economic and social conditions, America should be free from inequality. Within American culture, this mode of exceptionalist thinking has had, if anything, more traction than the descriptive mode. Displacing from the present to the future the latter's vision of what Irving Howe calls "the American myth of a covenant blessing,"[5] exceptionalist thinking harnesses the energy of nationalist fantasy for the more grounded work of historical scholarship, sociological study, and labor literature. Although labor literature aims to dispel the ideological descriptions of American exceptionalism, that literature's plot resolutions, tonality, and ethical vision place it fully within exceptionalism's prescriptive ideology. Indeed, labor literature is never more fully within the domain of exceptionalism then when it angrily denounces the failure of the American promise. Its contradictory relation to exceptionalism is possible because the two ideological functions of exceptionalism are of a different order: whereas the descriptive ideology is retrospective and posits a stable set of conditions that can be falsely represented, the prescriptive ideology is prospective and dynamic, conforming to what Fredric Jameson calls an "ideological act . . . with the function of inventing imaginary or formal 'solutions' to irresolvable social contradictions."[6] This means that while the manifest content of labor literature is anti-exceptionalist, the form adheres to the exceptionalism's logic of imaginary resolution—and imaginary resolutions cannot create permanent closure. The genre's repetitious nature thus indicates its inability to exit from a system whose precepts it denounces but whose logic underwrites its terms of denunciation. Accepting America's promise, labor literature cannot but reproduce its nationalist ideological framework.

The problem of reproducing the veil of class ideology by displacing it from content to form is not limited to literary representations of labor; it finds its way, almost as insistently, into scholarly criticism. For instance, a number of studies follow Tompkins's reclamation of sensation and sentiment by focusing on the abilities of particular writers to create cross-class bonds through a sympathetic gaze.[7] These studies largely miss, however, the degree to which sympathy, as a representational mode, lies within the social relations of capitalism. It is not, therefore, a mode of connectivity that can be imported from some domestic realm of imagined immunity from capitalist class processes. On the contrary, as Thomas Haskell argues, capitalism created the "cognitive style" that made the broad structures of humanitarianism and the specific mode of sympathetic connection possible. Before capitalism revolutionized global market relations, individuals had much narrower perceptions of "their causal connection[s]" and hence of their "moral responsibility" to others beyond their immediate family and community. It was capitalism, in other words, that created the cognitive sphere within which it made sense for individuals to feel emotionally linked to others with whom they had little or no previous contact.[8] Sympathy replaced obligation as market relations supplanted older norms of caste and custom. It is the affective tie of class cultures. Indeed, according to Adam Smith's *The Theory of Moral Sentiments* (1759), sympathy works precisely like a market relation, since it constitutes compassion through what Julia Stern calls a "reciprocal ocular exchange." "By attempting to imagine the predicament of the Other," explains Stern, "the compassionate subject circulates fellow feeling back to the suffering object, who then reflects it back to the subject again."[9] This "mirror of sympathy" famously lies at the heart of the liberal subject whose reciprocal bonds with others now extend beyond the family to encompass fellow citizens of the secular nation-state. This does not, of course, mean that sympathy and sentimentalism are in any absolute sense regressive emotional responses to suffering and, specifically, to the specter of exploitation. But neither does it mean that one can simply assume that sympathy is always or even usually a progressive step toward the amelioration of suffering. Since it is the emotional currency of the very system of relations that produces class suffering, the discourse of affect may, in Ann Cvetkovick's words, "serve to contain resistance. . . . Rather than leading to social change, the expression of feeling can become an end in itself or an individualist solution to systemic problems."[10]

Other studies of class and labor in American literature have avoided the problems entailed in analyses of cross-class representation by focusing on one emblematic author or on a narrowly circumscribed period (the "Red thirties" has always been a proving ground here).[11] Although such tactics have produced a number of luminous recuperative studies, they have, for different reasons, failed to probe many of the more fundamental disjunctures between culture and class. Indeed, inasmuch as these studies tend to make class appear to be the particular property of some individual or decade, they have added to these systemic troubles; they have, that is, tended to repeat the conventional ploy indicated by *Margret Howth*—pulling back the veil to give us a glimpse of the unrecognized and unknown specter of class inequity.

Although this move continues to exert some power (literature departments now regularly teach Rebecca Harding Davis, Tillie Olsen, and other recuperated authors), it has not brought us closer to understanding the way class, as a process of exploitation and as a set of social relations structured by that process, pervades culture as a whole. The sentimental move that finds poverty veiled in the dark den of national unconscious and then rushes to bring it into the light fails to comprehend the extent to which it is itself already structured by class relations.

The long history of socio-exposé narratives—which runs from the city mystery novels of the 1840s, through Jacob Riis's *How the Other Half Lives* (1890), to Michael Harrington's *The Other America* (1963)—must (at minimum) force a consideration of the political inefficacy of such a maneuver and should cause us to wonder at the meaning of a tradition of poverty's discovery. Might such discovery serve, ironically, to root the far more general ills of capitalist exploitation in what has come to seem the familiar tableau of poverty? Whatever the intention, the objectification of class in person, period, or identity can only serve to further mystify the extent to which class always exceeds these embodiments and superintends our own processes of recognition as an ideological accompaniment to capitalism's actual processes of exploitation. Class is not, in other words, what we find on the other side of the veil in Davis's "den," or in Upton Sinclair's "jungle," or in Steinbeck's Hoovervilles. Class is what structures the veil itself, what shapes our modes of mediation, and what prompts both the act of unveiling and the too-hasty resolution of class conflict that comprises the denouement. If we are to understand the repetitions within the labor narrative as symptoms of a larger trauma of class in the United States, if we are to understand how this trauma structures even the literature of high modernism (which seems to have nothing in particular to do with class), we need to shift our focus from the referent to the act of signification, from the writers to their discourse, from the content to the frame.

FRAMING CLASS

This method of reading class in the labor narrative may become clearer if we turn to a visual image from *You Have Seen Their Faces* (1937), a documentary book about southern tenant farming by Erskine Caldwell and Margaret Bourke-White. As William Stott notes, *Faces* was published late in the documentary movement of the Depression era, when "the economic weakness of Southern agriculture and the inhumanity of the tenant system" had already "been treated in a score of books and hundreds of articles."[12] Caldwell had, in fact, written a number of these himself, including two novels: *Tobacco Road* and *God's Little Acre*. While these novels enjoyed a good deal of popular success, reviewers criticized Caldwell for his saccharine renditions of southern life and his overtly sensational depictions of rural poverty. In response, Caldwell proposed to "show that the fiction I was writing was authentically based on contemporary life in the South."[13] Collaborating with Bourke-White, a famous *Fortune* magazine photographer, Caldwell attempted to corroborate the authenticity of his vision, to prove that his fiction was, paradoxically, not fictional at all.

You Have Seen Their Faces emerged, then, at the end of the ninety-year period I chronicle in this book, at the moment when the superabundance of poverty's signification created a crisis of authenticity that signaled the conclusion of a more naive tradition of labor representation. The problem facing Caldwell and Bourke-White was not how to unveil poverty to an unsuspecting public but how to unveil it in a way that would increase the force of its representation, that would give this public a deeper sense of what they had already seen. Such a project is evident in the book's title, which self-consciously references the "looks" of nineteenth-century cross-class representation even as it resigns them to a continual past tense. The title promises to complete a voyeurism that has previously remained superficial (it seems to say, "You have *only* seen their faces"), while it recognizes that, by the late 1930s, the voyeuristic view is always a review. Though redundancy and unveiling may seem to be at odds here, as objectification and affect seemed with Davis, they are, once again, complementary. What creates the force in Bourke-White's photographs—the sense of having a powerful knowledge of the class Other—is her attention to the ritual of unveiling itself. Essential for Bourke-White is not simply that poverty "may at most times be represented almost without restraint," as it has been from the Renaissance onward,[14] but that nonrestraint becomes a subject in its own right. In short, her point is not to unveil poverty but to unveil poverty as something that is always already the object of signification.

Nowhere is this clearer than in Bourke-White's photo entitled "Natchez, Mississippi" (fig. 1). Here a woman and a man perform a set of domestic activities (she cooks; he smokes) that are, in and of themselves, unremarkable. Yet they perform them in a one-room house that lacks a fourth wall—like the set of a play (*Tobacco Road* perhaps, which was adapted for the stage and played in packed houses throughout the midthirties). While Caldwell and Bourke-White construct a narrative (ventriloquized in the caption) to explain this absence, the story is as mystifying as the image itself. Why would anyone "like it better the way it is now"? What is the benefit of self-exposure? If these questions remain unanswered, the viewer's benefit is, at least, arrestingly clear. Not only are we given a privileged view into the domestic realm, but we are shown the extent to which such a view necessarily reiterates other representational techniques that have previously broached the division between

NATCHEZ, MISSISSIPPI. "I spent ten months catching planks drifting down the river to build this house, and then the flood came along and washed the side of it off. Doggone if I don't like it better the way it is now."

MISSISSIPPI, UNITED STATES—1936: Sharecroppers living in a house without sides from Margaret Bourke-White's book *You Have Seen Their Faces*. (Photo by Margaret Bourke-White/Time & Life Pictures/Getty Images). Bourke-White and her co-author, Erskine Caldwell, fabricated the quotes featured in this and other captions.

the public and the private. The theater is, as I suggested, an obvious antecedent here; but the sentimental novel, with its easy trespass into the familial realm, may be the more significant point of departure. The difference between this photograph and the sentimental novel is, however, that this scene of unveiling is static; unlike Davis's tale of ingress, this photo captures a "den" that is always in the process of exposure. It thus functions to put our own invasiveness into play, to thematize our own pleasure in looking, in a manner that *Margret Howth*, for instance, does not.

Our own pleasure in looking is tangible, to reiterate an earlier point, because of, not despite, the sympathy we may feel for the victims of flood, poverty, and voyeurism. Looking into this house from our own positions as privileged viewers (presumably more affluent and well housed), we see a scene that is comfortably familiar, we see ourselves in more unfortunate circumstances, making the best of it, making a home. There is a certain fantasy, then, which takes the form of transposition rather than identification; the way that class appears as performance in this scene invites us to imagine ourselves with similar qualities of endurance, fortitude, and stoicism. We like to like the poor. It allows us to experience our own economic fragility, our own position within relations of exploitation, in a manner that is not endangering. This is why we like to look.

For such viewing experiences to do their cultural work, however, we require more than sympathy; we require commensurate quantities of differentiation that are apparent in Bourke-White's various compositional techniques of control. Within "Natchez, Mississippi," the evocative normalcy of the characters on the left is balanced—scopically and figurally—by the sordidness of the objects on the right. They, too, may be read through the antecedence of the sentimental narrative that repeatedly discovers an unregulated domestic economy underlying the poverty of the working class and the poor. The unmade bed suggests a promiscuous blurring of domestic activities (we cannot not know that this couple eats, sleeps, and copulates within this one room). The unordered objects on the floor convey a lack of distinction between utility and waste. And the split box announces the crucial message: at least within these unveiled scenes, poverty is constituted not through a lack of objects but through a lack of their regulation. Unordered these threaten to split the box; they may have split the house. Similarly, uncontrolled poverty threatens to rend the representational divide. This is why the framing mechanisms—the crop of the photo, the frame of the house, the frame of the box—are necessarily so predominate. If we are titillated by the exposure of our visual pleasures, we must be commensurably distanced from their points of reference. This is also why this photo has such an odd aura of stasis: the self-reflexivity of Bourke-White's technique does not make these characters seem more alive; it makes them seem moribund. They appear, finally, like animals in a diorama, like one of the habitat groups on display in a natural history museum.[15]

This analogy to dioramic representation should help return us to the theoretical point under consideration: the location of class within such representations. For just as "nature" within the dioramic construction is evidently a product of culture, "poverty" in Bourke-White's image is clearly a product of photographic presentation. Thus we find class not in what is revealed (the nobility of the domestic duo, the disarray of objects) but, rather, in the operations of revelation. Class does not refer to the objects within the visual frame; it refers to the act of framing, to a set of social relations and ideological processes through which these objects come into signification in the first place. This shift from object to process does not turn class into a discourse (the post-Marxist position) or make discourse into the totality of relations (the postmodern position). Rather, it holds representations accountable as operations deeply implicated in the exploitive relations they seek to document. Walker Evans makes much the same point when, in conversation with William Stott, he accuses Caldwell and Bourke-White of a "double outrage" toward the subjects of their book, arguing that the representation serves "[n]ot only to cheapen them, but to profit by them, to exploit them—who had already been so exploited."[16]

THEORIZING CLASS

But what does it mean to find class in the act of framing rather than in the objects being framed? What does it mean to insist on a double outrage—a repetition of exploitation enacted by representation itself? Although these two questions are deeply connected, it seems necessary to explore them separately in the next two sections because the terms *class* and *representation,* as well as *culture,* are routinely invoked without much thought about their specific meanings and interrelations at different historical moments and in different critical traditions. *Class,* in particular, is currently being "rediscovered" by literary scholars, who, consciously or not, deploy it in a manner that diminishes its analytical potential. In their attempts to animate the silent member of the triumvirate of race, class, and gender, they take class to be an identitarian principle that names a subject position: one is a member of a class in the same way that one is a member of a race or a gender. While this helps integrate class into what Nancy Frazer calls a "politics of recognition"[17]—a politics that aims to bring subordinate groups into the social and cultural mainstream—this recognition depends on some set of normative qualities that must be understood to already define the social visibility of the subjects in question. Thus the social constitution of these class qualities, the way in which they are given meaning by the social relations of production, remains outside the parameters of analysis. In short, this conception of class tends to rely on, rather than to critique, the reifications and objectifications that one finds in cultural images of poverty—what I have variously called, the "look," the "glimpse," or the "gaze."

Despite these analytic shortcomings, this particular understanding of class—as a location within a social hierarchy—has had a long history both inside the academy and within common discourse. As Raymond Williams notes, *class* has conveyed this meaning since its emergence within the English lexicon during the late seventeenth century.[18] The industrial revolution was one instigation for the rapid adaptation of this term, but the conceptual shift was also brought about by the popularization of Enlightenment rationality. The taxonomic impulse, which so evidently shaped Isaac Newton's explorations of the physical world and so clearly supplied the categorical principles behind Denis Diderot's *Encyclopédia,* fueled the movement to understand human social groups in terms of measurable attributes and capacities. The cognitive modality of classification, which by now seems a natural part of rational thought, suggests that class must name a set of hierarchical metrics within the human sciences, just as the table of elements specifies a definable totality of material within the physical sciences.[19] Something like this modality predominates currently within sociological, historical, and literary examinations of class that (often unknowingly) derive their politics and methodology from Weberian social analysis. Max Weber's core theories—that classes are relational rather than oppositional, that "[c]lass situation is . . . ultimately market situation," and that "life-chances" and market capacities determine this market situation[20]—may seem distant from current scholarship. Yet they resonate powerfully behind current scholarly trends: the multiplication of classes within sociological analysis; the focus on consumption, rather than production, as the site of social relations; and (once again) the notion that class specifies an identitarian subject position (reflective, Weber would say, of the subject's socially determinate capacities). Despite the notable sophistication of these scholarly enterprises, they still regard class as a thing, a property, whose stasis founds a descriptive and methodological web of meaning systems and social interactions.

One of the more significant limitations of this critical tradition is that it does not (indeed cannot) understand the concept of class as a product of class struggle itself and, therefore, as a signifier with historically heterogeneous meanings. *Class* was not the only—or initially even the most popular—taxonomic term for social hierarchy. The terms *rank, order,* and *station* all preexisted it and served quite adequately to demarcate a system of feudal distinctions organized around bloodlines, inheritance, homage, and divine right. The concept of class arose only with the ascendant bourgeoisie and with what Williams describes as their "increasing consciousness that social position is made rather than merely inherited. All the older words, with their essential metaphors of standing, stepping and arranging in rows, belong to a society in which position was determined by birth."[21] Mobility, ascension, self-fashioning—concepts that now seem to actually exceed the meaning of class—were once integral to its function, to its ability to express the vision of self and society at the heart of the bourgeois insurgency.

In this era (roughly 1750–1850), to be of a certain class was precisely not to be of a specific rank. Class conveyed independence and earnest self-construction. Thus, as odd as it sounds to contemporary ears, the existence of the concept of class was completely consonant with the new political values of liberty, autonomy, and independence. Indeed, this understanding of class may have been most evident during the early antebellum era in the United States, where (as countless critics have noted) bourgeois ideology developed free of any residual feudal antagonisms. Within early Republican discourse, class was understood to be part of the "natural" operations of society, a fluid marker of potential far preferable to the static, "unnatural" distinctions of caste that held sway in Britain.[22] Though I will argue in chapter 2 that this understanding of class hampered attempts to understand the economic and social effects of industrialism, it is important to note its initial power as a political concept. Until the 1850s, even workers were able to adopt this more fluid language to articulate their interests as a "producing class," in opposition to those who would exploit their labor (the "possessing class"), limit their rights, or impede their mobility. Thus, at the moment of its inception as a conceptual term, *class* was already a "struggle concept."[23] It emerged from a taxonomic mentality whose own historicity belied its claims of permanence and stability, and it empowered others to agitate and to think dynamically about social position.

I think we can usefully locate Marx's evolving theory of class within this historical moment, when new ideas about self and society both instantiated and superseded taxonomic modalities. As numerous commentators have noted, Marx uses class in different ways given different contexts.[24] In historical writings, such as *The Eighteenth Brumaire of Louis Bonapart* and *The Civil Wars in France,* and in agitational texts, such as *The Communist Manifesto,* Marx often stresses class's descriptive capacity, using it to denote groups of people in social conflict. In his later, more theoretical texts, such as *Capital, Theories of Surplus Value,* and *Grundrisse,* Marx emphasizes class as an analytical category with dynamic ramifications. Here, class clearly refers to a process, the production and distribution of surplus labor power, or what Marx alternately terms "exploitation." Stephen Resnick and Richard Wolff note that "[i]ndividuals and groups are then approached by Marx only partially, 'only in so far as they are the personifications' of aspects or 'moments' of the class process."[25] Individuals and groups still, of course, act in socially and politically meaningful ways with regard to the class process (E. P. Thompson's "class ways").[26] But these ways do not emanate from some essential, determinate class identity.

Here I follow the lead of Resnick and Wolff in seeing this concept of class as process as the most productive and ultimately the most radical of the various concepts in play both within and outside of Marxism.[27] Not only does it emerge from and motivate a dense theorization of the workings of capital, but it does so with an elegant simplicity that testifies to its (and our) historical moment. It emerges, I contend, from a substratum of Enlightenment thought that brought to the fore the radical social constructivity of identity and social situation. It stands opposed to theories of class that seek to memorialize the more taxonomic theories of that era. Though typically (and perhaps erroneously) differentiated from Marx's earlier Hegelian idealism and humanism, the concept of class as a process also reverberates with the revolutionary energies that circulated around the dynamic movements of workers in Europe and the United States. Inasmuch as this concept locates exploitation in processes that are constructed by individuals and groups, it enables strategies of resistance that do not depend on static notions of self or enshrined and immovable identities. To place its radical antiessentialism at the heart of a class analysis (as I do in this text) is thus to insist that class be understood apart from its various personifications, objectifications, and reifications—as a process that may depend on but can never be reduced to social systems of differentiation and the ideological appurtenances of cultural representation.

More pragmatically, perhaps, understanding class in this manner alleviates some of the persistent problems that have beleaguered and beguiled those who approach class from the Weberian perspective of social hierarchy and identity. Despite the ever more sophisticated methods of calibration these scholars develop to factor occupation, skill level, autonomy, income, and net worth into class identity, they constantly face the problem of individuals who move between and outside of established rubrics. How does one situate a truck driver who owns his or her own rig? What about plumbers who earn more than teachers? Critics of this sociological methodology (who believe themselves to be critics of class per se) can thus contend that class analysis consists of an egregious system of economic essentialism that necessarily fails to accurately map the social sphere of a heterogeneous nation, such as the United States. We are "a people not class," claims Michael Kazin in one recent critique of identity-based class analysis. Class is a "rhetorical abstraction" that can be used neither to predict the behavior of wage earners nor to describe the politics of the labor movement. "It is time," Kazin concludes, "for the US left to shed [this] grand and fond illusion."[28]

But if class cannot—in and of itself—describe the behavior and politics of wage earners, neither can it be written off as an illusion, immaterial to the realities of workers and to the hard-fought battles of the U.S. labor movement. Its obvious inadequacy as the essential determinate of subjectivity does not leave it historically inert. On the contrary, the Knights of Labor, the Industrial Workers of the World, and the Congress of Industrial Organizations, groups that Kazin dismisses as "essentially middle class" (an uncanny return in this critique of class),[29] were all centrally concerned with class as an object of their battles. They struggled for greater control over the extraction of surplus value from labor power. That these struggles failed to radically transform the class process is tragic; that these wage earners may have identified with some image of the "middle class" is ideologically significant. But neither point elides the central role of class, as a process of exploitation, in the constitution of these struggles—or in labor history in general. As Resnick and Wolff suggest, we need to make "the term class struggle . . . refer to the object of groups struggling, not to the subjects doing the struggling."[30] By doing so, we enable a type of class analysis that is dynamic and dialectic, not essentialist (grounding class in identity) and deterministic (grounding the utility of class analysis in the predictable behavior of these identities). We avoid, in other words, an undialectical dependence on what Peter Stallybrass calls "the purified subject of the working class"[31]—a figure who is retrospectively erected to legitimate radical struggles but whose very insubstantiality leaves these struggles open to dismissal.

An antiessentialist conception of class argues against the paradoxical commonplace that class mobility makes class irrelevant within the United States. Unlike Kazin, who grounds a critique of class in the labor movement's defeats, celebrants of mobility often ground their critique of class in labor's successes. In the spirit of Abraham Lincoln, who famously claimed, "the man who labored for another last year, this year labors for himself, and next year he will hire others to labor for him,"[32] these critics chart income and net worth over several generations to show that economic stratification was the exception rather than the rule. Yet even if this were the case (and there are a number of studies that claim otherwise), the class process remains integral to such formulations. As long as surplus value is extracted from labor power, class continues to be a relevant phenomenon both for workers and for social and cultural critics. Erik Olin Wright makes this point rather directly when he writes, "you can change all of the actual individuals in a factory in the course of a generation and yet the class structure of the factory could remain the same."[33] Such factors as job mobility and generational income disparity are also relevant, but not in the way studies of mobility typically understand them to be. The flow of workers through various jobs masks but does not negate the role of class in the extraction of surplus value. Martin Burke alludes to this masking effect when he writes, "the experience of the working class in the United States was one of anticipation, not exploitation," since workers often pinned their hopes on an escape from the wage labor system.[34] To understand this slight of hand, where capitalists conceal exploitation with the promise of future freedom, we need to avoid repeating this displacement in our own methodology. Mobility changes the experience of class, but it does not make it go away. Repressed or otherwise hidden, the trauma of class will be unveiled again during the next economic downturn or when fetishized images of poverty return to fashion.

All of my preceding arguments have in common, finally, a desire to move away from an understanding of class that sees it as an ontological category, roots it in identities and taxonomies, and thus perpetuates what Fredric Jameson calls "the error of substance and substantiality."[35] In making class a thing and in making workers *the thing*, we reify a process and blind ourselves, ironically, to ways in which this process always already works through reification. Workers are no more the embodiments of class than women are the embodiments of gender or African Americans the embodiments of race. Arguments to the contrary (or arguments that proceed from an unacknowledged acceptance of the contrary) will reproduce the same error that essentialists routinely make—ascribing to people properties that derive from them but that are not contained within them. The movement away from essentialism in studies of gender and race—as in the shift from race to "race" in Henry Louis Gates's *"Race," Writing, and Difference*—has been nothing short of paradigm shifting.[36] A comparable move from class to "class" would sim-ilarly insist that when historical actors and political agents are named (as in "the working class"), we always understand them to be positioned within a process that does not comprise the totality of their subjective constitution.[37] Indeed, the extent to which this process attempts such a totalized inscription needs to be the subject of our critique.

REPRESENTATION

From the foregoing discussion, it should begin to be clear why conven-tional readings of the economic novel, of labor literature, or even of working-class literature should prove inadequate to the task at hand. Despite their political agendas, they proceed from an identitarian understanding of class that consequently prescribes an identitarian method of textual analysis and an inevitable set of conclusions. "[T]he conventional sociology of literature or culture," writes Fredric Jameson, "which modestly limits itself to the identification of class motifs or values in any given text, and feels that its work is done when it shows how a given artifact 'reflects' its social background, is utterly unacceptable."[38] It is unacceptable, I would add, not only because identification and reflection are predicated on essentialist notions of class but because this predication means that the processes of representation (here identification and reflection) must somehow be understood to remain themselves unaffected by class and the social relations of production. Class is, in this case, what has already happened; it is a set of identities, structures, or, at best, relationships that have determined the "social background" that texts then "reflect" with greater or lesser degrees of fidelity. Empiricism becomes the handmaiden of essentialism, and together they function to cordon off from analysis exactly what is most at issue: the imbricated relationship between class processes and textual representations.

This cordoning off is not, moreover, without its political implications. To understand class as always antecedent to textuality is to limit the polit-ical agency of critical analysis to the (aforementioned) repetitive acts of recognition (to the notion that there are, in fact, class motives or values in texts). There are two likely repercussions of this approach. First, one can invoke a pluralist politics of recognition, wherein these newly visible class motives and values add to the diversity of our cultural "mosaic." This approach is favored by the nascent working-class studies movement, which, through identifying lost or neglected aspects of "working-class culture," endeavors to make sure that "the working class [will] be invited to the diversity banquet."[39] Clearly the leaders of this movement are making tactical use of the prevailing liberal discourse. But the cost of this maneuver may outweigh the benefits. To receive an invitation to the diversity banquet, one must be willing to conceive of class as an identity that is not only essentialized but worthy of celebration and affirmation. Having affirmed class identity, do we not run the risk of affirming those very processes of exploitation that engender class diversity in the first place?

This is one of the very significant differences between class and race, gender, and sexuality. Whereas race, gender, and sexuality can, arguably, name social relationships that are not structured by an unequal distribution of power (this is the dream of pluralism, after all), class—by any definition—can only name a structure, process, or position of inequality. John Guillory writes:

> [W]hile it is easy enough to conceive of a self-affirmative racial or sexual identity, it makes very little sense to posit an affirmative lower-class identity, as such an identity would have to be grounded in the experience of deprivation per se. Acknowledging the existence of admirable and even heroic elements of working-class culture, the *affirmation* of lower-class identity is hardly compatible with a program for the abolition of want.[40]

Be that as it may, since 1993, when Guillory published his argument, a number of books have been written that struggle to achieve just this kind of linkage. Arguing both that any action toward abolition needs to be prefaced by a period of recognition and that working-class culture can be defined in ways that do not foreground the experience of deprivation, these critics mount an argument for a recovery movement on par with the cultural recovery movements undertaken within women's studies and African American studies programs.[41] The problem, however, is that the action of recovery is not without its own implications in the class process. Looking backward at a working class that was, we are told, more collaborative, more politically committed, more socially engaged, and more culturally relevant prompts examinations that are, depending on the position of their authors, either nostalgic or elegiac. These examinations are themselves so infused with a psychological want (what Vivian Gornick identifies as a species of romantic attachment)[42] that they can easily gloss over the continuity of economic wants that should prompt a more abolitionist spirit.

Second, in contrast to the pluralist celebration of class diversity, one can move from an act of recognition to a statement of repudiation (that class motifs and values exist in texts but evidence a system that is intolerable). This approach, needless to say, is far preferable to the first and roughly characterizes much of the tradition of leftist literary study, at least until the rise of working-class studies in the 1990s. However, the problem here is of a more theoretical nature. Though one might assume that a textual unveiling of poverty would prompt the reader to repudiation and action, such a result is neither necessary nor necessarily efficacious. There is no requisite link between epistemological realism (which claims to know a poverty heretofore hidden from view) and political radicalism (which takes actions against economic systems of exploitation). The presumption of just such a link (as in the assertion "If they only knew . . .") is purely idealist. It is idealist in the simple sense that it takes at face value an implied state of previous innocence that is hardly tenable given the broad tradition of unveiling, and it is idealist in the more complex sense that Louis Althusser and Étienne Balibar employ when they chastise classical economics for its "empiricist idealism" that "confuse[s] thought with the real, by reducing thought about the real to the real itself."[43] In other words, those who seek to renounce exploitation simply by representing it fail to recognize the fundamental discontinuity between the real and various attempts to represent it. Moreover, to the degree that this approach also proceeds from an understanding of class as an antecedent referent to a subsequent representation, it tends to foreground a politics that is predominately cultural (since what it understands as class in these motifs and values it discovers always stands temporally *behind* us). Unless class processes are understood to be imbricated in the continual present of textual representation—to be always in evidence, always shaping cultural frames of reference—our political agency will be delimited to pluralistic celebrations or ex post facto denunciations.

It is important to insist on class as a process that is indelibly intertwined with the text's diachronic movement, since it is possible, in contrast, to read class as merely part of the literary mode of production or as simply a discursive context through which to explain the text's use of various themes and tropes. The former method is best illustrated by the various studies of authorship that tie the changing discursive norms of realism and naturalism to the professionalization of writing. While these books—almost without exception—do a fine job of establishing the material conditions for literary form, the political and theoretical horizon of class always remains foreshortened. Class is, once again, something that has happened and that then remains intact, crystallized in the textual manifestations of changing authorial labor practices.

This form of scholarship is, however, ultimately of more utility than the approach taken by such authors as Wai Chee Dimock, Michael T. Gilmore, and Mary Poovey, who, in their essays in *Rethinking Class: Literary Studies and Social Formations,* find class to be a discursive artifact, important inasmuch as it and classificatory thinking explain various obsessions of eighteenth- and nineteenth-century literature. Part of what Dimock, Gilmore, and Poovey attempt to do is valuable: using certain poststructuralist precepts, they strive to craft a "class analysis" without either a "universal determinant" or a "privileged historical subject"—goals I share.[44] But for them, this antiessentialism ends up deconstructing *class* as a meaningful term. "How can we continue to use the word with any sense of political efficacy," ask Dimock and Gilmore in their essay, "when its instrumental expression—'class struggle'—has ceased to be a vital historical force?" (1). Here they draw upon the post-Marxism of Ernesto Laclau and Chantal Mouffe, who situate class struggle as one among several contingent "articulations" of equally contingent social movements.[45] There is, within this theory, no reason to find class struggle a priori more vital than antiracism, antisexism, or anti-imperialism. And if, according to Dimock and Gilmore, no one is bothering to articulate class as the focus of struggle, then it may have no force whatsoever.

But Dimock and Gilmore's question implies even more than this. Presumably they recognize the continued existence of exploitation and resistance to exploitation as historical forces. They mean that those doing the exploiting and the resisting no longer do so under the sign of "class struggle." Thus Dimock and Gilmore pose the ontological question, does class exist if no one understands themselves to be acting as if it does? If, they contend, class no longer names an "objective identity" (3), can it name anything at all? Perhaps, answers Poovey in her essay, class is but the economic manifestation of a certain "mode of apprehension" (42) that emerged out of Enlightenment "classificatory thinking" (19). Classificatory thinking, according to Poovey, was a particularly damaging way to understand the world, since it "reproduced *as inequities* the social differentiations it purported simply to describe" (19). Class—or rather, "class"—is the root of the problem. Once we, like Dimock and Gilmore, come to see it (the term, within this argument, is also the object) as "an analyzable artifact" (2), the problem of class will simply go away. Or to be more precise, we will understand it to have already ceased to be operational beyond the purview of Enlightenment rationality. This form of thinking is what Althusser and Balibar call (in contrast to empirical idealism) "speculative idealism"—the tendency to "confuse thought and the real by *reducing* the real to thought, by '*conceiving the real as the result of thought.*'"[46] However empowering such idealisms must seem to be, they are, in the end, unable to sustain a politically efficacious and analytically sharp class critique.

A dialectical theory of class and culture must begin, instead, by understanding these two processes to be continually intertwined in an overdetermined relationship, where each combines with additional processes to provide the conditions of existence for the other. Neither process is primary, and neither is the exclusive causative agent of the other. Class processes and the economic sphere are determining factors that shape acts of representation and the cultural sphere—just as "belief in and thinking by means of specific conceptual frameworks are cultural conditions of existence of the capitalist fundamental class process."[47] This theory of an overdetermined relation between class and culture has, to my mind, a number of advantages over the approaches previously noted: it neither postulates nor implies the antecedence of class, and it thus avoids empiricism, economism, and idealism; alternately, it does not, like working-class studies and some variants of cultural studies, find culture to be, in any particular way, a resource of hope or a privileged site of rebellion. These latter approaches move too quickly from a specific rejection of economic determinism to a general underestimation of the permeability of economic forces. A theory of overdetermination helps us see that class should not be relegated to the moment of a text's generation—to the means or modes of cultural production—but, rather, that it must be understood to imbricate the text itself, to inhabit its structure, and to effect its trajectory as a symbolic act.

This does not mean, moreover, that one need eschew the insights of poststructuralism that Dimock, Gilmore, and Poovey find so useful. Indeed, overdetermination functions precisely to connect an antiessentialist theory of class to a poststructuralist understanding of discourse. Though there are, at this historical juncture, numerous variants of poststructuralist theory (some of which do, in fact, lead to a post-Marxism), all can be said to share an initial presumption that objects, forces, and processes do not exist prior to or apart from the systems of signification that give them meaning. Accordingly, the experience of class in textual representation is never anterior to or dissociable from the conceptual frameworks and the discursive tools that make it legible. It does not follow from this understanding, however, that class is merely an effect of culture or language. On the contrary, class can be shown to have an objective reality, to describe a process whereby surplus value is extracted from labor power. However, it can only be shown to have this reality through means that are already discursive and thus bound up in a system of signification. This system of signification is itself overdetermined, which is to say that it is structured by the mode of production. This distinction is crucial in many respects, since it allows us to articulate a theory of the relationship between class and culture that is simultaneously materialist and discursive. It allows us, in other words, to understand how class can be both an objective reality and a discursive construct, a reality whose objective effects are unknowable but for, in Judith Butler's words, "a temporal process which operates through the reiteration of [discursive] norms."[48]

Both the temporal and the reiterative aspects are important here, since together they call attention to the fact that this relationship is not only mutually determinant but also responsive to (and responsible for) historical change. Changes in the mode of production—which determine the way class functions in a given society—both produce and are produced by changes in these discursive norms. Thus what Fredric Jameson calls "the system of production of signs and codes"[49] is roughly correspondent—viewed historically—to the structure behind a society's economic system, to the way it produces and distributes economic value. Of course, the task of literary and cultural criticism is to explore and define the nature of this correspondence in a way that is both subtle and nonreductive. To posit a correspondence between the mode of production and culture or between class and its representations is not, to anticipate a certain objection, to assert that cultural texts cannot vary in the degree to which they enable or interfere with class processes—clearly they can agitate for a different process of distribution. Rather, positing such a correspondence asserts that cultural texts' semantic distance from the signs and codes of the predominate mode of production can only reach a certain limit before these texts cease to make sense, to be viable as symbolic acts in what Butler calls "the domain of cultural intelligibility."[50]

The correspondence between mode of production and culture may be demonstrated through the example of the realist novel, which arose sometime in the middle or late eighteenth century (depending on the account), as market capitalism came to predominate in Europe and the United States. Georg Lukács, Ian Watt, and Nancy Armstrong have each argued that this coeval emergence was, in fact, no coincidence—that, rather, literary realism arose in tandem with the middle class, whose individualistic values it uniquely expressed.[51] We may, I think, also draw the correspondence in a less identitarian manner, by pointing to the way that market capitalism itself corresponds to the formal logic of textual realism—how, for instance, its production of and dependence on atomized and alienated subjectivities matches this genre's stress on individuation through characterization. Realism's epistemological stress on the empirical, on the "hard facts" and realia of the referent, also corresponds to the bureaucratic rationalism of the marketplace under capitalism, to the newly predominate values of quantification and predictability.[52] One may postulate, thus, that if this mode of production changes and if these values no longer predominate, the realist novel (and epistemological realism generally) will become a residual form and will no longer function as the norm from which other forms deviate.

The correspondence between mode of production and culture not only works to help map the limits of a cultural form but also gives us insight into the textual conventions of a given moment—in the case of the present study, into the particular ways in which class is figured in American narratives of labor. As I have already noted, the texts that I will consider in the chapters that follow evince a decided propensity to understand class through a process of unveiling and textual remediation. Class is revealed in this cycle in the objectified bodies of the poor or of workers. It is thus stabilized, made available for a process of sympathetic identification that leaves the reader affected by the poverty of the scene but not cognizant of the extent to which this scene is discursively constituting the poverty it seeks to mimetically represent. These textual conventions correspond, I contend, to the process of commodity reification that Jameson argues is the "cultural dominant or form of ideological coding" specific to the capitalist mode of production.[53] In this sense, reification names the structural correspondence between the dominant mode of class processes and the dominant mode of cultural configuration. It provides an interpretive key, a way of understanding and theorizing the obsessions and repressions of these narratives of labor.

REIFICATION

We are, I would conjecture, most used to thinking about reification in an abstract sense, as the process through which men and women who live and work within a capitalist society become alienated from others and themselves. According to Marx, this process derives from the "commodity form" that "reflects the social characteristics of men's own labour as objective characteristics of the products of labour themselves, as the socio-natural properties of these things." Thus the "relationship between the producers . . . take[s] on the form of a social relation between the products of labour."[54] Yet reification also describes a historically specific pattern of intersubjective consciousness: the way in which people living under capitalism conceive of their world as a set of objective realities that preexist and predetermine their own sensuous activity. Carolyn Porter writes:

> The reifying process endemic to capitalism produces a new kind of world and a new kind of man. It generates, on the one hand, a "new objectivity," a "second nature" in which man's own productive activity is obscured, so that what he has made appears to him as a given, an external objective reality operating according to its own immutable laws. On the other hand, it generates a man who assumes a passive and "contemplative" stance in the face of that objectified reality—a man who seems to himself to stand outside that reality because his own participation in producing it is mystified.[55]

We can add for present purposes that such a man will tend to have a particular relationship to both class and discourse, comprehending the former as an inherent, objective attribute of individuals and the latter as a process through which this attribute is revealed. Though this man may understand himself to have a social or moral stake in the conditions of the classed Other, these conditions will appear to be external and objective, existing at a distance from his own economic and discursive activities.

Of course, the point of this is to note that the narratives of labor that men and women in capitalist society produce also tend to replicate the nexus of reified relations within that society. They replicate these relations most obviously at the structural level, where class processes are reified into fetishizations and objectifications of poverty and workers, what Ann Cvetkovich calls "the literalization of capital's structures as a process of figuration."[56] But they also replicate them temporally, when they produce a set of discursive norms that perpetuate this vision. It is no accident, thus, that the most affective moments within labor narratives are also those moments when class is most objectified or materialized as an identity. The intersubjective connections between the reader (or the reader's cipher in the text) and the classed Other follow a trajectory delineated by reification. It is in this sense, also, that we can call reification a form of "ideological coding" or, following Foucault, a "productive discourse," which is to say, a discourse that produces the relations it names. As with any productive discourse, our analysis needs to be both contextual and genealogical, not so that we may discover the specific class process that is indicated by the reified textual formulation (though this information is of interest), but so that we may better understand the discursive means through which this operation takes place. While reification names the general correspondence between the dominant mode of class process and the dominant mode of cultural configuration, we need to further specify the other forces and processes that abet in this interchange, to understand, for instance, how structures like gender and race comply with the reduction of class into fetishes of poverty and labor.

The goal of this critical exercise is not to castigate these fetishized representations in favor of some more correct configuration but, rather, to understand them dialectically as tremendous efforts to comprehend class through the signs and codes available—efforts that inevitably fail according to some absolute criterion but that nonetheless avail further investigation. What Henry Krips notes about the fetish can stand as well for other reified forms: "The function of the fetish is as much that of a screen as a memorial. That is, it stands in the place of that which cannot be remembered directly. It substitutes for that which is and must remain repressed."[57] We can, however, work indirectly in order to recount the conditions that made repression necessary, to comprehend, in other words, the cultural logic that grants power to the repetitive unveilings of class in its reified forms. Fetishization, reification, and objectification—concepts that I have variously used to explain the particular way that class is textualized—are all mediations that do not reveal class as an ontology or as an identity but that nevertheless testify indirectly to the way that class processes inescapably permeate the textual field. They are repressions, as Krips would have it, of the class process that structures signification in such a way as to mystify their own presence. But in turn, they memorialize this repression in a way that enables us to disentangle this representational nexus, to understand the evolving symbolic means through which capitalist class relations secure their conditions of existence. Even the most reified textual forms, in sum, are dialogic and multivalent. They are blocked expressions of a social relation, but they nevertheless can be rearticulated so that they relate the conditions of their blockage.

But we must ask importantly: Does such a method of reading work to disrupt these conditions, or does it merely reproduce, at a more theoretical level, the same strategies of unveiling that I criticize throughout this chapter? The initial answer must be that it may do both: while I hope that this new way of reading class and literature produces new ways of struggling against capitalist relations, the present book is a critical study, with the obvious political limitations of such a format, and I am wary of claims for the broad-reaching effects of cultural interventions. We should recognize, too, that any study of reified relations must inhabit this realm to no small extent and operate within its discursive norms. There is no Archimedean point outside the social relations of capitalism, and hence, as Laura Kipnis reminds us, there is "no transcendent, privileged cultural space on which to stand that is *outside* capitalist reification."[58] To insist otherwise is but to reify one's method rather than one's subject matter. Nevertheless, the location of agency within the process of critical cultural production and analysis remains at issue. What would constitute a disruption of the cultural conditions that make capitalism possible? More specific still, where is the point of political possibility within the overdetermined relations between class and culture? That the present study tells a tale of complicity and co-optation rather than resistance and progressive challenge is in some sense prescribed by its authorship during the height of late capitalism. However, this does not, to my mind, obviate the need to proceed with a political commitment to socialism and an ethical commitment to insist on keeping the foregoing questions open.

THE POSITION OF CULTURE

It is worth noting, in contrast, that for many on the academic left, particularly those within the field of cultural studies, the question of cultural agency is essentially settled: culture constitutes a potent resource for radical change, even if resistant cultural texts by necessity still operate within capitalist social relations. Though this conjuncture is, to my mind, mostly untenable (even if one erects Gramscian notions of counterhegemony as a sort of alternative backdrop), it is nevertheless worthy of critical consideration. The position of culture within the evolving field of cultural studies has everything to do with its relationship—usually unarticulated—to this field's understanding of class and the history of class struggle. Hence my present reorientation of class analysis toward an antiessentialist method requires a move away from cultural studies and from what I argue is its tendency toward cultural essentialism. That this cultural essentialism was the tactic cultural studies took to remedy the limiting economic determinism of essentialist Marxism is one of the more ironic aspects of the recent history of the academic Left.

The progressivism and resistance ascribed to culture within cultural studies has a great deal to do with this field's origins in postwar Britain, in the work of Raymond Williams, Richard Hoggart, and, to some extent, E. P. Thompson. As Bill Readings has argued with great clarity, the British university system was then invested in an understanding of (English) culture derived from F. R. Leavis who saw culture, and particularly literature, as the best way "to heal . . . [the] split" caused by industrialism "between mass civilization and the organic community of the *Volk*."[59] Though Williams, Hoggart, and Thompson rejected the conservative and quietist implications of this theory of culture, they shared Leavis's belief in its ability to achieve what Readings calls "a vision of social wholeness."[60] This agreement is all the more remarkable since Williams, Hoggart, and Thompson's operative definition of culture differed significantly from Leavis's. Whereas Leavis and the English academy in general adopted an Arnoldian notion of culture ("the best which has been thought and said in the world"),[61] Williams, Hoggart, Thompson, and subsequent practitioners of cultural studies borrowed ethnographic notions of culture popularized in the 1930s by anthropologists and sociologists. For them, culture was not something you gained but something you already had; it was a name for traditions, rituals, and daily habits that defined specific social bodies. Hence workers need not aspire to become "cultured," since they already had an endogenous culture, rich in its own traditions.[62]

While this vision of culture effectively destabilizes the older, hierarchical model (in which some have culture and some do not), its effect is to make culture even more integral to and affirmative of subjective identity. Whereas it was possible for Leavis to see an Englishman in need of culture (this was the problem after all), it was not possible for Thompson to feel similarly about the English working class. Their very existence as a class presupposed a set of cultural attributes. "Class happens," writes Thompson famously in *The Making of the English Working Class,* "when some men, as a result of common experiences (inherited or shared), feel and articulate the identity of their interests as between themselves, and as against other men whose interests are different from (and usually opposed to) theirs."[63] Hence culture is no longer a supplement to either class or identity; it is both class and identity. This is what Readings objects to when he complains that "the class struggle is always already a cultural struggle" in the work of these scholars, that they "refuse to understand culture as the ideological effect of the class struggle as motor of history."[64] Readings does not mean, however, that culture should be understood as merely the superstructural reflection of the mode of production. Neither do I. Rather, I want to problematize the disappearance of class—as an actually existing economic process—into culture within cultural studies and to note also that as class becomes de-essentialized within this body of work, culture is, perhaps as a consequence, essentialized.

The other genealogical background to cultural studies is, of course, the broad historical arch of Western Marxism. Though a full recounting of this history is beyond the scope of the present study, it is significant to note that Western Marxism has also focused considerable attention on culture (which it understands in the objective sense, as literature, the fine and performing arts, and mass media). This focus derives, in part, from the absence of cultural critique in Marx and most of the orthodox Marxism coming from the Soviet Union after the 1930s. However, the critique of culture also has its origins in the centrality of ideology as a concept (continually under development and revision) that explains both the subjective nature of life within capitalism and the particular position of Western Marxism outside (in both a spatial and existential sense) socialism and revolution. "The hidden hallmark of Western Marxism as a whole," explains Perry Anderson, "is that it is a product of defeat. The failure of the socialist revolution to spread outside Russia, cause and consequence of its corruption inside Russia, is the common backdrop to the entire theoretical tradition of this period."[65] The failure of the socialist revolution can be explained in multiple ways, but in the work of Georg Lukács, the Frankfurt school, Antonio Gramsci, and Louis Althusser, it is often understood to be due to the relative success of a capitalist ideology that persists, within Western Europe and North America, in mystifying workers' real conditions of existence and preventing them from seeing the enormous contradictions of consumer capitalism. Culture—which Lukács, Gramsci, Althusser, and others had once hoped might serve as a vehicle for revelation (if not radicalization)—has increasingly come to seem allied with capital, especially as advanced communication technologies have come to mediate between culture's producers and consumers. Thus culture has come to stand as the sign for the absence of working-class class consciousness (though not class itself) and overt struggle.

While culture's meaning within cultural studies is, as I have noted, exactly the opposite, it nonetheless emerges from a similar sense of the defeat Anderson describes. Responding as well to the decline of the organized Left, the practitioners of cultural studies in Britain, such as Stuart Hall and Richard Johnson, find in culture both the last bulwark against capitalist hegemony and the last best indication that the working class is still capable of resisting the ideological effects of capitalist relations. This stance became even more accentuated in the 1980s, when John Fiske, Lawrence Grossberg, and others began to publish a series of texts arguing for the productive, active, and resistant relationship that consumers have to the mass media.[66] Their studies of popular sports, consumer commodities, and syndicated television all testify not to the culture industry's rule over working-class subjectivity but to the ever new and resistant practices that workers and others (the class focus starts to blur at this point) can exercise through resistant and active mass consumption. The backdrop of Thatcher in Britain and Reagan in the United States is certainly not coincidental. Writing in the shadow of Thatcher's vicious attacks on unionized labor within the heavy industries and Reagan's landmark suppression of the Air Traffic Controllers Strike (1981), cultural studies scholars found little to hope for in either the political or economic spheres. Cultural struggle—here understood as a relatively autonomous practice of individual consumption—displaced class struggle as the locus classicus of popular agency. But even if this allowed these critics to resolutely find the glass half full—to write passionately about the agency of the subject within late capitalism—it simultaneously dematerialized exploitation as the central constitutive moment within class formation. To the extent that the subject's primary "cultural identity" arises within acts of resistant consumption, the subject's relationship to production and economic class processes remains unacknowledged. If, in other words, Williams, Hoggart, and Thompson tend to see culture as class, then Fiske, Grossberg, and their followers tend to see culture instead of class, which, of course, amounts to much the same thing.

The rise of cultural studies and of "culture" as fundamentally constitutive of both individual and group identity has had effects that are broader than many realize. Even Fredric Jameson, the preeminent Marxist scholar in the United States, argues that the critic's ability to revitalize the dormant political possibilities contained in the kinds of memorializations, repressions, and reifications that I have been discussing is what makes cultural criticism a politically important act. There is, he argues, a "political unconscious" that lies within the literary text, some "active relationship with the Real" that the text carries as an "immanent subtext." Critical intervention can reconstitute this subtext as a political consciousness, "project[ing] its . . . Utopian power as the symbolic affirmation of a specific historical and class form of collective unity."[67]

Jameson grounds much of this theory of immanent Utopianism on his particular understanding of reification. The dynamic of reification, he writes,

> is a complex one in which the traditional or 'natural' . . . unities, social forms, human relations, cultural events, even religious systems, are systematically broken up in order to be reconstructed more efficiently, in the form of new post-natural processes or mechanisms; but in which, at the same time, these now isolated broken bits and pieces of the older unities acquire a certain autonomy of their own, a semi-autonomous coherence which, not merely a reflex of capitalist reification and rationalization, also in some measure serves to compensate for the dehumanization of experience reification brings with it, and to rectify the otherwise intolerable effects of the new process.[68]

In other words, reified forms do more than testify to the destructive processes of capitalism. Distilled within them are "pieces of the older unities," synecdochic crystallizations of the past that serve to compensate for present horrors. Capitalism produces, in this sense, cultural and symbolic acts that always surpass their "specific ideological mission" of "legitimating a given power structure."[69] Though they are isolated and atomized, they transcend their moment of cultural production, hearkening back to traditional unities as a recombinant way of "projecting" a Utopian future.

Given this formal aspect of culture under capitalism, the political task of the critic is clear: "A Marxist practice of ideological analysis proper, must in the practical work of reading and interpretation be exercised *simultaneously* with a Marxist positive hermeneutic, or a decipherment of the Utopian impulses of these same still ideological texts."[70] Jameson's reading of reification thus opens up a space of dialectic possibility within the confines of the literary text. With his methodology, the texts of the past can be reactivated and milked for their Utopian impulses, an activity that transforms the critic into an activist or, at the very least, into an archivist of immanent possibility. Once again, culture is thus awarded an extremely important role. It not only constitutes, in Walter Benjamin's words, a "document of barbarism," but by doing so, it documents the possibility of barbarism's cessation; it provides the only map to the realm of freedom, which lies, Jameson tells us laconically, within the realm of necessity.[71]

Yet as appealing as this program has proven, I adumbrate it here in order to problematize it and to differentiate it from my own claims. Any attempt to mount a critical intervention must correlate such an intervention with the particular role granted to culture within the critic's theoretical system. Although those who work in cultural studies found the critic's agency within the blocked potentialities of culture, where they find what appears to be presently unavailable in other realms, my own view is less optimistic. While I do understand cultural forms as symbolic acts that continue to have a political impact beyond their moment of inception, I do not think that we can so consistently integrate this impact into a positive hermeneutic. Not every subtextual longing is for a lost unity; not all unities are worth longing for. We might, in fact, understand the predominant role of culture in a quite different manner—not as an alternative to the "intolerable effects" of capitalism (or even as a resource of hope), but as yet another register of these effects. Just as economic processes do not escape the effects of culture, culture cannot escape the economic. To award culture a privileged position outside of these effects risks both idealism and cultural determinism. While the reified forms that I have been discussing can be read critically, what they predominately reveal are the technologies of mystification that helped shape their vision. "The cultural event is . . . not the mark of political crisis," writes Peter Hitchcock, "but perhaps more significantly a process that seeks to avoid such confrontation."[72] Its tendency, in other words, is toward consolation and amelioration of the contradictions within the political and social sphere, a tendency that is aided by other forces within capitalist relations but that need not be abetted by our own misplaced optimism.

I concur with Jameson that reified forms "serve to compensate for the dehumanization of experience reification brings with it," but not that this "rectif[ies] the otherwise intolerable effects of the new process." Culture does play a compensatory role, but in most cases, it does so in such a way as to prevent, rather than enable, anything worth calling rectification. Indeed, until the 1930s, representations of labor in the United States so overwhelmingly tended to enact fictitious resolutions to real struggles over class that this may accurately be called their "cultural work." The question of culture's compensatory value, to take a somewhat different tact, must be articulated in more specific terms: who, exactly, is compensated for which dehumanization? Surely, we cannot mean that those who inspire such fetishistic accounts of their physicality—Davis's "swarming" masses or Caldwell and Bourke-White's photographic subjects—are in any way compensated for their economic exploitations. On the contrary, these people are, as Evans noted, doubly victimized. We must conclude that those who initiate this second victimization, this memorialization of class as object, are themselves compensated. Let us not forget that writers and artists are also subject to capitalist class relations. Their fetishizations of wage workers and those with no work may well be a displacement, a way of reckoning with their own positions and social relations under capitalism. Our readerly investments with these forms may also give us some compensation, depending, in this case, on our willingness to suture with these texts along the lines they prescribe. "What draws the reader of a novel," wrote Walter Benjamin, "is the hope of warming his shivering life with the death he reads about."[73] In either case, this compensation has a conciliatory ideology, which works to substitute phantasmatic rectifications (sympathy, affect, inclusiveness, a harmony of interests) for more efficacious political ruptures. "The persistent spectacle of a minor culture's suffering," concludes Lauren Berlant, "allows ineffectually preemptive collective mourning for massive and ordinary systemic failures of the nation, failures of imagination and action to which national subjects seem patriotically addicted."[74]

What is needed, in the face of this conciliatory ideology, is a steadfast refusal to be conciliated, compensated, or otherwise distracted by imaginative displacements meant to cover over the systematic causes of exploitation. When it comes to textual representations of labor, what this means, in particular, is that we need to resist being interpellated into the text's affective apparatus of identification. Indeed, "disidentification" would be a more productive critical stance, since it would lead us to explore the structural causes for inequity. Sympathetic investments in the objectified figure of the class Other are, at best, an entry point into this sort of structural and discursive analysis. Often, however, their fetishistic qualities mitigate against precisely this operation. This does not mean, of course, that we need to forgo sympathy for the actual victims of capitalism. But rather, that we should not mistake representations for real people. Further, we need to understand that since sympathy follows the lines of connection already drawn by the social relations of capitalism, it can favor structures of identification formed along racial, gender, and heteronormative lines. The next chapter expands on this last point by showing how racialized sympathy acts to forestall the development of a critique of class.

"Discovering Some New Race"

"Life in the Iron Mills,"
Whiteness, and the
Genesis of the
American Labor Narrative

Race has become a trope of ultimate irreducible differences
between cultures, linguistic groups, or practitioners of specific
belief systems, who more often than not have fundamentally
opposed economic interests.
—Henry Louis Gates, Jr.,
Loose Canons: Notes on the Culture Wars

The price of culture is a Lie.
—W. E. B. DuBois, *The Souls of Black Folk*

THE IRONY OF WHITE SERVITUDE

Writing to James Fields, assistant editor of the *Atlantic Monthly*, Rebecca Harding Davis expressed concerns about the title of her forthcoming story "Life in the Iron Mills." Testing the merits of other titles, she asked:

> What would you think of "Beyond"? I should like something suggestive of the subdued meaning of the story, but if you do not approve of that, how would, "The Korl-Woman" do? I would be sure to read an article with that caption in the hope of discovering some new race,—of Hottentots perhaps. However, I shall be satisfied with your choice—whatever it may be.[1]

This letter, which is commonly cited in critical studies of Davis's work, is usually read through the lens of feminism. A young and relatively little-published writer, Davis seems at once "playful," as Sharon Harris argues, and deferential, foreshadowing her later willingness to fit her critical vision into Field's limited appetite for gritty social realism. Yet, written on January 26, 1861, during that brief span of time between the secession of the southern states and the outbreak of the American Civil War, the letter's reference to "some new race of Hottentots" should not be considered incidental or irrelevant to the story's content.[2] Rather, as I will argue in this chapter, this "playful" reference is an indication of Davis's racial politics, the "subdued" racial content of this and other early stories of American industrial labor, and—most important—the developing relationship between the racialized language of discovery and the relatively new practice of cross-class representation.

Indeed, though Fields may have envisioned other contexts for this story, Davis was probably correct in her assessment of its place in the literary market and its more general discursive affiliations. While Fields, in the postbellum era, would replace sensationalism in the *Atlantic Monthly* with a more genteel literary realism, the cultured readers of the northeast at midcentury still regularly digested their travel literature, exotica, and urban sketches with liberal doses of physical caricature and pseudo-scientific theories of racial hierarchy. In this, they were joined by working-class urban audiences, who, through blackface minstrelsy and such institutions as P. T. Barnum's American Museum, also sought what Eric Lott calls the "racial pleasure" of otherness.[3] The African Hottentot, widely regarded as the "lowest exemplum of mankind on the chain of being,"[4] was frequently featured in the more sociological and physiological examples of this discourse and served—as Davis's letter implies—as a convenient point of reference. Davis, one might conclude, was being realistic; readers expected to discover the spectacle of liminality through a highly conventionalized and often racist set of discursive norms.

But if "Life in the Iron Mills" partakes of an antebellum discourse of racial discovery, it does so obliquely and in ways that are largely symbolic. Looking for a new race of Hottentots, one finds instead only the "smoke" and "clinging . . . greasy soot" that forms its simulacra.[5] In the world of what Davis would elsewhere term "the tobacco-stained commonplace,"[6] race is everywhere, although African American characters are not. Except for two brief references to "mulatto" women, Davis populates "Life in the Iron Mills" with "flesh begrimed" (12) white mill workers ("with a pure unmixed blood" [15]) and more affluent white observers.

Even the Korl Woman, a statue that figures the terrible hunger of work-ing-class life, turns out to be "a white woman of giant proportions" (31), carved out of industrial material with an eerie "flesh-tint" (32). Rising out of the soot and blackness and gesturing with outstretched white arms toward the sky, she is nothing so much as a racial figure for working-class possibility. Standing as she does in the center of what we have come to consider a germinal text of American industrial fiction, she casts a long white shadow that we have yet to fully see.

In what we might call the irony of white servitude, Davis employs lin-guistic conventions that invite readers to discover a "new race" but that instead gives them a new class (the working class) whose white bodies are inscribed with uncanny signifiers of blackness. Yet the substitution of race for class is more complicated still. While these signifiers are a crucial means of demarcation in an era that otherwise lacked the language to convey the social and physical effects of the new regime of industrial labor, they are unstable, transitory, and ambivalently applied. Davis means to jar readers through an initial moment of misapprehension: instead of discovering black slaves, they find industrial laborers whose bodies mimic the physical determinism of chattel servitude by bearing similar marks of bondage and oppression. Yet like other northern critics of factory labor, Davis has no particular desire to collapse race and class into one signifying system. Although blackness initially denotes the ter-rain of exploitation, it is ultimately disavowed, replaced by other, seem-ingly more essential metaphors of agency, possibility, and promise. Whiteness in particular emerges (through the smoke and greasy soot) as a new way to invoke what Davis calls "the promise of the Dawn" (65)—or, put less metaphorically, the promise that the working class will not be forever excluded from the political and social prerogatives of nine-teenth-century white skin privilege.

While Rebecca Harding Davis's short story serves as the locus of this analysis, this chapter argues that the discursive effects of working-class whiteness—or, indeed, of whiteness generally—exceed the bounds of this or any particular text. Whiteness, the figurative corollary to the white skin privilege, plays a determinate role in American culture, serving as a blank space within which a number of the contradictory premises of cap-italism and colonialism can be fictively resolved. "The problem of poverty is not repressed," argues Amy Schrager Lang, "but rather trans-lated into a vocabulary that makes its redress possible, if not inevitable."[7] Seemingly insurmountable economic conflicts between capital and labor, like equally intractable political contradictions between freedom and slavery, are enfolded into a racial process with its own adjudicating logic. Hence whiteness and the broader concept of "race" emerge in the nineteenth century as principle sites for the process of reification I discussed in chapter 1, the particular means through which textual representations of labor both manifest and remediate the discordant presence of class. Whiteness, however, is a reification of a very particular kind. It is not fixed, limited, or even visible in the same way as the demarcation we know as blackness. Yet its openness, indeterminacy, and flexibility constitute its chief ideological strengths. This was plainly the case during the antebellum era, when inhabitants of the United States witnessed the concomitant operation of industrial labor and chattel slavery and had to account for both the commonalities and differences between workers and slaves. Thus the presence of slavery at the moment of industrialization, one of America's most significant "exceptional" conditions, must stand at the foreground of any historical account of the inception of the American labor narrative and should comprise one of the principle lenses through which we read subsequent representations of labor in this nation. The irony of white servitude, I hope to show through a history of the origins of the American labor narrative and a detailed reading of "Life in the Iron Mills," is one of the most prevalent and ultimately most detrimental modes of social criticism developed to apprehend class in the United States.

At its inception, this mode of criticism reflected both the changing social conditions of the late antebellum period and the limited discourses of social critique. The irony of finding workers in the place of slaves registered a clear shift in the demographics of the labor force and in the relationship between these two modes of production. During the crucial decade of the 1850s, concludes George Taylor, America experienced "the emergence of the wage earner." For the first time in U.S. history, those who were dependent on wages (*dependent* was a word pivotal in political and literary discourse) outnumbered those who worked for themselves or had other means of support. During this same era, the number of wage earners also surpassed the number of slaves. Nevertheless, the plantation, rather than the factory, still served to symbolically link persons to broad systems of dependency within the American imaginary.[8] This linkage was reinforced (if it was not, in fact, partially produced) by the free labor, antislavery movement, which, in Eric Foner's words, "by glorifying northern society and by isolating slavery as an unacceptable form of labor exploitation," may have "served to justify the emerging capitalist order of the North."[9] Indeed, the working-class wing of this movement was fully capable of critiquing slavery while simultaneously using racism to constrain African Americans to an underclass in the North. During the 1850s, in short, northern political and economic discourse was singularly unable to account for or critique class segmentation in terms of class itself. Race became an alibi; racial tropes of dependency filled the void.

A homologous displacement, I argue here, affected the emergent literary discourse of anti-industrialism. Following the well-worn path of sentimentalism and relying, for visibility, on the veritable cult of Harriet Beecher Stowe, anti-industrial critics sought to broaden the scope of literary reform to include the plight of wage laborers. Yet that tactic was problematic: by the 1850s, the language of sentimentalism and its structures of sympathy were so oriented toward issues of race and slavery that anti-industrial social critiques tended—consciously or not—to be made in racial terms. Hence the sentimental critique of the exploitation of labor ends up carrying the baggage of a racial logic that equates whiteness with freedom and blackness with slavery. Thus such critique can find no fully adequate language for a kind of labor that is neither completely free nor precisely enslaved.

FREE LABOR

Until the 1850s—despite the abundant presence of bonded labor, slave labor, and children and women whose labor was in no meaningful way free—the concepts of freedom, work, and labor shared strong discursive affiliations.[10] In early America, labor was not understood as punishment for sin, as it had been in medieval Europe; nor was it typically associated with deprivation, as in *ponos*, the ancient Greek word for both labor and pain.[11] Labor was, rather, turned into a virtue, through what Daniel Rogers calls "a momentous act of transvaluation." Under the dictum *Laborare est orare* (To work is to pray), continues Rogers, "work itself was prayer."[12] This act of transvaluation began in the sixteenth century, as Calvinism—particularly Puritanism—established a doctrinal connection between work in one's calling and spiritual salvation. "That every man should have a calling and work hard in it," writes Perry Miller, "was the first premise of Puritanism."[13] This transvaluation broadened and affected secular ideology in the eighteenth century, as the American Enlightenment turned sacred calling into civic duty. Together, sacred and secular valuations of labor formed what Max Weber famously labeled "the Protestant work ethic." Indeed, the term *ethic,* which connotes an internally consistent moral code, captures one of the more salient aspects of this conception: labor was an act valued in and of itself—valued intrinsically—above what it could or did achieve in the world. The loss of this intrinsic valuation, which came about with the advent of a new capitalist ethic and the turn to extrinsic valuations for labor, prompted a search for an adequate language for labor in the 1850s and, more generally, propagated what we now call the "labor narrative."

The intrinsic valuation of labor within the Protestant ethic emerged from one of the central doctrinal features of Calvinism: predestination. According to the Puritan church, only the elect would enjoy salvation; the rest—the preterite masses who were damned—could do nothing to alter their condition. Unlike the process of confession, remorse, and restitution in Catholicism, for Puritans, sanctification came only from the favor of God. Hence work—or, indeed, "good works"—could not function as a means of attaining deliverance. To believe otherwise was to ascribe improper agency to humankind. Nevertheless, work in a calling had to be performed as a sign of election, as part of the anxiously maintained system of conduct that, it was hoped, gave evidence of God's grace. An "unwillingness to work," Weber wrote, was immediately recognized as "symptomatic of the lack of grace." Even if the combination of diligent labor and asceticism led to the accumulation of wealth, such worldly goals could not be labor's purpose: "hard, continuous, bodily, or mental labor" was "ordained as such by God," and hence "labor must . . . be performed as if it were an absolute end in itself."[14] To accept Puritan doctrine was thus to accept work as inherently meaningful, as the manifestation of God's wishes, and as part of the covenant of the devout.

Although such a stringent ideology did not survive, fully intact, the fall of the Puritan theocracy, the concept of the inherent value of work at a calling (or, in secular terms, at a useful occupation) continued to shape labor discourse in the early nineteenth century. The Republican Party would, in the early 1850s, bring this attitude to its apotheosis, unifying disparate political interests around the glorification of labor and gaining electoral victories with the platform of "Free Soil, Free Labor, Free Men." But even before the sectional dispute prompted such aphoristic links between labor and freedom, writers from a variety of political perspectives insisted on the organic and intrinsic, if not the salvational, value of work. While the Republican William Evarts could claim, "labor, gentlemen, we of the free States acknowledge to be the source of all our wealth, of all our progress, of all our dignity and value," no other than

Daniel Webster, the great Whig orator, could announce that "the laborer of the United States is the United States."[15] Each political party competed to draw from labor's auratic power. Even such labor radicals as George Henry Evans, Robert Dale Owen, Thomas Skidmore, and Fanny Wright distinguished their version of the labor theory of value from contemporary European models through an almost metaphysical celebration of "producerism." In their excoriations of the idle capitalist and their exaltations of the inherent valor of hard work, one heard more than an echo of their Puritan forebears.[16]

While such a broad range of people considered labor a singularly virtuous activity, intrinsically meritorious even to the most menial hireling, the labor narrative as such could not develop. The labor narrative requires more friction, the projection of an Archimedean point from which to venture external critique. Neither the presence of wage work (already common by the nineteenth century) nor even the introduction of factory labor (the first factory opened in 1790, and the Lowell mills were internationally famous by the 1820s) were sufficient conditions to prompt critical literary representations of the conditions of labor—that is, to challenge the linkage between labor and freedom. These kinds of representations would not arise until large-scale shifts toward a mechanized labor process in the 1850s and 1860s began to fundamentally transform the way labor was or was not accorded value.

We get some sense of the imaginative terrain that predominated before this shift in *The Factory Girl,* a novel Sarah Savage published anonymously in 1814. Virtually unknown to scholars a generation ago, this volume has more recently garnered some attention as "the first novel about factory work written in America."[17] However, that assertion is true only in the most limited sense. Though the title does suggest that the book will feature sketches of factory work or at least describe the social ramifications of factory labor, Savage gives us no information about what goes on inside a cotton mill. Rather, in a plot that would come to fill many Sunday school primers, the text dwells on Mary Burnham's sense of "filial benevolence" and on her desire to enact this benevolence within the more public realm of the factory in order to make virtue "appear amiable and desirable to others."[18]

> "O how happy I shall be," said she almost audibly, "when I see my dear grandmother sitting at her tea-table, enjoying her favorite repast, which I have earned for her."—The glow of filial benevolence kept her unusually cheerful through the day, and it was not till she united with her grand-

mother at night, in petitions for divine protection, amidst the temptations and difficulties to which she might be exposed, that she remembered there was any labour, or were any privations, attending her new situation; and the recollections of this only served to increase the fervency of her desires, that she might be blessed with healthful activity, and persevering diligence in the discharge of her duties. (10)

It is tempting to conclude from the preceding passage—with its stress on desire emanating from privation and its celebration of diligence in the face of temptation—that Mary Burnham is somewhat the martyr, anxious to prove devotion through a test of hardship. But to read the novel through this lens is to romanticize what is actually a rather less-gothic paean to the Protestant work ethic. Mary's temptations prove minor (she is invited to a dance), and the privations remain undescribed. Martyrs would typically be tested through more extraordinary circumstances. Savage asserts that there is nothing particularly unusual in Mary's labors; it is her public, persevering diligence in the discharge of them that allows her to realize their value and that makes them worth noting. "Let your light so shine before men," quotes Savage to elucidate, "that they may see your good works and glorify your Father, which is in heaven" (21). Such sentiments lead Thomas Lovell, a recent critic, to conclude that "Mary's participation in the work of the factory" serves chiefly to provide "an opportunity for a fuller practice of her religious principles"; in short, "work . . . expands the operation of virtue."[19] It might be more accurate, however, to conclude that for Savage, work and the operation of virtue are not yet distinguishable acts. Despite the new context of the factory, the former is really only the physical manifestation of the latter—and as such, it either eludes representation or, given the hegemony of the Protestant ethic, simply does not require it. *The Factory Girl* is thus a labor novel without labor—or, to be more exact, a labor novel where the laborious exercise of virtue so predominates that work as an exogenous activity, something in operation apart from a moral typology, simply does not exist.

Daniel Rogers argues that discourses that valued labor according to extrinsic, instrumental criteria did not begin to circulate until "the transformation of labor undercut . . . mid-nineteenth-century assumptions about the moral preeminence of work."[20] This transformation entailed both the growing predominance of factory labor and the increasing tendency of wage work to create class segmentation. But perhaps more significant, it also involved the rise of a capitalist ethic that would wed these structural developments to a new ideology of labor. Unlike earlier formations, labor does not have an intrinsic value within the regime of capital; it is valued only instrumentally. Thus, as Jonathan Glickstein records in *Concepts of Free Labor in Antebellum America,* "the capitalist ethic undermined" claims "that hard and useful labor possessed an inherent moral value. . . . In its insistence that manual labor was a mere commodity, with no 'value' other than that established by marketplace supply and demand, the capitalist ethic highlighted the strictly calculative or instrumental dimension of work just as the most conservative formulations of the work ethic strongly subordinated that dimension."[21] Work, in other words, was worth either what it could garner in wages or achieve in profits—depending on one's point of view. Older, intrinsic values, such as religious piety and civic duty, became residual elements of labor discourse—to be mobilized at times as part of a radical critique of alienated labor, but more often to be remembered with nostalgia.

What capitalism and its ethic had created, Marx noted long ago, was not only a new concept of labor but a new concept of the laborer: the "free laborer." "This worker must be free in the double sense," Marx wrote, "that as a free individual he can dispose of his labour-power as his own commodity, and that, on the other hand, he has no other commodity for sale, i.e. he is rid of them, he is free of all the objects needed for the realization of his labour power."[22] If freedom in the first sense allows Marx's free laborer to continue to believe that his work reflects volition and autonomy, conditions that crucially distinguish him from the slave (who, in being owned, cannot sell his or her labor power), freedom in the second, negative sense calls this distinction into crisis. Not only is the free laborer free of land and machinery to otherwise realize his labor-power, he is now free of the ethical or moral imperatives that would give such labor any intrinsic value. Like the slave in this regard, his motivations are purely extrinsic: as with the whip, so with the wage. In this sense, to be a "wage slave" in the nineteenth century was not to be forced to labor—in other circumstances, labor could be "the basis for the constitution of the self."[23] It was, rather, to be forced by new systemic exigencies to labor without virtue, to labor only because of external pressures and only for external rewards.

As the capitalist ethic depreciated the moral, intrinsic value of labor in favor of extrinsic measures of profit and productivity, it simultaneously opened up labor and the laboring body to extrinsic representation. Labor became something to represent; not simply the sign of election or the enactment of civic duty, it was recast as an action multiply configured by external determinations and complexly operating within systems of external reward. Does one labor like a slave, and does that reflect on the ontological status of one's political freedom? Such questions had meaning for the first time only as labor and freedom were fully elucidated as distinct concepts and could thus be mediated through competing philosophies of their relation (free labor, slavery, socialism). Capitalism did not create slavery; but the capitalist ethic did create the discourse within which slavery could mark the fall from more meaningful forms and conceptions of labor. In creating the free laborer, ironically, capitalism invited labor to be measured through and against the rubric of chattel servitude, which, in antebellum America, was defined by race.

RHETORICAL FIGURES FOR SLAVE AND WAGE LABOR

This rubric was something Rebecca Harding Davis knew well; in her world the "tragic story" (50) of industrial labor could never be considered outside of the rubric of slavery. Raised since the age of five in the border town of Wheeling, Virginia, Davis experienced wage labor and slavery in the same physical space and as interconnected products of America's ruthless drive toward agricultural and industrial development.[24] "Our village was built on the Ohio River," she would later recount, "and was a halting place on this great national road, then the only avenue of traffic between the South and the North." This traffic included more than simply "passengers from the East" and "merchandise for the plantations." The political, economic, and cultural systems of the South and North came together in this antebellum borderland: "Sectional pride or feeling never was so strong there as in the New England or low Southern States. We occupied the place of Hawthorne's unfortunate man who saw both sides."[25]

Early in "Life in the Iron Mills," the narrator (who is never given a name or a gender) similarly deliberates on this dual vision, dwelling once more on the Ohio River and on a kind of traffic it creates between the South and the North. Here, however, the exchange is rendered in figural terms, through the mediation of what Leo Marx has called a "symbolic landscape."[26]

> From the back-window I can see a narrow brick-yard sloping down to the river-side. . . . The river, dull and tawny-colored . . . drags itself sluggishly along, tired of the heavy weight of boats and coal-barges. . . . When I was a child, I used to fancy a look of weary, dumb appeal upon the face of the

> negro-like river slavishly bearing its burden day after day. Something of
> the same idle notion comes to me to-day, when . . . I look on the slow
> stream of human life creeping past, night and morning, to the great
> mills. Masses of men, with dull, besotted faces bent to the ground . . . skin
> and muscle and flesh begrimed with smoke and ashes; stooping all night
> over boiling caldrons of metal, laired by day in dens of drunkenness and
> infamy; breathing from infancy to death an air saturated with fog and
> grease and soot, vileness for soul and body. (12)

Although present-day critics have largely missed the connection,
readers of the *Atlantic Monthly* may have recognized a debt in this passage
to British industrial fiction, specifically to Charles Dickens, who in the
"Key-Note" to *Hard Times* similarly wrote of a mill town with "a black
canal" where "smoke and ashes" marked the buildings "red and black
like the painted face of a savage."[27] For Dickens, who must have felt himself to be safely removed from both blacks and savages, the simile is
mostly illustrative, a way to mark the presence of the barbarous forces of
industrialism through an offhand reference to absent barbarians. In
Davis's story, however, the same rhetorical figure becomes more menac-
ing and far more invasive. Unlike the well-disciplined topography of
Dickens's Coketown, the "negro-like" river that cuts through the heart of
antebellum America cannot so easily be contained within the landscape.
Such slavishness is too near at hand; the "masses of men . . . begrimed
with smoke and ashes" too perfectly mimic their racial backdrop. "Laired
. . . in dens" and "breathing from infancy to death an air saturated with
fog and grease and soot," they inhabit conditions that threaten, in fact,
to perpetuate a generational servitude more typically associated with
blackness and slavery in the United States. Like the river that bears "its
burden day after day," the "slow stream of human life creeping past,
night and morning," seems likely to become a constant feature of the
narrator's vista, a naturalized accompaniment to the already "natural"
presence of slave power. Indeed, the rhetorical figure is so potent in this
different atmosphere that it must as quickly be retracted: "My fancy
about the river was an idle one," continues the narrator.

> [I]t is no type of such a life. What if it be stagnant and slimy here? It
> knows that beyond there waits for it odorous sunlight,—quaint old gar-
> dens, dusky with soft, green foliage of apple-trees, and flushing crimson
> with roses,—air, and fields, and mountains. The future of the Welsh pud-
> dler passing just now is not so pleasant. To be stowed away, after his grimy
> work is done, in a hole in the muddy graveyard, and after that,—*not* air,
> nor green fields, nor curious roses. (13)

The meaning of this strong racial metaphor—and this equally strong retraction—within Davis's own opening keynote has been regularly discussed but, unfortunately, just as regularly misconstrued. Reading the "odorous sunlight," the "quaint old gardens," the "air, and fields, and mountains" as symbols for the end of slavery, a number of critics have noted the antithetical position of the wage laborer, who is, according to Jean Pfaelzer, "fixed in an interminable present, despite the obvious irony that he is white, male, and not a slave."[28] While Pfaelzer rightly notes the ironic counterposition of wage and chattel labor in this passage, their relationship is not quite what she and others imply. The "odorous sunlight" and accompanying symbols should not be taken as Davis's (or anyone's) vision of postemancipation America. During the 1850s and 1860s, even the most ardent abolitionists envisioned a future in which African American "freemen" would join their white brethren in freely contracted wage labor—labor that many acknowledged would be industrial, rather than agricultural, in nature. Once freed, the "Negro" would be required to work, writes William Jay, "but labor is no longer the badge of his servitude and the consummation of his misery, for it is voluntary. For the first time in his life, he is party to a contract. . . . In the course of time, the value of negro labor, like all other vendible commodities, will be regulated by supply and demand."[29] As Davis would later note in her postemancipation novel, *Waiting for the Verdict*, "the regulation of supply and demand was not without its own horrors. "[H]omeless, shelterless, breadless, friendless, and moneyless" is how Frederick Douglass, in 1855, described his first days of liberty; "toiling, overworked, disheartened, [and] longing for relief," echoed Harriet Wilson four years later, in her "sketches from the life of a Free Black" in the North.[30] African Americans were greeted, suffice it to say, with "graveyards" more often than "roses." Davis's sunny image was, I would argue, more likely borrowed from pro-slavery apologists, who frequently contrasted the futures of the wage slave and the chattel slave in precisely these terms. Without the paternalistic care of a loving master, they asserted, the wage slave was always destined to be "stowed away," while the chattel slave could look forward to "sunlight" and a rosy retirement after his "weary" work was done.

> While, nestling near, to bless their humble lot,
> Warm social joys surround the Negro's cot,
> the evening dance its merriment imparts,
> Love, with his rapture, fills their youthful hearts,
> And placid age, the task of labor done,

> Enjoys the summer shade, the winter sun,
> And, as through life no pauper want he knows,
> Laments no poor-house penance at its close.[31]

Read in this historical context, Davis's rejection of the racial metaphor proves just as fraught as its initial application. Since slave and wage labor do not occupy different points on a historical continuum, their "streams" are contiguous and, at least in terms of the representations they generate, often confluent. Thus, if, in Amy Schrager Lang's words, "blackness is widely understood in the mid nineteenth century as a state of becoming," then what it is "becoming" in Davis's passage is not liberated (as Lang argues here) but universalized.[32] "Race is a product of history, not of nature," Barbara Fields concludes; at this juncture, its historical role is to mark the uneasy naturalization of labor's determination.[33] Unhinged from any fixed referent, "blackness" traffics between modes of production and comes, momentarily at least, to characterize the conditions of white wage labor. This characterization, rather than the passing of slavery and the "interminable present" of wage labor, proves most ironic and ultimately promotes the narrator's unconditional rejection of this "type" for wage labor. The rhetorical figure's seeming applicability must be denounced; looking through the narrator's back window, readers must find, once again, a new class rather than a "new race."

But what exactly does it mean to see a new class? What are the signs that establish its visibility? This problem haunted the labor narrative throughout its various revisions and reformations in the nineteenth and early twentieth centuries. The figurative norms for the representation of slaves had been, in contrast, well established by the 1850s. Marked as Other by tropes of blackness, a conventional set of physical attributes, and even an orthographically denoted dialect in the text, their visibility was never in question. Indeed, the slave's visibility always already functioned within a scopic regime of object and viewer that precisely mimicked the dyadic relationship between slave and slaveholder (a representational corollary to what W. E. B. DuBois would later call "double-consciousness").[34] As property of another, the slave was both capital and labor; though physically distinct and singularly embodied, he or she nevertheless defined, by extension, the power of the master. The slave's visibility hence both ensured and was ensured by the dominant mode of power. But as Frederick Douglass sagely noted, "the difference between the white slave, and the black slave, is this: the latter belongs to *one* slaveholder, and the former belongs to *all* slaveholders, collectively."[35] Even as the cash nexus sundered preindustrial ties of paternalism, it inaugurated new forms of bondage that were mediated in such a way as to make them more difficult to represent. "Not even the inhabitants of a manufacturing town know," writes Davis, "the vast machinery of system by which the bodies of workmen are governed" (19). Such knowledge is prevented by the fact of governance itself, which negotiates a relationship that has previously appeared organic. Although the wage worker sells his or her labor power, he or she is not capital's laborer; the bond is always articulated through some intermediatory vehicle. Within liberal capitalism, this is, of course, the contract. But there is no equally established representational vehicle. Though ambiguously applied and ambivalently received, the figurative signifiers of race are one way to fill this void, one way to coalesce and make visible the seemingly arbitrary signs of wage servitude.

In *The Wages of Whiteness: Race and the Making of the American Working Class,* David Roediger examines not only the racism prevalent in the antebellum labor movement but the highly fraught traffic in racial metaphor that circulated within antebellum labor discourse. In speeches, handbills, and newspapers, workers consistently used figural language to compare the new forms of dependency wrought by industrialism with the more "traditional" bondage of chattel slaves. Yet as he documents, such comparisons "cut hard" and "cut in two ways" in a nation founded on the ideology of republican freedom.

> [C]hattel slavery stood as the ultimate expression of the denial of liberty. But republicanism also suggested that the long acceptance of slavery betokened weakness, degradation and an unfitness for freedom. The black population symbolized that degradation. Racism, slavery and republicanism thus combined to require comparisons of hirelings and slaves, but the combination also required white workers to distance themselves from blacks even as the comparisons were made.

In certain instances, this "distance" could be constructed internally, as in the phrase *white slavery,* one of the era's most common racial metaphors. Here, the suggested alliance built around the word *slavery* is undercut by the modifier *white.* Hence, the "enslavement" of whites rather than the enslavement of people emerges as the root problem. More often, however, such distance is achieved through a cycle of comparison and disavowal—as in "Life in the Iron Mills." Roediger notes: "As long as slavery thrived, any attempt to come to grips with wage labor tended to lapse into exaggerated metaphors or frantic denials of those metaphors. Only with Black emancipation could a more straightforward critique of wage slavery, and a fierce battle over the meaning of *free labor* develop."[36]

Although Roediger is ultimately more interested in the actors and actions behind the exaggerated metaphors and frantic denials, his adumbration of this cycle helps to clarify the ways in which racial discourse functions within the antebellum labor literature of the North. Racial figures and tropes are seldom either unambiguously applied or universally denounced. Rather, as in Davis's keynote, they lend affective power to the industrial critique while hesitantly marking the degree to which "the vast machinery of system" (19) shapes the classed bodies of the industrializing labor force. Importantly, this cycle reveals not the fusion of race and class into one stable descriptive language of servitude (for none exists) but, rather, a repeatedly aborted attempt to measure economic exploitation through a racial lexicon. These attempts are repeated because, as Roediger notes, "in this slaveholding republic . . . the bondage of Blacks served as a touchstone by which dependence and degradation were measured."[37] They are inevitably aborted, however, because this scale of measurement can finally only dissolve one notion (class) into the other (race), collapsing the distinction that gives the irony of white servitude its critical edge. Not only do "white slaves" require black slaves for their rhetorical existence, but, more important, the hegemonic period of free labor discourse requires this unstable figural relationship to paper over the large-scale absence of a critical language of economic exploitation.

TYPES

The very elusiveness of Davis's opening can also be taken as a symptom of this more general linguistic absence. Her decision to include the narrator in the text and to have that narrator create and then reject a "type" for industrial labor calls attention to the difficult project of finding an appropriate language to describe the incipient working class. "Throughout the 1840s and 1850s," notes Amy Schrager Lang, "scholars, legislators, journalists, reformers, and writers of every political stripe ventured their opinions about the nature and ramifications of class in America."[38] Yet these authors were often as reluctant as Davis to assign industrial laborers a fixed type. Despite mounting evidence to the contrary, most political and cultural organs in the North continued to stress the exceptional social mobility of America, adding their voices to the free labor coalition. All that limited the worker, according to this ideology, was the extent of his or her desire to rise. To assign a worker a fixed type—which is to see class as an economic, rather than a moral, structure—was to contradict the northern and nationalist ideology of American exceptionalism. It was, moreover, to fix in writing—in type—what most authors and critics anxiously guarded against: the rigid stratification of the English class system.

As much can be gleaned from American responses to British industrial fiction. Like Dickens's *Hard Times,* the works of Disraeli, Gaskell, Kingsley, and Eliot sold well in the United States during the 1840s and 1850s and provided many Americans with their first (albeit mediated) exposure to industrial capitalism. Yet unlike Romantic poetry, which had seemed to transcend national affiliation, these industrial novels were read as irrefutably foreign.[39] The problems they described and their very modes of description were thought to have originated in a British caste system. Lacking an aristocratic past, the United States should be immune from both the fact and the language of economic determinism. Metonymy and typology, which the British novelists used to depict social status through physical representation, were never as comfortably adopted by antebellum American writers, who, as Henry James noted, emphasized instead "the absence of a variety of social types."[40] For instance, the term *hand,* which serves as a metonym for wage laborers in British industrial fiction (just as *head* metonymically represents management), is explicitly rendered multivalent in "Life in the Iron Mills": "two or three dirty hands" beseech a comrade to come drinking (16); an overcultivated gentleman is described as having a "white hand" (29); the mill owner's son wishes to "wash my hands of all social problems" (35); and Hugh Wolfe stretches his "hands to the world, that had given so much to them" (45). As I will show, though Davis wrote of "skin and muscle and flesh begrimed with smoke and ashes," she refused to use even this language to fix these figures in perpetuity. For Davis (as for most American writers), that moment of class unveiling, that discordant discovery of wage labor in the promised land, had to be followed by a promise of social amelioration, and this promise needed to be communicated in the figural language itself.

In "The Tartarus of Maids," one of the most inventive early explorations of class and figuration, Herman Melville goes so far as to make the absence of standard metonymic tropes a major theme. Published in 1855 in *Harper's Magazine* as a companion piece to "The Paradise of

Bachelors" (which satirizes an elite London men's club), this tale of female operatives in a New England paper mill is part of three diptychs that Melville wrote in rapid succession to contrast poverty and wealth in the United States and England. This format would become standard fare in U.S. magazines during the nineteenth century, since its ironic counterposition of poverty and wealth served to establish the desirability of a detached and morally superior middle terrain. Typically both sketches are narrated by the same character, whose ability to decipher the signs and codes of class difference remains unquestioned. Wealth is rendered desirable but dissolute, poverty terrifying in its very legibility. Yet unlike the rural American poor in Melville's "Poor Man's Pudding and Rich Man's Crumbs" and the English working-class theater audience in his "The Two Temples," the maids prove surprisingly difficult to represent. Eluding the facile language of reform that Melville both invokes and subverts in the other sketches, the maids seem, as Newton Arvin has written, oppressed in an "indirect and enigmatic sense."[41] The enigma here lies not in the mode by which the maids are oppressed (which is rather straightforward), but again in the inability of language to express that oppression's figurative dimensions. Melville's narrator tells us that not only are the maids silent and haunted by an "unrelated misery," but they are "blank,"[42] sapped of strength, vitality, and even fecundity by the mechanized process they ceaselessly serve.

"At rows of blank-looking counters sat rows of blank-looking girls, with blank, white folders in their hands, all blankly folding blank paper" (328). Replacing more delineated figuration, blankness helps constitute a number of different contextual and thematic issues. Melville is, as Michael Newbury has recently demonstrated,[43] concerned during this period to establish his own authority at the expense of the scribbling mob of women who he, like Hawthorne, blames for his failure to gain literary popularity. These blank-looking girls blindly folding blank paper may, in this sense, comment on those mill girls who, during the 1840s, famously wrote *The Lowell Offering*, a journal that largely served to praise factory work for the cultural and religious opportunities it afforded women from rural backgrounds. Melville, who could not but align the mechanical fabrication of paper with the mechanical fabrication of prose, was less sanguineous about the effect of industry on authorship. Inasmuch as the factory drains the humanity from its operatives, it ensures that the outcome of their operations will be evacuated of any marks of creativity.

But blankness also raises the specter of barrenness, of maidens turned to maids, having ceded their "natural" reproductive powers to the engine of industry. This particular theme lends the sketch a gothic tone, as Melville, following Mary Shelley, explores the "instinctive horror of going back to the source of life only to discover that 'life' is obsolete, that the 'artificial' and 'mechanical' has triumphed completely over the 'natural' and 'organic.'"[44] This horror matches the horror one encounters in "Tartarus's" companion, "The Paradise of Bachelors"—that is, the rather less-gothic discovery that those men who are supposed to be in power, managing the British Empire with efficiency and potency, are intoxicated and debauched, rendered impotent by the very homosocial rituals that they believe demonstrate their manhood. In both sketches, the sexual, gynecological, and scatological imagery is extreme; that it stands intact is testament to the credulity of *Harper's* editors and the willful blindness of the Victorian readership. But Melville is up to more here than adolescent pranks or the simple contraposition of hypertrophic states to warn against the dangers of deprivation and excess. He is slipping into one of this era's most common reifications, through which gender and the gendered body is made to stand in for a discourse of economic exploitation. "In Tartarus," writes Robin Wiegman, "the women's very blankness is symptomatic of the inability to be represented except as or by the phallic, making them the tame ministers to the expansion of a masculine economy."[45] Thus Melville's figuring of workers in "Tartarus" as barren maids in service to a machine "with a vertical thing like a piston . . . rising and falling" (238) and "two great round vats . . . full of white, wet, wooly-looking stuff" (331) gives this sketch a critical momentum yet also contains its political critique within what Wiegman correctly argues is a heterosexual model of the natural order.

Despite these limitations, Melville distances himself from his narrator in "Tartarus" to use the trope of blankness (with all its sexual connotations) to pose profound questions about the status of subjectivity and the role of race in a new industrial regime. If the maids can be expressed only as blank, do we read this as a disfiguring absence (as Wiegman's Lacanian language suggests), or is this the blank slate of liberal individualism? Should we read the blankness as a lack or, rather, as the freedom of the not-yet-inscribed? "Looking at the blank paper continually dropping, dropping, dropping," the narrator remarks, "I could not but bethink me of that celebrated comparison of John Locke who, in demonstration of his theory that man had no innate ideas, compared the human mind at birth to a sheet of paper; something destined to be scribbled on, but what sort of characters no soul might tell" (333). Though one can, of course, stress the latter part of this sentence—the lack of pre-determination celebrated by Lockeans during the American Enlightenment—the mention of birth must once again remind readers of the factory's circumscriptions. Just as birth and reproduction are no longer the prerogatives of the maids, blankness is no longer an originary state. In this sketch, it, too, is the outcome of the machine, which, with "unbudging fatality" (333), continues always to produce the blank page. Though Melville's inattention to the social relations of capitalism that underlie this machine deserves note, this inattention does not obscure Melville's message: having so recently escaped the heavy fear of spiritual predetermination through the aid of the Enlightenment, we risk being determined anew by industrialism. Worse yet, Melville implies that such determination will be practically undetectable, since even as industrialism produces bodily deformations (such as barrenness), it produces a "white-washed" (324) surface, a blank demeanor that misleadingly signals freedom rather than constraint.

That the freedom of indetermination can be falsely represented as well as actually signified by whiteness suggests that Melville's racial figuration of industrialism surpasses in complexity the cycle of comparison and denial that Roediger discovers in political texts and pamphlets. If, as I have mentioned, we find in the phrase *white slave* both an acknowledgment and a rejection of the similarities between free labor and slavery, we find no suggestion that whiteness could ever be produced. It is understood, rather, as natural and eternal. Thus Melville's insight in "Tartarus" is important. Nevertheless, such an insight does not lead him to decouple whiteness from its duties of signification. Race, like gender, stands in for class, even if race is more complexly understood. Looking at two maids passing unmarked paper through an apparatus designed to "rule" each sheet, the narrator remarks of the girl inserting the paper, "I looked at the first girl's brow, and saw it was young and fair," while he remarks of the girl receiving the paper at its destination, "I looked upon the second girl's brow and saw it was ruled and wrinkled" (328). As with his use of blankness, Melville's pun in this passage is multivalent, linking the new regime (the "rule") of the machine to the marks on a paper meant to govern the wayward writing hand (which is itself a symbol of the intractable subject). But both meanings of the term *rule* meet on the maid's face, which itself bears the marks of the industrial process, codifying its physical effects through an epidural lexicon that should, given the contrasting emphasis on whiteness, be understood as racial.

Indeed, the sexual and gynecological themes in "Tartarus" also fold into the domain of racial figuration—if we understand race broadly, as a taxonomy of people based on epidural differentiation or lineage. Such factories as the one the narrator visits or the famous Lowell mills employed unmarried women for a specific reason: to avoid replicating England's Manchester and Liverpool, where operatives commingled with other operatives and produced a permanent class of laborers (according to a eugenicist narrative of proletarianization). This eugenic vision and its consequent management principles (not hiring married operatives; forbidding operatives to marry) were largely successful in avoiding class segmentation (though not, of course, class processes) until the 1850s, when managers replaced native-born farm women with immigrant laborers who would work for less under harsher conditions, with their families by their sides.[46] In short, reproduction—or, earlier, its lack—was always included within a broad conception of the industrial labor process. Its inclusion could only be sustained by a eugenicist logic that comprehended class position as the result of breeding, that is, through the broad lens of race.

Less abstractly, however, Melville's point is not that whiteness needs to be understood as a social product of capitalist ideology (though he comes close) or that this labor process has a eugenicist component (though he does recognize this) but, rather, that the (re)generation of white skin—of freedom—has been grotesquely caricatured by mechanization. If it now takes "only nine minutes" (322) rather than nine months to produce the blank page, this "punctuality and precision" (332) comes at a considerable cost. We are no longer able to distinguish between the unmarked and the constructed-as-unmarked, between the existentially free and the formally "free"—the latter epitomized by the freedom of free labor, a freedom that more nearly means its opposite. However, whether unmarked or merely blank, it is, for Melville, the inscriber that matters most. Whether machines or men, those who write on these pages have the power to determine what is "destined to be scribbled" on or about the human mind.

As Melville's mediation on the blank page of working-class subjectivity might suggest, although industrial critics in the North recognized some of the changes wrought by class segmentation, they were largely unwilling either to engage (directly) in the language of class or to practice the more familiar British habit of typification. Indeed, during the 1850s, the only group of American authors who seemed to feel entirely comfortable assigning wage laborers a fixed type wrote from the slaveholding South. Responding to pressure from abolitionists, such writers as E. J. Stearns,

William Gilmore Simms, and George Fitzhugh developed, in Eric Foner's words, "a striking critique of northern labor relations."[47] Using a crude labor theory of value, these pro-slavery critics argued that the greater profits of northern industrial labor proved that wage workers were at least as exploited as plantation slaves. "For the man who lives by daily labor," stated Senator James Hammond, "and scarcely lives at that, and who has to put out his labor in the market and take the best he can get for it; in short, your whole class of manual laborers and operatives, as you call them, are slaves."[48] Fitzhugh added famously that wage workers were slaves "without the rights of slaves"—that because wage workers lacked the protection of paternalism, they were "slaves without a master."[49] At their most extreme, the pro-slavery writers would go further still in assigning workers this type, arguing that class and race were mere points on the same "natural" spectrum of servitude. Looking to England, where "the so-called free system of society has had the time to work out its results," William Harper foresaw in the English worker a racial future for the American wage slave: "With calfless legs and stooping shoulders, weak in body and mind, inert, pusillanimous and stupid," they were doomed to breed a race that perpetuated their own worst physical defects.[50]

Although these writers have been carefully examined by Eugene Genovese, Larry E. Tise, and others, the fact that southern apologists used fiction to add imaginative depth to their anti-industrial critique has largely eluded notice.[51] This is shortsighted: whatever we may think of their politics, any study of early American industrial fiction must count southern apologists' texts alongside the works of Herman Melville and Rebecca Harding Davis. While the pro-slavery novels never achieved high circulation, their numbers made them a force in the creation of a literary critique of industrial capitalism and ensured their influential role in shaping the discourse of class in both the North and the South. In the 1850s, for instance, at least twenty-seven pro-slavery novels included explicit attacks on the northern and British wage labor system. Many of these novels, such as William L. G. Smith's *Life at the South, or "Uncle Tom's Cabin" as It Is,* responded explicitly to Harriet Beecher Stowe's phenomenally popular *Uncle Tom's Cabin,* supplying what George Frederick Holmes suggested was a "counter-irritant."[52] But unlike northern novelists, pro-slavery writers had no problem finding a type for the life of the wage laborer. The greater imaginative freedom of fiction allowed them to figuratively show, not merely pronounce, that wage workers were, in fact, slaves.

Yet crucially, to invoke Fitzhugh's maxim, these novels give us wage workers who are slaves without the rights of slaves. For instance, in Mary H. Eastman's *Aunt Phillis's Cabin,* Ann, a servant (unlike Phillis, a slave), has neither a cabin nor the domestic sanctity that such space is here meant to suggest. "I'm an orphan, and poor; that's why I'm scolded and cuffed about," she reports, before Mrs. Brown, her employer, does indeed strike "the poor girl in the face." "They are nothing but white niggers, after all, these Irish," Mrs. Brown offers by way of explanation. Unlike the "real niggers," who are more tractable (and who are seldom beaten, Eastman reports), the "lazy, good-for-nothing Irish" require constant "teaching."[53] Indeed, a number of pro-slavery novels feature Irish immigrant laborers prominently, which is no doubt an effort to play off the virulent anti-Irish sentiment in antebellum America. These characters serve as perfect foils for the pro-slavery position, since their enslavement to capital can be so conveniently figured through an enslavement to whiskey or to the pope.

In *Uncle Robin in His Cabin in Virginia and Tom without One in Boston,* John W. Page makes an explicit theme of the comparison between the conditions of Irish laborers and black slaves. Dr. Boswell's new, northern wife comes to accept slavery after a tour of an Irish "shanty," complete with all the clichéd horrors of a British industrial novel.

> It was as stye indeed; there lay the mother in one corner on a dirt floor, with nothing between her and the floor but an old worn out blanket, and half covered with something that looked like a black stained saddle-cloth. She was shaking with an ague. There were, in another corner, six children, half naked, and shivering as if they too had agues. The filth and stench was insupportable, and Mrs. Boswell had to make her escape to the fresh air as soon as possible.

Mrs. Boswell finds Uncle Robin's slave quarters, in contrast, "neat and comfortable," leading her to the inevitable conclusion: "If slaves have more learning than free people, more religion than free people, and have better houses to live in than free people, I think the difference is in favour of slaves."[54] Dr. Worthington shares these same sentiments in Charles Peterson's *The Cabin and Parlor.* After narrowly saving the life of a poor white child ("little Alfred") whose respiratory illness came from a forced daily walk "through fog and dew," the doctor tiredly concludes: "I sometimes wish, when I see things like this, or am over-worked myself, that we were all niggers. The Lord knows, a black skin, in these nineteenth century days, is quite a blessing."[55]

The characters in Matthew Estes's *Tit for Tat,* unfortunately, cannot agree. In part of this Byzantine novel, Estes relates the tale of a five-year-old white boy stolen from his father and sold into "slavery" as a chimney sweep. This choice of occupation is far from incidental. It allows Estes to show, in scene after graphic scene, how servitude permanently reconfigures the bodies of young "climbing boys." After one young boy is recovered from a hot flue, for example, Estes writes:

> Shriveled, shrunk, blackened—not a particle of his hair left upon the sufferer's head—not a single hair left upon his eyebrows—his lips blistered and swollen—his cheeks crushed and blackened—nothing but the bright, bright eyes still moving, distended with pain, and the mouth uttering continual cries of agony, denoted that it was a human being, and not a large lump of charred timber.

More often these boys die a slower death: "They slept upon heaps of soot," and "by their constant contact with the soot they laid the seeds of a most revolting cancer, which frequently terminated their existence under circumstances of the most offensive suffering."[56] No matter what the process, the result is always the same: they work like slaves, turn black, and die. They meet their death, as the first passage surely reveals, in the throes of some nightmarish caricature of blackface—swollen, blackened, and barely articulate, only the "bright eyes" attesting to some faint humanity. In the pages of *Tit for Tat,* it is, in fact, never completely clear whether the climbing boys die from their labor or from their blackness. This uncertainty is the point. For the pro-slavery industrial novelist, blackness was not a metaphor to be disavowed; it was a way to portray figuratively the link between race and class, slavery and wage labor.

THE WHITENESS BENEATH

After the preceding examination of the paradigm that turns class into race, we may return to Davis's "Life in the Iron Mills" with a better understanding of the significance of the author's invocation and rejection of metaphors of blackness. Although her comparisons between slave and wage labor contain, in Catherine Gallagher's words, "a certain proslavery residue,"[57] Davis is careful to distinguish her vision from that of Eastman, Page, and Peterson. Smoke, ashes, and blackness are equally able to mark bodies and objects in Davis's text, but they penetrate only to a certain point. They serve, to reiterate Roediger, as a "touchstone," but not as

essential determinants. Consequently, the narrator conspicuously alter-
nates between a figural language of comparison and one of disavowal—
between, for example, an insistence that "the idiosyncrasy of this town is
smoke" (11) and a demand that we "look deeper" and ask ourselves: "Is
that all of their lives? . . . nothing beneath?" (14–15). We are told several
times that the narrator can give us "only the outline of a dull life" (13) but
that "whatever lies beneath you can read according to the eyes God has
given you" (23). On almost every page of this short story, the prepositions
beneath and *under* match and subvert the nouns *smoke* and *ashes* and the
adjectives *black* and *dark*. This reveals not, as some have claimed, a realist
text marred by residual sentimentalism or the mimetic lacuna of errant
Romanticism but, rather, an industrial narrative infused with racial language and propelled by a pedagogical purpose.[58] In each instance of comparison and denial, we are being taught how to read past the metonyms,
metaphors, and types of racial servitude to a site of indetermination and
possibility. What lies beneath the outline, the smoke, and the ashes—and
what is implied even in one of the other titles Davis suggested for this
piece, "Beyond"—is an unmarked space of possibility and promise, not yet
fully legible, but clearly symbolized by dawn, sunlight, and whiteness.

While this is certainly the "subdued meaning" of many of the narrator's direct addresses and almost belligerent ruminations, this unmarked
space is most apparent in the *tableaux vivant* that Davis uses repeatedly to
illustrate her text. In one such tableau, the narrator describes Deborah,
a "deformed . . . hunchback" (17) cotton mill worker, who has previously
seemed to figure the physical deformation of industrial labor and thus to
serve as an emblem, in Rosemarie Garland Thomson's words, of "the
unredeemed, subjugated body that impedes will."[59] Within industrial
fiction, the body usually registers the weight of exogenous social forces
and hence becomes evidentiary of that over which it has no power. At
this point in the narrative, however, Deborah's body is made less legible
and thus works to trouble such notions of evidence and typicality.

> Miserable enough she looked, lying there on the ashes like a limp, dirty
> rag,—yet not an unfitting figure to crown the scene of hopeless discom-
> fort and veiled crime: more fitting, if one looked deeper into the heart of
> things,—at her thwarted woman's form, her colorless life, her waking stu-
> por that smothered pain and hunger,—even more fit to be a type of her
> class. Deeper yet if one could look, was there nothing worth reading in
> this wet, faded thing, half-covered with ashes? no story of a soul filled with
> groping passionate love, heroic unselfishness, fierce jealousy? (21)

Once again, the narrator's gestures initially seem ambivalent and at odds. As soon as we are told of the "ashes" and are given the simile of the "limp, dirty rag," this language is undercut by exhortations to look "deeper into the heart of things." Yet even at this deeper level, where Deborah seems "fit to be a type of her class," matters are not so simple. There is, the narrator implores, more to it than that, something "deeper," something only "half-covered with ashes."

In an important essay on class, gender, and metonymy, Wai Chee Dimock argues that "Life in the Iron Mills" constitutes "one of the most interesting variations on the practice of metonymy in the nineteenth century." In particular, she finds in Deborah's tableau "a relation of impermeability, indirection, or nonalignment [where] certitude extends . . . only to what is verifiably there, not to what is unverifiably not." Resisting, if not in fact revising, a long Western tradition of reading classed bodies metonymically, Davis creates a situation where "Deborah emerges less as an identity than as the impossibility of identity. She cannot be read metonymically for just that reason, for her identity is both overflowing and undersaturated, both unexhausted by her materiality, and only partially accounted for by its determinations."[60] While Dimock is certainly right to note the importance of this scene, which presents us with a deeply embodied character whose form, nonetheless, exceeds the account of its determinations, this new figural "relation" hardly points to the "impossibility of identity" itself. Situated in the historical context I have outlined, it indicates, rather, a new, racially inflected logic of deferral: responding to a figural system that aligns marked bodies with chattel slaves, Davis gives us instead a character whose true self—whose true "story"—lies in her potentiality, in that unmarked space as yet unread through her thoroughly marked body. This potential is, furthermore, the condition on which Deborah is, at the text's conclusion, brought into the realm of middle-class redemption. A Quaker woman (whose own "homely body" [61] features preternaturally "white fingers" [62]) recognizes the promise others have missed and removes Deborah from the smoky mill town to the country, where "long years of sunshine, and fresh air, and slow patient Christ-love . . . make healthy and hopeful this impure body and soul" (63). Whiteness thus solves the problem of determination that metonymy leaves unresolved. In their economy of figuration, metonymic signifiers, such as the terms *hand* and *head,* can only signify specific locations within a broader social relation that the system posits as both organic and static (Dimock's complaint). Hence the degree to which an author uses the body to register the affects of industrialism is precisely the degree to which that body becomes a type. However, by invoking a racial system to differently configure both the individual body and the social realm, Davis and other antebellum critics of industrial labor replace metonymy with indeterminance and thus hold out the possibility for redemption.[61]

Although differently articulated, the same "relation of impermeability, indirection, or nonalignment," the same disjunction between embodiment and determination, is apparent in Hugh Wolfe, the mill worker and artist who serves as Davis's other main character. Like Deborah, Hugh lives a begrimed existence centered on constant labor. Yet unlike her and his fellow mill workers, Hugh already manifests a "finer nature": "down under all the coarseness of his life, there was a groping passion for whatever was beautiful and pure" (22–23). In his "off-hours" (32), he expresses this passion by chipping korl (industrial waste) into sculptures, which, though "rough" and "ungainly, . . . show a master's hand" (64). When one of these sculptures is discovered by several middle-class visitors, Hugh comes to believe that it is "his right to live as they,—a pure life, a good, true-hearted life, full of beauty and kind words" (46). After all, he knows God "never made the difference between poor and rich" (47). While this kind of class mobility may, according to free labor ideology, be his right, it is not his destiny. After being arrested for theft and imprisoned, he commits suicide.

What interests me about Hugh's narrative is once more the figurative language used to describe the laboring body and, through that body, class difference. Again class becomes visible through racial markings, which instigate an anxious search for what lies beneath. When, for instance, Hugh hears the middle-class visitors speaking, he listens "more and more like a dumb, hopeless animal, with a duller, more stolid look creeping over his face, glancing now and then at Mitchell, marking acutely every smallest sign of refinement, then back to himself, seeing as in a mirror his filthy body, his more stained soul" (30). Class, like race, manifests itself relationally. Mitchell, who is "spending a couple months in the borders of a Slave State, to study the institutions of the South," establishes the other end of the figural spectrum. His whiteness—"the contour of [his] white hand"—conveys "the impalpable atmosphere . . . [of] the thorough-bred gentleman" (29) and consequently allows Hugh to understand his own blackness, to read his body through its extraneous markings and to wonder at the condition of his soul. Thus taught, Hugh begins a process of introspection, an operation of stripping away, a search for what lies beneath.

The slow tides of pain he had borne gathered themselves up and surged against his soul. His squalid daily life, the brutal coarseness eating into his brain, as the ashes into his skin; before, these things had been a dull aching into his consciousness; to-night they were a reality. He gripped the filthy red shirt that clung, stiff with soot, about him, and tore it savagely from his arm. The flesh beneath was muddy with grease and ashes,—and the heart beneath that! And the soul? God knows. (40)

Set within the Christian mythos that Davis obviously means to invoke, this scene constitutes a mortification: in this purgation, a sinner (or, indeed, a slave, for this event is part of the paradigmatic structure of the slave narrative), having become cognizant of iniquity, attempts to strip away those outer signs of defilement. Yet Hugh's "sin" is not impiety but physical impurity. His very proximity to the ashes and soot of industrial production have excluded him from the ranks of the "thorough-bred" and ensured his own initial lack of class and race "consciousness." Once he understands that the outer markings of industrial servitude only obscure and do not preclude his right to "a pure life," he begins an anxious attempt to exfoliate the physical signs of determination, to decodify his body—or, indeed, to racialize it differently. In the discourse of antebellum labor narratives, the "right to live as they" entails, most immediately, the right to look as they. Whiteness as a signifying agent of class mobility—as an internal, residual sign of an unmarked soul—is thus (not incidentally) conferred at the moment in which, as the plot makes clear, the possibilities of such mobility are denied. Unless, like Deborah, one escapes from the factory into the chimera of Edenic agrarianism, recuperation is impossible. Unlike the sinner and the slave, the wage laborer finds no salvation in industrial America.

The force of this disjuncture between class stratification and race privilege (what Roediger calls the compensatory "wages of whiteness") is not, at least in "Life in the Iron Mills," lost on the white workers. Toward the end of the narrative, as he languishes in his cell, Hugh sees a series of different scenes through the "narrow window of the jail" (54). Like the narrator, the reader, and the mill visitors, he is now a viewer—occupant of a privileged position within the visual economy of realist discourse. Yet ironically, what Hugh sees is his exclusion from "the world and the business of it"—from, that is, his rights as a free white laborer in the public sphere. This exclusion is made abundantly clear in two linked visions. Fixating first on "a dog down in the market," Hugh envies the animal's ability to walk "after his master with such a stately, grave look!—

only a dog, yet he could go backwards and forwards just as he pleased.
. . . Why the vilest cur, yelping there in the gutter, had not lived his life,
had been free to act out whatever thought God had put into his brain"
(55). In case antebellum readers missed what must have been an almost
obvious link here between animals and slaves, Davis reinforces the relationship in Hugh's next "look" out the window. As the market closes, he
notices a "tall mulatto girl, following her mistress, her basket on her
head," walking with "a free firm step," with "a clear-cut olive face" and "a
scarlet turban tied on one side" (57–58).

Like the "stately" dog, the girl's movement ("free" and "firm") both
enacts and metaphorizes her freedom and, in contrast, Hugh's stasis.
Thus, in another form, the "negro-like river" again leaves the town
behind, abandoning Hugh to his "hole in the muddy graveyard." This
time, however, the conceit wears a human face. Growing "suddenly . . .
grave" at the sight of Hugh's "haggard face peering out through the
bars" (57), the girl registers a shock of awareness, a momentary suggestion, perhaps, that the irony of the situation is not lost on those even further excluded from a "right to live as they." But if this instant of recognition (this return of the gaze) suggests identification and invites mutual
comparison or even compassion, such undertones of the political
unconscious fall on deaf ears. Hugh's ability to recognize the grim irony
of this situation—or the irony of white servitude more generally—rests
on a newfound racial identity that precludes such a connection. The
mulatto woman who walks past his cell, like the tropes of blackness that
run through the story, can never, according to this formulation of racial
subjectivity, emerge from the backdrop. Shadowy, ephemeral, reified,
and overdetermined, these figures can finally only construct their alternative: the symbolic freedom of whiteness.

Davis assures us symbolically that Hugh finds this whiteness in his
death. After his visions (or his temptations to continue the motif), he
turns his carving tool on himself and dies in one last attempt to recover
what lies beneath. Freeing himself from any sense of cross-racial
identification, parodying through self-immolation the mill visitors'
desires for self-made men, he bids for entry into the figural realm of
racial purity. Indeed, his death scene is nothing so much as an account
of his racial purgation—salvation by way of spiritual transfusion.

Fainter and fainter the heart rose and fell, slower and slower the moon
floated from a cloud, until, when at last its full tide of white splendor
swept over the cell, it seemed to wrap and fold into a deeper stillness the

dead figure that never should move again. . . . Nothing . . . moved, save the black nauseous stream of blood dripping slowly to the pallet floor!" (61)

Of course, the final manifestation of what lies beneath—of the potential for working-class creativity and self-representation—is Hugh Wolfe's sculpture "the Korl Woman." This working-class figure carved from industrial refuse is, as most readers note, an important internal critique of the industrial process. Carved from surplus material from the iron milling process, she mimics and subverts the relations through which profit is carved out of surplus labor. Rising out of the waste, she seems to ask: "Is this the End? . . . nothing beyond?—no more?" But in a more specific sense, she is also an externalized figure for the sculptor. Through her "wolfish face," "the spirit of the dead korl-cutter looks out, with its thwarted life, its mighty hunger, its unfinished work" (64). Perhaps it should not surprise us, then, that the Korl Woman is so resolutely white—"the white figure of a woman . . . , white of giant proportions" (31). She is, finally, all that Hugh was but could never actually become. While he has passed into the "white splendor," she remains behind, in the narrator's study, "a bare arm stretched out imploringly" (64) to "command the darkness away" (65).

As Toni Morrison has insightfully demonstrated, "mute" white forms like the Korl Woman frequently haunt the conclusions of antebellum narratives. They rise with a striking regularity "whenever an Africanist presence is engaged"—whenever, that is, the "problems of human freedom" are encountered in the reified terms of race. Like the other figures of "impenetrable whiteness" that Morrison investigates, the Korl Woman functions "as both an antidote for and a meditation on the shadow that is the companion to this whiteness—a dark and abiding presence that moves the hearts and texts of American literature with fear and longing."[62] The fixity that is slavery and the determinism that is blackness confront here a white figure that is neither contained by her mode of production (she rises out of the waste) nor limited by her creator's talents and vision. Like the perfect whiteness of the figure who appears at the end of Edgar Allan Poe's *Narrative of Arthur Gordon Pym,* the terrible whiteness of Melville's whale, or indeed the sheety whiteness of his mill girls, the Korl Woman is multivalent—never reducible to one meaning and never exhausted by one reading. Each affluent visitor to the iron mill gives an interpretation. All the readings are allowed to stand, though none is complete, in and of itself. The Korl Woman may, in this sense, be the closest Davis comes to giving us a "type of such a life"—a type that is, perhaps impossibly, never fixed and ever free. In this, she embodies the promise that Davis found in the thwarted lives of Wheeling's working class—the potential she saw in them to extricate themselves from the determining blackness that threatened their bodies, minds, and souls; the potential she saw for them to become fully and completely white.

"BEYOND"

As "Life in the Iron Mills" closes, we are left with one last encounter between darkness and light: now back in the frame tale, we witness the narrator ensconced in a library, writing what we may assume is the conclusion of the text. Surrounded by the accoutrements of literary pretension—"a half-moulded child's head; Aphrodite; a bough of forest-leaves; music; work; homely fragments, in which lie the secrets of all eternal truth and beauty" (65)—the narrator labors through the dark night and into the impending dawn. The narrator is also accompanied by the Korl Woman, "hid behind a curtain," all that "remains to tell that the poor Welsh puddler once lived" (64). Haunted, perhaps, by the legacy of this family as much as by this enduring figure of the workers' racial potential, the narrator, too, works to turn night into day. In an exercise that cannot be anything but cyclical given Davis's diurnal metaphor, the narrator repeatedly brings the dark tale of grease and soot into the light and thus repeatedly exposes the underlying whiteness that should unify workers and readers through the text's fervent mediation.

Yet the importance of this scene extends beyond Davis's immediate context and into the postbellum era. As I will discuss in chapter 3, the United States underwent a stunningly rapid industrialization after the Civil War. During this period, other authors writing from other libraries continually confronted class segmentation and, with surprising regularity, perpetuated the legacy of Davis's final scene by relying on the language of whiteness. Even without the impetus of chattel slavery (and without the aid of a white woman in the closet), they depicted (and "resolved") class segmentation through the use of racial tropes. For example, in *The Silent Partner,* Elizabeth Stuart Phelps, the most immediate heir to Davis's reformist vision, draws attention to Sip's "little brown face" on six occasions to mark the character's class difference from Perley, the novel's upper-class protagonist.[63] Readers of this text know that the brewing class conflict is resolved when Sip is cleaned up a bit and reveals herself to be as pearly as Perley. Less obviously but no less importantly, Hamlin Garland's work shows that this paradigm inflects what is commonly known as American regionalism. When regions collide (as they often do) in Garland's work, their contact is marked by corporeal evidence of what we might now call "uneven development." In "Up the Coulee" (to cite but one instance), Garland uses racial tropes to testify to the different class histories of two brothers—one of whom has stayed on the farm while the other left for the city. The last sentence reads, "The two men stood there, face to face, hands clasped, the one fair-skinned, full-lipped, handsome in his neat suit; the other tragic, somber in his softened mood, his large, long, rugged Scotch face bronzed with the sun and scarred with wrinkles that had histories, like saber cuts on a veteran, the record of his battles."[64] The brothers' identical origins allow racial markers to attest to both their class difference and their "innate" commonality. Class structures are both marked and erased in one economical figure.[65]

One could, of course, go much further in marshaling texts to evidence the enduring presence of racial tropes in class-conscious literature, citing perhaps the whole genre of American naturalism, along with the works of various realists who read class decline ambivalently and hesitantly through bodily markings. But no matter how many examples one gathered, the paradigm would generally be the same: for American writers who saw racial formation and class formation arise at the same period, race and class have never been fully separable. Blackness is used to give evidence of class difference, which then instigates a search for what lies beneath. Inevitably, what lies beneath is a whiteness that can be claimed as common property in a nation economically divided.

The relationship between race and class in these instances is, as Roediger and others imply, compensatory: workers become white at the moment in which their class status is fixed. Their racial identity does not redouble their class identity (contrary to what some critics maintain) but evades it, becoming a blank screen for the projection of those American fantasies of uplift. Finally, race becomes a mode of social identification that avoids more painful economic realizations. At the level of literary representation, in particular, the interplay between race and class is considerably more complex than the current shorthand—"mutually constitutive"—will allow. Especially when race is understood to include whiteness as well as its more visible Other, race has a far more complex and potentially pernicious connection to class than is frequently thought. It is, to borrow an often quoted passage from Stuart Hall, "the modality in which class is 'lived,' the medium through which class relations are experienced, the form in which it is appropriated and 'fought through.'"[66] This last oblique gesture toward revolution (fought *through*) is, I think, more optimistic than the evidence I have presented in this chapter permits—to experience race as a modality of class is often not to experience class at all.

Voices of Insurgency

Strikes, Speech, and
Social Realism

There will come a time when our silence will be more powerful
than the voices you strangle today.

> —August Spies's last words before being hanged for
> conspiracy in the Haymarket incident

Words, words, words! how to make them deeds . . . with me they
only breed more words.

> —William Dean Howells, *Selected Letters*

The word in language is half someone else's. . . . the word does
not exist in neutral and impersonal language, . . . but rather it
exists in other people's mouths, in other people's contexts, serving other people's intentions: it is from there that one must take
the word, and make it one's own.

> —M. M. Bakhtin, *The Dialogic Imagination*

THE "MAN WITH THE KNIFE"

In the twenty-third chapter of his best-selling study *How the Other Half
Lives,* Jacob Riis changes his rhetorical strategy. The preceding chapters
have been largely documentary, using descriptions, illustrations, and
photographs to represent the degradations wrought by poverty on the
various inhabitants of the New York tenements. Working toward his concluding suggestions for urban reform, Riis attempts, however, to bring
these images closer to the reader, to augment previous calls for humanitarianism with a bald appeal to self-preservation. He offers the following
illustrative story:

A man stood at the corner of Fifth Avenue and Fourteenth street the other day, looking gloomily at the carriages that rolled by, carrying the wealth and fashion of the avenues. . . . He was poor, and hungry, and ragged. This thought was in his mind: "They . . . have no thought for the morrow; they know hunger only by name, and ride down to spend in an hour's shopping what would keep me and my little ones from want a whole year." There rose up before him the picture of those little ones crying for bread around the cold and cheerless hearth—then he sprang into the throng and slashed about him with a knife, blindly seeking to kill, to revenge.

Although "to-day he is probably in a mad-house," according to Riis, "the man and his knife . . . spoke . . . the warning. . . . They represented one solution of the problem of ignorant poverty versus ignorant wealth that has come down to us unsolved . . . —the solution of violence. There is another solution, that of justice. . . . Which shall it be?"[1]

While such dramatic enactments of class insurgency are rare in Riis's relatively restrained study, they are common in sociological and literary texts from the late 1870s and 1880s. In these texts, as in Riis's sketch, when poor or working-class characters look across the economic gulf, they are unfailingly provoked into angry "thought[s]" and "blind," vengeful actions. These characters may not premeditate their acts, but their authors clearly do, recounting them in order to make palpable what might otherwise remain distant. Just as Riis's "man with the knife" breaks through the sacrosanct space that divides him from "wealth and fashion," Riis's prose becomes sensationalistic, threatening to release the blind vengeance of "ignorant poverty" on his comfortable readership. Seemingly, all that contains these men with knives are the writers themselves, who, having conjured forth the irrational figures, proceed to label them as such, remove them to the "mad-house," and translate their "blind" actions into vocal "warning[s]." We might, then, call this the "rhetoric of extortion." Though reformists such as Riis seem to propose a choice between "the solution of violence" and the "solution . . . of justice," the decision is pretty much already made, and it is enforced by the very violence that "justice" is invoked to control. In this circular maneuver, acts of insurgency—often the solitary acts of working-class agency in these texts—are almost instantaneously converted into authorial power.

In this chapter, I will be concerned with examining the discursive nature of working-class insurgency and the ways in which this insurgency is rendered in narrative discourse. As men with knives (or, more commonly, with pickets) acted according to a discursive rationale, by speaking loudly from the political and social margins, men with pens quickly responded, creating a dialogic relationship that is revealing in both its manifest content and its formal operation. To be sure, during this period, novelists and journalists also responded with hysterics and histrionics (the cry "insurgency" carried a particularly dramatic resonance in the decades after the Civil War and in the years immediately following the Paris Commune); but their reactions were often more subtle and more manipulative. Like Riis, political reformers and political conservatives regularly transposed the physical and verbal violence of working-class insurgency into their texts in an effort to give weight to their political projects and to make their realism more forceful.[2]

The "economic novel"—that elusive variant of social realism—was particularly invested in this transliterate enterprise. Though such writers as Rebecca Harding Davis and Herman Melville began to represent working-class characters in the antebellum era, their modes of figuration were, as I have noted, both sentimental and problematically inflected through a racial lens. And, inasmuch as they were placeholders for a future elaboration of (white) working-class possibility, their characters were either literally or effectively mute. It remained, thus, for the "economic realists" of the late 1870s and 1880s to bring working-class characterization to its fruition and, in particular, to come to terms with an active, vocal, and politically motivated working class. Indeed, realism's shift in focus from morals to economics (or, as some have suggested, to a "moral economy")[3] owes considerably to the historical development of working-class articulation. As workers came to voice their demands as members of an economic class, realists felt pressure to accommodate these enunciations within a cultural topography that was, consequently, increasingly shaped by the struggles between capital and labor. But as I argue throughout this book, such accommodation takes some rather deceptive forms. Many of this era's most trenchant defenders of narrative inclusivity (the so-called democracy of literary realism) were paradoxically also the most invested in maintaining a hierarchy of political voices. Circumscribing working-class demands for autonomy and social equality within a system of economic hierarchy was, therefore, the project not only of the era's business managers but also of its cultural managers. Just as in business relations, including the voices of labor did not ensure the growth of economic justice. Working-class articulations, even working-class "elaborations of insurgency" (to use Gayatri Spivak's term),[4] could be translated, paraphrased, and co-opted—their force left intact, but their referent significantly altered.

One might demonstrate this process of translation in a number of different ways. In this chapter, I focus on the labor strike as both an emblematic instance of insurgent working-class expression and as a new representational problem for such "economic realists" as Thomas Bailey Aldrich, John Hay, and William Dean Howells. As Fay Blake documents in *The Strike in the American Novel*, although the strike was ushered into American literature by authors committed to the new project of realism, "the novelists were not at all interested in either accuracy or authenticity. They needed a violent clash between two contending forces. Never mind that all but a handful of real strikes were settled amicably. All the fictional strikes were violent. Never mind that most of the real strikes were won [by the strikers]. All the fictional strikes were lost."[5] If, however, middle-class writers exaggerated the frequency of labor violence and the victories of management, they did so for political expediency, not, as Blake suggests, for literary sensationalism. The physical violence in their novels reflected their sense of the latent violence of the insurgent labor movement. By projecting their antipathy toward working-class articulation onto a localized "violent clash" that could be "resolved" in favor of social order, these novelists compensated for their sense of a more general disorder between the classes. Further, by depicting class conflict solely through reified clashes between individual managerial heroes and individual proletarian villains, these realists participated in a struggle over the legacy of republicanism, the antebellum ideology of producerism, political independence, and artisan labor practices. While workers used the strike in an effort to maintain these working-class values and to resist the rapidly encroaching structures of industrialism, realists endeavored to transliterate these values into the radically circumscribed ideology of liberal capitalism.

THE STRIKE AS DISCOURSE

Although the earliest representation of a strike in American fiction, Martha Tyler's *A Book without a Title, or Thrilling Events in the Life of Mira Dana,* was published before the Civil War (in 1855), the strike did not become a major literary theme until the 1870s.[6] This reflects its slow ascension as a tool of working-class action. "[U]ntil the mid-1840s," notes David Montgomery, "far more people expressed their grievances through riots than through strikes." Before the proliferation of large factories and the consequent reorganization of urban space, most workers lived in small towns with defined centers that served as the loci of class politics. Hence most insurgent events—such as price riots, actions against corrupt banks or railroads, and violence toward "racial or religious foes"—took place outside the workplace.[7] This focus shifted between 1845 and 1860, as new types of factory labor and new labor disciplines made the workplace a site of contention and made the strike a significant tool. While the Lynn Shoemakers Strike of 1860—the first to garner significant national attention—marked the strike's new power as an economic, political, and symbolic weapon, the Civil War and the contentious politics of Reconstruction delayed its implementation as a broadly configured instrument of national protest and mass organization. Not until the so-called Gilded Age, when the nation was hit by the longest economic depression to date and by high-level scandals in Washington and in the banking industry, did the strike come into its own.

In the years between the Great Railroad Strike of 1877 and the Pullman Strike of 1894, the country experienced an unprecedented number of strikes, boycotts, and work stoppages. According to the U.S. commissioner of labor's conservative estimate, there were over seven thousand strikes in the 1880s. The Great Upheaval of 1886 included 1,412 strikes alone, involving more than 407,000 workers—a significant portion of the nation's industrial workforce.[8] Not only did the number of strikes impress observers, their location also demanded attention. While antebellum strikes most often occurred in isolated industrial communities, such as Lynn and Lowell, late nineteenth-century strikes were not so geographically contained; they frequently affected national commerce and disrupted daily life across entire regions. Perhaps most important, these later strikes had a more political character, as was demonstrated by the vituperative rhetoric of the strikers and the lack of correlation between strikes and business cycles. Workers in this era did not simply react to the pressures of an unregulated economy (as consensus historians have long maintained); they struck as part of a broader political exercise of their growing numbers and power.

While the numerical evidence of strike activity has always clearly testified to the importance of such mass actions, scholars and observers alike have long debated the strike's more qualitative aspects. Consensus historians were not alone in arguing for a narrow economic interpretation of strike activity. Early labor historians, who were equally invested in discovering a clear trajectory toward the consensual harmony of business

unionism, understood the strike in similarly economic terms.⁹ To contemporaneous observers, however, strikes were anything but rational
efforts toward economic improvement. *Harper's Weekly* was not alone
when it asked why "honest workmen" who "claim to know their own
interests" repeatedly "put the bread and butter of their wives and children" in the hands of "despotic" strike organizers "whom they have
learned that they cannot trust?"¹⁰ Other periodicals were even less generous in their attitude toward the rationality of strikers and strike leaders. Reacting to the Great Railroad Strike of 1877, the *Independent,* a New
York religious weekly, announced, "If the club of the policeman, knock-
ing out the brains of the rioter, will answer, then well and good; but if it
does not promptly meet the exigency, then bullets and bayonets, canis-
ter and grape . . . constitute the one remedy."¹¹

These loose depictions of the anarchistic and irrational strike gained
scholarly credence in 1896, when Macmillan brought out the English
translation of Gustave Le Bon's landmark psychological investigation
The Crowd: A Study of the Popular Mind. For Le Bon, the crowd was an
organic creature, "formed of heterogeneous elements, which for a
moment are combined" into "a new being which displays characteristics
very different from those possessed by each of the cells singly." In this
collective form, the crowd possesses neither individual nor communal
rationality but depends instead entirely on external stimulus. According
to this theory, the crowd's susceptibility, rather than its mass nature,
makes the riot and the strike threatening to the social order. "How slight
is the action upon them of laws and institutions," laments Le Bon, "how
powerless they are to hold any opinions other than those which are
imposed upon them. . . . it is not with rules based on theories of pure
equity that they are to be led, but by . . . what produces an impression on
them and what seduces them."¹² American observers of the strike found
Le Bon's seduction theory of the popular mind particularly appealing,
since it helped them reconcile their fear of the masses with an abstract
celebration of egalitarianism.¹³ Honest workmen were not to blame;
their simple minds were seduced by the "impressions" wrought by foreign agitators and itinerate labor organizers.

The strike emerged, then, both as a potent tool for class insurrection
and as a social action whose meaning was anxiously debated by nonstrik-
ing observers, managers, and capitalists. Since strikes, boycotts, and work
stoppages were a major component of working-class culture during the
1870s and 1880s, debates about the meaning of strikes were, in effect,
debates about working-class culture itself—particularly inasmuch as

working-class culture is a culture of struggle. At issue was the legitimacy of class solidarity within a nation where the dominant ideology dictated instead the individual "freedom" of association enshrined in the right to hire and fire at will. By translating the strike into "the mob," observers were able to ignore labor's insistence on collective political agency. They saw collectivity as coercion and called, ironically, for the intervention of state militias. "[I]t is the image of the mob itself which is ideological," concludes Fredric Jameson. "[A]nxieties about property and about the well-nigh physical violations of intimacy are . . . exploited and abused for essentially political purposes, in order to show what monstrous things happen when social control is relaxed or weakened."[14]

While early respondents to the strike saw either economic self-interest or mob psychology, scholars have more recently made significant gains toward understanding the strike in terms of a collective political articulation. In particular, the rise of discourse analysis has provided a means of escape from the strictures of the rationality/irrationality dyad, giving us a way to theorize what David Montgomery identifies as "the qualities of strikes which cannot be couched in the form of demands, let alone won in the terms of settlement."[15] Most centrally, as Montgomery and other new labor historians have argued, the strike should be understood as a class-specific act of expression. "As a working-class event within public life," writes Alan Trachtenberg, "'strike' represented a defiance of the cardinal norm of everyday life: compliance with the authority of employers. The strike was a rupture, a release, an act of negation. . . . It was moreover, a collective act, embodying a recognition that the freedom which arose from negation belonged to a common group."[16]

Though ultimately incomplete as a theory of the strike, Trachtenberg's concepts of rupture and negation usefully delineate part of the strike's expressive structure. As an act of negation—a moment of cessation in an industrial world ceaselessly in motion—much of the strike's power came from its ability to reveal what typically remained veiled. Rupturing the "norm of everyday life," the strike displayed not only the authoritarian relationship between management and labor but labor's potential ability to change that relationship. The strike was also revelatory in a more mediated fashion. During these acts of negation, the industrial labor process was revealed in all its dubious glory. As Rachel Bowlby has argued, by the late nineteenth century, consumerism was already displacing producerism as the main mode of social interchange.[17] The strike disrupted this displacement. Although the strike was a negative act of production, it was producerist all the same, and it served to reaffirm the social bonds of collective labor. Because it disrupted the process of production at the cite of production, the strike was inimical to both consumerism and the commodity form. The commodity was a reification of labor power; the strike abrogated that process. The commodity embodied a theft of labor power in the form of profit; the strike made manifest both that theft and its habitual mystification.

Strikes were, however, more than simply ruptures or acts of negation and revelation. At their most carnivalesque, they embodied the germ of an alternate social organization—founded on cooperation rather than competition. Strikes were thus positive, constructive, and constitutive articulations of a working-class presence. In an era when successive groups of non-English-speaking immigrants repeatedly reconstituted the working class, the strike was an especially important cross-lingual expression of collectivity. Gayatri Spivak has argued that within the "social text of imperialism, . . . elaborations of insurgency stand in place of 'the utterance.'" Although the contexts are different, working-class insurgency operates in a similar fashion. Within the "social text" of late nineteenth-century political culture, the strike stood "in place of" more traditional utterances. Set against the economic and political regime of the post-Reconstruction state, which actively negated the interests of labor in an effort to expand the dominance of corporate capitalism, the strike emerged as a negation of a negation. As a dialectical response, an "elaboration," it asserted, a "counterpossibility" to the economic silence demanded of industrial subjects within a capitalist democracy.[18] Indeed, many workers struck for precisely such a space of counterpossibility. During the Great Upheaval of 1886, strikers across the country agitated for the eight-hour day, chanting, "Eight hours for work, eight hours for rest, eight hours for what we will!"[19] In opposition to an industrial regime that divided the day narrowly between production by labor power (working) and the reproduction of labor power (sleeping, eating, and procreating)—a division that addressed workers exclusively as workers—strikers fought for an equal measure of time completely outside of what Marx called "the realm of necessity." By translating an Enlightenment concept of "the will" as uniquely constitutive of human subjectivity ("eight hours for what we will") into a class-specific response to the circumscriptions of industrial work processes, workers asserted their rights to eight hours within "the realm of freedom," a realm presaged by the strike itself.[20]

Although this sort of discursive theorization of the strike has yet to win many adherents among historians, a group of historical sociologists have made considerable progress toward refining and applying discourse analysis to what they term "repertoires of contention."[21] According to Charles Tilly, who introduced this term, understanding strikes, riots, rallies, and other collective actions as parts of a repertoire avoids both "spontanist" theories of working-class revolt (which find collective actions fundamentally unpredictable and unknowable) and modernization theories of collective action (which see collective actions progressing teleologically toward some specific goal). "The word *repertoire*," writes Tilly, "identifies a limited set of routines that are learned, shared, and acted out through a relatively deliberate process of choice. Repertoires are learned cultural creations, but they do not descend from abstract philosophy or take shape as a result of political propaganda; they emerge from struggle." Like Spivak in this regard, Tilly sees strikes and other less insurgent actions of contention as dialectical aspects of cultural struggle. These actions are collectively meaningful, inasmuch as they are neither simply reactive nor simply spontaneous; but their specific meaning, indeed their very character, is historically contingent: "At any particular point in history, . . . [people] learn only a rather small number of alternative ways to act collectively. . . , adapting each one to the immediate circumstances and to the reactions of antagonists, authorities, allies, observers, objects of their action, and other people somehow involved in the struggle."[22]

Tilly's insistence on the historical dialectics of the repertoire gives cultural critics a needed theoretical context for our understanding of the strike as a form of working-class discourse. While we have previously considered the strike as an instance of speech that embodies alternate modes of social organization, we can now begin to place this speech within a larger sociolinguistic system that complicates the strike's social significance. As Tilly notes, because the repertoire "takes its meaning and effectiveness from shared understandings, memories, and agreements, however grudging, among parties," it "resembles not individual consciousness but a language."[23] Language is, as Bakhtin has stridently argued, always both the site and the product of struggle.[24] Thus, for all of its intrinsic revolutionary promise, the strike's broader meaning emerged extrinsically through a larger, historically determined set of discursive structures through which participants, antagonists, and observers struggled for interpretation. Put simply, strikes were discursively meaningful in two linked, but potentially conflicting, ways: in an abstract sense, as elaborations of insurgency, their mere existence acted as a counterpossibility to capitalism's regime of working-class silence; but in a more specific sense, their meaning was determined by the historical dimensions of a larger cultural struggle. Thus, while strikes were always acts of working-class speech, that fact did not ensure their larger cultural meaning. Like the "man with the knife," their existence and even their particular platform could be contested, translated, and appropriated to fit the requirements of other political and cultural narratives.

REPUBLICANISM IN THE INDUSTRIAL AGE

From the point of view of capital, the need for such acts of appropriation was never so high as during the era in question. The strikes of the late 1870s and 1880s were the most insurrectionary in the country's history. Part of the pitched tenor of their discourse was economic in origin. As Trachtenberg argues, the "violence of feeling often registered in the speeches and writings of labor spokesmen arose in large part from the dawning sense of discrepancy between political promise and present condition, between rhetoric and the facts of daily life."[25] Yet the sense of discrepancy went well beyond the bread-and-butter facts of daily life, to encompass larger social issues. In the decade and a half following the end of Reconstruction, workers struggled to establish and maintain a voice in national debates that set political policy in the newly industrialized country. Their strikes, writes Montgomery, were part "of a continuous, largely unsuccessful, effort by American workers to intervene on their own behalf in the reshaping of national social and political life in a period when no ideological consensus legitimized the state."[26]

While a lack of ideological consensus did not necessarily signify a lack of political control, it did provide the opportunity for radical contestations of the dominant discourse that had failed to take into account the needs of workers. Labor, as a broad political constituency, had been attracted to the Republican Party in the late 1850s because of its espousal of a "free labor" platform. This platform reflected an older producerist ideology that held, in the words of Abraham Lincoln, that "[l]abor is prior to, and independent of capital," that "in fact, capital is the fruit of labor."[27] In the years during and after the Civil War, however, the Republicans repeatedly declined to act on these sentiments. Though labor organizations supported the radical wing of the Republican Party as it passed bills and amendments strengthening the federal government (the Homestead Act, the Legal Tender Act, the National Banking System, and the Fourteenth Amendment—making citizenship a federal right), these changes failed to produce dividends for the working class. Despite its continued promise to uphold the ideology of free labor, the Republican

Party increasingly chose to use federal power in order to aid the development of big business. When, in the Compromise of 1877, the Republicans exchanged Reconstruction and federal military protection of southern blacks for the presidency, any illusions of federal advocacy for
workers were irreparably lost. Organized labor realized that they needed
to struggle with (and not through) the Republican Party in an attempt to
preserve free labor values within the coalescent national state.[28]

Given the increased power of the federal government and its clear
advocacy for capital over labor, it is hardly coincidental that 1877
brought both the end of Reconstruction and the Great Railroad Strike,
the single most insurrectionary collective action in U.S. labor history.
The strike was both unorganized (in any centralized fashion) and
unplanned; but this did little to reassure corporate presidents, stock-
holders, and government officials. Rather, the spontaneous "insurrection" (as the secretary of war quickly labeled it)[29] demonstrated both the
precarious nature of civil society and the government's general inability
to combat civic rebellion. Indeed, while the extent of the strike reflected
a broad discontent among laborers ("It spread," wrote the editor of the
Labor Standard, "because the workmen of Pittsburgh felt the same
oppression that was felt by the workmen of West Virginia and so with the
workmen of Chicago and St. Louis"),[30] the success of the strike was due
to the depth of labor's support within local communities and even state
militias. In particular, as Eric Foner notes, the strike "exposed the deep
hostility to railroads—symbols and creators of the new industrial order—
that permeated many American communities."[31] In town after town, railroad companies were unable to operate scab trains because of the defeat
or dissolution of militia forces and the presence of large crowds of labor
supporters. As workers took over social authority in communities across
the nation, they demonstrated the extent of their grievances and the
lengths to which they were willing to go in order to participate in the
restructuring of the industrial nation. "This may be the beginning of a
great civil war in this country, between labor and capital," reported *The
Pittsburgh Leader,* imagining the worst: "It only needs that the strikers . . .
should boldly attack and rout the troops sent to quell them—and they
could easily do that if they tried."[32] The strike, as a discursive act, spoke
loudly to a nation unaccustomed to such violent forms of assertion.

Moreover, as discursive acts, this and subsequent strikes had a historically particular character. During the Gilded Age, workers saw themselves as the legitimate heirs to the American republican tradition and

demanded the rights and privileges of this legacy. Even as newly formed corporations claimed to embody the spirit of the laissez-faire Republic and used this language to argue against any restriction of their "freedoms," labor mobilized for different, more class-conscious notions of "freedom" and "republicanism." In striking for autonomy, workplace control, the preservation of the craft system, the eight-hour day, and other issues involving class mutualism, workers struggled not only for their rights to a fair wage but for their interpretation of national history, the significance of their "revolutionary heritage," and, thus, the meaning of insurrection itself. Leon Fink summarizes:

> The common terms of antagonists in the Gilded Age should not be allowed to obscure their ideological differences. The period may profitably be seen as a struggle for hegemony over the republican inheritance. It is a measure rather of the stakes of the conflict than of consensus among the contestants that the enemy—no matter who is doing the accusing—is described as alien, interloper, threat to the Republic, etc.[33]

The actions of 1877 suggest that in the struggle for hegemony over the republican inheritance, the labor strikes of the Gilded Age held a twofold significance: at the same time as the presence of these strikes acted as "utterances" of resistance to state and corporate control over social and political life, the content and structure of these strikes embodied the very principles of republicanism that workers attempted to defend. In terms of content, the strike speeches, for example, continually insisted on a labor theory of value, the primacy of the producing classes, and the mutual interests of all workers. "All you have to do," said one speaker at a rally in East St. Louis, "is to unite on one idea—that the workingmen shall rule the country. What man makes, belongs to him, and the workingmen made this country."[34] On a more structural level, it is significant that the 1870s and 1880s were not only the era of the Great Railroad Strike and the Great Upheaval but also the era of countless smaller sympathy strikes. Although national in scope, strike waves were built through a succession of sympathetic responses from relatively autonomous groups of workers—an organizational manifestation of the republican regard for mutualism and political decentralization. Commenting on nineteenth-century "repertoires of contention," Tilly has identified a unifying set of structural characteristics that accord with this observation.

> As compared to their predecessors, the nineteenth-century forms had a national, modular and autonomous character. They were *national* in often referring to interests and issues that spanned many localities or affected centers of power whose actions touched many localities. They were *modular* in that the same forms served many different localities, actors, and issues. They were *autonomous* in beginning on the claimants' own initiative and establishing direct communication between claimants and those nationally significant centers of power.[35]

Strikes and other acts of insurgency, in other words, managed to structurally express republican dissent within an era of rising corporate centralism.

FICTIONAL MEDIATIONS: FROM STRIKE TO STRIKE NOVEL

Tilly's description of nineteenth-century repertoires of contention not only describes the key characteristics of mass action during the period but provides a map of the strike's expressive structure—the form through which it and other insurrectionary conflicts related to the larger social and cultural formation. This is particularly valuable because when strikes are read against the realist strike novel, this side of the dialogic relationship is frequently ignored. Even critics as astute as Amy Kaplan have not always granted working-class forms of discourse the same power of "social construction" as the realist novel. Yet if, as Kaplan claims, we need to see "the production of the real as an arena in which the novelist struggles to represent reality against contradictory representations," then we need also to acknowledge the formal complexity and social vision of these competing expressive forms.[36] Such an acknowledgment will, moreover, help us to understand one of the pressures that stimulated the American novel's rapid change in form and compass. Like the strike, which had significantly enlarged its purview after the Civil War, the realist novel of the 1870s and 1880s struggled to become more national in scope and more democratic in content. Indeed, by focusing on characters who individually or collectively typified national traits, the realist novel (as opposed to its progenitor, the regional narrative) attempted to be both "modular" and "autonomous" as well. In more general terms, the strike novel was part of what Wai Chee Dimock refers to as "a nineteenth-century cognitive style" that arose in response to the expanded social world of industrial America. As an expressive representation of social interactions, it helped readers "to adapt not only to an expanded geographic universe but, even more crucially, to an expanded causal universe, in which human agency, social relations, and moral responsibility all had to be redefined."[37]

Of course, the strike novel had its own distinctive ways of adapting to the expanded causal universe of the late nineteenth century. In this new social order, where the impersonal forces of industrialism, national commerce, and mass immigration increasingly impinged on people's lives, the novel played a relatively conservative role. Whereas strikes attempted to enlarge their scope and sphere of influence, the strike novel—like other economic novels—was concerned with circumscribing and superintending social relations. Indeed, what made the economic novel "economic" was not its concentration on financial and commercial themes (the subject of very few economic novels) but, rather, its understanding of human relations as fundamentally based on rational, predictable, and thus containable systems of organization, governance, and dispensation. The strike novel—that is, the economic novel about the strike—took on the task of limiting the strike's expansive version of social interaction in the new industrial world. While the strike threatened to rupture the normative structure of everyday life, the strike novel resisted this structure by diverting and then assimilating its expansive, insurgent force into its own imaginative economy.

The three strike novels I will discuss in the remainder of this chapter—Thomas Bailey Aldrich's *The Stillwater Tragedy* (1880), John Hay's *The Bread-Winners* (1884), and William Dean Howells's *A Hazard of New Fortunes* (1890)—are in varying degrees successful in their attempts to tame and assimilate the strike into the world of economic realism. Each novelist explicitly or implicitly responds to the actual events of a labor insurrection (Aldrich and Hay depict the Great Railroad Strike of 1877; Howells reacts to the Haymarket Riot and a New York City streetcar strike), but each does so through the mediating strategies of thematic displacement, narrative containment, and caricature. Responding to the Great Railroad Strike of 1877 and to working-class struggles for republicanism, Aldrich and Hay counter with a co-optation of republicanism. In place of the strikers' expansive vision of working-class mutualism and collective economic striving, they give us silver-tongued foreign agitators, corrupt secret societies, and uncontrollable forms of working-class popular culture. *A Hazard of New Fortunes,* Howells's well-known reaction to the Haymarket Riot and the judicial murder of four anarchists, is similar in its strategy of displacement, containment, and caricature. Though it lacks the venomous denunciations found in Aldrich's and Hay's texts, the novel operates through a comparable moral economy. In the "economic chance world" it describes, workers, Christian socialists, and anarchists are all represented, but their political claims and insurrectionary speech are rendered incomprehensible and relegated to the background.[38]

While critics as varied as Daniel Aaron, Edwin Cady, and Walter Benn Michaels have cast Howells in progressive terms,[39] I include *A Hazard of New Fortunes* with such obviously antilabor novels as *The Stillwater Tragedy* and *The Bread-Winners* in order to foreground a less obvious thematic pattern and a linked congruency in plot. In thematic terms, all three novels deal with insurgent working-class actions by converting them into highly affective and dangerously seductive speech. As I have been arguing, strikes and other insurgencies are a kind of discourse, but one that depends greatly on its contextual reception for its cultural meaning. As insurgent discourse is converted into seductive speech in these novels, it is radically decontextualized, flattened, and—finally—reified to the point of caricature. Even as they represent insurgency to a readership unused to such topics, these novels deny its causes, lampoon its authenticity, and misrepresent its intended effects. Moreover, each of these novels pairs working-class insurgents with a protagonist from the ruling class (Hay) or from the ascendant middle class (Aldrich and Howells). While only the title of *A Hazard of New Fortunes* alludes to the fact, each of these novels is about the hazards and impediments faced by those who would lead industry into a period of economic growth and liberal capitalist organization. If, as Howells would later write, "the facts of finance and industry and invention" are valuable to fiction only as they can be dealt with "as the expressions of character," then we should examine the political ramifications of these ruling- and middle-class characters' economic fates.[40] Considered as literary exercises in disbursement—as imaginative acts of resource allocation—these novels are in accord with the history of the rise of a managerial sector. In short, by folding insurgent effect into literary affect and by charting the rise of a new managerial ethic, these novels publicize, simplify, and even ennoble their own account of class relations in the Gilded Age.

ALDRICH'S NEW REPUBLIC

As well as distinguishing itself as the first antilabor novel by a major American writer, Thomas Bailey Aldrich's *The Stillwater Tragedy* was one of the first American strike novels and an influential model for subsequent middle-class representations of working-class insurgency.[41] Aldrich was, however, an unlikely candidate for these dubious honors. His popularity in the 1860s and 1870s was due to his light lyric poetry, his witty short stories (in the style of O. Henry), and his "boy book," *The Story of a Bad Boy*. Published in 1880, a year before he replaced Howells as editor of the *Atlantic Monthly*, *The Stillwater Tragedy* was meant to be Aldrich's transitional work. He wrote to the poet E. C. Stedman: "I am three chapters deep in a novel of different cast from any fiction I have attempted lately. Tragedy this time. I have observed that the writer of comedy, however artistic he may be, is thought less of than the dull fellow who does something sombre, badly. I am going to get my humor a suit of sables."[42] *The Stillwater Tragedy*, the novel that brought the labor strike into the homes of the genteel readers, was to establish its author as a serious, "sombre" writer of realist fiction.

Yet if Aldrich wanted this pioneering attempt at economic realism to be both serious and somber, the result fell somewhat short. Though not exactly comedic, *The Stillwater Tragedy*, like Aldrich's other pieces, approaches its subject in a parabolic, almost allegorical manner. Written largely in the year after the Great Railroad Strike, the text depicts this strike (involving the railroad and heavy industry) only through its effects on a picturesque New England village and a small artisan shop. "In the face of the conflicts and the frenetic tempo of an industrialized society," observes Fay Blake, novelists "were recalling longingly the serenity of rural and village life." Blake continues:

> Villages by the hundreds had ceased to exist, swallowed whole by the demand for "hands" in the growing number of factories and mines, but the novelists were still describing villages. In Thomas Bailey Aldrich's *The Stillwater Tragedy*, for example, the iron mills of Stillwater are in the dim background while Aldrich lovingly describes the bucolic, paternalistic Slocum Marble Yards.[43]

While Blake is certainly correct, her perceptive criticism misses the broader political thrust of Aldrich's "longing." By displacing the strike from the mills (where, the narrator admits, the "smelters and casters . . . *are* meanly paid")[44] to the marble yards, Aldrich is able to shift the reader's attention from wage issues to matters of political control and social order. Although Aldrich does indeed long for a paternalism of sorts, his political vision is not simply nostalgic. Haunted by the image of unruly workers who cannot be restrained by either the bonds of personal obligation or the duties of responsible citizenship, Aldrich calls for a new, more vigorous form of control—a paternalism, perhaps, but one that draws its rationale and its ethics from the "laws" of the market. Appropriately enough, the hero in this forward-looking tale of village paternalism is not the father but the son—the business manager.

The "tragedy" in *The Stillwater Tragedy* does not, consequently, have anything in particular to do with the strike (which has more ameliorative consequences). Rather, it lies in the town's lack of paternal order and industrial growth. The novel opens with the death of Leonard Tappleton ("the richest man in town" [2]) and the murder of the wealthy miser Lemuel Shackford. While Shackford's "mysterious" fate provides the novel with its convoluted detective plot, Tappleton, who is never mentioned again, would be an utterly gratuitous presence were it not for the fact that his demise doubles the town's paternal losses. As the name *Stillwater* implies, these losses have made the village stagnant—its order lacking and its industry sluggish. Rowland Slocum, owner of the marble yards and the novel's only other patriarch, cannot fill the void. This "fairest and gentlest man that ever breathed" (138–39) is a weak-willed businessman who still feels obligated to his workers and thus runs his yard "full-handed for a twelve month at a loss, rather than shutdown, as every other mill and factory in Stillwater did" (140). Indeed, his superannuated business practices leave him under the control of the sinister Marble Workers' Association. "'I am the master of each man individually,'" he declares, "but collectively they are my master'" (64).

Because of his mistaken allegiances to preindustrial business practices, Slocum is wholly unable to exert control over the form and rate of the marble yard's growth. The Marble Workers' Association successfully perpetuates a craft system by limiting the number of new apprentices. "This is the way of it," as one worker explains: "Slocum is free to take on two apprentices every year, but no more. That prevents workmen increasing too fast, and so keeps up wages" (60). From the association's point of view, this is a form of controlled industrial growth. Their knowledge (in some sense, a form of capital) is controlled by master craftsmen, their wages are relatively sheltered from market forces and rise according to experience, and their community grows at a stable and economically healthy rate. But to Slocum, this situation seems stifling, and to Aldrich's narrator, it seems positively unnatural.

The system of this branch of the trades-union kept trained workmen comparatively scarce, and enabled them to command regular and even advanced prices at periods when other trades were depressed. The older hands looked upon a fresh apprentice in the yard with much the same favor as workingmen of the era of Jacquard looked upon the introduction of a new piece of machinery. Unless the apprentice had exceptional tact, he underwent a rough novitiate. In any case he served a term of social ostracism before he was admitted to full comradeship. Mr. Slocum could easily have found openings each year for a dozen learners, had the matter been under his control; but it was not. . . . So his business, instead of becoming a benefit to the many, was kept carefully pruned down for the benefit of the few. He was often forced to decline important contracts, the filling of which would have resulted to the advantage of every person in the village. (63–64)

Although complaints against limits put on the "natural" growth of capitalism are now familiar, in 1880, this discourse was just beginning its rise to dominance. Along with legal formalism, which similarly found support for pro-corporate legal interpretations in the supposedly fundamental laws of nature, economic defenses of the free market depended on—as they co-opted—republican ideals of natural duties, rights, and obligations.[45] Aldrich is not tentative in his encomium of the free market, but he is careful to tie market freedom to the precarious "organic" freedom of late nineteenth-century village life. By commanding "regular and even advanced prices," the Marble Worker's Association actually disassociates itself from the "natural" cycle of the economic boom and bust. Since Slocum cannot accommodate new "learners" in times of economic growth, his business stagnates. This, as Aldrich explains, is not simply a conservative way to manage an industry. It is a form of Luddism, an irrational avoidance of mechanical modernity. Apprentices are, in this sense, the actual embodiments of the new. Limiting their ranks to two a year (a number that symbolizes a conservative procreative plan) merely replicates the existing structure of the industrial family. Limits on a business's freedom to multiply are thus not only limits on the natural endowments of individual "learners" but limits on the health of the village and, by implication, the strength of the republic.

This unnatural situation is tested—and eventually overturned—by Richard Shackford, the novel's main protagonist (and a suspect in his cousin's murder). Anticipating Teddy Roosevelt by two decades, Shackford embodies the chief characteristic of the "new man" and speaks in tribute to unshackled opportunity. He is clearly Aldrich's mouthpiece for self-reliance and "free labor" as it will be translated and rearticulated according to the needs of liberal capitalism. On his return from the sea, he casts off any claim to privilege and fortune and begins as an apprentice in Slocum's yard. This does not go over well with the other employees. But the narrator reports: "Richard's pleasant, off-hand manner quickly won them. He had come in contact with rough men on shipboard; he had studied their ways, and he knows that with all their roughness there is not a class so sensitive" (78). Richard, in other words, returned from abroad able to tame the savage beasts at home. In defense of his rapid rise from apprentice to yard manager, a position that sets him even more concretely against the Marble Worker's Association, Shackford volunteers:

> Every soul of us has the privilege of bettering our condition if we have the brain and the industry to do it. Energy and intelligence come to the front, and have the right to be there. A skillful workman gets double the pay of a bungler, and deserves it. Of course there will always be rich and poor, and sick and sound, and I don't see how that can be changed. But no door is shut against ability, black or white. Before the year 2400 we shall have a chrome-yellow president and a black-and-tan secretary of treasury. (139)

In place of a republican belief in producerism and mutual rise, Shackford gives us a premonition of the liberal capitalist ideology to come: rights are reduced to the "privilege" to compete; "industry" is not shared but innate (like "the brain"). This, according to Shackford, may never eradicate the difference between "rich and poor," but it will eventually produce a desegregated ruling class. The rhetorical slippage from class to race is not accidental. Shackford, like many future "progressives," uses a disingenuous call for racial equity (a condition that will not manifest itself for five hundred years) to sell his theory of innate class inequity. According to this slippery reasoning, trade unions are not unlike slaveholders: both inhibit the rise of "skillful workmen" into positions of power.

Like other managerial heroes in strike novels of this era, Richard Shackford is paired with a working-class antagonist. Such a pairing allows Aldrich to show readers which attributes are desirable and which—like the propensity to organize strikes—are "misfortunes" (141). Torrini, a "swarthy" (141) Italian labor agitator, shares a number of characteristics with Shackforth: "He was a man above the average intelligence of his class; a marble worker by trade, but he had been a fisherman, a moun-

tain guide, and what not, and had contrived to pick up two or three lan-
guages, among the rest English, which he spoke with purity. His lingual
gift was one of his misfortunes" (141). Like Shackford, Torrini is an
intelligent, virile, and competent outsider. During his travels, he has
picked up the kind of talents that should ensure his easy rise. Yet his foreign nature, his "indolent" (141) manner, and his tendencies toward
seductive speech make him a perpetual outsider. Like liquor, his other
misfortune, Torrini's lingual "gift" endangers order and control in Stillwater. Holding forth in the tavern after work hours, his increasingly dissolute words introduce the idea of a strike to the otherwise content
"American" workers. "There was never any trouble to speak of among
the trades in Stillwater till he and two or three others came here with foreign grievances," remarks Shackford, who laments: "These men get
three times the pay they ever received in their own land, and are treated
like human beings for the first time in their lives. But what do they do?
They squander a quarter of their week's wages at the tavern . . . and make
windy speeches at the Union" (138).

Assigning the blame to the power of liquor and to persuasive foreign
agitators most obviously serves to disassociate labor insurgencies from
either economic forces or the agency of the working class at large. It was
a tactic frequently practiced in contemporaneous magazine articles and
newspaper editorials. But in this text, as in *The Bread-Winners* and *A Hazard of New Fortunes*, it has an additional purpose. Working-class action
and management reaction becomes a struggle over affective speech and
representational control. In *The Stillwater Tragedy*, the strike—as an
event—receives scant representation. Its violence, its insurrectionary
intent, and even the change it brings to the village are understood solely
in terms of unregulated speech. Shackford explains to Slocum:

> Every man naturally likes his pay increased; if a simple fellow is told five
> or six hundred times that his wages ought to be raised, the idea is so
> agreeable and insidious that by and by he begins to believe himself
> grossly underpaid, though he may be getting twice what he is worth. He
> doesn't reason about it; that's the last thing he'll do for you. In his mood
> he lets himself be blown away by the breath of some loud-mouthed dem-
> agogue, who has no interest in the matter beyond hearing his own talk
> and passing round the hat after the meeting is over. (172–73)

The danger here is not the pecuniary "nature" of the individual working-
class "fellow." That is usually kept in check by "reason" and the market

("what he is worth"). Rather, the danger comes from the "breath" of the "demagogue" and from the insidiously repetitious quality of insurrectionary speech.

In marked contrast, Shackford does not share Torrini's particular misfortune. Even in his bumbling courtship of Slocum's daughter, he is frequently unable to speak. He cannot verbally seduce Margaret and neglects to consult Slocum about his romantic intentions. "I intended to do so," he admits, "but my words got away from me" (119). When responding to the workers' strike demands, he does little better. Though he is able to tell them that Slocum will take as many apprentices as "the business warrants," this is the last statement he can convey: "The words were not clearly off Richard's lips when the foreman of the shop in which he was speaking picked up a couple of small drills, and knocked them together with a sharp click. In an instant the men laid aside their aprons, bundled up their tools, and marched out of the shed two by two, in dead silence" (176–77). Though ability to command men with one's voice, with mere words, was an attribute shared by many nineteenth-century literary heroes (Captain Ahab is perhaps the most obvious), in this instance, and in strike novels generally, persuasive speech is the province of the working class. Managerial heroes, such as Richard Shackford, rely instead on character, self-control, and a fundamental sense of fidelity.

In *The Stillwater Tragedy*, the strike plot and the murder plot come to similar ends. The strike plot is not so much resolved (which would suggest that insurrectionary discourse can have productive ends) as it is quelled. Standing resolute, refusing to negotiate, Shackford simply waits for the breath that blew into the workers to pass back out of them. In the face of discursive affect, he remains true and unwavering. Torrini, we are told, gets what he deserves. After "striking" Shackford (the only physical manifestation of strike violence in the book), he loses his hand in an industrial "accident" and dies. "They have cut off the hand that struck you, Mr. Shackford" (263), he says on his deathbed, in case the symbolism is not otherwise clear. Likewise, though Shackford is always suspected of murdering his rich cousin, this misunderstanding is similarly settled. Shackford refuses to defend himself and lets those who are unconvinced by the detective's narrative (another instance of affect) put together the "facts" of the case. Ultimately, the economic rationale of this novel rewards such resoluteness. The conclusion finds Shackford calmly awaiting his cousin's estate, already in possession of Slocum's yard and Slocum's daughter.

HAY AND THE WORLD OF AFFECT

While *The Stillwater Tragedy* may have been the first novel to characterize working-class insurgency in terms of affective speech, John Hay's *The Bread-Winners* is notable for bringing this motif to its apotheosis.[46] Like Aldrich's novel, *The Bread-Winners* responds to the events of 1877. But Hay brings class struggle from the village into the industrial city of Buffland (its name is a combination of *Buffalo* and *Cleveland*) and investigates its influence on urban politics. While Aldrich mitigates the role of affect through a countervailing search for fact (the detective plot), Hay immerses the reader in affect through a twisted plot of romance and seduction. Hay somewhat disingenuously subtitled his book *A Social Study* and promised to give his readers "an absolutely truthful picture of certain phases of our social life."[47] But the ambiguities of romance play a central and symbolic role in his conception of the dangers of the new industrial order. Just as romance brings unlikely pairs together and puts them at the mercy of irrational affective forces, urban industrialism forces the classes into an uncomfortable proximity and puts those who should rule in the political minority. In Hay's novel, affect becomes uncontrollable, and its force—more than the force of the working-class itself—must be resisted and contained.

Hay stages this drama of affect by structuring *The Bread-Winners* around a group of chance meetings, attempted seductions, and scenes of violent class conflict. The novel opens as Maud Matchin, a young and conceited working-class seductress, comes to ask Captain Farnham for a job, an imposition the reclusive Farnham feels acutely. Farnham initially fails at finding her work, because, as a "rich and honest" gentleman from one of Buffland's leading families, he is unaware of the patronage system in the city's political machine.[48] After he does succeed in finding Maud a job, she tells him that she wants not just his help but his love. Recoiling from the offense, Farnham rejects her, opening up the plot to a convolution of jealousy, romance, and politics. Offitt, a labor reformer, lusts for Maud and turns Sam Sleeny, an honest worker in love with Maud, against Farnham. Farnham meanwhile falls in love with Alice Belding, the wealthy and refined girl next door, and chances on a secret meeting of the Bread-Winners, a group of insurrectionary labor radicals. At their instigation, the local unions join the national strike, forcing Farnham to organize a militia of Civil War veterans. Spurred on by his own jealousy and by Maud's frustrations due to her unrequited love, Offitt robs and attempts to murder Farnham, in the process implicating Sleeny. In the end, justice prevails: Sleeny is exonerated, and he and Maud are united; Farnham and Alice consolidate their fortunes through marriage; and the Bread-Winners are all harshly punished.

Compared to Aldrich's controlled portrait of economically stagnant unions and changing village life, *The Bread-Winners* brims with a palpable sense of vengeance, anger, and fear. Hay saw strikes as inherently violent. "[N]o important strike has even been carried through without violence," he wrote, " and . . . no long strike has ever ended without murder."[49] Hay responded, consequently, with violent denunciations. Part of this violence of feeling was, no doubt, due to Hay's personal stake in national politics and labor relations. After being admitted to the bar in 1861, he became Abraham Lincoln's private secretary, a post he held until the president's death. From then until 1881, he occupied a series of governmental positions, including assistant secretary of state. After the Spanish-American War, he was instrumental in retaining the Philippine Islands and, in 1901, in securing the rights to build and control the Panama Canal. He is most often remembered, however, for a different imperialist victory—the Open Door policy toward China. His attitudes toward domestic labor relations were imbued with a similar concern for order, control, and access. After his 1874 marriage to Clara Stone, the daughter of the rich industrialist Amasa Stone, his finances were intricately tied to the fortunes of Lake Shore and Michigan Railway. When that railway's workers participated in the 1877 strike, he saw the action principally as a threat to national order, proclaiming that "a profound misfortune and disgrace has fallen on the country."[50] *The Bread-Winners* is in large part his response to this "disgrace" and his call for resistance to impending anarchy.

Hay's fear of a workers' conspiracy against order may have also emerged from his belief that the ruling class was already in a self-induced state of political disorder and needed to join with the newly forming professional-managerial class in an effort to manage working-class insurrection. Within the city of Buffland, for instance, the wealthy have little interest and even less ability to control the course of municipal politics. A week after the strike, they have already returned to their insular habits and willful naïveté.

> The rich and prosperous people, as their manner is, congratulated themselves on their escape, and gave no thought to the question which had come so near to an issue of fire and blood. In this city of two hundred

thousand people, two or three dozen politicians continued as before to govern it, to assess and to spend its taxes, to use it as their property and their chattel. The rich and intelligent kept on making money, building fine houses, and bringing up children to hate politics as they did, and in fine to fatten themselves as sheep which should be mutton whenever the butcher was ready. There was hardly a millionaire on Algonquin Avenue who knew where the ward meetings of his party were held. There was not an Irish laborer in the city but knew his way to his ward club as well as to mass. (246–47)

Although Brook Thomas reads the preceding passage as a condemnation of private gain and an appeal to "republican and Lockean notions of virtue," Hay's call for the rich to, as Thomas puts it, "participat[e] in political life" is motivated by less-lofty sentiments.[51] This image of rich sheep waiting to be slaughtered by hordes of machinating Catholics marks Hay's histrionic reaction to the postbellum rise of political power among Irish immigrants. He calls attention to this within *The Bread-Winners* when he notes that all attempts to wrest control from the Irish machine have failed miserably. An honorary position on the library board is all Farnham has to show for his efforts: "He and some of his friends had attempted a movement the year before, to rescue the city from the control of what they considered a corrupt combination of politicians. They had begun, as such men always do, too late, and without any adequate organization, and the regular workers had beaten them with ridiculous ease" (55).

Political channels are, in fact, so completely blocked that when the strike unfolds, Farnham must eventually organize a counterinsurrectionary militia of Civil War veterans. But before the captain's return to martial readiness, he, too, epitomizes the indolence and impotence of the unwary rich. Both his body and his house are "marked . . . with a kind of serious elegance" (6). His face "had the refinement and gentleness of one delicately bred, and the vigorous lines and color of one equally at home in field and court"; and his hands "had the firm, hard symmetry which showed they had done no work" (5–6). His history, too, bears the mark of an odd sort of powerlessness: his parents "had died in his childhood," then, as an "officer in the army," he "had served several years upon the frontier, had suffered great privations, had married a wife much older than himself, had seen her die on the Plains from sheer want, though he had more money than he could get transportation for" (8). Farnham is at heart, of course, a strong-willed frontier hero (a

Shackfordian manager hidden beneath a Slocum-like exterior); but his earlier efforts to save his wife from want, himself from privation, and the nation from the Indian threat have left him only too willing to remain ensconced in his library.

The lack of ruling-class political power creates a vacuum in the world of Buffland. Without the strictures of a "natural" class hierarchy, all citizens, rich and poor, are left at the mercy of any number of affective and seductive forms of literature, speech, and amusement. In this regard at least, Hay has followed Aldrich's lead, using the setting and subplots to augment the political force of the strike plot. Yet if Aldrich's village of Stillwater is stagnant, Hay's industrial city is on the brink of anarchy. The impudent Maud, for instance, was once "good-natured" (22) and the pride of her family: "She was so full of life and strength that, when she had no playing to do, she took pleasure in helping her mother about her work" (22–23). However, these pleasures are now replaced by the tawdry "dreams and fancies" of the "weekly story-papers" (a working-class cultural form that, as we shall see, also troubled Howells). In these, "she was wooed and won a dozen times a day by splendid cavaliers of every race and degree" (24). Not only do these fantasies convince her to eschew domestic service in favor of high school (an improprietous act of class ascendancy), but their rags-to-riches plots inspire her tasteless advances toward Captain Farnham.

Sam Sleeny, who Hay assures us is Maud's proper mate, is no less plagued by improper sentiments toward the ruling class. After seeing Farnham and Maud together, he descends into a fit of mad hatred: "He hated Maud for the beauty that she would not give him, and which, he feared she was ready to give to another. He hated Saul, for his stolid ignorance of his daughter's danger. He hated most of all Farnham for his handsome face, his easy smile, his shapely hands, his fine clothes, his unknown and occult gifts of pleasing" (73). It is this last bit of hatred, rather than any political or economic rationale, that prompts Sleeny to join the Bread-Winners. While "he knew and cared nothing about . . . Labor Reform, . . . his hatred of Farnham was easily extended to the class to which he belonged, and even to the money which made him formidable" (81). Farnham's money may make him "formidable," but it does not protect him from the power of seduction. Much of his rather awkward courtship of Alice Belding is conducted "without premeditation, almost without conscious intention" (160). He is regularly so entranced by her charms that he is unaware of the actual conversation, "an operation of . . . mind, like that familiar to the eaters of hashish" (159). Of course,

Farnham has the good graces to be seduced by one of his own class. He is not as attentive as he might be to the raging chaos around him, but he does manage to save that day. Maud and Sleeny are less lucky (and apparently less deserving). Their union occurs only after a lengthy course of trials and tribulations. In short, like many lesser-known novels of the era, *The Bread-Winners* features a swoon on almost every page. However, unlike these "vulgar and unhealthy" (24) romances, Hay's novel inserts a moral and political message: the working-class insurrection finds allies in minds easily led; consequently, political chaos comes to those who live in a state of social laxity.

Of course, the evils of insurrection require an actual perpetrator, a catalyst to solidify the broadly felt social decay into an actual event. Hay goes to extraordinary lengths to provide his readers with a personage appropriate to this task. Andrew Jackson Offitt, Hay's version of the labor agitator, is a wild amalgam of caricatures. At once a raving anarchist and a Jacksonian populist (which Hay evidently understood to be anarchism's precursor), his very physiognomy projects all that Hay finds odious.

[His face] was a face whose whole expression was oleaginous. It was surmounted by a low and shining forehead covered by reeking black hair, worn rather long, the ends being turned under by the brush. The mustache was long and drooping, dyed black and profusely oiled, the dye and the grease forming an inharmonious compound. The parted lips, which were coarse and thin, displayed an imperfect set of teeth, much discolored with tobacco. The eyes were light green, with the space which should have been white suffused with yellow and red. It was one of those gifted countenances which could change in a moment from a dog-like fawning to a snaky venomousness. (74–75)

Offitt's "gift" is every bit as significant as Torrini's in *The Stillwater Tragedy*. While Torrini's loquaciousness reflects his inebriated disposition, Offitt's mutable countenance demonstrates his two-faced personality. His pat incantations of insurrection—"We are goin' to make war on capital. We are goin' to scare the blood-suckers into terms"—are really only attempts to gain money and the much sought-after Maud. "He rattled off these words," Hay assures, "as a listless child says its alphabet without thinking of a letter" (78). As listless and unconscious as these words may be, they have a dramatic effect. Soon after Offitt converts Sleeny to the cause, the Bread-Winners instigate a general strike.

As in *The Stillwater Tragedy,* the Great Railroad Strike in *The Bread-Winners* is depicted solely in terms of affective speech. Hay, in fact, surpasses Aldrich by including the actual words of the strikers and strike organizers. For instance, the following passage of strike rhetoric, as Hay later informed the *Century,* was taken "almost word for word from a Cleveland paper of July 1877."[52] As Farnham prepares to defend his mansion, a friend and fellow counterinsurgent reports:

> there was a fellow in front of Mouchem's gin-mill, a long-haired, sallow-looking pill, who was making as ugly a speech to a crowd of ruffians as I ever heard. One phrase was something like this: "Yes, my fellow-toiler"— he looked like he had never worked a muscle in his life except his jaw-tackle,—"the time has come. The hour is at hand. The people rule. Tyranny is down. Enter in and take possession of the spoilers' gains. Algonquin Avenue is heaped with riches wrung from the sweat of the poor. Clean out the abodes of the blood guiltiness." And you ought to have heard the ki-yi's that followed. (218–19)

Hay's representation of the strike is both discursive and co-optive. Taking on insurgent discourse as such by surrounding it with other discourse, he contests both the presence of affective speech and its form and incendiary content. Without exception, he frames these quotations within the consciousness of a ruling-class character. Thus, while these quotations may be accurate representations of working-class speech, they are always presented as indirect quotes, always already contained within a derisive enclosure. An appeal to working-class solidarity is, in this instance, actually interrupted by a counterreading. Importantly, Hay does nothing to mitigate or disrupt the speaker's call for violence. Though rendered simply in almost inarticulate sentences, it stands intact, rationalizing Farnham's own violent actions.

Hay's description of the strike brings a certain clarity to his repeated condemnations of affect. If strikes are motivated by neither economic nor political rationale, then they are entirely the result of words of agitation and seduction. This assertion not only serves as evidence against the validity of working-class actions; it disproves their very possibility. In Hay's view, strikes, like Maud's pretensions and Sleeny's politics, are not the deeply felt articulations of rational working-class desires; they are the actions of mobs who are all too easily led. Workers may be conscious, but they are far too pliant to have anything like a class consciousness and far too obedient to act with a collective will. They are akin, rather, to Le

Bon's crowd—an organism entirely without rational thought, waiting to be directed. Hay's reactionary logic serves also as a rebuttal to the republican claims of the strikers of his era. As Alexander Hamilton asserted a century before, republicanism (working-class or otherwise) depends on a citizenry whose behavior accords with a certain understanding of rationality. If they are to be self-governing, political subjects must have a uniform and relatively stable sense of duty to the republic. Affect disturbs any such equilibrium. Not only does it deteriorate the moral character of the nation, but its ubiquity and power construct a citizenry who are constantly falling prey to nefarious people and their contrary notions of governance. In the face of this, men like Captain Farnham must not only resist the violent results of affective speech, they must counter with their own discourse of authority and acts of political management.

Like unruly children, what the workers in *The Bread-Winners* most need is steady work, strong discipline, and wise words from their betters. During the strike, when there was "a general cessation of labor, . . . there were curious signs of demoralization, as if the spirit of work was partially disintegrating and giving way to something not precisely lawless, but rather listless" (191). Sleeny, in particular, needs work in order to be his honest self: "Not until he became interested in his work did he recover the even beat of his pulse and the genuine workmanlike play of his facilities. Then he forgot Farnham . . . and enjoyed himself in a rational way with his files and chisels and screwdrivers" (92). Of course, sometimes workers are not so compliant, in which case the rod must be the rule. Faced with rioters, Farnham and his men make "rapid play with their clubs," after which "the crowd began to feel the mysterious power which discipline backed by law always exerts, and they ran at full speed up the street" (233). In Hay's Buffland, as in Aldrich's Stillwater, democracy and consensual rule no longer function. Here, the republican values of mutualism and communalism are relics of an artisanal past. Listlessness must be mét by work, violence by violent discipline, and affect by other words of persuasion. In a letter to the *Century,* Hay went so far as to advertise his own novel as the ultimate source of moral persuasion, power, and control. Responding to a critic who claimed that permanently valuable literature must "support justice against prejudice," Hay wrote:

> If I would make one working-man see that, in joining a secret society which compels him by oath to give up his conscience and his children's bread to the caprice or ambition of any "Master Workman" or "Executive Council," he is committing an act of folly whose consequences he cannot

foresee, and placing himself in the power of an utterly irresponsible despotism, I should be better satisfied than if I should turn out . . . permanently valuable work.[53]

HOWELLS AFTER HAYMARKET

During the years following the publication of Hay's best seller, a number of new strike novels appeared on the national scene. In 1886 alone, major houses published Edward Fuller's *Complaining Millions of Men,* George Dowling's *The Wreckers,* Martin Foran's *The Other Side,* Robert Grant's *Face to Face,* Ross Clinton's *The Silent Workman,* and Frank Stockton's *The Hundredth Man*—all of which featured strikes prominently. This subgenre did not reach its literary pinnacle, however, until after the height of strike activity, when, in 1890, William Dean Howells published his monumental economic novel *A Hazard of New Fortunes.* Indeed, *Hazard* marks not only the high point of the strike novel but something of a transitional point as well. Anxiously attempting to reestablish a moral ground in the midst of increasing class violence, Howells nonetheless saw more clearly than either Aldrich or Hay that the new economic and social structures of liberal capitalism would require pluralistic means of cultural representation and less-martial means of control. Thus his novel betokens the new world of liberal capitalism and is less parochial in its purview and less judgmental in its tone. Indeed, it resembles nothing as much as the expansive social novels of British, French, and German realism, as it makes a pioneering bid to translate European notions of the heterogeneous social sphere into American letters.

In *Hazard,* Howells gives his readers not only capitalists and workers but an entire social scene, including a dizzying array of managers, philanthropists, socialites, writers, aesthetes, genteel Southerners, and foreign revolutionaries. These characters are not flung together through the contrived orchestrations of a detective plot or a romantic entanglement but, rather, share a defined space and (for the most part) labor together on a national magazine. *Every Other Week,* "the new departure in magazines" (183), is, in this sense, more than a mere plot vehicle. Through it and through the thoughts of its writers, editors, owners, and artists, Howells foregrounds the struggle between the competing concerns of labor and management and the competing goals of politics and aesthetics within an industry that was broadening its readership, modernizing its means of production and distribution, and focusing on new topics. For Howells, the struggles in the management of this magazine are emblematic of the problems facing the larger project of American realism in a space newly defined by liberal capitalism: In an attempt to base the American novel on social grounds, how can one reconcile the disturbances and class conflicts brought about by the competing "needs" of business and industry? In the attempt to transcribe the voices of the American people into the confined space of a magazine or of a realist novel, how can one include those voices that threaten to rupture that space?

Howells wrote *A Hazard of New Fortunes* after a long, painful period of personal tragedy and political reflection. The ponderousness, the weightiness, and the new uncertainty of his vision in *Hazard* reflected his mood during what Edwin Cady has called "the black time" after the death of Howells's daughter.[54] This loss, coupled with his uneasy ruminations on the larger political injustices of industrial life, had inspired Howells to take a tortured journey through the novels of Tolstoy and the socialism of Laurence Gronlund's *The Co-operative Commonwealth. Annie Kilburn* (1889), Howells's eulogy to the philanthropic impulse, was the first literary manifestation of his new attitudes. That novel, he later explained, was a plea "for justice, not alms."[55] When Howells wrote *Hazard,* his next substantial reflection on American social ills, he drew on one additional event for inspiration. In 1886 and 1887, during the worst of his daughter's illness, he had made a failed attempt to rally support for the anarchists convicted in the Haymarket incident. In addition to recapitulating the stark social vision of *Annie Kilburn, Hazard* was Howells's attempt to come to terms with the lessons of the Haymarket incident and to reconcile its troubling challenges to the social novel.[56]

Even if the Haymarket incident and subsequent trial had not deeply influenced Howells, these events would be a necessary touchstone for an examination of representations of working-class insurrection. As Carl Smith has recently demonstrated, the representations of the bombing, "the Haymarket trial, and the public discussion that surrounded it, were the site of a conflict over whose words and descriptions were the right ones."[57] Who had the correct description of American society and the American system of justice: the anarchists and their supporters within the labor movement or the police and the prosecution? In addition to the public discussion, the Haymarket incident also prompted a judicial and political reconsideration of the legality of working-class insurrectionary discourse, a consideration based on the court's new understanding of this discourse's relationship to insurrectionary action. Responding both to the events of the Haymarket Riot and more generally to the anarchist tactic of "propaganda by the deed," courts and legislative bodies began to define insurrectionary speech as insurrectionary action—as something that was prima facie affective and thus, according to their understanding at that time, unprotected by the Constitution.[58]

In the Haymarket case, the domain, the power, and the proper place of speech was, for both the anarchist defendants and the government prosecutors, the major issue of contention. Even the initial confrontation between the police and workers was partially the result of differing interpretations of the meaning of speech. The workers who gathered in Haymarket Square in Chicago on May 4, 1886, to protest a recent police shooting of unarmed strikers were already beginning to disband when Samuel Fielden, the final speaker, concluded his address. Calling on workers to shed their illusions about making progress through legislative means, Fielden exhorted:

> The law is only framed for those who are your enslavers. . . . You have nothing more to do with the law except to lay hands on it and throttle it until it makes its last kick. It turns your brothers out on the wayside and has degraded them until they have lost the last vestige of humanity, and they are mere things and animals. Keep your eye upon it, throttle it, kill it, stab it, do everything you can to wound it—to impede its progress.[59]

According to Paul Avrich, who has written the definitive account of the Haymarket incident, these remarks stirred the police to action, convincing them that the speaker was calling for a direct attack on their forces. As a line of officers confronted the speaker, an unidentified person threw a bomb into the midst of the police, killing one officer and wounding several others. The police responded by firing indiscriminately into the crowd and, as autopsies later showed, into each other. Eight police died, and estimates of the civilian casualties from gunfire number as high as fifty. Despite the casualties, Inspector Bonfield, the officer in charge, defended his actions as a legitimate response to incendiary language.[60] Fielden, for his part, contended that he meant his statements figuratively: "If you take the metaphors from the English language, you have no language at all. . . . It's not necessary . . . that because a man says 'throttle the law' he means 'kill the policeman.'"[61]

But what if he does? What are the legal and political consequences of calls for insurrectionary action? Of concern primarily to economic novelists before 1886, the relationship between insurrectionary words and insurrectionary actions became central in the ensuing Haymarket trial, which was a trial of affect more than it was a trial of criminal action. Although the police devoted much of their forces to finding the bomber, going so far as to illegally interrogate a number of suspects, the perpetrator was never discovered.[62] All eight of the anarchist leaders who the police eventually arrested had alibis. Several were even at the rally, in plain sight, far from where the bomb was thrown. But faced with the lack of a credible suspect, lawyers for the prosecution advanced the novel legal theory of a "constructive crime." Contrary to all legal precedent, the state claimed that even if no physical evidence and no direct testimony linked the defendants to the perpetrator, their speeches and writings revealed a conspiracy of influence.[63] "Although perhaps none of these men personally threw the bomb," asserted Julius Grinnell, attorney for the prosecution, "they each and all abetted, encouraged and advised the throwing of it and are therefore as guilty as the individual who in fact threw it."[64] Courts had not heretofore so cavalierly linked encouragement and advice with either abetting or committing a crime. The Haymarket case, which the prosecution won and which survived appeal, marked a turning point in the courts' handling of speech. Words instigated deeds; demagogues were to blame.

It was undoubtedly this aspect of the Haymarket case that commanded William Dean Howells's attention during his period of isolation at Lake George after his daughter's death. To this author and editor who had devoted his career to championing the cause of realism in literature—who had brought the disharmonious voices of new characters and new authors to the reading public—this attack on freedom of speech was intolerable. He made a principled and almost solitary stand on behalf of the defendants. He wrote a letter to his friend George Curtis, editor of *Harper's Weekly*, in a futile attempt to change that magazine's opinion of the incident, arguing that the defendants "are condemned to death upon a principle that would have sent every ardent antislavery man to the gallows." A week later, Howells was more direct: "These men are doomed to suffer for their opinion's sake."[65] Howells was quick to add, in statements both public and private, that he did not agree with these particular opinions. He argued that violence was not the correct course of action for either the state or its citizens. Rather, he contended, there must be an open tolerance of a plurality of opinions. Like a realist novel, the public sphere must be a space of democracy, even if that meant it was frequently cacophonous. Nevertheless, the innocence of the defendants was, at least for Howells, strikingly clear. The issue was not their political or economic beliefs; the issue was speech, and speech must be defended.

But as I have noted, the inclusion of insurrectionary speech does not preclude its management and containment. Rather, as the public sphere expands and becomes more rancorous, authors tend to match inclusively with increasingly rigid structures of order. Howells faced a paradox with regard to the Haymarket case. While steadfastly maintaining the defendants' rights to voice their political opinions, he may have found validity in the prosecutions' claims about the power of affect. An editor and writer for nearly a half century, Howells ardently believed in the written word's ability to shape behavior. Thus Howells struggled to find an adjudicating mechanism, some sort of moral economy that could both permit speech but limit its shape, power, and purview. A *Hazard of New Fortunes* is the product of this political and aesthetic struggle; it maintains the spirit of Howells's earlier defense of insurrectionary speech; but as a representational structure, it presents this defense within a highly ordered economy. Its characterizations, its strategic use of dialect, and its strong sense of proper aesthetic order give Howells a way to channel and redirect the demands of expansive speech. Indeed, although Howells believes himself a defender of freedom of expression, the message of *Hazard* is not dissimilar to the message of the Haymarket trial: the problem is not speech per se but affective speech, speech with what the courts would call a "bad tendency" to arouse the working class.[66]

Within the world of *Hazard*, the working class is given an almost unprecedented amount of representation, presence, and even expression. The Marches, Howells's middle-class protagonists, seem to live mostly in a city of streets, where each narrative turn brings the possibility of a chance encounter with a working-class character. Such encounters serve a crucial purpose. They allow Howells to include alternate and even contesting voices, while simultaneously containing them within a middle-class character's point of view, the narrator's point of view, or even, finally, an omniscient description that blurs the distinctions. For instance, on his way to meet a coworker, Basil March, the new editor of *Every Other Week*, stops to ask directions from a "shabby-genteel ballad-seller." At first, March simply includes this "character" within the picturesque sketch that he seems always to be preparing for the magazine: "He decided simultaneously that his own local studies must be illustrated and that he must come with that artist and show him just which bits to do. . . . He thought he would particularly like his illustrator to render the Dickensy, cockneyish quality of the . . . ballad-seller . . . whom he instantly perceived to be, with his stock in trade, the sufficient object of an entire study by himself" (160). Unfortunately, this "object" has already "rendered" himself and his "shabby" East Side neighbors in his own ballads.

> [The ballads] were mostly tragical or doleful; some of them dealt with the wrongs of the working man; others appealed to a gay experience of the high seas; but vastly the greater part to memories and associations of an Irish origin; some still uttered the poetry of plantation life in the art-less accents of the end man. Where they trusted themselves, with syntax that yielded promptly to any exigency of rhythmic art, to the ordinary speech, it was to strike directly for the affections. . . . March thought this not at all a bad thing in them; he smiled in patronage of their simple pathos. . . . He bought a pocketful of this literature, popular in the sense that the most successful book can never be. (161)

Although this encounter is but one of many in a text obsessed with cross-class meetings, it is notable because of its focus on competing forms of working-class representation that exceed the comprehension of the text's main characters. The ballads are hardly revolutionary—"tragi-cal or doleful," they eulogize rather than radicalize. Still, in dealing with "the wrongs of the working man," they are clearly beyond March's own aesthetic parameters. Even in those moments when March's vision focuses on economic disparity—moments that critics have cited as evi-dence of a changed outlook[67]—he is far from seeing such "wrongs" as wrongs. According to March, in the "economic chance world in which we live and which we men seem to have created" (380), wrongs come from no particular agent. They "belonged to God" (380) or to the "law-less, Godless . . . huge disorder" (160), which, of course, is essentially the same thing. Mrs. March is even more devoted to theoretical sleights of hand in order to disavow the wrongs of the working class: "I don't believe there's any *real* suffering—not real *suffering*—among those people; that is, it would be suffering from our point of view, but they've been used to it all their lives, and they don't feel their discomfort so much" (60). As Wai Chee Dimock notes, many doctors were also convinced of this dif-ferential "calculus of suffering," which served to rationalize unequal access to medical care, anesthesia, and adequate food and shelter, as well as serving to comfort the genteel sensibilities of the upwardly mobile professional-managerial class.[68]

Yet if the ballads speak of the wrongs of the working man in a tone that challenges this dominant discourse, they do not speak freely. Or perhaps more accurately, their freedom to speak is contingent on their encapsulation within March's experience. As the passage moves between March and the narrator, blending these voices ambiguously, the voice of the ballads is circumscribed, turned into an expression of nostalgia, "artless" in its "accent" of the local. Even when Howells writes of the ballads' power to "strike directly for the affections," he distances this judgment with three modifying phrases. The hesitancy he finds in their "ordinary speech" may be more of a projection than a description; for he is nothing if not hesitant to ascribe them real power. The ballads have, moreover, an odd sense of materiality that helps contain their discursive force. In a text that continually works to separate the real from the ideal, they are distinguished by their notable, even excessive, reality. This, one would think, should add to their value within Howells's most "realistic" novel; but the lines are otherwise drawn. The "sense" in which these ballads are popular is merely the "sense" in which they can be bought by the "pocketful"—an act that makes them seem more incidental than expressive. Before the narrator describes their subject matter, they are, in fact, introduced as props for March's "study" of the "ballad-seller": the narrator observes that the latter's "stock in trade" were "strung singly upon a cord against the house wall and held down in piles on the pavement with stones and blocks of wood" and that "[t]heir control in this way intimated a volatility which was not perceptible in their sentiment" (160). In this observation, Howells protests too much. Howells's efforts to tie the ballads up, hold them down, and pocket them give evidence of a volatility that consequently requires repeated acts of control.

Howells invokes similar measures of control with regard to Lindau, a German socialist who is clearly meant to invoke the spirit of Haymarket and the challenge of dissenting speech. Lindau's translating job at *Every Other Week* is, as Amy Kaplan has noted, the key to the meaning of this character: "Lindau himself is represented as a translation, an amphibious figure who speaks both English and German and who acts equally at home in his tenement and in the Marches's new apartment."[69] Though he lost a hand in the Civil War and is therefore symbolically "American," his manners, political views, and speech clearly mark him as foreign, as an element that would, in most novels, require assimilation. *Hazard* does not, however, move in that direction. Rather, it renders Lindau's speech in dialect, positioning him permanently on the border between commonality and difference, inclusivity and expulsion. Even as the reader is informed that Lindau lost his hand for his country, Lindau interjects, "What gountry hass a poor man got, Mr. Marge?" (82). The conjunction of Lindau's radical sentiment and his garbled speech is, of course, not incidental. Every metamorphosed vowel and consonant mark both his speech and his ideas as heretical and, as a consensus of characters observe, "violent" (165, 253, 277). His voice is expressed but simultaneously contained. By characterizing him as a linguistic anomaly within the American scene, Howells can let his views stand as provocations that require no answer.

Indeed, while Lindau serves as more than a mere prop in *Hazard*, his role is narrowly confined to provocation. For the most part, he serves to bring other, more affluent characters into an ongoing debate about the merits, dangers, and limits of free speech. Like Torrini in *The Stillwater Tragedy* and Offitt in *The Bread-Winners*, Lindau is a catalyst whose own political actions and beliefs are murky. Readers know he is a socialist because other characters say he is a socialist; beyond that, there is no evidence. We never see him engaged in collective political struggle. This does not, however, seem to matter a great deal. Within the novel, it is not the content but the fact of socialism that threatens to interrupt the making of "new fortunes." This is dramatized during Lindau's introduction in the novel. While March is busy wondering how he knows the "tall, shabbily dressed, elderly man," Fulkerson, March's companion and employer, is interrupted by the vision of another German socialist.

> "See that fellow?" Fulkerson broke off and indicated with a twirl of the head a short, dark, foreign-looking man going out the door. "They say that fellow's a socialist. I think it's a shame they're allowed to come here. If they don't like the way we manage our affairs, let 'em stay at home," Fulkerson continued. "They do a lot of mischief, shooting off their mouths round here. I believe in free speech and all that, but I'd like to see those fellows shut up in jail and left to jaw each other to death. *We* don't want any of their poison." (74)

Of course, this and similar passages are hardly meant to represent Howells's own opinions about such matters. Rather, Fulkerson's crass views, his own accent, and even the italicized "we" in the last sentence work to distance the author from such vocal illiberalisms. The point of *Hazard* is, on the contrary, that "they" are already "here"; and although "they" shoot "off their mouths," as long as this remains a figure of speech (as long as "they" are speaking and not bombing), "they" must be tolerated.

Hazard's tolerance of dissenting speech proves, however, to have clear limits. These are mutually defined by the two central events in the novel. The first of these—March's defense of Lindau's speech during a gathering of the magazine's employees—has long been understood as a recapitulation of Howells's own defense of the Haymarket anarchists. After Dryfoos, the magazine's rich, ill-mannered benefactor, recounts his heroic destruction of a union, Lindau responds: "'That was vile treason,' said Lindau in German, to March. 'He's an infamous traitor! I cannot stay here. I must go'" (296). Mirroring Howells's previous actions, March later defends his employee's right to hold his opinions: "We don't print his opinions, and he has a perfect right to hold them, whether Mr. Dryfoos agrees with them or not" (313). While one cannot deny that in the face of his own tenuous economic circumstances, March has demonstrated principles of honor, this should not blur an important fact: Lindau made his comment in German to March, thinking that only his friend would understand. It is private speech and is thus protected under the principles that March, Howells, and the United States Supreme Court share. As March importantly notes, *Every Other Week* does not print Lindau's opinions and thus does not make them public. Lindau deserves and receives tolerance within the moral economy of the novel.

During the novel's climatic streetcar strike, however, Lindau oversteps the bounds of tolerable dissent and is promptly punished. When policemen begin to club the strikers, Lindau yells: "Ah yes! Glup the strikerss—gif it to them! Why don't you co and glup the bresidents that insoalt your lawss, and gick your Boart of Arpidration out of toors? Glup the strikerss—they cot no friendts! They cot no money to pribe you, to dreat you!" (368). A nearby policeman, in turn, strikes Lindau, crushing what remains of his arm and fatally wounding him. The resonance with *The Stillwater Tragedy* is all too clear: just as Torrini loses his hand in the earlier novel, here the machinery of power takes the hand that struck them. In this instance, March is equally unambivalent. Lindau went too far: "'I could almost say he had earned the right to be wrong. He's a man of the most generous instincts, and a high ideal of justice, of equity—too high to be considered by a policeman with a club in his hand. . . . It's the policeman's business, I suppose, to club the ideal when he finds it inciting a riot'" (375). Importantly, the question in this novel is never whether Lindau is actually right. His gross error is always presumed self-evident. The question is merely, does he have a right to be vocally wrong? In this case, the answer is no. This situation requires a different relationship between "business" and speech. Lindau's high ideals are, in fact, irrelevant if he can be shown to have incited a riot. His rights are suddenly not inalienable but "earned." Even so, they prove to be an inadequate protection. This type of speech is public and must be controlled by the state.

In his distinction between private protection and public regulation, Howells reiterates the dominant position of courts at the turn of the century, when, as in *Gompers v. Buck's Stove & Range Co.*, they distinguished between private speech, which enjoys the protection of the First Amendment, and "verbal acts," which contain "a force not inhering in the words themselves, and therefore exceeding any possible rights of speech which a single individual might have."[70] But despite this consonance, Howells's position is driven by less-juridical goals: He seeks to regulate that aspect of society that seems most in need during this era. Though private society in *Hazard* has been infiltrated with such radicals as Lindau and such boors as Dryfoos, the matrons and masters of the social scene evidently have the matter in hand. It is the public sphere that most requires attention. The police—a presence in all three strike novels—are the most obvious enforcers; but the novelist himself does not hesitate to assist.

Removing both Lindau and Conrad (a Christian socialist and Dryfoos's unlikely son) through their deaths in the course of the strike, Howells regulates the challenge of dissenting speech and adjudicates the resources of this economic fiction. Critics have traditionally understood these deaths as acts of punishment—not only for Lindau's provocation, but for March's aestheticism and Dryfoos's hubris. Yet if the novel acts as an adjudicating mechanism in this regard, these punishments do not seem to fit the crimes. Lindau's provocation is hardly on par with the Haymarket defendants' calls for revolution, March's desire to see the picturesque in poverty is not far from Howells's own stance, and the death of Dryfoos's Christic son seems like an exaggerated means of demonstrating the shallowness of Dryfoos's materialism. The deaths of the novel's two dissidents, the chastening of Dryfoos (the novel's rapacious capitalist), and the reeducation of March (its symbolic idealist) promotes a political and economic logic rather than a moral agenda. Howells eliminates the "extremes" of the political spectrum, leaving the newly pragmatic March to head *Every Other Week* and to serve as a standard-bearer for the newly established corporate dictates of liberal capitalism. March's ascendancy and Dryfoos's exit are meant to signal the triumph of those with a certain type of principles over those with mere economic principal; March's "new fortune" is earned through labor and honor, while Dryfoos's was won through union busting and oil speculation. But this is just a post facto rationalization for the novel's final act of reorganization: when March becomes editor and co-owner of *Every Other Week,* he immediately "dispenses" with a number of employees who had previously "seemed indispensable" (429), trimming the workforce and streamlining the organization of the magazine to make it more profitable.

This reorganization is significant for the overarching message of *Hazard.* Throughout the novel, *Every Other Week* has been more than a business venture: it has symbolized the political dreams of its editor and publisher and has more broadly served as a token of Howells's commitments to more egalitarian labor practices. When the novel begins, March and Fulkerson have high hopes for a new kind of literary egalitarianism. Before they settle on *Every Other Week,* they try out such names as *The Syndicate* and *The Mutual* (10). As these references to political republicanism may suggest, their initial idea is to take submissions from all parties, paying them a share of the profits: "The thing was a new departure in magazines; it amounted to something in literature as radical as the American Revolution in politics: it was the idea of self-government in the arts, and it was this idea that had never yet been fully developed in regard to it" (183). Yet by the novel's close, this adventure in republicanism has become a symbol for the increasing corporatization of journalism and the arts. Once fully in control, March and Fulkerson are faced with the inevitable decisions of all business owners, they initiate "reforms . . . for a greater economy in management" (428). Like the realist novel itself, the magazine's national scope and democratic content require more, not less, managerial supervision.

This relationship may be said to summarize the plot of all three of the strike novels considered in this chapter. Widening their purview, broadening their vision, and heightening their claims, they all follow Lindau's command never to "forget the boor!" (165). Unfortunately, the poor are as garbled a presence in the novels as they are in Lindau's speech. Their voices are apprehended, but only as instigations for further management. Heard now through the realist strike novel, workers and the poor are not as inarticulate as Davis's iron puddler or Melville's factory girls, but they might as well be. The power of their presence and the strength of their claims are made to serve other masters. Thus the strike novel is best understood as a coercive, but not a repressive, force. By following the strike's expressive structure while narrowing its discursive means, the novel channels and contains what might otherwise prove anticonsensual. The "voices" of the insurgent class are heard through literary ventriloquism, but their dissonance is rendered in "foreign" tones.

Middle-Class Melancholy and Proletarian Pain

The Writer as
Class Transvestite

The struggle of classifications is a fundamental division of the class struggle. The power of imposing a vision of divisions, that is, the power of making visible and explicit social divisions that are implicit, is the political power *par excellence:* it is the power to make groups, to manipulate the objective structure of society.

—Pierre Bourdieu,
In Other Words: Essays Toward a Reflexive Sociology

Strong and infinitely appealing are the basal elements of existence, and yet mysterious, evasive, receding like a spectre from your craving grasp.

—Walter Wyckoff,
The Workers: An Experiment in Reality

STEPHEN CRANE'S EXPERIMENT

On a rainy winter night in the depression year of 1894, Stephen Crane "went forth" dressed in "rags and tatters . . . to try to eat as a tramp may eat, and sleep as the wanderers sleep." His experiences in New York City's Bowery Mission that night provided the basis for his sketch "An Experiment in Misery," which confronted readers of the *New York Press* with an unusual journalistic message: much of what they thought they knew about poverty was invalid. "You can tell nothing of it unless you are in that condition yourself," he wrote, "It is idle to speculate about it from

... [a] distance."[1] Like the "squads of well dressed Brooklyn people, who swarmed toward the Bridge" (248) after their daily work in Manhattan, Crane's middle-class readers were geographically and culturally divided from those in rags and tatters, unable to conceptualize how the poor really "feel" (862). The sketch's fictionalized account of one middle-class youth's disguised journey into the world of poverty attempts to bridge this distance, providing Crane's readers with a study of class subjectivity in transformation. What Crane wishes to show is not "how the other half lives" but how misery, as a class-specific social force, shapes perception. His young and impressionable protagonist serves as a gauge of this environmental effect: apprehending misery (as well as luxury, in a paired sketch) as an exogenous condition to his own experimental body, and then interpreting the outcome to his readership. The point of the journey, as the youth tells his elder friend, is not to actually become "a tramp," but to "discover his point of view," to momentarily take his guise in order to "produce a veracious narrative" (862).

Working toward such ends, Crane carefully depicts the youth's representative change through a gradual movement into economic abjection. "Trudging slowly" along the streets dressed in an "aged suit" (862), the youth is "completely plastered with yells of 'bum' and 'hobo'" and cast into "a state of profound dejection" (283). Later, in a lodging house, he feels the alteration deepen as "his liver turn[s] white" from the "unspeakable odors that assail him like malignant diseases with wings" (287). However unpleasant, such misery does produce the desired sociological reward: during the long night, the youth stays awake watching "the forms of men . . . lying in death-like silence or heaving and snoring with tremendous effort" (287), and he then "carv[es] biographies for [them] from his meager experience" (289) in poverty. In their class now, but still not of it, he is able to distinguish "an utterance of meaning" in each "wail of a . . . section, a class, a people" (289). The mediatorial role he assumes through this ability to discern meaning and translate perception allows him to arrogate the cultural power of authentic social knowledge. First internalized and then incorporated, the distance that once stood between him and such "sorry humanity" (862) now constitutes his own expanded and thus authoritative perspective.

I have termed such tales of temporary guise "class-transvestite narratives," a phrase that best describes their attempts to close epistemological gaps through cross-class impersonation.[2] Although Crane's experiment is the best known of this type, its methodology and goals were hardly unique. Between the depression of the early 1890s and the reforms of the 1910s, an impressive number of white middle-class writers, journalists, and social researchers "dressed down" and entered what Jack London called (in his undercover narrative) the "human wilderness," in order to traverse with their bodies what they saw as a growing social gulf.[3] They joined early sociological surveys, progressive social movements, and a series of reform efforts, in an attempt to repair the ruptures made evident by the insurrectionary class struggles I discussed in chapter 3. Like Crane, these disguised investigators recognized the inherent difficulty of social knowledge in an economically segmented society: perceptions based on a sympathetic middle-class point of view were for them as inaccurate as those informed by the sensationalized reports in the daily press. Recognizing the impossibility of both an Archimedean point outside a classed subjectivity and what William James called the particular "blindness" of "looking at life with the eyes of a remote spectator,"[4] these explorers attempted to move inside and collapse the distance between subject and object into one performative, narrational body.

These authors thus conceived of their own bodies both as objects of social forces and, consequently, as sites of social knowledge—the value of the experience depended on the very authenticity of the misery the experiment produced. Authenticity was an ascendant social value during the late nineteenth century, as technological changes as varied as the first instances of mass production, the birth of photography, and the revolution in ready-made clothing made fabrication, duplication, and impersonation ever more common occurrences. Just as objects could be fabricated seemingly at will, the body itself seemed suddenly malleable—classified and shaped through naturalist narratives, medical texts, penological studies, and other discursive systems. Indeed, as Crane's experiment makes clear, the tractable body of the "class transvestite" is almost preternaturally prone to such forces—"plastered" with epithets, "assailed" by "diseases," but nevertheless still awake and able to "carve biographies" from the undifferentiated "wail" of the poor. Their ability to remain observant in the midst of subjection distinguishes these class-transvestite narrators from the other classed subjects of this era's literature and marks their works as middle-class texts about the working class and the poor. Throughout their journeys to the realm of misery, these narrators never relinquish their role as translators of experience and mediators between knowing and being. This is also what makes their consequent narratives distinct: while most documentaries about the working class and the poor produce knowledge through the distancing rhetoric of the social spectacle (as in the newspaper report, the photo documentary, and the muckraking book), these class-transvestite narratives reverse this process, producing authentic knowledge—and performing authenticity itself—through the act of embodiment.

An examination of such a move and its cultural motivations does not, of course, supplant the valuable body of scholarly work that uses Jean Baudrillard, Guy Debord, and Michel Foucault to examine representations of the working class and the poor in terms of "the spectacle." Giorgio Mariani—with the agreement of Rachael Bowlby, June Howard, and others—argues (with admirable critical acumen) that "the dramatic industrial development of the decades following the Civil War marked a definitive shift from an economy of production to one of consumption . . . [in which] all men and women were to be addressed as consumers."[5] As consumers, the people constituted themselves in and against a society that tended to reduce objects (and other subjects as objects) to spectacles for consumption. Within such a visual economy, the urban proletarian and lumpen proletariat functioned crucially to define the limits of middle-class propriety by embodying the essence of impropriety. Thus, in Howard's words, "We encounter the brute [Howard's shorthand term for the popular image of workers, tramps, and the poor] in its far-flung manifestations as a creature perpetually outcast, yet perpetually to be cast out as it inevitably reappears within self and within society."[6]

These readings make political and psychological sense out of the scopophilic gaze evident in many texts, but they are incomplete; they identify one mode of apprehension and from it generate a comprehensive cultural theory. In this regard, Howard's work is fuller than most. Through an examination of American literary naturalism, she identifies both a compulsion for narrational distance from the scandalous masses ("naturalism and the spectator") and an almost contrarian "libidinal investment . . . [in] the image of the proletarian as brute."[7] As she notes in her detailed exegesis of these antinomies, the libidinal investment in the "brute" chiefly serves to raise the stakes, since the carefully maintained boundaries between the self and the Other both express and repress (or express through repression) not only a desire for the "brute" but a desire for something like the libido itself. Yet I think that the recurring figure of the class transvestite suggests a different solution to these formal and cultural antinomies, in effect turning this model on its head. For some middle-class writers and investigators, a libidinal investment in the working class and the poor is not so much repressed as it is rearticulated as a mode of apprehension in and of itself. In such acts of apprehension, the middle-class subject does not maintain the boundaries of subjectivity by ostracizing the Other but, rather, performs a subjectivity which is sufficiently plastic to momentarily embody the Other. Some, like Crane's "youth," to put the matter simply, find it more expedient to take in, rather than "cast out," the brute.

By entering into the realm of misery rather than casting out the miserable, these narratives set up a model of integration and social incorporation that accorded with the ameliorative ideology of the Progressive Era. In each narrative, the presumption is both that these realms are sufficiently exotic as to require a disguise, a journey, and an "experiment" and that such difference can be effectively assimilated through sartorial means alone. According to the class transvestite, underneath the clothing and sumptuary habits of the economic Other lies an essential sameness, a common humanity that requires only recognition and understanding for an inevitable amalgamation. These presumptions of similitude derive, in no small part, from nineteenth-century ideologies of social mobility and egalitarianism. Yet in class-transvestite narratives, these vestiges of working-class republicanism are inflected and embodied in far less progressive ways that ensure that acts of amalgamation remain superficial. Mobility resides with the narrator alone, and egalitarianism becomes his or her ability to manipulate vestments during strategic moments of entry. The class transvestite's journey "down" thus ultimately serves to echo and circumvent other journeys "up," reducing mobility to a mere play of cultural signs. "Slumming," concludes Peter Hitchcock in a discussion of a related mode of cross-class discovery, "is the process through which one explores economic inequity only to return to that place and space that guarantees it."[8]

Following this journey through its various sites of integration and to its various objects of interest, I use this chapter to examine how containment through embodiment operates and to analyze the social and political changes it underwrites. After a brief history of transvestite narration, an examination of Jack London's and Josiah Flynt's appropriation and integration of the despised tramp will serve to outline the machinations of this process. The tramp, along with the itinerant worker, was the primary (though not the exclusive) object of the male explorer's interest. Shorn of the web of social relations maintained in stable working-class communities, he was a ripe target for such sociological study. Alvan Francis Sanborn's incursion into the lodging house provides another, more semiotic version of the same paradigm. The lodging house, Sanborn informs us, is where the itinerant comes to rest, founding and relying on a special kind of cultural community. From these examples, the discussion moves to a theoretical model, suggesting that these writers' search for sociological authority serves, in part, to reconstruct their manhood or womanhood in the face of what Jackson Lears has called the "crisis of cultural authority."[9] Whereas men like London and Flynt searched for authenticity among the "rustic" tramps, women such as the Van Vorst sisters and Cornelia Stratton Parker sought their political voice in the settlement houses and the textile mills. The discussion concludes with an examination of contemporary explorations of working-class culture, drawing analogies between the translation of class into a cultural category in the Progressive Era and the new labor history. By looking at the discursive construction of class identity in these texts, I assert that what we call the "class struggle" is always also a struggle over the very terms of class analysis—a struggle over the meaning of "class" itself.

TRANSVESTITE JOURNEYS

Undercover explorations of the working class and the poor have had a long history in Europe and the United States. Their earliest conceptual antecedents were the Saturnalian festivals of ancient Rome, where revelers reversed "high" and "low" social and cultural forms in a ritualistic venting of tensions, an aspect of the festival that was retained in other rituals well into the early modern period. Cross-dressed social investigation owes more, however, to the epistemological problems created by industrialism, urbanization, and immigration, which mapped "high" and "low" onto a series of static spatial relations, such as the factory floor and the city neighborhood. As the workplace increasingly became a site of subterfuge and the city a place of mystery, the newly forming middle class looked to periodicals and eventually to more-academic texts for information about those whom they no longer felt they knew. Thus disguised investigation began in earnest after the first period of intense industrialization and proletarianization, when British journalist James Greenwood published "A Night in the Work-House," the first recorded study of this kind (1866). This was followed in turn by the more sociologically oriented work of Charles Booth in Britain (1887–1903) and Minna Wettstein-Adelt and Paul Göhre in Germany (1890s), all of whom copied Greenwood's methodological example in their attempts to bring empiricism to the newly forming study of the urban poor.[10]

This mode of investigation also began in the United States during the late 1880s and 1890s. Because of more social mobility and an unending desire for sensational accounts of all sorts, class transvestism immediately experienced a level of popularity entirely unprecedented in Europe. Such reporters as Annie Laurie and Nellie Bly went undercover to investigate working conditions in fruit canneries, factories, and urban hospitals. Inspired by their example, Walter Wyckoff undertook a more sustained exercise in undercover political economy. His two-year journey as a "manual proletaire" took him from New Jersey to the Pacific and resulted in the two-volume work *The Workers: An Experiment in Reality* (1897–98) and a professorship at Princeton. Though less academically inclined, Josiah Flynt, author of the enormously popular *Tramping with Tramps* (1893), also had intellectual leanings. In his study, he tried to rectify the positivist leanings of contemporary penology by interpreting the psychological dimension of vagrant criminality. Making good use of his own material, he later worked as a railroad detective and a crime reporter. Like Flynt, Jack London initially employed this methodology in his "hobo writings," though he later expanded his purview to include the industrial proletariat. In all of his accounts, London focuses on the tensions between intellectual and manual labor—perhaps most passionately in *The People of the Abyss* (1902), his disguised journey through London's East End.

After the turn of the century, these class-transvestite experiments increasingly tended to be practiced by women.[11] In part, this shift reflects the draw of the settlement house movement among women who subsequently insisted on a link between social reform and experiential knowledge. But this shift also reveals the force of the new muckraking magazines, which competed for readers by offering documents—sociological, confessional, and fictional—of middle-class women who briefly lived "working-class" lives. A number of these documents were later published in book form. Some, like Cornelia Stratton Parker's *Working with the Working Woman* (1922), garnered national attention. Others, like Bessie and Marie Van Vorst's *Women Who Toil* (1903) (a personal favorite of Teddy Roosevelt), became grist for political debate.

Of course, this type of undercover investigation did not grind to a halt with the close of the Progressive Era. Such writers as Whiting Williams continued to draw on their proletarian journeys well into the midcentury.[12] Additionally, the recent discovery of Frederick C. Mills's account of his tenure as an undercover investigator for the California Commission of Immigration and Housing demonstrates a (largely undocumented) governmental use of this tactic. Before becoming an economist at Columbia University, Mills spent two months in "the world of the submerged" in order "to investigate" and record "the activities of the Industrial Workers of the World."[13] Yet such occasional and institutional accounts aside, class-transvestite investigations in the popular press greatly decreased in the 1920s, with what Paul Boyer has termed a move toward "secularism" and "professionalism" in "the urban moral-control movement." Within this broad ideological shift, not only were such individual efforts at mediation displaced by government-sponsored institutions, but the once problematic economic and ethnic heterogeneity of the city was, as Boyer notes, increasingly "treated as a positive social gain, adding to the richness and creative diversity of American life."[14] When class transvestism reappeared in the 1930s, at the impetus of another economic downturn, similar journeys through the lives of the working class and the poor carried the weight of a new middle-class self-consciousness. The specific and vocal articulations of labor and leftist organizations provoked such anguished apologias as James Agee and Walker Evans's *Let Us Now Praise Famous Men* (1941) and such politically evasive parodies as Preston Sturges's film *Sullivan's Travels* (1941).[15] The naive assumptions of Crane and his contemporaries—perhaps even the belief that one could personally mediate between classes—would never again enjoy such unequivocal popularity.[16]

The historicity of such attempts at integration is, however, integrally linked to their complex cultural work. The events that popularized this mode of representation suggested the need for socially redemptive models of engagement and assimilation. Though the participant/observer had occasionally visited the pages of the urban gothic novel and the detective story earlier in the nineteenth century, the cross-dressed investigator did not appear with regularity in the U.S. press until around the 1893 depression. This five-year economic collapse followed two decades of recurring strike waves and labor militancy (see chap. 3), producing a set of social and economic forces that changed the dimensions and perceptions of urban poverty. As Paul Ringenbach documents in *Tramp and Reformers,* during the renewed "discovery of unemployment" in this depression, the lines between tramps and workers and between skilled American craftspeople and recent immigrants blurred under the pressure of penury's seemingly indiscriminate mobility.[17] The once secure native working class and the emergent middle class seemed suddenly at risk from the rising tide of massive unemployment.

Under the pressure of these conditions, the tramp arose as a leading emblem of the indiscriminate effects of the industrial downturn. "To many observers the hobo seemed the most obvious manifestation of the economic dislocations and social maladjustments of the times. He was ubiquitous and easily identifiable—the least common denominator of unemployment, parasitism, crime, and vice."[18] All of these factors made him an obvious choice for undercover examination. Tramps had, of course, previously haunted America's political unconscious: along with slaves, Native Americans, and the Irish, they sporadically peopled the mythic barbarians at the gate of the Protestant work ethic. Francis Wayland, the normally sober dean of Yale Law School, made just such a synecdochic leap in 1877 (appropriately enough, the year of the Great Railroad Strike): "As we utter the word Tramp, there arises straightaway before us the spectacle of a lazy, incorrigible, cowardly, utterly depraved savage."[19] By the midnineties, such rants had reached a new level, as "the spectacle" grew to unprecedented numbers and began collectively to make organized political demands. In 1894, "General" Coxey and his "industrial army" marched across the country planning to present Congress with a "petition in boots." Though their specific petition was for the enactment of Coxey's Good Roads Bill and Non-Interest Bearing Bonds Bill, their implicit appeal was for general political recognition. Such recognition was not forthcoming, and their demands were answered instead by police action and political derision.[20] As C. S. Denny, the mayor of Indianapolis, commented some months later, vagabonds, like "wife-beaters," had "no right to claim an existence in this country" and therefore "should have no legal protection." If existing vagrancy laws failed to stop the flow of tramps into urban centers, argued Denny, then municipalities should "substitute the whipping-post for the prison."[21]

In the face of such blatant hostility, Jack London's exploration, appropriation, and subsequent depiction of these abject figures is particularly relevant—both for what he achieves and for how he does so. One of Coxey's less-disciplined cadre (he left the "army" long before it reached Washington), London had other, less-collectivist ways of soliciting public recognition for the unemployed.[22] According to the young London, who, in 1897, wrote "The Road," the tramp suffers most from a lack of understanding and appreciation. Labeled a vagrant by "the law" and a "Vag" for short, just "three letters . . . stand between him and the negation of being," placing him "on the ragged edge of nonentity."[23] Pulling him in off that edge and affirming his existence requires, not unexpectedly, a certain amount of authentic information, supplied in this instance by London's firsthand experience traveling with the tramps. Though "we have met him everywhere," London reports, "we are less conversant with his habits and thoughts than with those of the inhabitants of the Cannibal Islands" (70). The tramp's sumptuary habits, London assures us, are actually much less exotic (and parasitic). Unlike the "stationary Negro population . . . of the South" (another synecdochic leap), the "tramp population," is "full of the indomitability of the Teuton" (71). Like other Teutons, tramps labor conscientiously, according to the dictates of their vocation. Those who might presume a lazy egalitarianism are, in this respect, greatly misinformed: "In this outcast world the sharp lines of caste are as rigorously drawn as in the world from which it has evolved" (71). London demonstrates this last point in his narrative by categorizing tramps into "classes" and "subclasses," charting the "tramp problem" in terms that would have been comfortably familiar to middle-class readers. Once they are categorized according to relative skill level ("efficiency" is the word London would come to use), these previously ostracized figures seem only to be slightly degraded copies of factory workers, as indeed they are for London. The "tramp problem" should be studied, he concludes, as an integral part of the relationship between capital and labor—not as a "surplus labor army" (as he would later assert), but as an unavoidable and generally harmless result of frictional unemployment.

Josiah Flynt's appropriation of these "human parasites," as he calls them, moves along similarly systematic lines.[24] But whereas London embraces economic and social means of integration, Flynt works from a psychological and criminological perspective. In *Tramping with the Tramps*, he draws on his "intimate" acquaintance with "notorious members" (3) of this class in order to challenge and indeed deconstruct the predominately phrenological foundations of contemporary penology. "We have volumes . . . about the criminal's body, skull, and face, his whimsical and obscene writings on the prison-walls, the effect of various kinds of diet on his deportment, the workings of delicate instruments placed on his wrists" (1). But "we" still do not understand the mental workings of these outcast characters. In order to comprehend their criminal status—that is, in order to rationalize what seems ethically and socially illegible—we need to augment this type of knowledge with more intimate data; in short, we need the authentic knowledge gained by studying them from "different points of view" (7). Yet, from inside the tramp's "point of view," Flynt, like Crane and London, becomes a good deal more sympathetic. The tramp's phrenological difference, Flynt immediately notices, derives from environmental, rather than biological, forces. Those tramps who have never been to prison, who are successful in their vocation, "if well dressed, could pass muster in almost any class of society. . . . [A]n uninitiated observer would be unable to pick them out for what they are" (8). What they are, in turn, seems also to be now in question. As Flynt's own narrative moves from "Studies" to "Travels" to "Sketches," these parasites lose a good deal of their once onerous status and (again) assume the characteristics of the society at large. Like London, Flynt finds that "vagabonds specialize nowadays quite as much as other people" (113) and that "success in vagabondage depends largely on distinct and indispensable traits of character—diligence, patience, nerve and politeness" (138). As he concludes his study, Flynt's sociological tone turns nostalgic, an indication that assimilation is, from his new point of view, already inevitable. For like "the Indian," the tramp is becoming part of the civilized norm: "The secrets of Hoboland are becoming common property, and the hobo is being deprived of a picturesque isolation which formerly few disturbed" (391). Criminological reforms are almost unnecessary, Flynt decides, as ethnographic incursions like his will integrate these marginal characters without the overt efforts of policy reformers.

UNDER THE GUISE OF REFORM

Josiah Flynt viewed reforms as unnecessary, but as Ringenbach documents in *Tramps and Reformers,* the discovery of the tramp and of his destructive mobility did indeed precipitate an escalation of urban reform efforts. And such reforms were, in a slightly different manner, also related to the inception of undercover reportage. If mobility arose as a new trope for the nation's fear of impoverishment, then recently inaugurated sites of reform, such as the settlement house and the lodging house, operated as compensatory locations of temporary repose. Following the 1893 depression, reform ideology shifted from moralism to environmentalism, a move that highlighted the importance of these contained residential spaces.[25] The goal, as Ruth Hutchinson Crocker explains, was to rehabilitate by example: "By 'settling' among the less fortunate, [reformers] would practice a true charity, sharing the day-to-day existence of the poor while showing them better standards of life and culture."[26] Yet despite these communitarian efforts, the settlement house and particularly the less-monitored lodging house often functioned quite differently, both for the residents and for social investigators. Within these newly demarcated spaces of repose, anonymity and transience were more often the norm—a norm on which undercover investigation depended for its existence. Before the large-scale poverty, urban migration, and immigration of the 1890s, journalists and writers would not have been able to pass for the working class and the poor with such apparent ease, since many of the unemployed and most workers lived in knowable communities where impersonation would have been difficult. Though reformers tried to avoid just this sort of institutional anonymity, the atomized clientele of the lodging house composed, in contrast, a class-specific realm that was of interest to middle-class readers and eminently penetrable by these proto-ethnographers.

At the same time that these anonymous realms provided the opportunity for class transvestism, they also helped to supply the material for such performances. Though settlement workers and other reformers may have tried to inculcate residents with middle-class cultural values, many boardinghouse patrons developed, out of resistance or perhaps out of felt necessity, their own systems of signs, codes, and sumptuary signifiers. To the naive investigator, like Crane's "youth," these appear to be mere disguises, sartorial rituals of the begging trade: the "men of brawn" when "dressed in their ungainly garments. . . . showed bumps and deficiencies of all kinds" (289–90). The fuller descriptions offered in such books as Alvan Francis Sanborn's *Moody's Lodging House and Other Tenement Sketches* reveal, however, a different level of symbolic functioning. To "the gang" at Moody's, clothing and manners signify each person's social place, both with respect to each other and within the larger Boston community: for example, Gus, "a gentleman bum," prides himself on "urbanity," and always "pretends to be adjusting a non-existent garter or suspender, when he is goaded to scratching by an uncommonly virulent bite."[27] Affecting a similar fraudulent history, "Barney" draws "money and sympathy" from fellow Irish immigrants with his "rich Irish brogue" (10), just as "Shorty," "a genuine working-man originally" (10), turns his biography into his pitch and persona. The disguise is, as Sanborn explains, both a way of securing one's living and a way of communicating within this space of transience, a means of vesting one's self with a history in an institutional realm that operates to deny it.

However, as Sanborn likewise demonstrates, the danger inherent in such a compensatory system of signs is that it offers a considerably heightened opportunity for adoption, inhabitation, and integration. To enter a community of people in costume, where one's history is so blatantly worn on the body, all that is needed is a "mien extraordinary eloquent of roguery or misery," but short of this, "a disguise is helpful" (1).

> When the time for going out came, I thoroughly grimed face, hands, and neck, donned several suits of worn, soiled underclothes . . . , a pair of disreputable pantaloons, a jacket out at elbows, clumsy, discolored shoes, and a hat that was almost a disguise in itself. In certain finishing touches I took a genuine artistic pride; these were a dingy red flannel fastened around the neck with a safety-pin, a clay pipe filled with vile-smelling tobacco, a cheapwhiskey breath, a shambling gait, and a drooping head. (2)

The preceding verbal minstrelsy is obviously meant as parody: from begrimed skin to soiled clothes to absurd accessorizing, it is played out as much for Sanborn's readers as for Moody's residents. The point is, however, that it effectively fulfills both roles. At least from Sanborn's point of view, his affectation mimics "the gang's" assumption of some bastardized notion of the authentic. Within this institutional setting, the organic community has been entirely replaced by a nexus of cultural signs. Ironically enough, this new system of cultural affiliation becomes a different mode of authenticity. Given the strictly superficial definition of class, Sanborn can claim that after one night, he has for all intents and purposes become "a cheap lodger." "Living does away with the necessity of playing at living," he opines (3). The sequential experience of "playing" and "living," we might also note, provides the class transvestite with a certain amount of comfort in economically troubled times: "Bums are, by general consent, the very dregs of society. Is it not, then, worth a bit of suffering to feel certain that the very worst that can befall you (in the world's view) is not so very bad after all?" (4).

Almost as an apologia for his crude act of appropriation, Sanborn closes his collection of sketches by describing an appropriation that is almost inarguably cruder. In "Among the Sandwich Men," he portrays the "type" of "bum" who works as a bodily advertisement (literally, as a sign) for the services offered to other "bums." This type's body appears so entirely determined by his environment that Sanborn can describe him only through a succession of similes to more substantial objects: "Irish Tim . . . is lean as a lilystem, his cheeks are like bog-holes, his lower jaw projects like a window-awning, and his gums are as guiltless of teeth as a freshly stropped razor" (165). Already forced to perform his subservience for his subsistence, it takes little training to teach him to more publicly do so, and when he wears a sign for—

ROAST TURKEY
with
CRANBERRY SAUCE, VEGETABLES,
and
TEA or COFFEE,
ALL FOR 25 CENTS (163)

—his slightly better-fed "mien" of "misery" can bring a profit to the petty capitalist as well. As this description suggests, Sanborn's understanding of transient communities as cultural sign systems ultimately takes an almost hyperbolic turn. Though similarly invested in the sartorial, few class-transvestite reporters would, in fact, replicate Sanborn's singular obsession with translating the sumptuary codes of the working class and the poor into such a clear hermeneutic. In their texts, the subcultural dimensions of transient life provide, rather, a sociological focus of study—a way of codifying and reconstituting these communities in discursive terms. But if such authors as Jack London and Stephen Crane were less rigid and ahistorical in their use of this culturalist strategy, they partook equally of its underlying ethnographic assumptions. Like Sanborn, they treated their subjects as spatially, sartorially, and socially distinct, as members of a class unified by cultural ties, rather than by communitarian, moral, or economic ones.

THE CULTURAL WORK OF THE CLASS-TRANSVESTITE NARRATIVE

This culturalist understanding of class has its own historical genealogy. In 1890, Jacob Riis initiated this shift, opening the way for imitators like Sanborn and setting a precedent for the way in which Progressive Era social scientists and reporters would understand the urban working class and the poor. In Riis's enormously popular *How the Other Half Lives*, workers and the poor appeared, for the first time, in explicitly cultural terms. The moral typology of the mid-nineteenth-century studies and the racial taxonomy that had haunted sociology since the antebellum era turned, with Riis, into a clear sociocultural lexicon. In this text, he created a classification based not only on neighborhoods and ethnicities but, more pointedly, on bodily signifiers and sumptuary habits. His use of photographs was, as Keith Leland Gandal notes, crucial in this lexiconic transformation. Until Riis's book was published, photographs of the city universally depicted broad topographical visions, celebratory panoramas free of poverty and urban crowds. Riis's photographic focus on the visual properties of the working class and the poor inverted this paradigm, representing the city as a bricolage of "scenes" that emphasized the visible, sartorial difference between the classes.[28] In *How the Other Half Lives*, the denizens of "the Bend" and "Hell's Kitchen" wear their class identities in easily discernible and subsequently simulatable fashion. Riis's invitation to "go into any of the 'respectable' tenement neighborhoods" and "be with and among its people until you understand their ways" thus reconfigures the urban topography in a new and important manner. Not only did he align "neighborhoods" with corresponding "ways," but he depicted these ways as singularly perceptible and thus available for middle-class understanding.[29]

Of course, the undercover investigators took Riis a bit more literally than he intended, actively incorporating what he had only categorized. While Riis's aspirations were primarily taxonomic, to provide readers with a map of discrete urban spaces, the class transvestite imparted a more dynamic experience of the spatial domain of the working class and the poor. Moving through a succession of transient places (such as rooming houses and temporary job sites) and transitional spaces (such as train stations and city streets), the investigator constructed an urban map that blends and flows. Indeed, in their journeys, the class transvestites commonly discovered not fixed neighborhoods and types but the mutability of classed space itself, the way in which a neighborhood can quickly change with the influx of immigrants from different countries of origin or workers lower in the economic scale, or, even more fundamentally, the way in which space both conforms to and contracts the positionality of the subjective observer. During one survey of London's East End, published under the title *People of the Abyss,* Jack London discovers, for instance, the multiple variability of the neighborhood he inhabits. According to its working-class inhabitants, it was once the home of "the better class of workers" but has now been "saturated" by "foreigners and lower-class people."[30] As London writes, the proletariat and the lumpen proletariat exist in an uneasy mixture that shifts from block to block and even from building to building. Part of the story of *People of the Abyss* is London's growing awareness of these different spaces and the sorts of unstable and shifting identities they underwrite.

Similarly, in class-transvestite texts, Riis's steady sociological gaze gives way to highly ambivalent narrative postures. Unlike Riis's study, which retains the pose of objectivity until its histrionic conclusion, such texts as Wyckoff's *The Workers* and London's *People of the Abyss* are rife with conflicting dispositions toward their subjects. Workers and the dispossessed appear to be alternately appealing in their seeming freedom and camaraderie and horrifying in their lack of self-regulation. Wyckoff, for instance, seems to have spent a good deal of his tenure as a "proletaire" anguishing between these two extremes. Regarding Clark, his temporary "partner," he notes: "It is strange . . . the closeness of the intimacy between Clark and me. . . . Perhaps men come to know one another quickest and best on a plane of life, where in the fellowship of destitution they struggle for the primal needs and feel the keen sympathies which attest the basal kinship of our common humanity." More typically, however, Wyckoff finds himself rebelling against the physical urgencies of these same "primal needs," especially when they include an "instinct" for "liquor and lust."[31] London, alternately, seems almost to find pleasure in inhabiting this ambivalence. He opens *People of the Abyss,* for example, with a chapter entitled "The Descent," which describes his initial horrified reaction to the population of the East End: "The miserable multitudes" who walk the "screaming streets" are like "so many waves of a vast and malodorous sea, lapping about me and threatening to well up and over me." Once in "costume," however, both he and his narrative tone change remarkably.

> All servility vanished from the demeanor of the common people with whom I came in contact. Presto! in the twinkling of an eye, so to say, I had become one of them. My frayed and out-at-elbows jacket was the badge and advertisement of my class which was their class. It made me of the like kind, and in place of the fawning and too-respectful attention I had hitherto received, I now shared with them a comradeship.[32]

The comradeship London describes, one would have to add, is borne not out of shared labor or a common history but out of bodily simulation. Like Sanborn's, London's painless metamorphosis belies an unstable notion of class identity that rests, at least in this moment, on superficial vestments.

Yet even here, during such instantaneous transvestite operations, ambivalence is evident. If the aim of the middle-class investigator is to map—and thus to rhetorically contain—the mysterious realm of the working class and the poor, then such an easy transition from observer to participant exposes, rather, the fragile border between the two. "I have been mistaken for a drunkard, and a detective, and a disreputable double of myself," complains Wyckoff, "I fear that the very success of my disguise is somewhat chagrining at times."[33] To put it differently, the act of clothing oneself with class-specific apparel involves a structural contradiction, since one presumes both a social dichotomy (the need to cross-dress) and a countervailing semiotic slippage (the ability to cross-dress convincingly). The presumption of difference is in part, certainly, a historical inheritance, renewed in the 1890s by the increasing social pressure of poverty and economic stratification. The semiotic slippage reflects, however, one of the cultural contradictions of capitalism—a comparatively new shift in the discourse of dress and fashion. Although sartorial signs had historically functioned to indicate social difference, the wide dissemination of ready-made clothing for men in the 1890s provided a site for contesting articulations of egalitarianism. (The "ready-made revolution" in women's fashion would not take place until the 1910s.) "In the nineties," as Claudia Kidwell documents, the "suit arrived," as an emblem of the industrial "democratization of clothing in America." Marketed widely and with explicit appeals to egalitarian sentiments, the suit became "a uniform which knew no class or economic group."[34] In coming years, the well-dressed gentleman, the worker, and even the tramp would favor the new "sack suit" as a normative statement of masculine fashion. Of course, as London's testimony indicates, class signs persisted, as a superficial display of individual history replaced more traditional dress styles as "the badge and advertisement" of class status. The fit, the material, and the degree of wear of one's "frayed and out-at-elbows jacket" gained increased, if less codified, significance.

While the discursive shifts brought about by the development of a mass-market clothing industry help explain the language of class transvestism, the ambivalences, contradictions, and slippages in these texts need also to be theorized in more general, structural terms. As Marjorie Garber demonstrates in her book on cross-dressing, "[o]ne of the most consistent and effective functions of the transvestite in culture" is to repeatedly expose such disconsonant moments, "to indicate the place of . . . 'category crisis,' disrupting and calling attention to cultural, social, or aesthetic dissonances." The figure of the transvestite marks, then, "a failure of definitional distinction, a borderline that becomes permeable, that permits of border crossings from one (apparently distinct) category to another: black/white, Jew/Christian, noble/bourgeois, master/servant, master/slave."[35] Though her study is broadly conceived, Garber is most interested in the category of gender. In her estimation, within this category, the "crisis" works toward progressive ends—denaturalizing the dichotomous and oppressive relations between socially constituted men and socially constituted women. The category placed in ontological crisis in the class-transvestite texts is, however, not gender but class, which appears to be both explicit and somehow mobile, constructed now through the production and replication of cultural signs rather than through the shared subjection to economic exploitation. Such a homologous reconstruction does not function toward similarly progressive ends. For what is erased here is not the socially constructed relations between bodily signifiers and political referents, which are in fact reinforced, but the systemic relations between lived experience and historically specific economic exploitation. In short, in class-transvestite texts, what Garber calls a "transvestite logic" deconstructs class as an economic referent and reconstructs it, in turn, as a function of cultural position.

Yet if class-transvestite texts put the category of class in crisis, the exposed ambivalences and contradictions are not sufficient to impair the function of the transvestite narratives. Rather, what Garber calls their "dissonances" structurally enable their cultural work. As we have seen with Crane, the dynamic movement of subjective identity through the symbolically figured poor avails an authoritative voice. Or put differently, sociological authority emerges out of the ability to have an authentic experience of poverty while retaining a supposedly middle-class ability for objective assessment. On this and other matters, Bessie Van Vorst is characteristically unambiguous: "My desire is to act as a mouthpiece for the woman labourer. I assumed her mode of existence with the hope that I might put into words her cry for help." Like the lodgers who "wail" in Crane's sketch, Van Vorst's "woman labourer" has no unmediated, intelligible means of communicating her "material" and "spiritual needs." The degenerative environment of the factory has left her reliant on narrational mediation. "It was probable my comrades felt at no time the discomfort I did," remarks Van Vorst, "As our bodies accustom themselves to luxury and cleanliness, theirs grow hardened to deprivation and filth. As our souls develop the advantages of all that constitutes an ideal . . . their souls diminish under the oppression of a constant physical effort to meet material demands."[36] Lacking Van Vorst's ability to straddle class identities—to draw on a distinction between inner sensibility and outer degradation—the "woman labourer" is not only unable to articulate her cries for "help"; she is, in Van Vorst's estimation, unable even to understand the dimension of her need. It is left to Walter Wyckoff to take this specific operation to its logical conclusion, revealing its discursively integrative function. Whereas Van Vorst uses mediation to promote understanding, Wyckoff resorts to blatant ventriloquism to enact a scene of social cooperation, as in the following remarkable address, given after his first week of physical labor:

> We are unskilled laborers. We are grown men, and are without a trade. In the labor market we stand ready to sell to the highest bidder our mere muscular strength. . . . We are here and not higher in the scale, by reason of a variety of causes. Some of us were thrown upon our own resources in childhood, and have earned our living ever since, and by the line of least resistance we have simply grown to be unskilled workmen.[37]

In the next dramatic turn, Wyckoff alternately speaks as a capitalist, eventually dissolving the so-called labor problem into a closet drama.

Such acts of ventriloquism are, however, only the most obvious textual function of these narratives. The construction of sociological authority is part of a more integral objective of reestablishing and reinvigorating middle-class cultural authority. If working-class impersonation seems to serve such a goal obscurely, then we must keep in mind the particularly transient and unidirectional characteristics of these experiments. The emergence of middle-class identity in the United States occurred in a profoundly relational process, a crystallization of a broad middling segment by means of constant reference to aristocrats and laborers.[38] More typically, such relations were of the differentiating sort; they tended to distance and marginalize the working-class Other (and, less frequently, the aristocratic Other) in an attempt to establish and solidify the moral territory of a bourgeois center. Strict rules of "social conduct," writes Karen Halttunen, helped the middle class solve "the problem of establishing and recognizing social identity in a republic based theoretically on the boundless potential of each individual."[39] Yet again, I think that these class-transvestite narratives offer another model of class relations, one of embodiment and integration rather than invidious distinction. With remarkable unanimity, they tell an alternate tale of a middle-class lack fulfilled through working-class experience, bourgeois ennui cured by way of proletarian pain. Facing a new industrial order, argues Jackson Lears, the middle class suffered a "crisis of cultural authority," compounded by a feeling that "life had become . . . curiously unreal." Reality and authority might be recaptured, then, by a "pilgrimage" through something like the "authentic."[40]

To put this sort of exercise in perspective, it might be useful to note that such models of reinvigoration through cross-identity inhabitation were not new in American culture. By the 1890s, a succession of marginal figures had already been appropriated as symbols of what was feared lost to an emergent nation. During the antebellum period, some members of the working class negotiated their "whiteness" and their masculinity through theatrical appropriations of the black body; and throughout this country's history, various authors have projected their anxieties over rampant industrialism onto the figure of the "vanishing native." Yet by the turn of the century, these fetishized receptacles had already begun to disappear—new, abstract models of corporate identity replaced older individualist embodiments. As Frederick Jackson Turner noted in 1893, after the closing of the frontier, one could no longer "strip off the garments of civilization and array . . . [oneself] in the hunting shirt and moccasin";[41] that is, one could no longer become an American by way of becoming a savage. Yet during the Progressive Era, one could still gain a semblance of such rustic vivacity through a journey into the urban frontier, arraying oneself, temporarily, in the garments of poverty's corporeal immediacy.

MEN IN DRAG AS MEN

The machinations of middle-class revitalization are most obvious in the highly gendered operations of the class-transvestite narratives. Teddy Roosevelt's call for a "strenuous life" echoes through the men's narratives, haunting the authors with fears of bookish effeminacy and over-civilization. As Melissa Dabakis writes, a "crisis of masculinity" provoked middle-class men in the 1890s to fear that "manliness was no longer an inevitable product of middle-class life and that the ideals of independence, self-reliance, competitiveness, and risk taking (essentially mythic constructions of an agrarian frontier) were becoming lost to middle-class men in an industrialized culture."[42] Such fears prompted a number of "man-making" movements, including not only the physical culture movement often associated with Roosevelt but also the founding of the Boy Scouts of America, an increased attention to hunting and fishing for sport, the inception of the craft revival, and a new martial ideal whose apotheosis was the Spanish-American War.[43]

Closer, however, to cross-class impersonation was the popularization of the "work cure," a masculine counterpart to the more famous "rest cure" developed by S. Weir Mitchell in the 1870s and 1880s.[44] Though the work cure and the rest cure both responded to neurasthenia—a hypothesized nervous malady associated with symptoms as various as hysteria, fatigue, depression, and irritability—advocates of the work cure postulated a diametrically opposed etiology and prescribed a similarly divergent regime of treatment.[45] According to such physicians as Herbert Hall and such physical culturalists as the champion wrestler William Muldoon, what most plagued middle-class men was not overwork but a lack of physical activity: exposed to the tensions and stresses that accompany jobs in management and the professions, these men had no concomitant bodily labor to act as a nervous release; thus they lacked the vital energy and virility that they required both for their own health and for the greater task of nation-building. Alcoholism and other forms of dissipation, which believers in the work cure understood to be the most common symptoms of neurasthenia among men, prompted a number of middle-class and wealthy men to seek help at Hall's community in Marblehead, Massachusetts, or at Muldoon's sanitarium in White Plains, New York.

Theodore Dreiser spent six weeks at Muldoon's sanitarium in the spring of 1903, after an extended bout of writer's block, depression, and poverty brought him to the point of nervous exhaustion. Before he consented to his brother Paul's plan to send him to the sanitarium (and to pay the bill), Dreiser spent a number of months living in rooming houses in Manhattan and Brooklyn and looking, in vain, for even the most menial labor.[46] Just before Paul's intervention, Dreiser had, ironically, finally secured a job with the New York Central and Hudson River Railroad, after having presented himself as a writer "in poor health" who "wished, in order to recuperate it, to obtain some form of outdoor work, preferably manual."[47] After his time exercising and being drilled by Muldoon, which Dreiser described, in his essay "Scared Back to Nature," as both humiliating and restorative, he took the job working with the railroad in order to carry through in earnest what had been originally only a ruse to secure work.[48] Still physically weak and totally unskilled in manual labor, Dreiser was eventually situated in a carpentry shop associated with the railroad, where he swept shavings and did other small jobs. Even this was a difficult task for him, as he describes in *An Amateur Laborer;* but his self-imposed work cure did seem to have the desired effect.

There was a comfort in carrying my basket of shavings to and fro, without anything more to think about. It was something to stoop and bend, when the mind was wearied with much thinking; to know that I had this one thing to do, ill or well. I have the cure for neurasthenia, I said to myself. I have the thing that will make me forget, and I went earnestly on carry-

ing my basket, filling and emptying it until my arms were . . . sore and my
back . . . tired.[49]

Dreiser found his "new relationship" to "the men who were working"
around him just as restorative as his shift from mental to physical labor.[50]
Compared to his own difficult and anxious musings, their lives seemed
simple and immediate, their comradeship earnest and invigorating.
Unfortunately, dipping into their world did not give Dreiser the heightened social consciousness he would eventually gain in the 1920s and
1930s—his essays from his period of unemployment, "On Being Poor"
and "The Toil of the Laborer," reveal a striking lack of empathy[51]—but
his journey did bring him back to the point where he could resume his
life as a writer.

Though London, Wyckoff, Crane, and others were less specifically
directed toward performing a work cure for their deficient vitality, they
similarly proceeded in search of a deferred masculinity, which was
dressed in the guise of an experiential authority and Arcadian authenticity. Wyckoff prefaces his two-volume *The Workers*, for instance, with a
description of an apocryphal meeting with Channing F. Meek, a man
outstanding in his "familiarity with practical affairs." "In our talk," Wyckoff writes, "I could but feel increasingly the difference between my slender, book-learned lore and his vital knowledge of men and the principles
by which they live and work." This barely euphemistic panegyric to vital
manhood stands, then, in place of a more formal, or informative, introduction. We are now to assume that we are fully apprised of the rationale
for Wyckoff's two-year journey. This is not the last time, moreover, that
he intones this theme, comparing his own masculinity to the masculinity
of others as a way to measure his physical changes and the alterations of
his appetite, desires, and moods. After working under the particularly
affecting command of one boss whose "mingled shrewdness and brute
strength . . . marked him as a product of natural selection," Wyckoff
begins to experience his previously dormant animality: "I was hungry,
not with the hunger which comes from a day's shooting, and which
whets your appetite to the point of nice discriminations in an epicure's
dinner, but with a ravenous hunger which fits you to fight like a beast for
your food, and to eat it raw in brutal haste for gratification."[52]

The libidinal basis for Wyckoff's continual process of masculine mod-
eling—his introjection of the object of desire as a cherished aspect of the
self—is made glaringly clear in "In the Logging Camp," the final episode
of his first volume on his journey. The evening after his first day at the

camp, Wyckoff discovers the presence of Dick or, as he is affectionately known, "Dick the Kid":

> He was the finest specimen of them all; not much over twenty, I should say, and grown to a good six feet of height, and as straight as the trees among which he worked. Through the covering of rough clothes you felt with delight the curves of his splendid figure, and the sinewy muscles in symmetrical development. And then the lines of his throat and neck were so clean and strong, and his face charmed you with its fresh beauty, and its expression of frank joyousness. No wonder that he was a favorite in the camp.

Despite his communal lapse into the second person, Wyckoff's ability to appreciate Dick's popularity, "the power which he had to hold the others," lasts for only a short time.

> I could endure the sight no longer; I went out to the mountain-road, and waited where I thought that Dick would pass.
> He was startled when I stopped him, and instinctively he clenched his fists. For a moment I had a vivid sense of my physical insignificance, as I realized how easily, with a single blow, he could smash in my countenance and make swift end of me.

Though Dick immediately identifies Wyckoff as "a sky-pilot," he responds to him with friendly talk rather than the physical annihilation that Wyckoff clearly substitutes for inhibited physical desire. Despite the lack of physicality, Wyckoff sums up his emotional position unambiguously: "I lost my heart to him completely."[53]

However, what makes Wyckoff's homoerotic attachment operative, what ensures that it adds to, rather than challenges, his fragile sense of masculinity, is the reversal he narrates as he closes this encounter. Ever sanctimonious, even in the presence of his manly ideal, he asks Dick if he "felt no sense of wrong in using lightly the name of the Almighty." Wyckoff quotes Dick's gentle suggestion that Wyckoff should expect to hear men swear in a logging camp, before paraphrasing their all-important parting in one sprawling, paratactic sentence.

> His face was even more attractive in its expression of manly seriousness when we stood on the roadside at parting, and he put a firm hand on my shoulder, and fixed clear eyes on mine, as he told me, in his frank, open way, that he wanted to make a man of himself and not be a drunken sot,

and that, in this new venture before him, he would honestly try, and would ask for help.[54]

Whether this part of the episode is true or apocryphal, it caps the volume by casting Wyckoff in the role of superior man in this act of masculine exchange. Having invested Dick with all the phallic power of the frontier hero and all the physical beauty of a Greek statue, Wyckoff humbles him while he elevates himself and the Christian morality he proselytizes. The passage renders two definitions of manhood distinct so that they can be more completely amalgamated: the manly physicality of the working-class Dick and the moralistic middle-class manhood that Wyckoff promotes and that Dick apparently wants to emulate. In hypostasizing their combination, Wyckoff sets the terms for his own growth from a "slender, book-learned" youth into the full and vital manhood of worldly experience.

Albion Tourgée also promotes the ideal of vital Christian manhood, in *Murvale Eastman, Christian Socialist,* one of the first novels by a major American author to use the theme of class transvestism.[55] Tourgée was a progressive writer and journalist best known for advocating the policies of the Radical Republicans in the Reconstruction South and for writing a series of novels in the 1870s and 1880s devoted to examining the effects of slavery and the "problem" of miscegenation.[56] In *Murvale Eastman,* Tourgée turns to the dilemma of materialism and to the growing divide between capital and labor. He contends that these two major forces of industrial society need to be reunited under the auspices of the Christian church, which, according to Tourgée, is the only institution in modern society that can effectively convince men of wealth and men of poverty that they should share an ethic of cooperation. But before the church can achieve this bond, it must undergo a "revival," which Tourgée describes in gendered terms as a "strenuous effort" to draw the "young men of the best families," who "seemed strangely indifferent."[57] Murvale Eastman, Tourgée's "square-shouldered, bronze-faced" pastor "with muscles like a whip-cord" (43), is exactly the man for the job. When the novel opens, Eastman has just returned to his post as pastor of a wealthy church called The Golden Lilies, from a mysterious absence during which he has worked as a municipal railway driver. While his moneyed parishioners rode unsuspectingly in his railway car, oblivious as usual to the presence of the working class, Eastman acquired valuable knowledge about the concerns of railway workers, knowledge that allowed him to settle a streetcar strike without violence: "While others were studying the strike from the outside, he went to work and studied it from the inside" (175).

When Eastman is not bound up in the novel's Byzantine detective plot and its equally complicated romance plot, he is similarly able to mediate between his parishioners and the estranged, though religious, working class. Having convinced the affluent of their duty to the less fortunate, he similarly convinces them of the necessity to share their place of worship with citizens of all economic backgrounds. Through his manly efforts, he gets the girl (the daughter of Eastman's rich nemesis), solves the mystery (concerning who really owns the land the church was built on—a scarcely veiled parable), and revives the church.

Though Jack London's odd combination of social Darwinism and Marxism bears little relation to Wyckoff's Temperance Union moralisms and Tourgée's muscular Christian socialism, he shares their desire for personal and institutional revitalization through a rebuilt masculinity. Indeed, much of London's oeuvre can be read as an appeal for regeneration through adventure, what Jonathan Auerbach describes as London's "male call."[58] Though London came from a working-class background (and claimed it repeatedly with pride), this did not prevent a considerable amount of anxiety over the "feminizing" effects of his subsequent literary success. In his fiction, this anxiety was manifested in continual attempts to incorporate the atavistic strengths of the wild dog or the Teutonic superman with the philosophical acuity of the cultured classes. In his introduction to *Sea-Wolf,* one of London's more overt syncretic exercises, John Sutherland writes: "The still-young man evidently feared that as 'Jack London, author' he was in danger of losing the manhood which he had laboriously earned by sweat, danger, and struggle. It is clear from various remarks he made that Jack identified both with Wolf Larson, the male 'brute,' and with the 'sissy' Van Weyden, the sexless and bloodless 'scholar and dilettante.'"[59] The point of *Sea-Wolf* is that neither end of this spectrum can survive in its simple state: Van Weyden's "small and soft" (38) muscles leave him victim to physical harm, while Larson, "a god in his perfectness" (129), suffers from a fatal brain tumor that signifies, for London, the ultimate sterility of his primitive social type. It is left for Van Weyden to progress from standing "on dead men's legs" (22)—a phallic metaphor that manages to capture both his economic parasitism and physical flaccidity—to standing on his own. This operation is achieved, appropriately enough, on Endeavor Island, where Van Weyden successfully reerects the masts of the *Ghost,* Wolf's wrecked ship. While this episode has been regularly read through its rather obvious phallic symbols, London's message is more socially oriented than most imagine. In order to raise a set of masts without an already erect fixed anchor, Van Weyden must demonstrate not only intelligence and physical strength but an unusual degree of planning and foresight. The same is required, London suggests, in the project of resurrecting middle-class manhood for men from the professional-managerial class, who cannot depend on either ritualized rites of passage or the support of other men.

Luckily, not all men of affluence have to be shipwrecked and dominated by a "man-god" in order to find their "legs." The world of the urban working class proves just as regenerative and vitalizing as the South Seas or the Klondike. In his 1909 story "South of the Slot," London tells the tale of Freddie Drummond, a sociology professor at the University of California who, like Van Weyden, "was a very reserved man."[60] Drummond devotes his professional life to crossing the slot that divides the neighborhoods and the classes of San Francisco in order to investigate the mysterious ways of the working class. Like other class transvestites—including, of course, London himself—his explanation for such journeys is rooted in the now familiar notion of the superior authority of experiential knowledge: "He endeavored really to know the working people; and the only possible way to achieve this was to work beside them, eat their food, sleep in their beds, be amused with their amusements, think their thoughts and feel their feelings" (260). Yet as London makes clear, Drummond's best-selling volumes of labor history, *The Tyranny of Labor* and *The Fallacy of the Inefficient,* demonstrate how thoroughly he misunderstands the class he is impersonating. The superiority of experiential knowledge proves a ruse; it is simply one more ideological structure used to secure capitalism's political authority. Yet despite his ideological affiliations with the capitalist class, while Drummond plays the part of Bill Totts, his alter ego, he participates in the physicality of working-class life with unrestrained gusto. "At first he had been merely a good actor," pretending pleasure in the (supposedly) libertine activities of the working class, "but as time went on simulation became second nature. He no longer played a part, and he loved sausages—sausages and bacon, that which, in his own proper sphere, there was nothing more loathsome in the way of food" (262). This unsimulated love of sausages foreshadows, predictably, the release of Totts's libido, which Drummond fears he cannot control. Drummond makes a last, desperate attempt to control his alter ego, by marrying himself to an adequate woman, who, in the story's concluding scene, watches in horror as Bill Totts literally emerges, a "riotous savage" (270), from Freddie Drummond's body, to crucially help striking workers block a group of scabs. This conclusion is interesting and, although London was probably unconscious of it, quite telling. Though London could imagine the amalgamation of the dilettante and the man-god in the remote world of the South Seas, he had more trouble projecting the successful combination of the libido and the cognito once these were more explicitly expressed through class metaphors. At war with each other within a capitalist society, the working class and its middle-class managers could not, for London the revolutionary socialist, simply combine. Their "transformation scene" (268) had to be more violent and, following the logic of London's politics, should have produced a new man of the revolution. But London was unwilling or unable to go this far, leaving his readers with a Bill Totts who remains unchanged. The violence of the transformation is, in fact, displaced onto Drummond's fiancée, from whose point of view the scene is narrated. Her obvious mortification illuminates the story's deeper message: the foundational trauma within "South of the Slot" comes not from capitalism's exploitation of the working class but from Victorian culture's emasculation of middle-class men.

London's investment in a vital manhood looms similarly throughout his depiction of the working class and the poor in *The People of the Abyss,* though the East End slums prove, in contrast, hostile to the type of "stalwart men" he had found in the South Seas and in his own "spacious West, with room under its sky and unlimited air for a thousand Londons." Of one blue-eyed English acquaintance destined to a "wretched, inevitable future," he notes:

> I was not surprised by his body that night when he stripped for bed. I have seen many men strip, in gymnasium and training quarters, men of good blood and upbringing, but I have never seen one who stripped to better advantage than this young sot of two and twenty, this young god doomed to rack and ruin in four or five short years, and to pass hence without posterity to receive the splendid heritage it was his to bequeath.

The amazing conflation of eugenics and erotics is not, of course, incidental. In London's disguised journey through London (a pun that unavoidably suggests a search for personal Anglo-Saxon origins), he repeatedly remarks on the bodily degeneration of the men "who are left" while England colonizes the world: "The strong men, the men of pluck, initiative, and ambition, have been faring forth to the fresher and freer portions of the globe, to make new lands and nations. Those who are lacking, the weak of heart and head and hand, as well as the rotten and hopeless, have remained to carry on the breed."[61] Racial dissolution was not an unfamiliar fear in 1903; it could be found within a wide variety of political positions and had, in fact, been used only two years before to connect a critique of English imperialism with a call to restart lagging urban reform efforts.[62] But as Robert Peluso has argued, London's racism has more to do with his feelings about the specific conditions of American masculinity in the face of its new imperialist ventures.[63] In order to avoid a similar degeneration of race and masculinity, London pointedly advises his readers in the "new lands" (who he repeatedly addresses as "dear soft people") to attend to their own urban poor, the biological foundations of national progress.

SISTERS

Class-transvestite narratives by women also use the undercover mode to explore the connections between gender and class. As I noted, these texts tend to come later in the Progressive Era, often deriving from reformist political activity and, often explicitly, responding to the preceding narratives by men. A number of the women who went undercover saw their efforts as a continuation of the methodology of the settlement house project, in which reformers lived with workers in working-class neighborhoods in order to teach by example. According to Jane Addams, who introduced the concept of settlement to the United States, reform under this model could achieve two things: by teaching vocational skills, sanitary practices, home management, and language and literacy, it could accomplish a degree of social restitution within the system of industrial capitalism; and by giving the "New Woman" of the 1880s and 1890s a moral purpose, it could battle the sense of "uselessness that hangs about them heavily." Though Addams was an early participant in and advocate of women's higher education, she felt that "the first generation of college women had taken their learning too quickly, had departed too suddenly from the active, emotional life led by their grandmothers and great-grandmothers," and "had lost that simple and almost automatic response to the human appeal, that old healthful reaction resulting in activity from the mere presence of suffering or of helplessness."[64] Registering the same sense of "leisure-class" (Addams's preferred term) ennui that echoes throughout the narratives by men, she takes this feeling in a different direction, advocating not only activity but emotion, which she associates with the more traditionally feminine traits of sentimentality, empathy, and maternalism. Thus, in her interpretation, while the "objective value of a social settlement" can be measured by the reforms it enacts and the education it imparts, the "subjective necessity for social settlements" (necessity, that is, from the point of view of the leisure class) must be understood more poetically.

> You may remember the forlorn feeling which occasionally seizes you when you arrive early in the morning a stranger in a great city: the stream of laboring people goes past you as you gaze through the plate-glass window of your hotel; you see hard working men lifting great burdens; you hear the driving and jostling of huge carts and your heart sinks with a sudden sense of futility. The door opens before you and you turn to the man who brings you in your breakfast with a quick sense of human fellowship. You find yourself praying that you may never lose your hold on it all. A more poetic prayer would be that the great mother breasts of our common humanity, with its labor and suffering and its homely comforts, may never be withheld from you.[65]

According to Addams, a visual link with the laboring people is too unidirectional, a bond with the waiter too brief; what one needs in order to secure an ongoing connection with humanity is to settle among labor and suffering itself.

Perhaps because of this agenda, the narrative tenor of women's class-transvestite texts is different from the tone of the men's texts. The fetishistic descriptions of the burly proletariat are missing, and in their place we find images of an endangered womanhood plagued by the mental and physical demands of manual labor. Laura Hapke writes: "The middle- and upper-class women who published the results of their undercover work pointed sympathetically to the chasm between their lives, in which cotton-mill, pickle-factory, or glove-counter work was a data-gathering interlude, and those of the women who remained behind. . . . [The authors] explored the tension in such encounters between class and gender identity, between sororal impulse and class condescension, and last but not least, between women as workers and as ladies."[66] Yet the tensions between workers and ladies were not so innocent (or so objectively rendered) as this statement might suggest. Such narrators as Bessie Van Vorst, Rheta Childe Dorr, and Cornelia Stratton Parker came to these encounters with their own particular investments. If we can reductively characterize the male paradigm as regeneration through incorporation, then we might characterize the female paradigm as legitimacy through redemption. Reformers, reporters, and writers, these female investigators found validation for their new status as "working women" through activities that could, at times, create gender consciousness but that preserved class distinctions. This much is indicated in Parker's brilliantly punning title *Working with the Working Woman*. Whatever solidarity emerges from the shared work activity is circumscribed by Parker's propensity to work "with" the malleable subjectivities of the working women—that is, to work those subjectivities into some semblance of middle-class morality.

To stress both the active and the descriptive connotation of Parker's title is, I think, altogether appropriate, for with remarkable unanimity, the female class transvestites foregrounded their participatory roles in the scenes they witnessed. Unlike their male counterparts, their goal was to reform, not merely pass through, the lives of "the unknown class." As Bessie Van Vorst states after coining this term, bridging the epistemological distance with authentic knowledge is not enough. One must supplement knowledge with moral commitment: "We must discover and adopt their point of view, put ourselves in their surroundings, assume their burdens, unite with them in their daily effort. In this way alone, . . . can we do them real good, can we help them to find a moral, spiritual, esthetic standard suited to their condition in life."[67] While for Walter Wyckoff and men like him, becoming a worker was already nearly tantamount to becoming a man, Bessie Van Vorst and women like her faced a more difficult negotiation of gender and class ideologies. As Carol Smith-Rosenberg remarks, "To place a woman outside a domestic setting, to train a woman to think and feel 'as a man,' to encourage her to succeed at a career, indeed to place a career before marriage, violated virtually every late-Victorian norm." One way to circumvent this violation of norms was, then, to formulate professional and political activity in the language of bourgeois domesticity, to rhetorically expand the ideological purview of the domestic realm: "A woman . . . did not have to bear children to fulfill her feminine nature. Women who sought to secure the health and happiness of working-class children through child-labor legislation, the public-health movement, visiting-nurse services, and educational reform . . . had assumed the role of public mother."[68] In other words, if men had to leave home to become real men, then women had to expand the home to become new women—to connect domestic and maternal values to social and public virtues.

As Van Vorst reports, such public mothers were badly needed: "The American woman is restless, dissatisfied. Society . . . has driven her toward a destiny that is not normal. The factories are full of old maids.

. . . For natural obligations are substituted the fictitious duties of clubs, meetings, committees, organizations, professions, a thousand unwomanly occupations." To more progressive middle-class observers, this substitution would belie changing economic conditions, the effects of a rapid industrial proletarianization of traditional women's work. Such an analysis is, however, clearly not Van Vorst's goal. Rather, her narrative fixates on the endangered status of working-class womanhood, relentlessly transferring economic pressures into moral shortcomings, political problems into physical decadence. Even the bodily "degeneracy" of the woman worker, she concludes, is the result of "moral and not physical" causes. Her "increasing sterility" derives from "the triumph of individualism" and "the love of luxury." Yet since these "two enemies" were previously fought from the woman's vantage point within the home, they should be now fought from without, according to Van Vorst, by more public maternalistic incursions.[69]

Of course, not all female class transvestites wrote with the same moralistic fervor, but an anxious investment in the female working-class body did consistently function as a unifying focus for their investigations. Unlike Bessie Van Vorst, Rheta Childe Dorr and her collaborator William Hard saw women's "industrial emancipation" as a progressive development—a movement that ran "parallel" to the "intellectual emancipation," which "took women of the 'middle class' from their homes to colleges and universities to study." According to their report, this linked departure did not relieve women from their duty as women. Rather, it called for "the establishment of the principle that the home itself must be socially developed and expanded." Recasting historical development as a sentimental romance plot, Dorr and Hard proceeded to push this domestic conceit to the limit, calling for social restitution in obviously charged language. Maintaining that "women, entering industry, are still women, with bodies that can easily be wrecked," Dorr and Hard claimed that industry, "still . . . temperamentally a bachelor, with energetic, exhausting, short-sighted, irresponsible, bachelor ways," must be taught to "marr[y] and settle down," so that "we shall see some housekeeping." After all, this housekeeping "is necessary for the preservation of the physical health of the woman workers" and "necessary for the perpetuation of an undebilitated human race."[70]

Given the overwhelming concern these narratives demonstrate for preserving the reproductive capacities of white working-class women, it is not surprising that all of the fictional accounts of female class transvestism contrast the degenerative effects of unregulated female labor with the regenerative potential of the romance plot. As Allison Berg writes, "the racial value of reproduction" was a common theme in women's fiction of the 1880s and 1890s and was frequently communicated by these narratives' push toward marriage and motherhood.[71] Indeed, Bert Bender goes so far as to claim that American literature from this period contains a "Darwinian unknown" that operates through courtship plots in order to promote late nineteenth-century theories of sexual and racial selection.[72] Love, in other words, was portrayed in this period not as an innocent connection between two like-minded spirits (as writers in the earlier, Romantic era presented it) but as the coming together of a man and a women to perpetuate the race.

These fictional narratives additionally reveal that the romance plot is also an able mechanism for negotiating the persistence of patriarchal power at a moment of changing middle-class gender ideologies. For the "new woman" heroine of turn-of-the-century industrial fiction, a concern with the working class—with the maimed bodies of girl laborers and the injustices inflicted on their families (present and future)—is always also a potent statement of her own understanding of a woman's duties and desires in the world of business and industry. While such a statement could be articulated along the lines of "public motherhood," that set of metaphors did not always lessen the perception that new women were challenging men's authority within a sector men had long been used to controlling. In this sense, labor reform novels by women are unlike sentimental antislavery fiction, which could draw on slavery's association with familial relations to mount a domestic critique. Labor relations were generally understood to be of specific concern only to the male factory owner and managers. Thus, unlike efforts to secure municipal reforms of housing laws and sanitary legislation, women who pressed for workplace reform in their fiction appeared to commit a significant and almost entirely unauthorized breach of gender convention. However, class-transvestite novels, which feature affluent women who go undercover and gain a special kind of authority, circumvent that set of problems. Often the daughter of a patriarchal industrialist, the heroine works in the mills or on the shop floor, which gives her sanction to act against her father or, more frequently, to convert him to her perspective. Her time in disguise also brings her into romantic relation with an appropriately progressive "new man"—a man of her own social class with a conventional understanding of marriage, to be sure, but one who is also dedicated to social welfare. Hence, these texts are at once progressive and traditional. They feature some of the most independent and socially conscious women of this era's fiction, but they simultaneously circumscribe within a softer, gentler patriarchy both this independence and the politics it prompts.

W. H. Little's *Sealskin and Shoddy* provides one of the more overt examples of these contradictions. Misidentified as a piece of "labor press fiction," it is actually a novella centrally concerned with the entry of a "new woman" of affluence into industrial management.[73] *Sealskin and Shoddy* is set in an unidentified western city during the strike year of 1886 and tells the tale of Mamie Symington, who, as the subtitle proclaims, leads a "triple life as a society belle, nurse and factory girl." Mamie Symington is the daughter of Paul Symington, who is president of Symington Clothing Company and who remains, for most of the novella, in absentia in Europe. Mamie Symington has just returned from completing her undergraduate studies at Mount Holyoke Seminary and comes to understand the subjective costs of her father's business as she (in disguise) nurses Lizzie Knowlton, a sewing girl unjustly dismissed from the Symington factory for her sickness caused by overwork. Symington decides to investigate the matter further by taking a series of jobs in the clothing trades (in yet another disguise) while spending her evenings nursing sick factory girls and poring over the accounts of her father's factory—much to the dismay of Herbert Standish, the inordinately harsh factory superintendent who hopes to marry Symington in order to elevate his position. Symington is aided in her quest to reformulate the factory around a plan of worker representation and profit sharing by Hal Hinston, a scholar of economics with progressive ideas who predictably becomes Standish's competition for Symington's affections. Hinston must first wait for Symington to win over her absent father to the cooperative plan, since, as she proclaims, "I will not disobey papa."[74] Indeed, though his absence has created the possibility for productive change, Mamie's father remains the ultimate authority who the major characters struggle to seduce to their own theories of labor management. Mamie is, however, the most persuasive, since she can draw on her empirical knowledge of the workings of both management and labor. For her efforts, Mamie Symington is named the director of the company's board and settles into a marriage with Hinston. Their marriage is also somewhat of a business venture, since "by accepting and wearing this ring," Symington agrees to share in Hinston's profits and "in all my future earnings."[75] However "progressive" this articulation of marriage is (and its invocation of progressive labor relations is meant to designate a move in this direction), it does not take Symington out of her father's house. Rather, Hinston and his father (who marries Symington's spinster aunt) move into the Symington homestead. Though hidden underneath the machinations of this overwrought plot, the message is clear: Symington's disguised investigation wins her the authority and the approval to reformulate the company's labor relations; nevertheless, she remains a subordinate to both her father and her husband.

Marriage was, of course, a standard plot element of late nineteenth-century and early twentieth-century serial fiction and dime novels, where it often enacted just such an ideological foreclosure of earlier gestures toward change and political expression.[76] But as the more "literary" class transvestite novel *Henry Worthington, Idealist* by Margaret Sherwood demonstrates, marriage regularly comes to mark the extent of the feminist imagination within this era's realist fiction. In *Henry Worthington,* Worthington and Annice Gordon, the novel's protagonists, each struggle to define themselves against—while remaining obedient to—their strong-willed and politically conservative fathers. Indeed, upon Gordon's return from college she pledges to "devote herself to her father always," while Worthington, for his part, had decided at age four that if God made the world, then "Father made God," a point of view that solved for Worthington "all abstract problems of philosophy and ethics."[77] But both Gordon and Worthington turn against their fathers—the former when she realizes that her father owns Smith's, a particularly exploitive department store, and the latter when his father urges him to stop teaching his students about local labor conditions. In each case, this rejection of the patriarch prompts a period of social investigation, as Gordon goes in disguise to study the conditions at Smith's ("there's no other way to find out" [63]) and Worthington carries out a series of economic investigations (because he is "tired of abstract existence" [59]). Predictably, they fall in love while engaged in their social work, their romance made possible by the blurred boundaries of disguise. But although Smith's is indeed as horrible as Gordon has been lead to believe, she momentarily returns to her father's defense when Worthington speaks against the store. Gordon eventually rejects her father and marries Worthington, after having realized the justice of the latter's accusations. Importantly, this tension and its resolution totally occlude the developing critique of class relations and exploitation. After Gordon chooses to ally herself with a progressive man, reject her father's money, and start over in the West, all mention of social reform (and even a half-developed plotline about a landgrab) is dropped.

Even *What Diantha Did,* a class-transvestite novel by Charlotte Perkins Gilman, participates in this pattern—cross-dressed exploration avails an expanded gender role that is eventually contained within the patriarchal marriage structure. Five years before she wrote *Herland* (1915), which fancifully set women in a society without men as a way to advocate communal living, shared child rearing, and socialism, Gilman used *Diantha* to explore another aspect of her social program: the industrialization of housework.[78] Fleeing her own tyrannical father and tired of waiting for her fiancé to be free of his financial debts and obligations to his spendthrift mother and sisters, Diantha disobeys both men and goes undercover as a house servant in order to study and improve on the economic organization of household labor. What she discovers is that the cooking of meals, the washing of clothes, and even such jobs as housecleaning can be more effectively managed by external teams of professional laborers. The middle-class housewife can be liberated from housework so that she may enjoy "higher" occupations, and the wives of capitalists can be free of nosy, bothersome house servants who (as we learn in a chapter entitled "Sleeping In") tempt the men of the house to sexual indiscretion. Capitalizing on her newly gained knowledge, Diantha begins a successful housework business and organizes local "girls" into a professional labor force. She earns enough to relieve her fiancé of his financial burdens and to convince him to marry her. But the book does not—indeed, cannot—end at this point. Though she has achieved financial success and has proven her business theories correct, she is overwhelmed with a desire to serve her husband and win his approval: "With marriage, love, happiness came an overwhelming instinct of service—personal service. . . . She wanted to wait on him, loved to do it. . . . She had a sense of treason, of neglected duty, as she left the flower-crowned cottage day by day."[79] Her husband concurs with her estimation of negligence, but he manages to use "the element of dissatisfaction in his married life" to fuel his work (on Lamarckian biology—a minor obsession of Gilman's), which takes him to Europe for extended stays. The novel ends, however, with him granting his approval in strangely transgendered terms ("As man to man I'm proud of you—tremendously proud of you") and with Diantha sinking to her knees as "she gave way to an overmastering burst of feeling": " 'Thank you!' was all she said, with long, deep sobbing sighs between. 'Thank you!—Oh—thank you!' "[80]

INVENTING WORKING-CLASS CULTURE

Both the foreclosed adventures in feminist liberation and the male class transvestite's libidinal investments testify to the way turn-of-the-century authors used the figure of the working class to achieve their own social goals. These goals were the establishment of an experimental authority based on claims to authenticity, the revitalization of self through adventures in adversity, and the establishment of new middle-class gender roles through a momentary assumption of the guise of the working class. Yet taken as a group and judged more abstractly, these narratives had other, perhaps more profound, effects on the understanding of class in America. In all of these accounts, the authors recast the discourse of class and class difference in new and more accommodating terms. From the abject to the integral, from community to signifying system, from shared work to shared morality, from economy to culture, the transvestite's recorded journey through the lives of the working class and the poor produces a translation that creates the discursive space for a fictitious resolution of material class conflicts. As Cornelia Stratton Parker asserts, these illusory "conflicts" derive principally from a limited perspective, the lack (echoing Crane) of an expanded "point of view": "A certain type of labor agitator, or 'parlor laborite,' prefers to see only the gloomy side of the worker's life. They are as dishonest as the employer who would see only the contentment. The picture must be viewed in its entirety—and that means considering the workers not as a labor problem, but as a social problem."[81] Considered as such—which is to say, considered apart from their relation to the mode of production—the workers as "social problem" are finally not all that problematic. Underneath their different clothing, different habits, and different idioms (underneath "class" as it is here conceived) lies a certain sameness, a common "humanity" that can be reconstituted and resurrected within a renewed, more harmonic notion of American culture.

To be sure, class transvestites were not the only or even the principal protagonists in this larger ideological transformation. Rather, the recognition, revaluation, and accommodation of "difference" within American culture—what we now call "cultural pluralism"—progressed slowly and unevenly at the turn of the century, through the popular press, academic departments of social science, and legislative bodies. With regard to the categories of race and ethnicity (its main targets), the discourse of pluralism was a qualified success; it gave some legitimacy to those struggling against nativist and racist policies, and it opened the way to broader movements for civil rights. Yet the specific ideological variant of class pluralism, or "industrial pluralism," underwrote other, less progressive structural and institutional changes. The price of a place at the table, a role within the new industrial regime, was a circumscription of working-class action within the dominant forms of political representation. "Out of the nadir of the 1890s depression," writes Leon Fink, "labor unions had revived, not on the basis of the inclusive, antimonopoly platform of the Knights of Labor but through the self-protective and politically conservative craft unionism of the AFL." Following this conservative trend, "industrial pluralists" connected such traditionally progressive actions as collective bargaining "not to the destruction of the capitalist order but to its reinvigoration," pressing for "legally sanctioned mechanisms of managed conflict between employers and workers."[82] The most popular mechanisms of management, we might add here, affected the lives of the unorganized and the unemployed as well. As Martha Banta has recently demonstrated, the mode of "scientific management" initiated by Fredrick Winslow Taylor in the 1890s had a wide sphere of influence, structuring and rationalizing both the workplace relations and the cultural experiences of the working class and the poor during this era.[83]

Banta's recent intervention not withstanding, the trend in much of the "new" labor history of recent years has been to find resistance to these newly codified structural changes in the 1890s within an autonomous realm of "working-class culture." Working after such British labor historians as E. P. Thompson and writing against older historiographic models of industrial consent, a generation of American historians has looked outside of the managed labor process for resistant pockets of "preindustrial cultural values." For Herbert Gutman, who first charted this theory in his seminal essay "Work, Culture, and Society in Industrializing America," the preindustrial was more than simply a romantic past, necessarily abandoned at the factory gates. It was, rather, an alternate system of working-class values, continually reasserted by the successive waves of immigrants and migrants to these industrial centers. Gutman maintained that this complex tapestry of political republicanism, ethnic communitarianism, and producer ideology formed a residual discourse (to borrow from Raymond Williams) that could and did create the basis for actions against the modernizing dictates of industrial capitalism. To the extent that this culture stood outside of economic and industrial dictates, it was unencumbered by the pervasive effects of workplace rationalization and corporatist management, free of the pluralist recognition, celebration, and accommodation of working-class difference.[84]

Yet I think that as a corpus, the class-transvestite texts offer a contrasting view to such culturalist approaches to the period. Long before

Gutman and others identified and explored working-class culture, the class transvestites had already found a particular use for such realms of autonomy. Though this nefarious precedent can hardly serve as a counterargument to the new labor history's reliance on culture as resistance—an interpretation founded on its understanding of the decades in question—it might at least operate as a methodological warning that one should continually be aware of the contextual and ideological implications of such a paradigmatic move. In the class transvestites' journeys through communities of the working-class and the poor in search of authentic cultural forms, we hear more than an echo of Frederick Winslow Taylor's own cross-dressed travels taken across the factory floor in order to discover, catalog, and colonize the workers' "mass of traditional knowledge."[85] Much like Taylor, the class transvestites believed that such cultural knowledge might be successfully colonized and utilized within the production and vitalization of new forms of middle-class authority.

The point of such an abrupt analogy is not, finally, that workers and the poor lacked a culture of their own (even a culture based on anti-industrial values) but, rather, that this culture, however formulated, was no more inherently resistant to appropriation than was the considerable skill base of industrial craft workers. Indeed, precisely the aura of authenticity and resistance surrounding working-class culture assured its fetishistic attraction to the class transvestite. Its sociological and journalistic value derived specifically from its supposed position of autonomy outside of the homogenized realm of the new industrial order. Once it was identified, mapped, and, to various degrees, appropriated, it could serve as part of a newly expanded point of view. The result of these discursive acts of imperialism was, furthermore, not simply the co-optation of working-class culture and the cultural practices of the poor but the co-optation of "class" as "culture"—an analytic sleight of hand, repeatedly reiterated, which underwrote the translation of class conflict into class difference and then into cultural difference. Once understood as a culture among many, the workers and the poor could be contained within a rhetoric of pluralism that celebrated difference even as it denied revolutionary visions of transcendence.

Modernism and the Aesthetics of Management

T. S. Eliot and Gertrude Stein Write Labor Literature

I have heard it said, in fact I believe that it's quite a current thought, that we have taken skill out of work. We have not. We have put a higher skill into planning, management, and the tool building, and the results of that skill are enjoyed by the man who is not skilled.
—Henry Ford, *My Life and Work*

A poem is a small (or large) machine made of words.
—William Carlos Williams, *Selected Poems*

THE CUBIST VISION AND THE LABOR PROCESS: A PROLOGUE

When the Armory Show opened in New York on February 15, 1913, it was the first major presentation of postimpressionist art in the United States and thus rapidly came to represent what J. M. Mancini describes as the "moment at which the 'new' vanquished the 'old' in American culture with a single and stunning revolutionary blow."[1] The battle between old and new was most evident in the controversy surrounding Marcel Duchamp's infamous entry in the Cubist Room, *Nude Descending a Staircase, No. 2* (fig. 2). Described variously as an "elevated railroad stairway in ruins after an earthquake," a "dynamited suit of Japanese armor," and "an explosion in a shingle factory,"[2] it became a lightning rod for popu-

Marcel Duchamp, *Nude Descending a Staircase, N. 2.* © 2005 Artists Rights Society (ARS), New York / ADAGP, Paris / Succession.

lar opinion and a touchstone for the public's response to the disassocia-
tive stimuli of modernity. "To have looked at [the Cubist Room] is to
have passed through a pathological museum," summarized Kenyon Cox
in *Harper's Weekly*. "One feels that one has seen not an exhibition, but an
exposure."[3]

When cultural historians recount the inception of modernism in the
United States, however, they usually dismiss such reactions in favor of an
alternate story of Duchamp's genius, the Armory Show's success, and, in
particular, modernism's rightful victory over Victorian gentility. If the
1950s version of this story depends on celebrations of modernism's formal complexities and if the 1970s version depends on its antibourgeois
aestheticism, contemporary narratives increasingly draw connections
between aesthetic and political radicalisms in the modernist era. The
Armory Show thus appears, in Mancini's words, as part of a "wider struggle by workers, women, and others for liberation in the first decades of
the twentieth century."[4] Once valorized for its purported transcendence
of history and politics, modernism now maintains its centrality, paradoxically, through appeals to the historical conjunction of alliance politics.
Pairing the Armory Show with the Industrial Workers of the World's
Paterson Strike Pageant in *New York 1913*, Martin Green concludes:
"The spirit of 1913 was an aspiration to transcend what most people
accepted as ordinary and so inevitable. It was the ordinariness of capitalism and liberalism and class hierarchy, in the case of the IWW strike; and
in the case of the Armory Show, it was old forms of art, appreciation and
beauty."[5]

Though I will eventually turn my focus to literary modernism—to its
epistemological links to labor management, to its roots in a reconcep-
tualization of working-class forms, and to the early works of T. S. Eliot
and Gertrude Stein—I begin with the Armory Show, Duchamp's *Nude*,
and their critical legacy, to introduce a different story of modernism's
relationship to class and labor in·the 1910s. In this story, modernism
neither evades history nor aids the working class through its ruptures,
fractures, and quest for a new cultural totality. These aspects of the
modernist project, I argue alternately, can be read as modernism's own
technique for apprehending and containing the dissonances of class
segmentation. They are not, therefore, an attempt to transcend "the
limits of the individual self," as Green would have it,[6] but a new way of
configuring that self—not an aesthetics of liberation, but an aesthetics
of management that was symptomatic of incipient configurations within
the industrial labor process. To some extent, this managerial tactic con-

tinued the efforts crystallized in the strike novels of the 1880s (discussed in chap. 3). But whereas realism co-opted working-class movements by adopting and then containing their strategies of articulation, modernism fragmented and systematized working-class forms in a manner that matched the new production processes of the twentieth century. As Louis Fraina noted in his reply to Kenyon Cox, the "New Art" is not "pathologic" but "expresses the vital urge of its age. . . . It is the art of capitalism. . . . Cubism transfers the technique of machinery, so to speak, to the canvas."[7]

We can measure Fraina's perceptiveness if we pair Duchamp's *Nude* with a quite different labor event of 1913–14, the implementation of modern line-production methods at Ford's Highland Park plant in Detroit.[8] Though not the only factory to apply Frederick Taylor's *Principles of Scientific Management* (1911)—observation, timing of each operation within the task, establishment of minimum unit times, and reconstruction of jobs with composite times as the standard—Highland Park was the first to combine these principles with uniform design specifications and the endless chain conveyer belt. As Stephen Meyer notes, the standardized design of the Model T enabled Ford's engineers to "specialize and routinize . . . work processes" in order to transfer skill from craft workers into "the design of sophisticated and complicated machines."[9] The conveyer belt then ensured that the repetitive and sequential nature of these processes would be enforced by the machines themselves, which now proscribed the pace and path of what had once been a series of complex operations completed by skilled craftsmen and their helpers. This constituted, in Harry Braverman's words, a significant division of "the unity of thought and action. . . . The subjective factor of the labor process is removed to a place among its inanimate objective factors."[10]

The epistemological significance of this division can hardly be underestimated; here we find the corollary to modernism's own aesthetic operations. For industrial engineers to design a mechanical process that would replicate the physical and cognitive skills of the craft worker, they needed to perform exactly the sort of objectification Braverman describes, comprehending the worker as a machine, whose motions could be traced and rationalized using precise chronological measures. For our purposes, the visual tracings of this objectification are the most immediately arresting, since they so clearly prefigure Duchamp's *Nude*. Using a rapid-speed camera technique developed by Eadward Muybridge and E. J. Marey, Frank Gilbreth (the inventor of time-motion studies) recorded "the paths of each of several motions made by various parts of the body and their exact distances, exact times, relative times, exact speeds, relative speeds, and directions."[11] Gilbreth's chronographs (fig. 3), like Muybridge's examinations of the human figure (fig. 4), thus give us a different way to connect Duchamp—and the cubist idiom generally—to the industrial culture of the 1910s. Such a comparison provides a visual record of both the aesthetic dimensions and the social permeation of management epistemology.

While it is generally known that chronophotography inspired Duchamp's cubism—that, in some general way, industrialism inspired modernism—this mode of figuration needs to be traced more specifically to changes in the labor process. Not only did new industrial technologies supply the tools to create atomized images, but at a more fundamental level, they supplied the problem that made such studies conceptually useful: how can the moving, working body be apprehended in a way that allows its most intimate physical knowledge—its knowledge of sensuous human labor—to be alienated from it and reinscribed in a process, a system, or a mode of representation? I think that Duchamp's *Nude*—and a good deal of early avant-garde modernism—speaks to this problematic. Duchamp does not attempt to represent the moving body holistically but, rather, to dissect movement as such, to reduce it to elemental static poses. By doing so, he makes a crucial transition from the norms of nineteenth-century portraiture to the analytic mood of avant-garde modernism. Rejecting the epistemology of realism, which grounds knowledge in the shared experience of the empirical, he instead vests the proprietary observer with a scientific comprehension of motion in the abstract—a comprehension superior to any held by the body itself. This shift is exemplary of what Anson Rabinbach sees as the "triumph of technology over sense perception"[12] and is predictive of other formally invested, self-referential modernist texts (which will exploit the spectacle of technical mastery along similar lines). Importantly, the triumph of technology also links avant-garde modernism to the epistemological dictates of Taylorist production methods and to the managerial systems that those methods underwrite. As Taylorism divides and separates each act of labor into conception and execution, Duchamp's *Nude* separates motion into cognitive and physical dimensions. As scientific management installs a system of administration that superintends these now disparate acts of labor, the *Nude* embodies a technical aesthetics that both fragments and links the divided object within its purview.

Frank Gilbreth's chronograph for time-motion studies, 1919. (Reprinted from Frank R. Gilbreth and Lillian M. Gilbreth, *Fatigue Study: The Elimination of Humanity's Greatest Unnecessary Waste: A First Step in Motion Study* [London: George Routledge and Sons, 1919].)

MODERNISM AND MANAGEMENT

What avant-garde modernism and scientific management have in common, in other words, is a similar understanding of the way formal apparatuses can function to systematize bodies, labor, and the stresses and tensions of class conflict. In scientific management, this is explicit. "In the past the man has been first," writes Taylor, but "in the future the system must be first." Taylor explains, "What constitutes a fair day's work will be a question for scientific investigation, instead of a subject to be bargained and haggled over."[13] Most avant-garde modernist texts that can be read as instances of a managerial aesthetics are, in contrast, neither as obvious nor as unmediated in their connections. These texts share, however, a substructure that connects them to the social and economic processes of industrial modernization and to Taylor's mode of resolution through formal procedures. As with Duchamp's *Nude*, this substructure typically entails two main innovations. First, avant-garde modernists express a commitment to atomization and fragmentation, a desire to separate the object, scene, or theme into a set of disparate, ele-

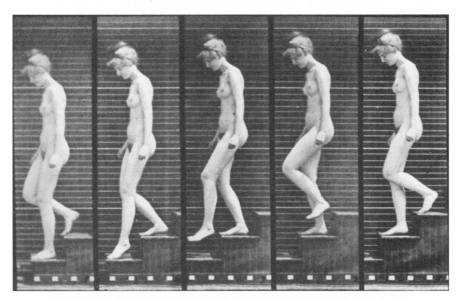

Eadweard Muybridge, "Descending the Stairs and Turning Around," 1887. (Reprinted from *Animal Locomotion: An Electrophotographic Investigation of Consecutive Phases of Animal Movements* [Philadelphia: University of Pennsylvania Press, 1887].)

mental parts. Second, they reconnect these parts through an external system, logic, or, in more familiar terms, aesthetic technique. T. S. Eliot, who serves as the initial example in this chapter, refines these moves further, subsuming the subjectivity of the poet and those whom he apprehends across the class divide within a system of coherences and affective relays that he calls the "objective correlative." Gertrude Stein, for her part, is similarly interested in avoiding subjectivity in favor of the logic of systemization. Her system, however, is made up of a collection of working-class types with fixed bottom natures who are put on display by Stein's highly formalized techniques of characterization and narration.

Eliot and Stein are also significant examples of modernism's imaginative affiliations with management, since their early work so clearly reacts to urbanization and immigration, the two socioeconomic factors that largely prompted the management revolution. Taylorism and Fordism arose, in particular, as a response to the new concentration of unskilled foreign laborers who were willing to work outside of the traditional craft system. Though avant-garde modernism was, as one would expect, less baldly instrumental, it was often no less functionalist. Modernists registered urbanization and immigration as the simultaneous pressures of proximity and difference (in Eliot's words, a "swollen . . . stream of mixed immigration bringing . . . the danger of . . . a caste system"),[14] which existent forms of literary representation could barely recognize, much less remediate. For the early Eliot, before his turn to the unifying idea of culture and much before his conversion to the Church of England, remediation could come through an aesthetic system that cushioned the shock of modernity by adding a measure of predictability and impersonality. For the early Stein, before her turn to the antirepresentational experiments of *Tender Buttons,* remediation could come from the scientific principles of Jamesian psychology that found the working class fixed in their class positions by their very habits of attention.

Of course, by referring to modernism as an aesthetic system—which, along with other systems, attempts to manage the economic and social pressures of modernization—I am proposing a substantially different method of reading class and labor in modernist literature. As I noted in chapter 1, most readings of labor literature proceed from an identitarian conception of class, where class denominators indicate a person's place within a social spectrum (lower class, middle class, upper class). Understandably, these readings then privilege realist fiction, which more accurately reveals these identities as they come into conflict. But as a result of this method, readers of labor literature, with a few conspicuous exceptions, have been unable to attend to nonrealist poetic and narrative forms.[15] I suggest, however, that especially when we look for modernism's relation to class, we should look not for traditional class characters and characteristics but for something one could call *class performativity:* the manifestation of the forms or logic of the class process within the cultural text, moments in which the deep structures and processes that configure and are configured by economic forces surface and are visible. This can give us a historical understanding of modernism that is, as Perry Anderson puts it, "conjunctural," composed of an "overdetermined configuration" of aesthetic forms and "key technologies or innovations of the second industrial revolution."[16] Placing modernism within this history—that is, within labor history—removes its aura of intellectual and aesthetic exclusiveness and grounds it in the lived history of its authors and readers. Though these authors and readers may not have understood the epistemological shifts of modernity as an "emptying of time-space,"[17] they could have hardly escaped the consequences of rudimentary shifts in the labor process that had fundamentally rationalized not only time and space but also the human body.

MODERNISM AS LABOR LITERATURE

Another way to understand the connection between shifts in the labor process, managerial modes, and the rise of modernism is through the lens of literary history—more specifically, through an examination of the way in which literature's apprehension of workers and those marked as class Other changes at the "moment of modernism" in the 1910s. Although it is rarely treated to the sorts of thematic examinations that more typically embrace the 1930s, the literature of the 1910s is surprisingly flush with representations of labor. This is the decade of Jack London, Theodore Dreiser, and Upton Sinclair's prominence (if not their best fiction) and also the era of *The Masses,* which introduced readers to a more urban school of labor writing through the fiction and poetry of Floyd Dell, John Reed, and Max Eastman. The year 1913 not only encompassed the Armory Show and Ford's triumph in Highland Park; it was the year of Vachel Lindsay's poetic odes to industrial Springfield, Illinois, in *General William Booth Enters into Heaven and Other Poems.* Two years later, Carl Sandburg followed Lindsay's lead, by praising Chicago ("hog butcher for the world") in *Chicago Poems,*[18] only to be echoed in 1918 by Sherwood Anderson's forgotten book of labor poetry, *Mid-American Chants.* Even Robert Frost, whose fame has largely served to disarticulate him from his roots in early populism, was heavily reliant on class representation. *North of Boston* (1914), the book that established his reputation and solidified his poetic voice, stages a series of long dialogues between northeastern rural "folk." Finally, and perhaps most surprisingly (since it has gone entirely without critical note), this era finds a number of American modernists constituting their aesthetic principles through poetic and fictive interactions with the working class: T. S. Eliot, Gertrude Stein, William Carlos Williams, and Ezra Pound in the 1910s; John Dos Passos and William Faulkner in the 1920s.

Of course, ever since the Romantic poets, formal innovations in literature have often been prompted by an apprehension of workers. William Wordsworth's movement toward a "natural language" in his interchanges with rural peasants, Émile Zola's attempt to ground naturalism in a taxonomic genealogy of the working-class family, Walt Whitman's expansive lines driven by a desire to encompass the "lowly," and even the urban expressionism of Stephen Crane—all conjoined literary experimentation with descriptions of work, workers, and the social divisions wrought by class. What distinguishes modernism's concern with the working class is, however, its distinct epistemological orientation. The motivational pressure does not arise, as it does in the nineteenth century and in the poetic populism of Carl Sandburg and Sherwood Anderson, from a greater desire to know, to reveal the sordidness of poverty, or to celebrate the (supposed) vital physicality of laborers. Modernism's propensity to make art from the experience of class has more to do with its drive to systematize and manage class referents that are already abundantly revealed. Indeed, as Walter Benjamin observes, the modernist responds to the urban masses with "fear, revulsion, and horror" rather than with anything like affective sentimentality. "The shock of experience," which, Benjamin suggests, "corresponds to what the worker 'experiences' at his machine," has "become the norm"—a norm from which one wants relief, not with which one wants greater intimacy.[19] Relief, at least for Benjamin's subject, Baudelaire, comes in a set of aesthetic tactics: transpositions, displacements, symbolisms. For American modernists who, I would argue, experience the shift toward machine processes as a more holistic cultural event, relief comes from articulating the aesthetic potential that lies within scientific management's formal system—in comprehending the way that the worker, once abstracted from a sentimental system of affect, can be used in a different, even more functionalist manner to vitalize new aesthetic structures.

The most obvious manifestation of this turn comes in modernism's different exploitation of the linguistic vernacular. As Elsa Nettels notes, by the late nineteenth century, American realism represented vernacular voices both to record and to contain the cultural otherness of immigrants and African American migrants to the North.[20] Such representations were driven by a realist epistemology that tied discursive revelation to control through technologies of linguistic rearticulation (as in the way William Dean Howells frames foreign voices with orthographic marks). But most modernists were only secondarily interested in exploring the vernacular for the purposes of verisimilitude. Modernism's utilization of the vernacular focuses, rather, on discourse itself, attempting to use the linguistic otherness of idiomatic speech to divest itself from the strictures of genteel English and to propel itself toward more complex, self-referential linguistic systems. In other words, modernism looks to the speech of workers—which was thought to have a fluid vocabulary and nonnormative syntactical patterns—to ground its own attempts to refunction literary forms. Michael North writes of modernism's relationship to the African American vernacular: "The real attraction of the black voice to writers like Stein and Eliot was its technical distinction, its insurrectionary opposition to the known and familiar in language. . . . Modernism . . . mimicked the strategies of dialect and aspired to become a dialect itself."[21] Though North circumscribes his analysis of the "dialect of modernism" with the metaphor of the "racial masquerade," the evidence suggests (indeed, his evidence suggests) that class structures modernism's interchange with the vernacular Other in just as profound a manner as race. Not only are Stein and Eliot's racial Others from the working class (as are all of North's examples), but their voices are interwoven with those of Irish and German immigrant workers and are joined by the class-inflected vernacular experiments of Frost, Sandburg, Faulkner, Anderson, and others.

It is important to stress, however, that modernism's reliance on the linguistics of class otherness goes far beyond its utilization of the lexical fecundity of the vernacular. As Pound's poetry certainly shows, one need not venture into the music hall to explode the hermetic strictures of genteel literature. Non-Western poetic traditions and passages from Latin, Greek, and Sanskrit can similarly destabilize and denaturalize the sentimental pretensions of the Victorian lyric. Rather, such modernists as Eliot and Stein—who literally discovered their aesthetic techniques as they moved through the working-class neighborhoods of North Cambridge, South Boston, London, and Baltimore—employ working-class forms (vernacular speech, artifacts, popular culture, and stereotyped characters) as tools in their efforts to shift from an aesthetics of reference to an aesthetics of self-reference and materiality. "Although there are many different accounts of literary modernism," explains Walter Benn Michaels, "probably all of them acknowledge its interest in the ontology of the sign—which is to say, in the materiality of the signifier, in the relation of signifier to signified, in the relation of sign to referent."[22] Put differently, modernism does not reject materiality (or indeed, in any a priori manner, materialism) but, rather, relocates materiality from the referent (the "real world" in realism) to the signifier (the materiality of language or of modernist linguistic practice). Working-class forms hence have functional utility because they carry with them an aura of a heightened materiality. They seem, in and of themselves, more "real"; thus their amplified reality (the vibrancy of working-class vernacular, the deep embodiment of the working-class subject, the hypermateriality of the smells and sounds of working-class neighborhoods), once transposed from referent to signifier, can add a physicality to the linguistic operations of the modernist text. But once transposed, this working-class materiality is also more easily managed. The otherness that once seemed foreign and inassimilable is reconstituted as a material property of language itself.

"DULL PRECIPITATES OF FACT": ELIOT'S WORKING-CLASS FORMS

If T. S. Eliot's poetry seems at first an unlikely example of the type of management aesthetics I have been discussing, that is in part due to the success of his tactics of self-censorship and self-fashioning. By all accounts a guarded person, Eliot defended himself against the invasions of modernity and the affronts of popularity by constructing, early on, a private persona for the public, a voice within his most confessional poems that could be taken as an authentic self. Thus conventional acceptance of Eliot as the poet of ennui, heroic failure, and the "refusal of assertion"[23] is not so much incorrect as insufficiently probing; it fails to take into account how assertively Eliot produced this disposition. Having now the benefit of facsimile editions of *The Waste Land* and especially of the publication of the long-suppressed "notebook poems" of 1909–17 (published in 1996 under the title *Inventions of the March Hare*), we get a very different sense of the poet. If the initial sections of the standard *Complete Poems and Plays* present the poet as staid, restrained, and prematurely aged, these early notebook poems offer us what we would have otherwise missed: the young, tortured, and passionate Eliot who is repulsed by a working class he nonetheless must enact symbolic violence on in order to construct his persona.

Indeed, the much-reported scandal of the notebook poems may only incidentally be the scandal of Eliot's misogyny and racism (which were, at any rate, famously "exposed" long before the publication of Eliot's notebook).[24] The more enduring scandal emerges from finding the poet of "ironic self-deprecation" practicing this pose against the backdrop of poverty, class stratification, and urban decay—the "waste land"— a trope that can now no longer be explained by reference to World War I or to Eliot's traumatic marriage (since these poems preceded both).[25] The fragments and waste that Eliot perpetually finds in his cityscapes are neither simply the objective renderings of postwar Europe nor the subjective expressions of the poet's mind. They are, more centrally, a mode of epistemological management (of disarticulation and totalization) that seeks to reconcile world and mind through a series of contextually resonant tactics. I argue, in particular, that the notebook poems stage a series of attempts to achieve personal and poetic coherence—attempts that reach fruition only as Eliot more completely systematizes his poetic method. Thus the "objective correlative," his most fully realized system of affective relays, marks the culmination of this process, a process of management that, for Eliot, is also a process of objectification and de-personalization.[26]

Although the working drafts, fragments, and prose segments that compose the notebook are not organized in any rigid fashion, they do consistently orbit around two central motifs—slumming and music—which illustrate Eliot's continual attraction to class themes and efforts toward systematization. If the act of walking through the urban decay of North Cambridge, South Boston, and London presents the poet with dis-articulate forms of class otherness—what Gregory Jay calls "the object world that dominates the lower classes"—then the caprice, the interlude, the love song, and the ballad afford a continual attempt to circumscribe this otherness within the traditional structures of high culture.[27] Eliot would, in fact, later claim that such antipodal tensions were endemic to the poet's work, since "the contemplation of the horrid or sordid or dis-gusting by an artist, is the necessary and negative aspect of the impulse toward the pursuit of beauty."[28] Yet in the 1910s, Eliot's "pursuit of beauty" manifested itself mainly in ironic attempts to restrain the mater-ial and corporeal within a suggestion of the harmonic—a cloying and, indeed, jarring frame for the paratactic iterations of working-class forms. The more general problem—as Eliot would later both elucidate and "resolve" in *The Waste Land*—is that modernity is so rife with excess that there is a continual incommensurability between the objects of the world, its artifacts and realia, and the subjective, cognitive, and aesthetic systems that order them. These systems do not disappear at the moment of modernity, but they then come to seem extrinsic and thus incapable of fulfilling their totalizing role.

As James Buzard notes, Eliot tried, in these slumming trips, to sur-mount this problem through the borrowed paradigm of ethnography, to gain "the privileged view of culture as a whole, a view denied to inhabi-tants."[29] But Eliot was largely unprepared to relinquish either his fasci-nation with materiality or his distancing mechanisms. The results, as they appear in the notebook poem "First Caprice in North Cambridge," are telling.

A street-piano, garrulous and frail;
The yellow evening flung against the panes

Of dirty windows: and the distant strains
Of children's voices, ended in a wail.

(13)

The problem here is not that these musical puns and motifs fail to knit the poem together. On the contrary, the doubled meaning of "caprice" (a whimsical slumming journey through North Cambridge or a whimsical musical composition) rather precisely prefaces the condescension of the final line: "Oh, these minor considerations! . . ." (13). The "street-piano" (which recurs throughout the notebook as a metonym for working-class culture) rattles nicely, but not discordantly. The overworked meter and end rhymes serve to mimic, if not exactly the freedom of a caprice, at least the effect of musicality. The problem, rather, is that the method so thoroughly overreaches and underappreciates the material that the poem seems finally like a study in bourgeois arrogance. Such endeavors were not, of course, new in 1909 (Eliot's dating for the poem). Eliot would have known such elegant ditties as Baudelaire's "Bash the Poor!"[30] But Eliot is no Baudelaire, and the speaking voice is not substantiated enough to sustain the arrogance that the frame provides. In fact, the speaking voice is not substantiated at all. It is the rhyme and meter—and, most particularly, the materiality of the objects themselves—that give this piece substantiality.

To put this somewhat differently, the objects in the poem stand in an ambiguous relationship to the poetic subject. They are, in one sense, maddeningly autonomous. Embodying the random violence of some past moment (through their brokenness) and insisting on passivity (through the passive voice), they exist, for Eliot, within a state of "sordid patience" (13)—that is, sordid in their patience rather than patient of their sordidness. Yet they are also forcefully present, reverberating with the jagged physicality of the urban, interdependent and coherent inasmuch as they renew a set of sentimental tropes of class otherness (wailing children, crowds, dirt) put into play by nineteenth-century industrial literature. If such tropes are more traditionally connected to the narrator and the reader through various apparatuses of affect, Eliot's goal is evidently otherwise. He attempts to disarticulate them—or to present them in their disarticulation—in order to push aside the weight of so much genteel sympathy and Victorian hand-wringing and to uncover the materiality of the words themselves. To give Eliot his due, there is a certain beauty within these urban pastoral rhymes ("broken barrows; / . . . tattered sparrows" [13] in the second stanza) that rises to the fore. Yet the beauty comes at the expense, one might say, of the children who wail rather than communicate their needs. Disconnected from such sensational designs, these wails can iterate the sounds of Eliot's urban caprice. But the ironic tone and arrogant stance required to sustain this form muffle, rather than amplify, the music.

We need the sonorousness of these working-class forms, Eliot insists regardless, because we need their vitality. Without the body (and for Eliot, the working class always implies the bodily), "[t]he pure Idea dies of inanition." It dies, he continues in "First Debate between the Body and Soul," through lack of incarnation—through the sterility of mental onanism.

> Imaginations
> Masturbations
> The withered leaves
> Of our sensations
>
> (64)

Our sensations are withered because we have cast them about unfruitfully (Eliot refers to "imagination's . . . defecations" [65] in the final stanza). We should, rather, find a way to make them more effective, a way that transliterates the animate wails of children into the inspired voice of Culture. Toward these ends—which are, perhaps, the central ends for the early Eliot—he stages a number of contrapuntal debates between upper- and lower-class forms, encounters that are once again mediated through musical motifs but that move us from the concert hall to the music hall. For instance, an untitled two-stanza poem fragment remediates the ennui of "torpid after-dinner drinks" (70) with the vitality of what would later be known as "lowbrow culture."

> What, you want action?
> Some attraction?
> . . . .
> Someone sings
> A lady of almost any age
> But chiefly breast and rings
> *"Throw your arms around me—Aint you glad you found me"*
> Still that's hardly enough—
> Here's a negro (teeth and smile)
> Has a dance that's quite worth while

That's the stuff!
(Here's your gin
Now begin!) (70)

According to David Chinitz, the "music hall was Eliot's chief site of contact with popular culture." His familiarity may explain why this fragment,
despite its limitations, goes further than the "classical" selections toward
enacting a dialogic relationship between "high" and "low" forms. As
Chinitz notes, "the appropriate slang," "snappy rhymes," and "syncopated rhythms" of the second stanza are done with a verve that matches
any similar experiments in Eliot's more mature poetry.[31] Yet, like in
"First Caprice," the individual formal aspects are a good deal less problematic than the inner machinery that makes them work. What gives
relief to "the after-dinner insolence" (70) (one of Eliot's stock
metonyms for bourgeois culture) is not merely the action and attraction
of the music hall but the very particular form of miscegenation it allows.

We would be wrong, in this regard, to ignore the structurally integral
role that misogyny and racism play within this cross-class encounter. The
musicality of the second stanza depends not just on the syncopated verbal cuts and chops, the quotational use of popular song, and the vernacular phraseology but, more fundamentally, on the use of racial and sexual fetishism. Indeed, inasmuch as the fetish ("breast and rings," "teeth
and smile") brings with it a specific system of signification—where parts
not only stand for things but incarnate the things themselves—it serves
as the poem's key figural form. In other words, the conspicuous materiality of the poem, its jazzy idiomatic mélange, reiterates and generalizes
the fetish's ability to materialize and contain (to contain through materialization) larger social relations. If the identity of the singer is random
("[a] lady of almost any age") but her physicality specific ("chiefly breast
and rings"), then so, too, for instance, is the quoted song lyric—one of
many, but thus all the more evocative of the indiscriminate physicality of
"low" cultural forms. The mélange is hence recuperative, but not
because, as Chinitz would have it, "the music hall is a rare venue in which
Eliot's modernist alienation is momentarily assuaged by a sense of genuine community."[32] Scopic dismemberment, rather than imaginative
communitas, assuages the poet's alienation. "The avant-garde rejection of
mimesis," writes Peter Nicholls, "is . . . clearly linked with a dismemberment of the body and its translation into inorganic form as a prerequisite
of original aesthetic perception."[33] As in "First Caprice," the disarticula-

tion of working-class forms from their previous symbolic systems here permits their recuperative reintegration into modernist poetic forms.

For Eliot, the working-class music hall, rather than being the utopic space that Chinitz seems to imagine, is a threatening realm that repeatedly captures the poet's attention only to engender consequent acts of violent intercession. The danger of the music hall is not the danger of cultural competition (of rising working-class configurations that threaten to supplant the oracular function of the poet), a familiar theory that Chinitz rightly disproves. The danger is decidedly more psychological; the music hall presents a community from which Eliot feels excluded, symbolically a community of the body, visceral in its exigency but repugnant to his sensibilities.[34] This explains the libidinal force of his disarticulations, the frequency with which the dismemberments of the class Other create fetishistic forms that energize the poem but exceed the poet's capacity to bring them into a fruitful relationship with the poetic voice. This issue is somewhat circumvented by the strength of the second-person address in the fragment above, though not in "In the Department Store," a brief notebook poem from 1915. This poem begins with an image of working-class autonomy—

> The lady of the porcelain department
> Smiles at the world through a set of false teeth.
> She is business-like and keeps a pencil in her hair
> (56)

—which eventually prompts the poet's closing reflection on his own ennui: "Man's life is powerless and brief and dark / It is not possible for me to make her happy" (56).

One of several notebook poems of failed sexual conquest, this text would be unremarkable if not for the conspicuous image of "false teeth" and the equally striking unlyricism of the final line. Throughout the 1910s and 1920s, Eliot repeatedly returned to images of women's mouths, the gossiping mouths of bourgeois women who had too much to say and the decaying, odorous mouths of working-class women whose orality more explicitly stands in for their frightening sexuality (as Lil so famously exemplifies in *The Waste Land*, lines 139–73). In this case, the false teeth objectify not only the character's sexuality but also her class pretensions, her desire to falsify the record of her life, to fill her own cavity with the marks of class mobility. The teeth that screen her smile hence serve as exteriorations of a class otherness that constitutes simultaneously her disturbing autonomy and her otherwise unexplained desirability. In some sense, their pretensions permit the poet's own within the final line—not the Eliotic confession of sexual impotency, but the altogether unjustified supposition on which it depends: that the woman is in actuality not already happy. Indeed, her presupposed emotional impotence begets and validates the poet's own and propels the adolescent philosophy of the final couplet. If the last line were not so resolutely unpoetic, so clearly a demarcation of the limits of Eliot's lyric, it would stand as one of the more revealing moments in his early poetry. As it is, it most immediately reveals the strain put on the poetic voice as it stretches to encapsulate the Other—the boundaries of Eliot's managerial imagination.

The problem with these poems of sexual conquest, in other words, is not just that connections between the self and the class Other are troped as sexual but that attachment itself is libidinized, a move that internalizes the chaos and anomie that Eliot sees in his surroundings. Connections between materiality and form, body and mind, and alienated modernist and community rely thus on a sexual adhesiveness that Eliot, for whatever reason, is unable to enact. The objectifications of class (the false teeth, in this case) are not integrated into a whole but stand, rather, outside of it—crystallizations of a powerlessness and an impossibility that verge into inconsequence. The pain of connection that prompted the distancing mechanisms of "First Caprice" and the fetishism of the music hall fragment give way to a corresponding pain of isolation, a state that threatens to silence forever the power of the poetic voice. For Eliot, two routes were possible given this impasse: he could work toward establishing identificatory bonds between the poetic voice and the working-class forms that surrounded it; or he could establish a formal system whereby these bonds would be both displaced and rationalized, whereby the connections between the dualities that plagued him would be safely prefigured and prescribed. Though readers will likely know that Eliot took the second option, famously describing this poetic system of affect as the "objective correlative," the class dimensions of this decision have largely gone unnoticed. Alternately, too few celebrants of Eliot's "extinction of personality" have paused to examine his brief attempts to take the other route and explore cross-class identification.[35]

TOWARD THE OBJECTIVE CORRELATIVE

The notebook poems do, in fact, show several attempts at an alternative form of cross-class poetics. Yet these attempts are halting and uncertain;

they occur only in poem fragments and are typically contained within the conditional tense. In an undated fragment, for instance, the poet begins on an existential note, asking, "Do I know how I feel? Do I know what I think?" before outlining two possible ways of answering these questions. The first way entails taking up "ink and paper," presumably to capture the substance of the poet's mind. Alternately, the poet imagines asking his porter for a drink and, under that pretext, discovering from him "how I think and feel" (80). In essence, the poet imagines an alternative to the reality he simultaneously enacts. Even as he does indeed take up ink and paper to try (unsuccessfully) to bridge ego, emotion, and cognition, he projects an external solution, a worker who can recognize his social being and, by doing so, grant him intrasubjective integrity. The problem, however, is that social interactions cannot so easily be prefigured. Relying on the Other for the essential connections of self means opening oneself to unforeseeable outcomes, the vicissitudes of alterity, a fact that Eliot finds socially disabling.

> If I questioned him with care, would he tell me what I think and feel
> —Or only "You are the gentleman who has lived on the second floor
>   For a year or more"—
> Yet I dread what a flash of madness might reveal
> If he said "Sir we have seen so much beauty spilled on the open street
> Or wasted in stately marriages or stained in railway carriages
> Or left untasted in villages or stifled in darkened chambers
> That if we are restless on winter nights, who can blame us?"
>
> Do I know how I feel? Do I know how I think?
>
>   (80)

As the near repetition of the opening questions might suggest, neither of the porter's imagined responses is suitable. If the first is merely the expected recognition of class difference, a propitious answer that politely recognizes the impropriety of such questions, the second ("a flash of madness") goes quite a bit further than the poet can comfortably contemplate. Everything in the second response circles around the meaning of "we," a crucial pronoun that either includes the poet in the porter's modernist denunciations of philistine culture or excludes the poet in a far more radical denunciation of bourgeois waste. The porter either robs the poet of the poem's best line or, more significantly, exposes the fraudulence of the poet's ennui and his poetic attempts at cultural recuperation. Whatever the case, the ambiguity is intolerable, and it leaves the poet contemplating (or perhaps committing) suicide in the fragment's final lines—an escape, one might say, not only from his own doubts but also from the impossibility of having them assuaged by the class Other.

Through his work in the notebook, Eliot finally arrives at a different, more systematic approach to correlate emotions and objects, a methodology that allows him to integrate the aura of materiality that surrounds working-class forms, while predetermining the forms' relationship to the poetic subject. The "objective correlative," as he terms it, removes the need for sentimentality or the variances of social connection; these it replaces with the rationalized functionality of a linear relationship. "The only way of expressing emotion in the form of art," Eliot famously explains in 1919, "is by finding an 'objective correlative'; in other words, a set of objects, a situation, a chain of events which shall be the formula of that *particular* emotion; such that when the external facts, which must terminate in sensory experience, are given, the emotion is immediately evoked."[36] This definition is, of course, one of the mainstays of modernist criticism; it is often revisited in literary histories of the period. Yet I want to stress two aspects of this poetic method that have received little attention: first, the objective correlative is, as Eliot defines it, practically a machine relation; second, Eliot fabricates it largely to rationalize his imaginative interactions across the class divide.

On the first point, it is probably enough to stress certain words in Eliot's definition, a definition that is as precise as it is, strictly speaking, unattainable. What Eliot imagines for these correlatives is a system of specific equivalencies, a "formula," that matches objects, situations, and events to artistic affect without either friction or waste. Such correlatives not only are empirically substantiable—"external facts" that meet the scientific criteria of replicability—but operate instantaneously, without the uncertain mediations of readerly interpretation. Merely to specify an object (the wail of a child, a set of false teeth) is to "immediately evoke" a specific emotion in all people, at all times, regardless of context. The objective correlative thus evades the painful Cartesian split between mind and body by fantasizing a world without the *cognito*, where sensory experiences bear formulaic relation to emotion, skipping entirely the Sisyphean struggle to know how to "think and feel." Such sublime robotics are possible, though, not because of the poet's manipulative abilities but because, for Eliot, humans are simply made this way. The artist must "find" the objective correlative just as the scientist must find the correct equation for the chemical reactions present in nature; such relations are understood to preexist and superintend their constitutive parts. In the terms I have been exploring in this study, the objective correlative is thus a managerial epistemology, both in the simple sense that it works to manage otherwise chaotic sensory stimuli and in the more specific way that it denotes a totalizing relation that depends on the prior delineation and rationalization of all objects and events into subsequently systemizable parts. "In the achievement of the objective correlative," writes Terry Eagleton, "the poet passes beyond the encapsulating limits of private, poetic experience into an impersonally integrated objectivity."[37] But such passage, we might add, gives the poet the numb efficiency of the machine.

The objective correlative is, notwithstanding its precise definition, an impossible method to sustain. Human systems do not function so efficiently, a fact that Eliot certainly knew. The invocation of the correlative in 1919, at the end of the decade of the notebook and of Eliot's slumming trips, reflects the pain of cross-class affect and is aimed at aiding the modernist subject caught within the uncertainties of social causality. Though the objective correlative does not remove pain from life or from art—indeed, it builds pain into the affective system—it does make that pain predictable, measurable, and instrumental. By doing so, it thus constitutes the final rejection of middle-class sentimentality and all that this connective mode brings to representations of the working class. It is a significant step in Eliot's long struggle to refashion the relationship between the poetic subject and the social domain, a struggle that was part of modernism's larger process of resituating labor and the pressures of class within new epistemological systems of management.

One final way to understand this refashioning is to turn briefly to "The Love Song of J. Alfred Prufrock" and note how the published version (1915 and 1917) uses some of Eliot's earliest experiments with the objective correlative to overwrite the markedly different class relations of the original notebook poem (written, probably, in 1911).[38] Prufrock is, of course, one of Eliot's more successful characters, a cipher for the poet's sense of social impotence and the measured introspection of a certain kind of modernist masculinity. Insisting that—

> There will be time, there will be time
> To prepare a face to meet the faces that you meet[39]

—Prufrock is the manager par excellence, a role that, given the context of the notebook, seems not only caused by the pain of social interaction but also erected to defend against it. The published version of the poem, however, gives us little explanation for Prufrock's plight. Whereas this absence authorizes innumerable critical readings and helps consecrate ambiguity as a chief modernist virtue, the poem did, in its earliest form, have a more substantial exploration of Prufrock's predicament.

In the published version, lines 70–74 encapsulate both Prufrock's attempt to sing his "love song" and its abrupt abandonment.

> Shall I say, I have gone at dusk through narrow streets
> And watched the smoke that rises from the pipes
> Of lonely men in shirt-sleeves, leaning out of windows? . . .
>
>   I should have been a pair of ragged claws
> Scuttling across the floors of silent seas.[40]

This gives us two disarticulated images that now, perforce, serve as correlatives (of class-inflected homosocial exclusion and of a consequent retreat to solipsism). But the original draft of the poem included, between these two correlatives, a separate section, "Prufrock's Pervigilium," that continues the abandoned song. Comprising thirty-eight lines, it is too long to quote in full and, at any rate, recapitulates many of the themes I have already discussed here. During the night (a *pervigilium* is a poem memorializing "a watching through the night"),[41] Prufrock hears the familiar "children whimpering in corners" and sees the familiar working-class forms: peeled oranges, newspapers, "evil houses leaning all together." But dawn ends the *pervigilium* rather remarkably—

> I fumbled to the window to experience the world
> And to hear my Madness singing, sitting on the kerbstone
> [A blind old drunken man who sings and mutters,
> With broken boot heels stained in many gutters]
> And as he sang the world began to fall apart . . .   (43)

—before it returns us to the second objective correlative.

> I should have been a pair of ragged claws
> Scuttling across the floors of silent seas . . .[42]

Comparable in its effect to Pound's later, more noted cuts to *The Waste Land*, the elision of these lines alters the poem considerably. The *pervigilium* provides something of a backstory, a contextual apparatus through which to better comprehend what would become, in the published version, disparate figurative allusions to the working class—that is, objective correlatives. In these final stanzas of the *pervigilium,* the class Other, personified, empathetic, even empathic, is rather the apotheosis of a very different kind of cross-class association—one that amplifies, rather than manages, social pain. In a recent introduction to Eliot, Helen Vendler has called the displacement of this image into the singing mermaids ("I have heard the mermaids singing, each to each") the most "brilliant moment" in Eliot's development as a poet.[43] Yet surely, it is other than that: the deeply intersubjective moment in the *pervigilium* is a road not taken, perhaps decisively, since it would have bonded the poetic subject not to the isolation of cultural retrospection but to the possibility of the social. Eliot's preference for the mere artifacts of working-class life—these correlative forms—is, finally, a preference for the fragmentary over the connective. Or rather, to return to the model with which I began, it is a preference for the fragmentary as a way of removing the self from the social process, a way of situating the connective apart from the percept in a managerial role.

STEIN'S WORKERS

While Eliot's notebook poems reveal some of the ways a managerial epistemology influenced the aesthetic innovations of high modernism, they are not alone in this regard. Writers from different backgrounds with different artistic affinities were similarly invested in word systems as a way to compose the working class. Gertrude Stein, who explored word systems with a rare tenacity, may serve as further illustration, triangulating this managerial process and giving us a better sense of its relevance to high modernism in general. A Jewish lesbian from California who repeatedly celebrated the cultural accomplishments of the middle class, Stein would seem unlikely to share many alliances with Eliot, whose misogyny and anti-Semitism were but the most noxious of his Anglophilic, monarchist, and elitist values. Indeed, within current revisions of the modernist canon, Stein is positioned as a sort of anti-Eliot, a representative ethnic and sexual Other whose deeply subjectivist discursive experiments somehow balance the preponderant masculine ennui and social nostalgia of an Eliot, a Pound, or a Stevens. Be this as it may, certain commonalties deserve note. Like Eliot, Stein expatriated herself to Europe to begin her literary career in earnest. Eliot went to Harvard; Stein went to Radcliffe College, where she was influenced by the luminaries on the faculty (most particularly, as I will discuss, William James). Finally, as was true for Eliot, Stein's first significant modernist innovations arose in conjunction with her attempts to apprehend the working class.

On this point, we might note that Stein's critics, like Eliot's, share a singular blindness to the significance of her early attention to workers. Although *Three Lives,* her first published book, presents a triptych of novellas that each focus on a female domestic laborer, the common gender of their protagonists, rather than their common economic and social positions, informs contemporary criticism. Feminists, in particular, draw attention to the lesbian subtexts of the novellas, to Stein's use of syntactical play to represent the constrained lives of her protagonists, and to the fact that her modes of narration and characterization derive from— and perhaps contest—William James's psychological theories (an influence I will explore along other lines). The apparent racism of the central novella, "Melanctha," has not gone without note and has caused some discomfort among those who would celebrate Stein's achievements. However, Stein's repeated association of refinement with whiteness and of sensuous pleasure with "the warm broad glow of negro sunshine"[44] has typically been dismissed or found to be peripheral to the text's accomplishments. I want to approach Stein from exactly the opposite perspective in the remainder of this chapter, arguing that her racism and elitism reflect a deeply essentialist understanding of subjectivity that forms the foundation for her aesthetic experiments. Indeed, set within the context I have been elaborating, which connects shifts in the labor process to shifts in the way modernists understood both the working class and aesthetic principles, Stein's experiments prove to be explicitly managerial—discovering fixed types of working-class subjects who can be creatively composed in texts that embody the systemic dictates of second-wave industrialism.

Stein understood, earlier and perhaps more fully than Eliot, that modern innovations, such as the managerial systems of Taylorism and Fordism, would proceed from method to material, rather than from content to form. The systems that link together relatively basic operations would thus become the ultimate bearers of signification. In *Three Lives,* the traditional causative progressions of realism are eclipsed by a holistic compositional structure; the plot moves not from action to reaction but ideationally or associationally, according to a systemic logic. Similarly, *Three Lives* begins to reveal Stein's use of language as a system bound less by the dictates of reference than by self-reference, intent less on an indexical function (pointing to something in the real world) than on a more self-contained iconic function (embodying the thing itself).[45] Such experiments could, however, only be launched on relatively stable ground. Just as the variegated patterns of a musical theme and variation typically rely on a simplistic initial melody, and just as early cubist still lifes fracture well-known forms, Stein's syntactical and narrational modes required a set of "simple" types (working-class immigrants or African Americans) whose weighty material presence and rich iconic value could underwrite her discursive play. Stein's understanding of subjectivity and psychology were, to put the matter differently, rooted in the nineteenth century—in theories of physiognomy, of presocial "bottom natures," and of racial and ethnic types—while her understanding of linguistic and discursive forms boldly inaugurated the literary avant-garde of the twentieth century. This differentiation is neither coincidental nor anomalous. As with Eliot, Stein's social conservatism—her views about race, class, and even gender—prompted her aesthetic radicalism. Her simplistic comprehension of character types permitted a totalizing, managerial structure and epistemology.

HABITS OF ATTENTION

As most critics acknowledge, Stein's conceptions of character types were largely formed by her early work with William James.[46] Stein first encountered James at Harvard in 1893, when she attended his lectures on psychology as part of an introductory philosophy course. During the next several years, Stein took two more courses with him (as well as five other psychology classes) before entering the Johns Hopkins Medical School, largely at his urging. Though she left Johns Hopkins without completing her degree and never continued her experimental work in psychology and neurology, she and James remained correspondents. Throughout her life, Stein credited him as a significant influence. He was, according to one recent critic, "Stein's one intellectual father."[47]

Yet in weighing James's significance for Stein, we should take care to note that the James of the 1890s, who "fathered" her, was not yet the more progressive James of later years. Though already a liberal pluralist, his 1890 *Principles of Psychology* and 1892 *Psychology: A Briefer Course* (which Stein used as a text in his class)[48] were marked by normative Victorian theories that reflected a deep class bias. Arguing for the psychological basis of possessive individualism, for instance, James claims that "a man's Me is the sum total of all he CAN call his, not only his body and his psychic powers, but his clothes and his house, his wife and children, his ancestors and friends, his reputation and works, his lands and horses, and yacht and bank-account."⁴⁹ James's theory of habit—the foundational concept of his psychology—is less obviously, but no less importantly, structured around class and class difference. James acknowledges that we all have habits that subsequently determine our experiences and our character, but he maintains that some few geniuses have the ability to escape habits' structures. The working class, in contrast, have no such escape and, moreover, are kept at work precisely by their habituation to manual labor.

James formulated his theory of habit at the same time (and perhaps for similar reasons) that Taylor began to divide the labor process into conception and execution. The structural parallels are not initially obvious, however, since for James, habit serves most clearly to connect the physical and the mental domains of subjectivity. Habits indicate that impressions traveling through certain "sensory nerve roots" into and out of the brain have been organized into "paths" that, over time, have deepened and become set (1). These deepened paths allow for sensory impressions to automatically trigger composite actions. "An acquired habit . . . is nothing but a new pathway of discharge formed in the brain, by which certain incoming currents ever after tend to escape" (1). Even "the most complex habits" are, James stresses, "nothing but concatenated discharges in the nerve-centers" (4). Thus, while habits indicate the presence of a mental pathway, at their most basic level, they are mechanical operations that are similar to the other machine relations I have been discussing. Once an activity has been conceived and tested (the formation of a new sensory pathway), it can be executed systematically and efficiently. By diminishing "the conscious attention with which our acts are performed" (6), habit "simplifies our movements, makes them more accurate, and diminishes fatigue" (5). Ultimately, James concludes, "the more of the details of our daily life we can hand over to the effortless custody of automatism, the more our higher powers of mind will be set free for their own proper work" (11–12).

In what is evidently a Taylorist fantasy of efficiency displaced from the factory to the individual, James envisions the self as its own tiered productive realm, where the monotony of repetitive manual labor ("the lighting of every cigar, the drinking of every cup, . . . rising and going to bed every day" [12]) can be handed over to the custody of automatism. This leaves the mind free for its "proper work," the conceptualization of new knowledge, new inventions, even new systems of psychology. Indeed, the effort to develop new mental pathways is precisely how the mind should employ its relative freedom, since even the mind's higher powers are liable to be affected—and ultimately limited—by habitual modes of thought, what James calls "habits of attention" (39). Though we need such habits of attention to act as "organs of selection" (38) and to keep us from encountering the chaotic stimuli of the world in a state of "sensational nudity" (181), these organs tend to act as normalizing filters, presenting the mind with sensations that can travel the pathways already formed within the nervous system. "In a world of objects thus individualized by our mind's selective industry, what is called our 'experience' is almost entirely determined by our habits of attention" (39). The degree to which we can control such habits—that is, the degree to which we can act as managers of our own subjectivity—is the degree to which we can remain free. Children and the insane escape absolute determination by the force of habits of attention, though they consequently suffer from a lack of these habits' screening operations. Geniuses, however, also escape and are in an ideal position, since they are supremely able to rely on the managerial powers of automatism (when they so desire) but are also able to exercise their attention on subjects that lie outside their realm of habituated perception. "Genius," James concludes, "means little more than the faculty of perceiving in an unhabitual way" (195). While others may be restrained by the circumscriptions their bodies enforce on them, geniuses (among whom Stein believed herself to be)[50] surpass these strictures.

For James and Stein, the managerial power of the genius stands in counterdistinction not only to the nongenius but particularly and markedly to the working class.

> Habit is . . . the enormous fly-wheel of society, its most precious conservative agent. It alone is what keeps us all within the bounds of ordinance, and saves the children of fortune from the envious uprisings of the poor. It alone prevents the hardest and most repulsive walks of life from being deserted by those brought up to tread therein. It keeps the fisherman and the deck-hand at sea through the winter; it holds the miner in his darkness, and nails the countryman to his log-cabin and his lonely farm through all the months of snow; it protects us from invasion by the natives of the desert and the frozen zone. . . . It keeps different social strata from mixing. Already at the age of twenty-five you see . . . . the little lines of cleavage running through the character, the tricks of thought, the prejudices, the ways of 'shop,' in a word, from which the man can by-and-by no more escape than his coat-sleeve can suddenly fall into a new

> set of folds. On the whole, it is best he should not escape. It is well for the world that in most of us, by the age of thirty, the character has set like plaster, and will never soften again. (10–11)

Though one notes (perhaps with appreciation) the shifting social referent for the pronoun "us" in the preceding passage, the ramifications of James's psychological system can hardly be so easily muddied. Within this system, habits, just like subjectivity itself, both mark and ensure class divisions.

The results of Stein's own experimental research largely accord with the psychological process James outlines.[51] Indeed, Stein builds on the social theory implicit in James's work on habit, demonstrating the presence of automatic functions and arguing that people can be divided into fixed types based on their ability to control their automatic functions. In the first of two articles published in the prestigious *Psychological Review*—"Normal Motor Automatism," coauthored with Leon Solomon (1896)—Stein reports on her attempts to demonstrate that "normal" subjects can be induced to exhibit "motor reactions unaccompanied by consciousness," or, in James's parlance, that their higher powers can be momentarily displaced, leaving only that part of the self given over to automatism.[52] Stein and Solomon explain that after "training," a subject can successfully write dictated words while simultaneously concentrating on reading a different text, then "[i]n a few hours" (497), the subject loses first "the feeling of effort" and then "the motor impulse" itself.

> We hear the word, and we know what we have written; that is all, this is the general condition of things throughout the experiment, after the preliminary training is over. The writing is conscious, but non-voluntary and largely *extra personal*. The feeling that the writing is *our* writing seems to disappear with the motor impulse. (498)

Once the possessive sense of personal identification ("*our* writing") disappears, small "intervals of complete unconsciousness" (500) are not uncommon. Stein and Solomon hence conclude:

> We have shown a general tendency, on the part of normal people, to *act*, without any express desire or conscious volition, in a manner in general accord with the *previous habits* of the person, and showing a full possession of the faculty of *memory;* and that these acts may go on just as well

outside the field of consciousness; that for them, not only volition is unnecessary, but that consciousness as well is entirely superfluous and plays a purely cognitive part when present. (509)

There are, importantly, fundamental similarities between Stein and Solomon's experiments in the "unconscious passage of sensation into motor reaction" (497) and Eliot's "objective correlative," which also postulates a system wherein consciousness is superfluous to the "formula" that guarantees that "external facts . . . terminate in sensory experience."[53] In both instances, the *cognito* does not come into play. One looks instead for a set of correspondences between stimuli and behavior that reside beyond, before, or outside consciousness itself. As with Eliot, this set of correspondences forms the essential element within Stein's conceptual and aesthetic apparatus in her earliest fiction. There is one substantial difference between the two systems, however, which helps explain their very different textual materializations. While Eliot is a universalist who believes that words, objects, and images evoke the same response in all people, Stein is a pluralist who recognizes that people display a variety of different responses to stimuli. In neither case is the cognitive faculty given much value—but for different reasons. Eliot finds it too painful, too unsure. Stein believes that it masks, rather than reveals, the truest aspect of personality and selfhood, which for her lies in the more basal relations between sensation and action. Both systems are in the broadest sense managerial, even if Stein's promises to accord a greater amount of flexibility. Both discover a system of relays that can be empirically "proven," statistically enumerated, and, most important, superintended.

In fact, while Stein's pluralism might lead one to imagine that her conception of subjectivity was nonessentialist and therefore considers social context (this, at least, is the typical assumption about pluralism), the situation is quite the reverse. Though Stein believed in psychological differences, she nonetheless understood these differences to be essential, quantifiable, and ripe for categorization. This, Stein explained some years later, was her real discovery in the psychology laboratory.

I was supposed to be interested in their [her subjects'] reactions but soon I found that I was not but instead that I was enormously interested in the types of their characters that is what I even then thought of as the bottom nature of them, and when in May 1898 I wrote my half of the report of these experiments I expressed these results as follows: In these descriptions it will be readily observed that habits of attention are reflexes of the complete character of the individual.[54]

Habits of attention, the subject's ability to employ and manage the automatic motor component of the self, are, in sum, the absolute reflex of his or her essential nature, a primary determining factor that does not change and that can, subsequently, form the organizing principle for a complete taxonomy of human types.

Stein refers, in the preceding quotation, to a second article, "Cultivated Motor Automatism: A Study of Character in its Relation to Attention," where she does, in fact, begin to formulate such a taxonomy. Using much the same method that she and Solomon developed for the previous experiment, Stein examines a group of Harvard and Radcliffe students in order to ascertain the "types of character that accompany a greater or lesser tendency to automatic action."[55] Since these students are racially and economically homogeneous, we cannot know whether Stein would have found a correlation between race, class, and bottom nature. But Stein does relate physical characteristics to psychological type, thus establishing the scientific basis for the essentialism that will ground *Three Lives*. Stein's "best subjects" (296), she quickly determines, are those who are able to disengage attention and allow for motor automatism. "The subjects who did the best writing" are subdivided further "into two large groups very different both in characteristics and method of response," which Stein calls "Type I and Type II."

[Type I] consists mostly of girls who are found naturally in literature courses and men who are going in for law. The type is nervous, high-strung, very imaginative, has the capacity to be easily roused and intensely interested. . . . Type II is very different . . . is more varied, and gives more interested results. In general, the individuals, often blonde and pale, are distinctly phlegmatic. If emotional, decidedly of a weakish sentimental order. They may be either large, healthy, rather heavy and lacking in vigor, or they may be what we call anaemic and phlegmatic. (297)

As Wendy Steiner notes, this particular grouping "does away with much of the store-house of conventionalized character implications" circulating in the 1890s: Type II, for instance, encompasses subjects with "exactly opposite characteristics"; they can be large and healthy or anaemic and phlegmatic and are grouped only by their common aptitude for automatic response.[56] Nevertheless, Stein's goal is precisely to spell out their character implications as she conceives of them—as measured by their ability to control their attention and thus as reflexes of their bottom natures.

Stein scholars tend to misunderstand both Stein's point in this regard and its subsequent ramifications for her literary work. The abundance of contradictory characteristics within each type does not, as Steiner concludes, connote a nonessentialist model. On the contrary, only the absolute fixity of Type II-ness allows Stein to circumscribe so many heterogeneous variables within the category. Similar acknowledgments of diversity ("black or white, rich or poor") often ground claims for essentialism ("we are all sinners in the eyes of the Lord"). This is a basic principle of nineteenth-century scientific taxonomy that Stein would have learned in her physiology courses, if not from James himself. Priscilla Wald reads the experiments in much the same fashion as Steiner, though for her, the heterogeneous variables demonstrate an underlying culturalism within Stein's physiological theories: "Outlining different character types that yielded categorically similar responses to her experiments with automatic writing, . . . Stein prepares for a conclusion that forms the basis of *The Making of Americans:* cultural factors determine preperceptions that shape the experience of the self."[57] While this may be the case in *The Making of Americans* (the point, I think, is debatable), it is decidedly not the conclusion Stein comes to in this instance. While she evidently believes that cultural factors play a role in determining preperceptions that shape experience, this is, for Stein, of secondary importance. What interests her are the deeper, precultural factors that indicate the degree of this determination. Though these factors appear to be heterogeneous, they include enough physical and racial "characteristics" to suggest that Stein believed that race marks essential differences in type. And her subsequent writing about (black and white) workers is so invested in the fixity of character typology that it might be most accurate to conclude that class functions as both a precultural and a cultural determinate within Stein's system.

It would be a mistake, therefore, to pass blithely over the fact that Stein's Type II subjects are "often blonde and pale" and are "distinctly phlegmatic." Such epidermal distinctions within a "white" population mean less a century after Stein's experiments, but during the 1890s, a decade that saw both an influx of immigration from Eastern and Southern Europe and the beginnings of the eugenics movement, differences between blonde and brown and between pale and dark weighed more heavily. Indeed, within the homogeneous population at Harvard and Radcliffe, pale blondes and Jews, such as Stein, were understood to inhabit opposite ends of the spectrum of "racial" diversity. Even within this small sample, who are at any rate accorded rather benign and idiosyncratic racial attributes, the connotation is obvious: physical types (blonde and pale) are in fact character types (phlegmatic), a precultural connection that is both revealed and reinforced by the degree to which they are able to direct and develop habits of attention. While Stein's further elaborations on these types (their propensity to daydream or to become lawyers, for instance) lend themselves to a culturalist (mis)reading, surely the conflation of physicality and mentality show otherwise. Stein believed (at least until 1912, after which it becomes difficult to ascertain) that one's bottom nature is a reflex of one's habit of attention and that habits of attention, however they may be subsequently modified by cultural pressures, reflect basic physical essences.

As Steiner chronicles, Stein persists with her typological schemas well into the 1910s, developing and modifying them in *The Making of Americans* (written between 1902 and 1911) and in *Many, Many Women* and *A Long Gay Book* (written between 1909 and 1912). In many ways, however, *Three Lives* was the most rigorous application of this principle to a select character type. In these other works, Stein attempts the extravagant task of encompassing the entirety of the taxonomy—of, as Steiner puts it, "describing the essential being of people and their relations to other people"[58]—limited only by nationality and gender (in the first two books, respectively). The three lives that compose her triptych are, in contrast, three extended explorations of one character type: the racially or ethnically marked female domestic laborer who lacks—as James notes of the working class generally—the ability to control her habits of attention. This does not mean that these three characters share the same superficial character traits—that they lack, in any meaningful way, individuality. As I noted, the cultural differences that constitute character traits are incidental to Stein's typology. What these characters share is the same inability to control their habits; once their character traits are constituted, their bottom natures prevent them from exercising (or even from imagining) any meaningful development or change. For Anna, Melanctha, and Lena, in other words, biology is destiny, since it ensures that they will not be able to challenge the economic and social determinations of their working-class lives. This is the sense in which we may meaningfully call the Stein of *Three Lives* a naturalist in the biologistic strain of Jack London or Frank Norris, even as we recognize her modernist will to innovate. Her innovations, which I consider in the next section, amplify, rather than challenge, the basic essentialist principles that compose her epistemological and managerial conceptions of subjectivity.

COMPOSITION

I am not the first, of course, to note the scientism of Stein's vision—her preference, in her early works, for taxonomy, quantification, and other positivist methods of characterization. In one of the earliest sustained responses to Stein's innovations, Edmund Wilson famously called her an "august human seismograph,"[59] an opinion that B. L. Reid seconded in his 1958 book-length critique of Stein's *Art by Subtraction:* "Her method, which at first glance seems intuitive and inspirational, is in fact nothing of the kind. It is the geared oiled functioning of the artist who has made himself [*sic*] as nearly as possible a scientifically accurate recording mechanism."[60] Clearly, Wilson and Reid object to Stein's antihumanism, to the way in which her early writing so completely endeavors to replace the subjective interpretations of art—that is, the "proper" role of the artist—with the accurate measurements of the machine. But neither Wilson nor Reid fully comprehend the degree to which the machine is itself an interpretive strategy, embodying the vision of its author while reflecting the larger epistemological shifts of modernity. What critics need to stress, to put the matter somewhat differently, is that Stein's mechanics are born out of a relationship between her understanding of the bottom nature of people and her developing experiments in "composition." And that properly understood, this relationship helps explain why "the first definite step away from the nineteenth century and into the twentieth in literature" was made on the backs of immigrant and African American working-class women.[61]

Though Stein never exactly elucidates the relationship between her literary innovations and her choice of subjects, she nonetheless foregrounds "Melanctha," her "Negro story," in all of her major statements on methodology. "Everything I have done has been influenced by Flaubert and Cézanne," she notes, for instance, in a 1947 interview.

Up to that time composition had consisted of a central idea, to which everything else was an accompaniment and separate but was not an end in itself, and Cézanne conceived the idea that in composition one thing was as important as another thing. Each part is as important as the whole, and that impressed me . . . so much that I began to write *Three Lives* under this influence and this idea of composition and I was more interested in composition at that moment, this background of word-system, which had come to me from this reading that I had done. I was obsessed by this idea of composition, and the Negro story . . . was the quintessence of it.[62]

The centrality of Cézanne in this explanation (which Stein repeated in other interviews and essays) has led critics to conclude that Stein's "Negro story" was an act of primitivism analogous to the primitivist experiments that were so formative for the postimpressionist avant-garde. For Michael North in particular, "Melanctha" functions as a primitive mask (similar to Picasso's masks) that both displaces and configures Stein's sense of expatriate alterity.[63] It is, according to him, a rewriting of a failed novel about a failed lesbian affair that inscribes what Stein herself identified (in another context) as her "Rabelaisian, nigger abandonment, Vollard, daddy side."[64] Such an explanation is accurate but, in and of itself, insufficient. As we have seen with Eliot, the desire to displace what must otherwise remain hidden or out of control onto the classed and/or raced Other is only half the story. Displacement must be accompanied by management if that which is displaced is to retain its operative value. For these early modernists in particular, to displace is not to cast out but to decenter and to rearrange—or, to use the word to which Stein returns insistently, to "compose."

It is worth noting, in this regard, that the term *composition* has a distinctive meaning within Stein's lexicon, a meaning that does indeed suggest the operations of displacement but that works against the anachronistic impulse of primitivism. Composition is, for Stein, a spatial or systemic process that is always contemporary in its historical outlook. As she writes in "Composition as Explanation," it is contingent on a specific "time-sense," put into place by "each generation."

> It is understood by this time that everything is the same except composition and time, composition and the time of the composition and the time in the composition.
>
> Everything is the same except composition and as the composition is different and always going to be different everything is not the same. Everything is not the same as the time when of the composition and the time in the composition is different. The composition is different, that is certain.[65]

Working once more from an essentialist conception of subjectivity, in which individuals, or at least their bottom natures, remain constant across time, Stein attempts to explain her theory of historical change. This is by no means an easy task, conceptually speaking, for someone with such faith in taxonomy—a faith that led her to maintain well into the 1930s that the "history of the whole world," "a history of human nature," could be represented through "enormous charts."[66] Nevertheless, historical change is a necessary part of Stein's aesthetic and philosophical system, if for no other reason than that any claims for contemporariness rely on it. According to Stein, the composition of elements rather than the elements themselves change across history. "Everything is the same except composition and time." People are the same. Their bottom natures are the same. Only their social composition and aesthetic compositions of their greatest artists constitute their generational affinities. "Nothing changes from generation to generation," she summarizes, "except the thing seen and that makes a composition."[67]

But what is the "thing seen" in the first decades of the twentieth century, and what ties this "thing" to the obsession that led to *Three Lives?* Stein ventures an answer to the first part of this question in "How Writing is Written," a lecture delivered to the Choate School in Wallingford, Connecticut, in 1935. Though relatively unknown, this lecture includes one of the rare instances where Stein relates her textual innovations to socioeconomic (rather than aesthetic) developments.

> [E]ach period of time not only has its contemporary quality, but it has a time-sense. Things move more quickly, slowly, or differently, from one generation to another. Take the Nineteenth Century. The Nineteenth Century was roughly the Englishman's Century. And their method, as they themselves, in their worst moments, speak of it, is that of "muddling through." They begin at one end and hope to come out at the other: their grammar, parts of speech, methods of talk, go with the fashion. The United States began a different phase when, after the Civil War, they discovered and created out of their inner need a different way of life. They created the Twentieth Century. The United States, instead of having the feeling of beginning at one end and ending at another, had the conception of assembling the whole thing out of its parts, the whole thing which made the Twentieth Century productive. The Twentieth Century conceived an automobile as a whole, so to speak, and then created it, built it up out of its parts. . . . The Nineteenth Century would have seen the parts, and worked towards the automobile through them.

Now in a funny sort of way this expresses, in different terms, the difference between the literature of the Nineteenth Century and the literature of the Twentieth. . . . [English writers] conceive of [literature] as pieces put together to make a whole, and I conceive of it as a whole made up of its parts.[68]

At first glance, this quotation would seem to cover much the same ground that Stein maps in the better-known Cézanne reference. Once again, she relates parts to the whole in a nonfocalized or decentric manner (a quality she refers to elsewhere as "distribution and equilibration");[69] once again, she aligns that new relationship to the moment of modernity, when linearity and narrative causality give way to simultaneity and systemization. Yet in this explanation, we move well beyond a localized reference to postimpressionist experiments with spatial value, to a broader grounding in the epistemological dictates of the new industrial process of production. Ford's cars replace Cézanne's apples as touchstones, just as the machine process itself overwrites any lingering evocations of organicism or holism. Indeed, not only does Stein acknowledge and celebrate her relationship to the norms and values of the assembly process, but within this explanation, process itself emerges as the governing trope of high modernist aesthetic experimentation.

The primacy of process has several ramifications. First, Stein suggests that the process of production is, in essence, the real avant-garde, creating compositional forms and systems long before artists and writers attempted such acts of contemporariness. Second, when these artists and writers eventually achieved contemporariness, what they, in fact, achieved is verisimilitude—not, of course, according to nineteenth-century norms of visual focalization, linear causality, "grammar, parts of speech, [and] methods of talk," but according to twentieth-century norms of atomization, fragmentation, and systemization. In other words, if Cézanne, Picasso, and Stein each in some way created a compositional pluralism—wherein "one thing was as important as another thing"—it is because they re-created in another format the basic dictates of industrial rationalization: "the conception of assembling the whole thing out of its parts." Finally, the primacy of process helps establish the character of modernism's link to modern capitalism. While leftist critics have typically understood high modernism to be part of capitalism's new consumerist regime—disarticulated and fragmented images that function as cultural commodities—this is clearly not Stein's understanding of the matter. She is interested, on the contrary, in aligning her writing with the process of production, with the new "conception of assembly" that made the mass commodity possible in the first place.

Since the factory serves, at least in this instance, as Stein's model for composition, it would make sense to claim that her early attention to immigrant and African American working-class characters derives from her producerist focus. As Stein well knew, immigrants and African Americans predominated within factories and other regimented workplaces. While they did not conceive of the process "which made the Twentieth Century productive," they executed its demands; their labor power was, as it has always been under capitalism, the true source of value. Yet Stein, like Eliot, understood workers and their value differently, choosing to focus largely on the un-Taylorized labor of domestic workers. Aligning themselves with the system—rather than with the systematized—Stein and Eliot saw these workers as one element among many, who were particularly useful for their iconic value and the rich array of material forms they could bring into the complex mechanisms of a modernist text. For Stein in particular, workers represented a relatively stable subject from which to launch a composition, since their "habits of attention"—as she understood them—prevented the sort of changes, developments, and growth that propel the more typically bourgeois protagonists of the bildungsroman. Indeed, what changes and develops within the pages of *Three Lives* are not the workers themselves (who are, on the contrary, strikingly consistent) but the highly stylized language that circulates around and through them.

Such is, I think, the implication of Stein's 1906 letter to Mabel Weeks, surely one of the more significant ancillary documents concerning *Three Lives.*

> I am afraid that I can never write the Great American novel. I dn't know how to sell on a margin or to do anything with shorts and longs, so I have to content myself with niggers and servant girls and the foreign population generally. Leo he said there wasn't no art in Lovetts' book and then he was bad and wouldn't tell me that there was in mine so I went to bed very missable but I don't care there ain't any Tchaikovfsky Pathetique or Omar Kayam or Wagner or Whistler or White Man's Burden or green burlap in mine at least not in the present ones. Dey is werry simple and werry wulgar and I don't think they will interest the great American publia.[70]

As Pricilla Wald notes, the "Great American novel" in question in Stein's letter is *The Making of Americans,* which Stein temporarily put aside to compose the three sketches that would become her first published work.[71] Clearly, however, the two texts are interrelated, at least for Stein, who evidently considered *Three Lives* to be antipodal—a text that literally and figuratively occupies the "wulgar" "margin" of that more grandiose project. But the margin of a composition is, of course, as important for Stein as the center. Thus her pun on *margin* is integral to her meaning: unsure of her ability to parlay her marginality into greatness, she "content[s]" herself with marginality itself.

Yet if "niggers and servant girls and the foreign population" are not only marginal but simple and vulgar, their simplicity and vulgarity prove (even within the preceding quotation) to be surprisingly enabling. They are the simple elements around which Stein will erect her aesthetic mechanisms, the vulgar bottom natures through which Stein will discover a literary language. Though Stein's tremendous condescension disallows any possibility for a more emotive, more sympathetic connection to her subjects, such identificatory bonds are, for her as for Eliot, beside the point. She does not "care [if] there ain't any Tchaikovsky Pathetique or Omar Kayam or Wagner or Whistler or White Man's Burden." She dismisses the romantic tradition in favor of the idiomatic, the iconic, and the elemental—cultural constructions that are appropriate to the new epistemological regime of the twentieth century. What Stein fears, interestingly enough, is being "missable" in her new endeavor, a pun that connects unhappiness to invisibility through some sort of simulated ethnoracial dialect.[72] But if the dialect allows her to iterate her fears, it also suggests their remediation—through the management of voice, the verbal acrobatics, and the careful aesthetic systems that would, in time, make her famous. "[N]iggers and servant girls and the foreign population" are, in other words, more than merely the projection of some repressed aspect of Stein's inner psyche. They are the simple and vulgar natures that Stein will work with and through in order to solicit interest from the "great American publi[c]a," the basic units through which she will compose her approximation of the principles of modernity.

THREE LIVES

The three texts that compose Stein's *Three Lives* need to be considered together, not merely as a progressive chronicle of Stein's efforts to create a style adequate to her aesthetic vision, but for the unity of vision that underlies this triptych. Though these three lives are indeed three separate lives, they are deeply bound by their typological commonalities. Either immigrant or African American, but in each case from the working class, the women Stein portrays are governed by the permanence of their "habits of attention." These habits are quite distinctive—Anna gains power through self-denial, Melanctha "wanders," and Lena is passive—yet they are similarly persistent. Each of these women is unable to develop or grow, to achieve self-consciousness, or, in any meaningful way, to resist her social determinations. Indeed, one might say that given James and Stein's understanding of psychology, these social determinations are always already fixed biologically for these members of the working class. If one wants an explanation for why Anna, Melanctha, and Lena are the way they are, one must settle, in other words, for an account of their bottom natures: their characters are manifestations of neurological "paths"; their linguistic worlds are iterations of physiological proclivities. An account of their bottom natures is hence also an account of Stein's stylistic innovations: her physiognomical characterizations, her delimited lexicon, her tactical use of free indirect discourse, and even her recombinant plotting.

Stein's fundamental innovation in *Three Lives* is her mode of characterization, a mode that relies on nineteenth-century physiognomical techniques but that takes these techniques in new directions, ultimately putting them at the service of her modernist project of linguistic materialization and authorial management. Physiognomy is, Graeme Tytler explains, "the idea that man's outward appearance, whether taken as whole or in parts, is a manifestation of his inner self"; it is "the art of knowing the inner man through the outer." Hence physiognomy both instantiates and relies on a system of observable correspondences between body and mind, physicality and mentality, and materiality and morality. "Beauty and ugliness," to take but the most obvious example, "are expressions of virtue and vice respectively."[73] One might just as well reverse the direction of the relation, since, according to physiognomical logic, virtue and vice are equally properties of beauty and ugliness. Only our greater access to the physical, or perhaps the nineteenth-century's preference for the observable, makes physiognomy so insistently a technique for reading from the outside in, for elucidating what comes to seem a simpler and more linear progression from the body to the embodied. Indeed, the ubiquity of this reading technique leads Tytler to conclude that "character description in the novel is, and always has been, by definition physiognomical."[74] Character description, at least within literary realism, always makes the individual legible through a set of shared physical signifiers that convey meaning through a generally accepted discursive code.

Despite the ubiquity of this technique, we should not lose sight of the tremendous amount of variation in physiognomical characterization. Within nineteenth-century American literature, the spectrum runs from Nathaniel Hawthorne's metaphysical meditations on stains and marks to Mark Twain's humorous caricatures, from Harriet Beecher Stowe's sentimental tableaux to the observations of Henry James's unreliable narrators. Stein, for her part, takes physiognomy to a different plane altogether in the early modernist period, by collapsing the physical and mental attributes of her working-class characters into strikingly concise, dramatically unambivalent pronouncements of temperament. This shift is easy to miss because Stein's method has been broadly popularized; but compare, for effect, the following five character descriptions from "The Good Anna" to the following passage from Henry James's "Daisy Miller."

pretty, cheerful Lizzie (39)

[M]elancholy Molly . . . was a tall, dark, sallow, thin-haired creature, and she was always troubled with a cough, and she had a bad temper, and always said ugly dreadful swear words. (39–40)

Old Katy was a heavy, ugly, short and rough old german woman . . . (41)

This Julia Lehntman was an unattractive girl enough, harsh featured, dull and stubborn . . . (55)

Mrs. Drehten . . . [was] large and motherly, with the pleasant, patient, soft, worn, tolerant face, that comes with a german husband to obey . . . (60)

Winterbourne had not seen for a long time anything prettier than his fair countrywoman's various features—her complexion, her nose, her ears, her teeth. He had a great relish for feminine beauty; he was addicted to observing and analyzing it; and as regards this young lady's face he made several observations. It was not at all insipid, but it was not exactly expressive; and though it was eminently delicate, Winterbourne mentally accused it—very forgivingly of a want of finish. He thought it very possible that Master Randolph's sister was a coquette; he was sure she had a spirit of her own; but in her bright, sweet, superficial little visage there was no mockery, no irony.[75]

Stein, evidently, is not interested in using the extended passages of physiognomical characterization that James and other realists of his generation employ to illuminate their more affluent characters. Perhaps her workers do not warrant such lyricism. Certainly, their affections have less pecuniary value, and thus their visages inspire no expansive exegeses, no attempts to ferret out the suitability of their temperaments. Stein's characterizations, unlike James's, do not contain moments of mediation. Without hesitation or modification, she spins together lists of adjectives ("heavy, ugly, short and rough") to present working-class character types whose vividness and verisimilitude depend on the immediacy of their physical presence rather than on their imagined interiority. This technique is only possible because their physical presence accords so exactly with their mental abilities and general temperament. Melancholy Molly is, of course, "tall, dark, sallow, [and] thin-haired," just as Julia Lehntman is both "unattractive" and, without fail, "dull and stubborn." Physiognomy is, in this sense, far more integral to Stein than to her realist predecessors. With Stein, physiognomy becomes, to use Peter Brooks's term, a mode of "hypersignification."[76] In these short descriptive phrases, she establishes the absolute and inviolate correspondence between physicality and mentality that translates her psychological principles into the ontological and epistemological precepts of her early prose.

Not only do Stein's characterizations lack the sort of mediatorial gestures practiced by earlier realists; they also exist outside of (and instead of) the traditional, realist arc of character development. Though melancholy Molly, the good Anna, and others appear frequently in this brief text, their names are seldom far from their adjectival tags, and hence they continually reappear as entities whose bottom natures are always supremely visible. Such recurrences are themselves part of Stein's general project, which was to replace realist development and elaboration with modernist repetition. But as I have been arguing, the ties between Stein's formal techniques and her understanding of working-class subjectivity need to be stressed. Unlike James, who places his bourgeois characters in complex social situations to have them grow, change, and develop through interaction, Stein's working-class characters are as fully realized in the beginning as they ever will be. They are like pieces on a chessboard, whose properties do not change during the course of the game. On the contrary, their properties make the game possible at the outset. The outcome—in this case, the plot—is less a matter of growth or introspection (much less suspense and surprise) than a matter of tactics and management, of effective authorial deployment and control.

This is what Donald Sutherland means, in part, when he draws attention to Stein's "impulse to elemental abstraction," to her radical shift toward "description in terms of the final and generic as against description by context and association."[77] Such realists as Henry James and such impressionists as Claude Monet work through the latter mode. When James presents a character or Monet a water lily, these are described through their contextual connections to social or atmospheric conditions (such as, in Monet's case, the refraction of light) and through their association with other characters or objects. Stein, like Cézanne and Picasso, radically disarticulates her working-class characters from such contextual affinities. She deploys physiognomy in its starkest form to present set essences—a move that constitutes both a return to an older, iconographic mode of representation (such as one finds in fairy tales or medieval religious paintings) and a radical shift to the generic and taxonomic dictates of machine epistemology (where one finds highly systematized parts). Put more simply, "the good Anna" is not good because she acts kindly toward other characters or because she is presented in contrast to bad characters (these things happen, but they are epiphenomenal); she is good because that is her bottom nature, held fast by an inability to alter her habits. The reader knows that she is good because that is her taxonomic affiliation (just as we know, as soon as we meet her, that Cinderella's wicked stepmother will act wickedly). Realists, such as James, believe in the centrality of context and association because they believe, in varying degrees, in the primacy of social construction in the formation of subjects. Stein's innovation, ironically, comes from a return to premodern models that reverses the relation. To whatever extent the social exists in *Three Lives*, it is "composed" entirely of types whose generic affinities preexist its formation.

Something of this essential difference is evident even in the distinct ways that Stein and James use point of view in their physiognomical passages. For James, interpretation is the central act, constitutive in its own right of subjectivity and social circumstance. In the preceding quotation from "Daisy Miller," Winterbourne's interpretation of Miller's physiognomy is significant because it reveals not only his sense of Miller's character (which may or may not be reliable) but also and more important, his own presumptions and patterns of thought. Indeed, Winterbourne's ability to "read" Miller is precisely at issue in "Daisy Miller," as are such interpretive acts throughout James's texts. Stein, in contrast, leaves no room for interpretation. Physiognomy is not the result of actions of observation, much less the mode by which one character reads another. It is the expression of an internal principle of nature. The narrator's eyes never move across the character's face, assessing its details, weighing its meaning, reading its temperament. Instead, the narrator presents the character as a physiognomical principle embodied, as a set of determined relations between body and mind. The physiognomical relation is not the result of an active process of knowing but, rather, the principle on which knowledge, in a reified sense, is based. All action—indeed, all aspects of the narrative—are predicated on such knowledge, which is, in turn, dependent on a physiognomical code deeply formed around gender, race, and class.

The different ways that race and class function are, in particular, integral to the taxonomic comprehension of female domestic labor in *Three Lives*. There is little doubt that Stein chose to examine German immigrant and African American protagonists to show a variety of female working-class types. Stein must have felt that she knew these types with some intimacy, having employed German immigrants in her home and attended the delivery of African American babies in Baltimore while studying medicine at Johns Hopkins. Whatever the basis of her judgments, Stein characterizes female German immigrants and female African Americans quite differently within *Three Lives*. Though Stein writes, on occasion, of an immigrant character who is "slatternly and careless" (40), the majority of these immigrants are careful and exacting, concerned with neatness, cleanliness, and economic frugality. Stein's African American women—whom we meet exclusively in "Melanctha"— have quite opposite characteristics. Freer and more emotive than Stein's immigrants, they partake in varying degrees of "the wide, abandoned laughter that makes the warm broad glow of negro sunshine" (87, 92, 195, 138, 169). Such freedom has a downside, however, since these characters tend also to be lazy and careless, depending on how deeply their nature reflects "the simple, promiscuous unmorality of the black people" (87).

As different as these characters seem, they nevertheless do share the same absolute predisposition toward permanence that I have been arguing more generally defines the working-class type within Stein's psychological taxonomy. While Melanctha wanders and the good Anna works herself to death, they are, at root, two different manifestations of the same deterministic class disposition: to be locked into whatever psychological habits first emerge. It does not seem to matter, actually, whether these habits are "natural" or social in origin. What matters is the extent to which the habits, once formed, superintend the subsequent existences of these working-class characters. While the deterministic plots of Stein's three stories—the way in which each protagonist's central characteristic foretells her demise—are the best evidence of this class disposition, Stein voices more localized explanations in several places. In "The Good Anna," she describes "Melancholy Molly" by drawing attention both to her nature and to her subsequent training, which has only superficially taken hold: "She was a tall, thin, sallow girl, aged twenty-three, by nature slatternly and careless but trained by Anna into superficial neatness" (40). In a similar passage in "Melanctha," Stein introduces Rose Johnson, who "was careless and was lazy, but . . . had been brought up by white folks and . . . needed decent comfort." Stein writes of Rose: "Her white training had only made for habits, not for nature. Rose had the simple, promiscuous unmorality of the black people" (87). This "Melanctha" passage may be confusing, since Stein here uses the term *habits* colloquially to refer to superficial attributes rather than to a permanent disposition. Nevertheless, the point should be clear: Neither Melancholy Molly nor Rose Johnson can move beyond their bottom natures. While their race may predispose them toward a particular nature, it is their shared class identity that makes it hold. And it holds, Stein tells us repeatedly, regardless of external circumstance.

Given the number of passages where Stein similarly discusses a racial or ethnic "nature" held firmly by class, one might further conceptualize the relationship between race and class in *Three Lives* as some sort of Aristotelian split between matter and form, where neither can be said to be primary or exclusively constitutive of the other. Race conveys a certain "nature," a sense of physicality and materiality; class conveys shape and delineation, congeals that matter into a socially recognizable form (a physiognomy), and secures that form firmly in place. Stein first describes the gentle Lena's body, for instance, in the following terms:

> Lena was a brown and pleasant creature, brown as blonde races often have them brown, brown, not with the yellow or the red or the chocolate brown of sun burned countries, but brown with the clear color laid flat on the light toned skin beneath, the plain, spare brown abundant straight, brown hair, hair that only later deepens itself into brown from the straw yellow of a german childhood.
>
> Lena had the flat chest, straight back and forward shoulders of the patient and enduring working woman, though her body was now still in

its milder girlhood and work had not yet made these lines too clear. (189)

Stein identifies Lena's body through both its racial and class aspects. On the one hand, Lena is "brown and pleasant"; on the other, she has the "flat chest, straight back and forward shoulders of the patient and enduring working woman." Her brownness ("brown as blonde races often have them") establishes a visible resonance, a material presence palpable in its detail. But such pure materiality is not fully realized without shape and form, without the bone structure and carriage that identifies her class as a worker. This shape is present in Lena's body, importantly, even before her work has really begun. Work, it is true, will make her class "lines . . . clear" (her "line-age"). But even without the clarity that adulthood will provide, her structure already records the life to which she was born and the destiny that she will fulfill.

Indeed, the physiognomical relationship between race and class, matter and form, and physical presence and definitional lineage has more general effects in *Three Lives,* orienting the stories toward different aspects of working-class life. Though all three stories are concerned with the interplay of racial and class characteristics, "Melanctha" focuses most centrally on love and sexuality, while "The Good Anna" and "The Gentle Lena" revolve around labor and labor relations. Melanctha works—we learn this in passing in the narrative—but Stein only tells us where and for whom and never records her experiences as a domestic laborer. What we do learn about are the details of her relationship with Jeff Campbell (and, less centrally, with others), through which unfold the psychological drama of two very different types trying to relate on an intimate level. Alternately, while both Anna and Lena have relationships, they are by no measure as fully explored as Melanctha's. Though we are told, for instance, that "Mrs. Lehntman was the romance in Anna's life" (50), this description substitutes for any more lengthy elaboration. Similarly, since Lena's marriage suffers from an almost total lack of connection, her love life and even her psychology remain hidden from view. What we learn in "The Gentle Lena" and especially in "The Good Anna" is what it is like to labor, to organize households, and to cater to the whims of others. It is as if Stein's decision to focus on these different working-class types also constituted a decision to segregate the internal and external aspects of working-class life accordingly, to institute some sort of authorial division of labor between a study of love and two studies of work, between a character whose bottom nature causes her to wander and two characters who are, by nature, destined to exhaust themselves working within confined domestic spaces.

Given Stein's focus on physiognomy, taxonomic determination, and the interweavings of race and class within this particular character type, her stylistic innovations seem entirely appropriate. The repetition of sentences and phrases, the limited lexicon, and the heavy use of free indirect discourse all forward Stein's particularly modernist aims of fragmentation or division, on the one hand, and systematic control, on the other. In this case, Stein intends to make language an integral part of materializing her characters' bottom natures and to bring that element of linguistic materialization under authorial control. It may be true that all authors attempt to control the worlds they create. But I argue, as I have with regard to Duchamp and Eliot, that there are dramatically different forms and degrees of artistic control; that this mode of early modernism is specifically concerned with the control, systemization, and management of working-class subjects; and that many of its aesthetic innovations can be usefully understood as part of this project.

Stein's most noted innovation—repetition—bears centrally on this interplay of separation and control, just as it clearly emerges from her typological comprehension of working-class subjectivity. The reiterative nature of various sentences in "The Good Anna" and "The Gentle Lena" and of the dialogue in "Melanctha" act as reflexes of the relative fixity of these characters' temperaments and processes of thought. To reiterate the passage "Anna led an arduous and troubled life" (37, 39, 44) is, as I noted, to shift from a realist mode of elaboration to a modernist mode of repetition. But it is also to echo powerfully the very dullness and flatness of such a life and thus to harmonize discursive elements of the narration with the basic psychological disposition of Anna's bottom nature. Lisa Ruddick and Marianne DeKoven each get at some of this when they differently harness feminism and psychoanalysis to argue that Stein's repetitions reveal an otherwise hidden, feminist unconsciousness within her characters.[78] They are right to match subjectivity and style. But Stein's conception of psychology is decidedly pre-Freudian, and her stylistic investment in complex subtextuality is surprisingly minimal. The complexities of Stein's prose are all, as it were, on the surface, in the compositional articulations she makes between the various elements in her texts.

Repetition must be understood thus principally *as repetition,* as evidence, as DeKoven observes, of a character's "fixed blocked mind struggling to free itself by going over and over the terms of its fixation until it has mastered them."[79] It is not symptomatic of something else—a different way of knowing or a covert resistance to phallogocentrism—nor is its meaning particularly symbolic. This does not indicate, however, that repetition elides such things as incremental change. On the contrary, as these phrases reappear in *Three Lives*, we see new meaning in them and have some sense of Stein's characters groping for comprehension and clarity.

> You got no idea Herman, how bad mama is feeling about the way you been acting Herman. . . . She says she never can understand how you can be so thankless Herman. It hurts her very much you been so stubborn, and she find you such a nice girl for you, like Lena Mainz who is always just so quiet and always saves up all her wages, and she never wanting her own way at all like some girls are always all the time to have it and your mama trying so hard, just so you could be comfortable Herman to be married, and then you act so stubborn Herman. (205)

But it is the repetitive groping, not the comprehension, that repetition serves chiefly to demonstrate, the groping of characters whose minds work in such a fashion.

Indeed, if any contextual connection is to be made with Stein's technique, it is not between repetition and some sort of *ecriture feminine* but—once more—between repetition and the epistemological dictates of mass production. Donald Sutherland made this connection in a commemorative appreciation of Stein's life, when he noted how "certain quite practical features of the twentieth century world," such as "mass production and series production, the assembly line and so on," correspond to Stein's "sort of composition." Long before Andy Warhol's series prints and the dubs of modern musical electronica testified to the repetitive nature of twentieth-century mass production, Stein glossed the assembly line with her infamous "a rose is a rose is a rose." No subsequent acts of artistic series production have as concisely captured what must have seemed an almost instantaneous shift from the organic and the romantic to the mechanized plentitude of modern replication. Sutherland, for his part, takes pains to assure his readers that such a transition in the process of production does not place "their individuality . . . at stake": "[I]f you have say a new Mustang it is your own Mustang, even if it is not fully paid for, and you go your own way in it and treat it as if it were unique. And even if there are thousands of suits exactly like the one you are wearing, it is still your suit, you are by yourself in it." After all, Sutherland says in his own repetition of Stein, "that thing is being that thing and not being just anything it is everything."[80]

But the consequences of repetition on the individuality of the consumer (or reader) are, if anything, a distant consideration with regard to *Three Lives*, where repetition is much more tied to the epistemological dictates of production than to whatever processes of consumption might ensue. Indeed, the connection between Fordist production methods and repetition is not even causal, in a simple and immediate sense. Unlike Kenneth Fearing and other proletarian poets of the 1930s, who would claim that Fordist production techniques also produced workers with minds and bodies bent by repetition, Stein sees repetition in a broader, more epistemological fashion, as a contemporaneous technology of composition that can function within her work to manage ties between characterization, plot (as it were), and style. Thus any predilection for repetition on the part of her characters precedes the repetitious nature of their actual labors. Though repetition is a class attribute in *Three Lives*, it is essentialized and presocial. This is what allows it to make the all-important synchretic connection between subjectivity and style.

The fact that repetition is, for Stein, simultaneously a presocial aspect of her characters and one of the most historically resonant aspects of her prose is, admittedly, something of a paradox. But she would claim throughout her career that repetition, like her other aesthetic innovations, was somehow endogenous to characters, objects, and even language itself; that all she did was to discover this internal principle of modernity lying deep in the ontological grain of the thing itself and then reflect it in her prose; that her contemporaneousness arose not from a break from mimesis but from a recognition that the process needed to move to a different level. Whatever one makes of this argument, it does have one particular consequence that deserves brief note here: to claim that repetition is an internal principle is to disallow, a priori, the kind of multivocality—the visible accretion of social meanings within language—that makes other literary texts fecund in their ambiguities. Like Eliot's "objective correlative," which endeavors to funnel the ambiguity of affect into a linear relation between the percept and the prescribed emotion, Stein works to evacuate language of the unpredictability of its own historicity, of "the multiplication of resonances and ambiguities" present in "conventional" literary language.[81] Though one might argue that the rose in "a rose is a rose is a rose" can never be divorced entirely from Blake's "O Rose thou art sick," this is clearly Stein's intent. As late as 1946, she would critique her own work for its unintentional falls into association. Of the sentence "Dirty is yellow," which appears in the prose poem "A Piece of Coffee," she writes: "Dirty has an association and is a word that I would not use now. I would not use words that have definite associations. This was an earlier work and none of the later things have this. This early work is not so successful. It is an effort and does not come clean."[82] Cleanliness is, of course, antithetical to those unfortunate associations surrounding the word *dirty* (which lead one to wonder about what sort of racial logic might have linked the concepts "dirty" and "yellow" in the first place), and thus it captures Stein's monumental effort toward linguistic precision. Unfortunately, such precision and control seem also to have prompted the elision of social multivocality from her language and the appropriation of material forms from her racial and working-class subjects into the linguistic systems of her prose.

Some brief comments on the other most noted stylistic elements of *Three Lives*—Stein's use of a limited lexicon and her deployment of free indirect discourse—may make this last point clearer, especially if we examine them together. More traditionally, critics have appreciated Stein's lexical choices but have neglected to comment on her narrative stance, since they assume that Stein was writing in the vein of nineteenth-century dialect fiction and that the stance would, perforce, be self-evidently realist. The generation of Stein critics who first clarified Stein's stylistic operations (Richard Bridgeman, Donald Sutherland, Catherine Simpson, and others)[83] recognized, however, how completely Stein breaks from the rhetorical mode of dialect fiction; her lexical patterns reflect mental (rather than verbal) processes, and her use of free indirect discourse ("third-person, past-tense rendering of speech or thought which approaches the verbal style of a character")[84] moves away from the simple assumptions of realism. Sutherland notes that even the "elaborate syncopations" of the prose rhythms are directed toward characterological, rather discursive representation: "As with the vocabulary, the simplification of the rhythm is there to carry and clarify something complicated. . . . The functioning of the attention of the characters in speech (which would be according to Gertrude Stein's early definition a reflex of their total character) goes on against a simplified verbal rhythm. It has to be simple to disengage the special personal emphasis and to carry a rhythm of ideas."[85]

This interpretation is true enough, but if we factor in the particular nature of these ideas and their relationship to the prose, other, more socially resonant results become clear. While the limited lexicon functions to exteriorize these characters' limited mental processes and to materialize these processes within the prose, free indirect discourse works to foreclose the possibility of any deeper or alternative linguistic territory. While Stein's bounded word choices establish, in Jayne Walker's words, "the narrowly restricted linguistic universe that confines the speech and thoughts of simple uneducated characters," the use of free indirect discourse ensures that "there is no escape from the linguistic and conceptual boundaries that restrict the characters' expression and their thought." In short, Stein combines "the verbal impotence of her characters . . . with a similarly restricted narrative idiom to create a poetics of impotence, of antieloquence."[86]

Given the admirable precision of Walker's explanation, we need only amend one observation to more deeply explore the operations of power embedded in Stein's "poetics of impotence." Though it is true that Stein's characters cannot escape from their "linguistic and conceptual boundaries," it is equally true (and equally important) that Stein's assumed readers can—and that they, in fact, exist well outside of these bounds, in an expanded linguistic and conceptual universe. The linguistic limits would not be recognizable as such if this were not the case, just as the stylized repetitions I have already discussed would not be a recognizable reflex of a particular character type were this type not at some taxonomical distance from the reader. In other words, Stein's renderings (re)produce a sociolinguistic difference, which is represented by the lexicon and enforced through narrative point of view. This difference makes Stein's style a "poetics of impotence," instead of a portrait of impotence or an impotently drawn portrait. The complex virtuosity of Stein's techniques thus stands outside of these characters' lives even as the techniques themselves function to deny the possibility of an outside. That denial does not mean that such an alternative space ceases to exist or to function crucially in the rhetorical structure of the triptych. It means, rather, that, like Eliot, Stein sets out to abrogate the traditional bridges of sympathy and sentiment that have posited such a space as a potential alternative to the "arduous and troubled" lives of the working class. That space becomes, instead, the place from which Stein manages her working-class forms.

The opening sentence of "The Good Anna," to take but one of many possible examples, establishes this distance immediately, as it delineates the difference between class power and efficacious language: "The tradesmen of Bridgeport learned to dread the sound of 'Miss Mathilda,' for with that name the good Anna always conquered" (37). Anna conquers in (and with) the name of another (her employer, who most critics see as a cipher for Stein) because her own name has no such power. Shorn of its ventriloquistic pretensions, her own voice cannot prompt action. Stein makes this fact apparent six paragraphs later, when Anna scolds her dog ineffectually (in her first recorded speech).

> Sallie! can't I leave you alone a minute but you must run to the door to see the butcher boy come down the street and there is Miss Mathilda calling for her shoes. Can I do everything while you go around always thinking about nothing at all? If I ain't after you every minute you would be forgetting all the time, and I take all this pains, and when you come to me you was as ragged as a buzzard and as dirty as a dog. (37)

Stein here uses not only a limited lexicon but one marked quite heavily by the minstrel tradition, which, like the music hall, gave early modernists a usable, if idiosyncratic, sense of working-class cultural forms. The comedic element of this first bit of dialogue stems from a particular minstral joke—already dated by 1909. Since Sallie *is* a dog, a derisive comparison to a dog cannot really have Anna's desired effect. What it shows is Anna's limited linguistic capacity—Stein's desired effect—and her self-important pomposity, which is reinforced by a complete lack of self-reflection. (She unknowingly compensates for her class position by berating her dog.) Though Anna's diction is marked as Other through her vaguely ethnoracial locution, which does not reflect any specifically Germanic syntactical patterns, her character traits are precisely rendered. Her simple bottom nature is demonstrated, in this instance, by her overly literal understanding of linguistic forms. Anna's metaphors tend toward tautology; unlike Stein, she has no poetics. Hence her lexical limits accurately define the shape of the life she has lived and the destiny her nature bids her to fulfill. Unable to comprehend her own powerlessness and her dependence on Miss Mathilda, insensitive to the subtly expressed needs of her family and lover, and ineffectual in her attempts to govern her own boardinghouse, Anna obstinately works herself to death. If, as I have argued, biology is destiny in *Three Lives,* these biologistics are apparent in the text's linguistic forms. Or, to put the matter somewhat differently, the poetics of impotence is also the poetics of predetermination.

Another joke, similarly drawn from the minstrel tradition, helps define the subjective terrain of "Melanctha," a story that also charts the obdurate naïveté of its central characters. In response to Melanctha's thoughts about suicide, Rose Johnson says:

> I don't see Melanctha why you should talk like you would kill yourself just because you're blue. I'd never kill myself Melanctha just 'cause I was blue. I'd maybe kill somebody else Melanctha 'cause I was blue, but I'd never kill myself. If I ever killed myself Melanctha it'd be by accident, and if I ever killed myself by accident Melanctha, I'd be awful sorry. (89)

Once again, Stein gives us "a systematic stylistic demonstration of the limits of rational discourse,"[87] as Johnson's repetitive language and circular logic lead her to a humorous impasse. But there is more at stake here than simple humor. Johnson's linguistic mistake derives from a deeper philosophical misunderstanding about Cartesian principles of selfhood. Conceiving of the epistemological being and the ontological being as separate entities, she thinks that the self as subject (who knows that she is dead) can exist beyond the self as object (who is dead). Stein may be gently mocking a kind of Christian faith in the afterlife or perhaps the transcendentalist strain within American romanticism, but her own views on the subject are all too clear. When the protagonists in *Three Lives* die, they are simply dead, barely remembered even by their friends and family. And when they are alive, they tend—particularly in "Melanctha"—to have too little appreciation for the ephemerality of this condition. "Melanctha" begins, for instance, with the title character assisting at the delivery of Rose Johnson's baby, who was "very hard to bring to birth" (87). But once the struggle is over, "Rose Johnson was careless and negligent and selfish, and when Melanctha had to leave for a few days, the baby died. Rose Johnson had liked the baby well enough and perhaps she just forgot it for awhile, anyway the child was dead and Rose and Sam her husband were very sorry but then these things came so often in the negro world in Bridgepoint, that they neither of them thought about it for very long" (87). There is, not to press the point overmuch, another minstrel joke buried in this piece of free indirect deadpan. Of course, "these things came so often" precisely because people do not think about them "for very long." Repetition once again replaces elaboration, prompting these characters to forget what will, consequentially, come again.

Indeed, a basic disjunction between the epistemic and the ontologic realms of the self emerges as the dominant bottom nature in "Melanctha," just as the misconstrual of power comes to thematically characterize "The Good Anna" (and an inescapable passivity indelibly imprints "The Gentle Lena"). Though the consequences are not as dramatic, Melanctha, like Rose Johnson, is also prone to forgetting or, as Stein writes repeatedly, "wandering." But unlike Johnson, such wanderings seem to define every dimension of her life. Ruddick writes:

> The references in "Melanctha" to the heroine's many "wanderings" have rightly been considered part of a sustained euphemism for sex, but one might as easily reverse the emphasis and say that sex itself stands in the story as a metaphor for a certain type of mental activity. Melanctha's promiscuity is part of an experiential promiscuity, an inability or unwillingness to approach the world selectively. Her sexual wanderings are part of a "wandering attention" [William James] that takes in experience without mediation.[88]

Beyond sexual and experiential wandering, we should also add a linguistic wandering to "the different kind of ways she wandered" (174). Like other aspects of her wandering attention, her limited linguistic constancy reflects an essential dissociation within her conception of the self. Melanctha, for instance, "did not know how to tell a story wholly": "She always, and yet not with intention, managed to leave out big pieces which make a story very different, for when it came to what had happened and what she had said and what it was that she had really done, Melanctha never could remember right" (98). Crucially, what she cannot re-member are the parts of the story relating to herself. Without what William James calls, the "Self-of-selves,"[89] she is unable to assimilate aspects of her past with her present and thus cannot correlate these various entities into a linear, causative narrative. At the lexical level, the preponderance of euphemisms that have no fixed referent also indicate a kind of promiscuous slippage (here within the narrator's free indirect discourse). When Melanctha is "wandering" to learn "various ways of working" (95) or to gain "wisdom" (101), it is never entirely clear whether the reference is to sexual, experiential, and/or cognitive activity.

Though Ruddick and others argue—once again—that these various types of wandering compose another, subversive way of knowing,[90] there is really no evidence to suggest that either Melanctha or Stein experiences them as such. On the contrary, Melanctha's indiscriminateness ensures that she cannot ever be happy: "Melanctha had not found it easy with herself to make her wants and what she had, agree. Melanctha Herbert was always losing what she had in wanting all the things she saw. Melanctha was always being left when she was not leaving others" (91). Her nonconstancy is also, in part, what ends her relationship with Jeff Campbell (who is perhaps another cipher for Stein). While Jeff (as

Melanctha characterizes him) is "always wanting to have it clear out in words, always what everyone is always feeling" (145), Melanctha (as Jeff characterizes her) is "never remembering anything only what you just then are feeling in you" and is "not understanding what anyone else is ever feeling, if they don't holler just the way you are doing" (152). Jeff laments that Melanctha's mental promiscuity means, in particular, that "I ain't got any way ever to find out if she is real and true now always to me" (149). In large part, he refers, of course, to questions of sexual fidelity. But his problems go deeper than that. He means also that he has no way to verify that Melanctha is, from day to day, the same person, the same subjectivity.

Such subjective relativism and such consequent linguistic ambiguity and imprecision are so distant from the values Stein otherwise promotes—immanence, essentialism, exactitude, and linguistic instrumentalism—that it is difficult to place Stein and Melanctha together as advocates for an experiential antirationality or for what DeKoven sees as some sort of "presymbolic, pluridemensional" knowledge of the body.[91] For Stein, on the contrary, knowledge comes not from the body but through the body, in what is empirically evident and subsequently reified in her taxonomic categories. Knowledge of the self means, in addition to conceiving of the self as a whole, knowledge of the self's bottom nature and, in some cases, its absolute fixity. Such is, I think, the message Stein telegraphs in the subtitle to "Melanctha," "Each One as She May." Here the "as" should be read as a relation of constitutive equivalence: Each is a one in acting as she may; and each may only act, at least in this world of the working class, according to her bottom and ultimate nature. Within this world, difference and pluralism—a plurality of types—is more tragic than it is liberatory. As Jeff Campbell realizes, without flexibility and change, growth and empathy, "each [is] not for the other but for ourselves": "Each man has got to do for himself when he is in real trouble" (150). In fact, the sole instance of intersubjective understanding, of a utopia articulated along pluralist lines, comes (and here we return full circle) as Stein waxes romantic about people's relationship to the machine.

> Melanctha liked to wander, and to stand by the railroad yard, and watch the men and the engines and the switches and everything that was busy there, working. Railroad yards are a ceaseless fascination. They satisfy every kind of nature. For the lazy man whose blood flows very slowly, it is a steady soothing moving power. He need not work and yet he has it very

deeply; he has it even better than the man who works in it or owns it. Then for natures that like to feel emotion without the trouble of having any suffering, it is very nice to get the swelling in the throat, and the fullness, and the heart beats, and all the flutter of excitement that comes as one watches the people come and go, and hear the engine pound and give a long drawn whistle. (96)

The railroad yard equally satisfies every kind of nature, by evoking a direct emotional response (a feeling, in Stein's words) that does not require work, ownership, or suffering (intersubjective relationships that Stein signals through the word "having"). Thus the railroad yard is not only literally a place where one encounters machines; as with Eliot's "objective correlative," it is a machine relation, animated by the utopian promise of sure emotional evocation without the uncertainty of social interaction. Indeed, the railroad yard may well be an objective correlative for satisfaction itself, since (Stein's nod to pluralism notwithstanding) it successfully gives that sensory experience to every kind of nature. Unlike "the warm broad glow of negro sunshine," which is less certain in these characters' lives than that racist metaphor would suggest, the railroad yard is a sure thing, "formulaic," to use Eliot's term, in its dependability. Yet in order for the railroad yard to serve this function—to serve as an aesthetic alternative to the profoundly unsatisfying lives of Stein's working class—it must stand outside these characters' lives in the rarified realm of art. Like the figure who descends in Duchamp's painting and the children who wail in Eliot's early poetry, the railroad yard animates and evokes only insomuch as it is a spectacle, as it has, paradoxically, already been estranged from the moving bodies, affective demands, and broader agency of the workers themselves. Perhaps this is but another way of saying that high modernism interacts with the working class through the time-honored techniques of alienation, reification, and fetishism. But if this is the case, then high modernism gives these techniques its own particular twist. Not only does it siphon off the auratic power of working-class forms for its own aesthetic radicalism; it systematizes these in a way that manages the challenges of class struggle.

The Fetish of Being Inside

Proletarian Texts and
Working-Class Bodies

The tenement is in my blood. When I think it is the tenement
thinking. When I hope it is the tenement hoping. I am not an
individual; I am all that the tenement group poured into me during those early years of my spiritual travail.

—Mike Gold, "Towards Proletarian Art"

She looked down on the great black sea of bodies, heads like
black wheat growing in the same soil, the same wind. Something
seemed to enter her and congeal. I am part, she wanted to say.

—Meridel Le Sueur, "Tonight is Part of the Struggle"

A "POLITICAL AUTOPSY"

In the winter of 1939, as the chaotic decade of the Great Depression
wound to a close, Philip Rahv, onetime Communist Party member and
coeditor of the recently disaffiliated *Partisan Review,* declared the proletarian literature movement a dead entity. Born out of an unnatural cou-
pling of aesthetics and politics, nurtured through its infancy by Communist Party "commissars," weakened by the vicissitudes of the party's
political "line," and finally "devour[ed] . . . [by] the political party that
fathered [it]," the literary movement that always seemed as much corporeal as discursive awaited only a "political autopsy." Rahv's vivisection,
argued with considerable trenchancy and verve in the conservative *Southern Review,* promised just such an inside view. Proletarian literature was,
according to Rahv, little more than a sham, a monumental bait and

switch where the party (always invoked in the abstract) lured sympathetic writers with the appeal of class solidarity and leftist pluralism but gave, instead, doctrinal marching orders. In a sentence that set the terms for years of subsequent scholarship, Rahv summed up his postmortem inquest: "It is clear that proletarian literature is the literature of a party disguised as the literature of a class."[1]

It would be hard to overemphasize the importance of this single, thin statement. Picked up three years later in Alfred Kazin's pathbreaking *On Native Grounds* and six years after that in Dixon Wecter's *The Age of the Great Depression*, Rahv's message began an impressive journey through the realms of literary criticism and political history. By the time Irving Howe and Lewis Coser reiterated it in *The American Communist Party: A Critical History* (1957), what once must have seemed tendentious appeared to be common sense—one among a handful of pithy indictments of literary and political Stalinism.[2] Rahv's claim has loomed equally large over more recent, left-oriented scholarship of the period. From Alan Wald's *Exiles from a Future Time,* to Michael Denning's *The Cultural Front,* to Barbara Foley's *Radical Representations,* to Paula Rabinowitz's *Labor and Desire,* to Rita Barnard's *The Great Depression and the Culture of Abundance,* the strategy has been either to exert great effort contesting Rahv's claim (by arguing, as have Wald, Denning, and Foley, that the Left of the 1930s was pluralist and/or the party nondoctrinal) or to assert the particular power of authorial transcendence (by arguing, as have Rabinowitz and Barnard, that Rahv was right but that certain writers rose above doctrine to produce art). Yet what has received far too little attention in this war-by-other-means is the deeper implication of Rahv's charge: that "disguise" and dissimilitude played a fundamental role in the period's negotiations between literature, politics, and class.

If we can allow for the biases prompted by Rahv's newfound anticommunism and look at specific authors rather than at an abstract party, we can see that, however intended, Rahv's statement does distill many of the central concerns of the thirties' proletarian literature movement. Though the movement was self-consciously proletarian, most of the authors involved in the journals and clubs that formed its institutional base were from the middle class, an aspect of their identity that occasioned no little amount of concern and self-criticism. By means of disguise, dissimilitude, sympathy, imaginative suture, literary self-flagellation, or actual economic self-dispossession, they sought to submerge themselves into the body of the proletariat, to achieve not only an epistemological but an almost physical integration with this emerging his-

torical agent. Though the party was indeed more pluralist and less doctrinal than Rahv's statement allows, it did promise to facilitate this integration, so that to write within its cultural domain was, as Rahv's syllo-
gism suggests, to write the "literature of class." "Literature must become
party literature," the *New Masses* quoted from an essay by Lenin; "literature must become part of the great proletarian movement."[3]

Essential to this assimilative operation was the multivalent nature of
the body in thirties discourse. As Rahv's autopsy makes visible, the body
was both individual and collective, physical and political, a literal corpse
and a literary corpus. The operation of melding these aspects together to
represent social suffering and class struggle in cultural terms was the
major innovation of the 1930s literary Left. Nevertheless, because of its
insistent focus on embodiment as the privileged site of class materialization, the movement's legacy was mixed. Visions of the working, suffering
body as the residuum of exploitation and the origin of revolutionary
hope could and did inspire authors to combine political radicalism, for-
malist invention, and epistemological self-consciousness into deeply
affective labor literature. Yet, however enabling, the movement's
reliance on mediating symbols—the party, the vanguard, the body—to
materialize class in literary form also led to the movement's downfall. Its
death was not at the hands of the party itself, as Rahv and others have
argued, though the party did little to combat its demise. Its death was by
co-optation, as the cultural nationalism of the Popular Front and the
state populism of the New Deal absorbed and redeployed the very tropes
that the movement had employed to agitate for revolutionary socialism.
Within these new cultural forms, the proletarian body became the American body (just as communism became Americanism) and performed
the same operations of mediation, though now between the citizen and
the state.

Foregrounding this discursive operation of mediation and integration not only helps explain the demise of proletarian literature; it also
provides a way to comprehend the relationship between the literature of
the 1930s (surely the decade most compartmentalized within American
literary scholarship) and earlier literary attempts to represent the working class. Both Granville Hicks and V. F. Calverton charted this relationship during the thirties itself, depicting the proletarian literature movement simultaneously as the apotheosis of critical realism and as a break
with the strictures of that identifiably bourgeois tradition. In this latter
regard, they saw it as almost prophetic, bringing forth a new literary form
appropriate to the objective conditions and subjective needs of a post-

capitalist culture.[4] Since that time, critics have argued principally about its relationship to the modernist movements that immediately preceded it, weighing proletarian literature's antimodernist celebrations of producerism and suspicion of formalism against its deployment of such modernist techniques as reportage, montage, and narrational intercutting.[5] Though I also find proletarian literature to be formally consonant with some aspects of modernism (particularly in how it treats language and how it uses the body), I do not think that it shares modernism's desire to fragment, systematize, and refunction working-class forms. On the contrary, it invests the working class with an almost auratic wholeness, at moments with a mythopoetic ability to achieve, through its struggle, not only communism but something akin to total psychosocial integration. Though this promise seemed, in the 1930s, precisely what oriented the movement toward the future, this idealization of wholeness, of integration through union with the working class, now identifies the movement as retrospective in vision. As I have argued in previous chapters, representations of workers and the poor in American culture have long tended to follow a repetitive cycle of unveiling and attempted assimilation. What is initially understood to be an epistemological disruption (the discovery of an unknown Other) is quelled by the production of a literary discourse of "knowledge" that can account for the intrusion. Each moment, each point of repetition, involves a different, though related, discursive construct. From the creation of a labor narrative of "whiteness" (discussed in chap. 2), to the transliteration of revolutionary rhetoric into realist prose (treated in chap. 3), to the momentary donning of working-class garb (examined in chap. 4), and even to the fragmentation and management of working-class forms (discussed in chap. 5), the struggle has been toward ever more intimate knowledge of the disruptive presence of the working class. The disguises, assimilations, and bodily inhabitations of the proletarian literature movement provide a culmination to this recapitulative paradigm, not only employing tropes and tactics that had been in use since the antebellum era, but also subverting some of these preexistent literary formulations through a new consciousness of the political limits and possibilities of literary form.

A comparison may clarify the new stakes. In 1894, Stephen Crane could journey undercover in order to "discover," "narrate," and circumscribe poverty's "point of view"; but by the thirties, the "experience" was more enveloping, and the "experiment" was less transitory and blithe.[6] Joseph Freeman, coeditor of the *New Masses*, explained in his introduction to a 1935 anthology of proletarian literature:

Often the writer who describes the contemporary world from the viewpoint of the proletariat is not himself a worker. War, unemployment, and a widespread social-economic crisis drive middle-class writers into the ranks of the proletariat. Their experience becomes contiguous to or identical with that of the working class; they see their former life, and the life of everyone around them with new eyes; their grasp of experience is conditioned by the class to which they have now attached themselves; they write from the viewpoint of the revolutionary proletariat; they create what is called proletarian literature.[7]

What Rahv and others would later "reveal," Freeman here forthrightly admits: proletarian literature is "often" written by a middle-class writer from the "viewpoint of the revolutionary proletariat." While Crane, Jack London, and others temporarily assumed the sartorial signs of the working classes in order to assimilate class difference into cultural pluralism, the proletarian literature movement attempted to take this gesture to a more radical conclusion, to assimilate the intellectual permanently into the hypostasized body of the forming revolutionary proletariat. Freeman's thesis is not so much that historical conditions have progressed to the point where there is a revolutionary proletariat (on this, he is hopeful but ambivalent) but, rather, that economic conditions have so deteriorated that middle-class writers develop a "viewpoint" or an "experience" that is "contiguous to or identical with" the working class. This theme was echoed throughout the Left in the early thirties, particularly in Lewis Corey's 1935 book *The Crisis of the Middle Class,* which drew structural as well as economic connections between corporatized and collectivized managers, clerks, professionals, and salesmen and the industrial working class. But the material and experiential background for contiguity was not, for many, a strict necessity. Granville Hicks recommended something far more voluntarist: "[Since] literature grows out of the author's entire personality, his identification with the proletariat should be as complete as possible. He should not merely believe in the cause of the proletariat; he should be, or should try to make himself, a member of the proletariat."[8] Hicks was only reiterating, however, the plan that Michael Gold, another editor of the *New Masses* and a tireless advocate for proletarian literature, had outlined in his 1930 "New Program for Writers." Gold suggested that each writer "attach himself" to an industry and "spend the next few years in and out of this industry, studying it from every angle, making himself an expert on it, so that when he writes of it he will write like an insider, not like a bourgeois intellectual observer." Only by doing so, he argued, can writers avoid becoming "tourists": "We must become more than that, part of industrial life itself, the tongue of the working class."9

To become the tongue of the working class in 1930 was not quite the same as becoming its "mouthpiece," as the Van Vorst sisters put it, three decades earlier.10 For one thing, by the early thirties, working-class writers were beginning to speak for themselves, as Gold well knew, since he grew up in poverty and wrote movingly about that experience. But more to the point, the epistemological focus of the proletarian literature movement was significantly different. Like class transvestites, proletarian writers sought entry into the domain of the working class, sought an authentic experience that would fuel honest and authoritative literature. But for the proletarian writers, knowledge no longer remained outside, in the supposedly objective world of journalism, sociology, or, more broadly, bourgeois society. The truth about society, knowledge of its inner workings, was available if and only if one wrote from the position of contiguity or identicality with the "revolutionary proletariat." Since "bourgeois claims of universality are an empty concept," argued Rahv and Wallace Phelps, "the class struggle must serve as a premise, not as a discovery" in imaginative literature.11

This form of Marxist cultural theory contained a number of idealizations that weakened its analytic ability: it entailed not only "workerism" (so-called since workers were seen as the standard-bearers of political truth) but, more generally, vanguardism (since the party garnered the same position of political privilege through its alliance with the revolutionary working class). But whatever its weaknesses, the Communist Party did not undertake this doctrine with either the deceit or the lust for power that Rahv's autopsy implies. Rather, proletarian writers and the theorists who sought to direct their efforts mounted a monumental and, in retrospect, quixotic effort to get around the power of capitalist culture and its reifications and to create a genuinely revolutionary proletarian epistemology. In the Soviet Union, Georg Lukács was also engaged in theorizing (and, under pressure, amending) a similar set of principles. In 1934, the *Partisan Review*, then still affiliated with the Communist Party, published his landmark article—translated as "Propaganda or Partisanship?"—which gave theoretical weight to this cultural doctrine. Discussing the contradiction between Balzac's bourgeois class sympathies and his withering critique of French society, Lukács argues: "The proletariat is not subject to this ideological limitation. For its social existence enables the proletariat (and hence the revolutionary proletarian writers) to transcend this limitation, to perceive the class relationships and the development of the class struggle behind the fetishist forms of capitalist society."[12]

Ironically, however, in their attempt to escape from the fetishistic forms of capitalist society, proletarian writers often ended up fetishizing the proletariat itself. The "literature of a class" became—to rephrase Rahv's epitaph—the literature of class identity and, through this stress on identity, the literature of class embodiment. The slippage between what we might now call "standpoint epistemology" and a belief in the recuperative powers of embodiment impoverished the proletarian literature movement in such a way that it could not maintain an autonomous theory of revolutionary culture in the face of its entry into the Popular Front coalition in 1935. Though a number of writers continued to work with proletarian forms (and a few continued to write from the standpoint of the revolutionary proletariat) into the latter parts of the decade, their energy, their tactics, and even their investment in the working body was absorbed into the populism of the Popular Front and into the romantic nationalism of the state culture propagated by the New Deal. Surveying the literary Left's evolution (or devolution) from radicalism to reformism, others have concluded that there was an unseen conservatism shaping the movement all along, that the inevitable culmination of the proletarian literature movement's youthful radicalism came in its sober "rediscovery of America" under the growing threat of fascism.[13] Yet the Left's susceptibility to liberalism had nothing to do with an inevitable historical progression and less to do with the threat of fascism than is typically imagined. Rather, the literary Left suffered from much the same malady that has plagued it throughout its development in the United States. Despite embracing Marxism as both a theory and as a political platform in the 1930s, the literary Left failed to develop a language of class sufficiently materialist to resist the co-optation of the liberal capitalist state.

BODIES IN PAIN

The fact that Freeman, Hicks, Gold, and others figured the insertion of the writer into the proletariat in bodily terms should not be altogether surprising. By the early 1930s, the decade already had a corporeal air to it. The presence of hungry families on breadlines, the public poverty of Hoovervilles, workers marching in demonstrations, and the violent repression of strikers all made untenable any lasting Victorian impulse to hide the body beneath the veneer of culture. Still today, when we remember the era, we tend to fixate on images of the exposed body as a register of social conditions: Dorothea Lange and Walker Evans's photographs of tired but resolute migrants and sharecroppers, John Steinbeck's literary veneration of Rose of Sharon's nourishing breast in *Grapes of Wrath* (1939), and paintings of muscular workers as ideal citizens in the murals of the Works Progress Administration. Even such scholars as Daniel Aaron and Barbara Foley, who agree on little else, are alike in their constant recourse to body metaphor. Aaron dismisses the entirety of the decade's literature because it "violated almost every literary canon and . . . positively reeked of the Depression," while Foley asks repeatedly how "the proletarian texts . . . manage to give fictional embodiment" to the politics of the Communist Party.[14]

There were compelling theoretical reasons for the preeminence of the body within the leftist discourse of the period. As bodies, bodily pain, and bodily violence became more visible, so did certain contradictions within capitalism. For liberals and New Deal policy makers, the contradiction (though this is not the term they would have used) was between America's promise of liberty, opportunity, and security and the reality of poverty, social determination, and fear. Within this contradiction, the body in pain is principally a site of deprivation, marking the absence of material resources (such as food and housing) and institutional guarantees (such as an old-age pension). This is the primary function of bodies in, for instance, the Farm Security Administration's photos of sharecroppers and migrants. It is also, as I will discuss, the primary function of the body within leftist discourse (including the discourse of the Communist Party) during the Popular Front era. During the early part of the decade, in contrast, many writers in and around the Communist Party conceived of the body more dialectically—not so much as a site of deprivation, but as a site of depletion, where absences measured the extent and duration of labor exploitation. Within this analytic framework, the working body is primary to both capital and the capitalist means of production, which live (as Marx famously put it) as a vampire on their working-class "hosts."[15] The vampires, of course, see it differently: "The rhetoric of capitalism insists that it is capital that makes things happen; capital has the magic property of growing, stimulating. What this conceals is the fact that it is human labor and, in the last instance, the labor of the body, that makes things happen."[16] Simply put, there was something radical about writing literature that showed working-class bodies making things happen, that reasserted the primacy of human production even within an era of great deprivation. The challenge was, however, to avoid romanticizing the laboring body and thus falling into the pastoral mode. Working bodies had to remain connected not only to production but to broad social forces that circumscribed their agency—a high-wire act that proved difficult to achieve.

In addition to these theoretical imperatives, there are specific historical reasons for the visibility of this era's biopolitics and for the way in which the body came to serve not only as a site of violence and exploitation but also as a vehicle for integration. As Michael Staub has recently argued, many of the specific tropes and rhetorical concerns of 1930s literature developed out of the intellectual defense and state execution in 1927 of two Italian American anarchists, Nicola Sacco and Bartolomeo Vanzetti.[17] As Malcolm Cowley later recounted, the relationship between the intelligentsia and the Communist Party in the thirties had much to do with the fact that disaffiliated writers—John Dos Passos, Katherine Anne Porter, Edna St. Vincent Millay, John Howard Lawson, Grace Lumpkin, Ruth Hale, and others—had been unable to prevent the actions of the Massachusetts Supreme Court. By the time of the Depression, "the intellectuals had learned that they were powerless by themselves and that they could not accomplish anything unless they made an alliance with the working class."[18]

Symbolically, the execution of Sacco and Vanzetti helped cast the subsequent events of the Depression in somatic terms, as a continuous assault on multiethnic and multiracial working-class bodies, foreign and diseased interlopers into the American whole. As Mike Gold and other leftists realized, the push for execution was only partially due to anti-Red hysteria; much of the bloodlust came from anti-immigrant and racist sentiment vociferously articulated by prosperous Northeasterners "flamed up into a last orgy of revenge" and "insane with fear and hatred of new America."[19] The new America that inspired such fear and hatred included not only Italians but Jews, the Irish, Slovakians, Hungarians, Latinos (Puerto Ricans and Chicanos, but also expatriate Mexican leftists), African Americans, Asians, poor white sharecroppers, and disaffected midwestern farmers—exactly the population that would form the rank and file of the various leftist movements. What these new Americans learned from the Sacco-Vanzetti case (if, indeed, they did not already know it) was that "old America," in conjunction with the American state, would not hesitate to amputate offending limbs, to officially sanction a nativist and racist violence that had been all too present in the discourse of the twenties but that had been limited to extralegal terror campaigns carried out by lynch mobs. The crash of 1929 and the Depression did, of course, intensify the pressures of poverty and unemployment on this sense of bodily otherness, but it would be a mistake to discount the symbolic importance—perhaps even the symbolic priority—of this violent moment of disunification and bodily disassociation.

Of crucial importance for the proletarian literature movement (just beginning to percolate in early pieces by Gold and others), the Sacco-Vanzetti execution also brought some of the first calls for a new kind of radical writing. If the body was going to be the site on which labor and capital (aligned with the state) struggled for dominance, then the body needed also to become the subject and object of the Left's future literary efforts. John Dos Passos, one of the most stalwart defenders of Sacco and Vanzetti, exhorted: "Sacco and Vanzetti must not have died in vain. We must have writing so fiery and accurate that it will sear through the pall of numb imbecility that we are again swaddled in after the few moments of sane awakening that followed the shock of the executions."[20]

Dos Passos himself made several attempts to produce this kind of writing in the late twenties and early thirties. Comprised of occasional pieces, political editorials, reportage, and lyric poetry, these attempts complement and stand in contrast to his extended efforts to reformulate the historical novel in the *USA Trilogy* (1930–36). Barely two months after the execution of Sacco and Vanzetti, he wrote one such piece, a lyric entitled "They Are Dead Now—" that responds to the (now ironic) battle cry that galvanized their defense, "They must not die!" In this poem, Dos Passos gauges the efficacy of battle cries, of words generally, and of literary texts specifically to achieve change by enacting an awakening. The poem begins:

> This isn't a poem
>
> This is two men in grey prison clothes.
> One man sits looking at the sick flesh of his hands—
> hands that haven't worked for seven years.
> Do you know how long a year is?
> Do you know how many hours there are in a day
> when a day is twenty-three hours on a cot in a cell,
> in a cell in a row of cells in a tier of rows of cells
> all empty with the choked emptiness of dreams?

It ends:

| Make a poem of that if you dare![21]

Though the tactic of antipoesis—vernacular poetry that denigrates its own art in favor of reality—became popular in the leftist poetry of the thirties and again in the sixties and seventies, Dos Passos's use of it is one of the earliest examples in American letters.[22] Antipoesis has the benefit of seeming to shift poetry away from the figural (metaphors and metonyms that inevitably accentuate the distance between signifiers and referents) to the material ground of ontology (where poems are the things they tell about). The poem, of course, cannot really move past representation—from personification into literal embodiment—just as Dos Passos cannot make Sacco and Vanzetti live by insisting on the present tense. Textual mediation presents a powerful limit to materialization, as René Magritte would convey two years later in his cynical reply to such fabrications, *Ceci n'est pas une pipe.* But whereas Magritte was content to puncture the idealizations of bourgeois realism with the acerbic wit of representational surrealism, Dos Passos's use of a congruent tactic depended on idealism as an entry point into something more radical, a negative dialectic where what was absent—Sacco and Vanzetti's lives, their literal bodies—could become the basis for a movement forward toward collective social action. In other words, antipoesis only seems to divide the ideal (dead letters) from the real (living men) and then only seems to privilege the latter. Used effectively, the tactic creates a recognition that the real is in abeyance, that the men are dead and that the movement failed to save them. Into this space of absence and failure, it substitutes its own presence, using its materiality (language) as a platform from which readers can build a movement that aims to realize the ideas of revolutionary socialism.

Dos Passos repeats this effort toward an inductive embodiment in the second half of his poem, where he works to transform the classic metaphor of inspiration (breathing in and thus being occupied by the spirit of another) to revolutionary purposes. Referring both to Sacco and Vanzetti's grisly electrocution and to their cremation, he writes:

| These two men were not afraid
| to smell rottenness
| in the air of Massachusetts
| so they are dead now and burned
| into the wind of Massachusetts.
| . . . .

Ten thousand towns have breathed them in
and stood up beside workbenches
dropped tools
flung plows out of the furrow
and shouted
into the fierce wind from Massachusetts.
In that shout's hoarse throat
is the rumble of millions of men marching in order
is the roar of one song in a thousand lingoes.[23]

Though less innovative and, I think, less successful than the tactic of antipoesis, this metaphor opens the poem significantly, saving it from becoming merely eulogistic. The idea, of course, is that as we move from smell to breath to shout to song, we similarly move from inspiration to collective struggle, initially through the body and then through song (which is a more physical and collective surrogate for the still-degraded poem).

As I noted, this set of figurative operations, the movement toward union and integrations through the body, would become central to proletarian literature in the thirties. Without a revolutionary movement with a strong cultural front, the bodily experiences of violence, hunger, racism, and exploitation would have remained private and disarticulated instances of deprivation, as they in fact appeared in the mainstream press well into the 1930s.[24] Communist Party publications, little magazines clustered around independent radicals, and a few left-liberal periodicals took it upon themselves to make visible the links between disparate acts of state violence and the different effects of economic exploitation—to read the body in pain as a collective and dialectical political text. Though such practices could turn fetishistic and could even objectify and commodify the poverty and violence they exposed, the tactical decision to use the proletarian body in this way can be defended on strategic grounds. This approach, however, has several weaknesses. Without an accompanying class analysis, it can be turned to many ends (not only to the cultural nationalism of the New Deal, but to the state capitalism of the Soviet Union and to the fascism of Spain, Italy, and Germany). It also, as Edward Dahlberg wrote caustically, invites not merely fetishism (where the body at least remains intact) but eucharism (where it nourishes a movement that supersedes it).[25]

This last problem has something to do with the proletarian literature movement's unqualified adoption of certain modernist principles—a practice that was, arguments to the contrary notwithstanding, both widespread and uncritical. Though movement writers by and large rejected the opacity and formalism of modernism, not to mention what they took to be its fundamental apoliticism, they tended to borrow (usually without acknowledgment) its stress on the materiality of the signifier as a way of meshing with the materiality of working-class life. This allowed them to make the same set of connections that Dos Passos negotiates in "They Are Dead Now—" between the physical body, the materialized body of the text, and the social body. Similarly, writers could use materialization to dwell on the connections (and differences) between the work of writing and manual labor. In the best instances, such connections were consciously examined, artfully tested, and expanded to include the larger class processes that determine (and are determined by) physical and discursive materialization. Too often, however, the writer and the proletariat appeared as such distinct and deeply essentialized class entities that materialization proceeded in an undialectical fashion, with any union seeming forced and wooden (as in the much decried "conversion endings"). Sometimes, despite their best intentions, authors were simply unable to materialize a cross-class union in their texts. This failure had the effect of turning the text back on itself, producing a highly self-conscious, if also self-critical, outpouring of ennui. Marcus Klein criticized this species of proletarian literature (thinking he was criticizing the whole genus) for dwelling phenomenologically on "experience." Klein argued that as in the modernist bildungsroman, "the hero of the new novel of the thirties was again and again an artist, and the issue was the shaping not of his politics but of his sensibility."[26] But another, more Marxist way of phrasing this same complaint would be to note the erasure of class at precisely the moment that many examples of proletarian literature turn to the proletariat.

INTERSECTIONS: DEATH, BIRTH, RAPE, AND MARCHING

One finds explorations of sensibility in remarkable places in the literature of the proletarian movement. They not only play a prominent role in the proletarian bildungsroman and in novels of middle-class questing, such as Waldo Frank's brooding *The Death and Birth of David Markand* and Lauren Gilillan's self-protective *I Went to Pit College;* they occur with striking frequency in cultural reviews, in discussions of the politics of cultural production, and in tendentious literary manifestos. Ironically, the more zealous and doctrinaire a work's stance is, the more prone the text is to collapse in on itself, since its author can be pulled toward obsessive self-criticism by his or her own obedience to the principles of workerism and political purity. One of the proletarian literature movement's best and most partisan writers, Meridel Le Sueur, fell into this pattern in a pair of texts she published in the *New Masses:* a manifesto, "The Fetish of Being Outside," that took issue with Horace Gregory's insistence on "objectivity" and "perspective"; and a piece of first-person reportage, "I Was Marching," that charted Le Sueur's integration into a strike.[27] Though both pieces advocate physical union with the proletariat for explicitly revolutionary purposes, both end up being most concerned with reformulating the artist's own emotional response to the world.[28]

Following the manifestos of Gold, Hicks, and others, Le Sueur begins "The Fetish of Being Outside" by arguing that in the present crisis, neither political nor aesthetic objectivity can provide a viable "point of view" (22): "You cannot be both on the barricades and objective at the same time. . . . you are likely to receive the bullets of both sides"(23). "The fetish of being outside" is, in her view, a "middle-class malady," at this point only a "hangover" from "nineteenth-century romanticism" and scientific Darwinism (22). What might have been tenable in the last century, when the bourgeoisie held uncontested hegemonic sway, is now chimerical, for "all this old ideology is dead" (23). Of its death, Le Sueur writes:

> Everyday I see people rotting, dying in this dead class like plants decaying in a foul soil. I feel I, myself, have rotted and suffered and threshed in this element of the bourgeois class like an organism in a decaying pool with the water evaporating about you and the natural elements of your body and desires in stress and your hungers decaying and rotting and stinking to high heaven. (23)

Such a hyperbolic use of the grotesque was not unusual in the pages of the *New Masses,* where "the dead body of bourgeois society," as Lenin put it, was frequently on display.[29] Just as leftist writers regularly drew the proletariat's ascendancy in corporeal terms, they repeatedly physicalized the bourgeoisie's present and eventual "decay." This passage is worth noting, however, for the sheer verbal aggressiveness of the trope, for the way Le Sueur sits paratactically on an image long after it has done its denotative work. Like Dos Passos, Le Sueur attempts to push language toward materialization. The breathless quality of the prose turns description into enactment, while the shift in voice from a confessional first person to an accusatory second broadens the claim. As "we" (she continually specifies the reader as a member of the bourgeoisie) watch Le Sueur rot on the page, we are to question our own bodily legitimacy, our ability to "stand" outside of the battle at hand.

While other manifestos merely call a for union with the revolutionary proletariat, Le Sueur's desire is to enact that transformation. Deconstructing the bourgeois fictions of objectivity—her first step—thus means decomposing the bourgeois body itself, since its boundedness, its very physical integrity as an object, stands in the way of "our" integration with the collective body. In this sense, "The Fetish of Being Outside" is not only argument and manifesto, it is an apologia—a public defection from putrescent bourgeois individualism.

> I do not care for the bourgeois "individual" that I am. I never have cared for it. I want to be integrated in a new and different way as an individual and this I feel can come only from a communal participation which reverses the feeling of a bourgeois writer. What will happen to him will not be special and precious, but will be the communal happening, what happens at all. I can no longer live without communal sensibility. I can no longer breathe in this maggoty individualism of a merchant society. I have never been able to breathe in it. That is why I hope to "belong" to a communal society, to be a cellular part of that and to be able to grow and function with others living in a whole. (22)

Le Sueur's desire to leave her "maggoty individualism" for a growing, functioning communal society is, of course, understandable. She sketches a relatively common feeling that is remarkably close to the process Vivian Gornick names "the romance of American Communism": "one merges by merging; whereby one experiences oneself through an idea of the self beyond the self and one becomes free, whole, and separate through the mysterious agency of a disciplinary context."[30] Striking, then, is not Le Sueur's desire for communalism but how close the form of this desire is to the ideals of nineteenth-century romanticism that Le Sueur has explicitly rejected. Indeed, Le Sueur and Gornick are far closer to Emerson than to Lenin in their approbation of a self beyond the self, a transcendental whole that alone can remove the quotation marks around the term *individual.* This recapitulation of romantic ideology might be another instance of the negative dialectic—of an attempt to build the new (communism) out of the rotting mess that is at hand (individualism)—were it not for Le Sueur's insistent focus on the (Emersonian) "I." As invested as she is in the "whole," this entity is surprisingly unrealized within the text. She imagines it as a sort of secret club to which she might "'belong'" (in quotes), or as an organic body within which she might have a cellular function, but never, in this manifesto, as something she must help build. Mostly, she conceives of it as a sensibility that she will acquire through the process of abdication.

Le Sueur describes the emergence of this sensibility through the trope of a difficult birth. Unlike those whose desire for objectivity will only produce abortive art, people who choose belonging and proceed with "full belief" will achieve regeneration. And the main product of this regeneration, aside from belonging, will be the capacity to supersede the sterile bourgeois point of view with a revolutionary new aesthetic vision.

> It is difficult [to leave the middle-class] because you are stepping into a dark chaotic passional world of another class, the proletariat, which is still perhaps unconscious of itself like a great body sleeping, stirring, strange and outside the calculated, expedient world of the bourgeoisie. It is a hard road to leave your class and you cannot leave it by pieces or parts; it is a birth and you have to be born whole out of it. In a complete new body. None of the old ideology is any good in it. The creative artist will create no new forms of art or literature for that new hour out of that darkness unless he is willing to go all the way, with full belief, into that darkness. (23)

There are a number of themes in this passage that resonate with other literary manifestoes of the thirties: an insistence upon the writer's alliance with the proletariat, the ominous and vague reference to a "new hour," and the reified counterposition of the proletariat's "dark passional world" with the bourgeoisie's "calculated, expedient world." Yet by linking these themes to a birth and a "new body," Le Sueur manages to layer in another message: The artist can have the clarity and artistic innovation of that new hour before it actually arrives if he is willing to "go all the way, with full belief." "Unconscious of itself," still "sleeping," the "great body" of the proletariat can nevertheless play surrogate for the revolution, begetting, in this instance, not communism but revolutionary creativity.

Several critics have argued that representations of such birthings are neither innocent nor incidental to the literature of the thirties. While "head boys," such as Mike Gold, famously looked for the "son of working-class parents" who "writes in jets of exasperated feeling," women authors, such as Le Sueur, used gendered language to theorize other, sometimes contradictory literary formulations.[31] "Their texts," writes Constance Coiner, "address the physiological and sexual experiences that shape women's lives—sexual initiation, pregnancy, childbirth, miscarriage, sterilization, battery, rape—at a time when these topics seldom appeared in literature."[32] Certainly, this is an apt observation. For Le Sueur, Tillie Olsen (*Yonnondio*), Agnes Smedley (*Daughter of the Earth*), and others, the themes of abortion, gender violence, sex, and birth provide highly productive figures for male dominance, bourgeois decadence, radical change, and aesthetic rejuvenation. Yet as even Gold's scandalously phallic quote surely shows, they were far from alone in using the body and its gendered functions to express both personal and political experiences. The "terms of the body" are not "repressed" in proletarian texts by men, as Paula Rabinowitz has argued;[33] they are exhibited at every conceivable opportunity (in texts by both men and women) in order to help materialize the text's ideological goals.

Moreover, the language of the body is not always as progressive and desublimating as Coiner and Rabinowitz seem to believe, even in texts by women. If we analyze the gender tropes in Le Sueur's birth scene, for instance, they reveal a structure that is not altogether dissimilar from the more obviously phallocentric missives of the period (and they reveal a meaning that is certainly no less onanistic). The middle-class artist is explicitly male, and the great proletarian body ("a dark chaotic passional world") is obviously female. Rabinowitz argues that Le Sueur's consistent feminization of the proletariat "inscribes female desire within history through a re-presentation of the masses as the maternal body."[34] Yet while the masses are clearly maternal, they have, in this passage at least, no apparent capacity for desire. In what is surely more like rape than blissful union, desire is clearly aligned with the male artist, who enters without consent and leaves without concern. The "birth" is similarly one-sided. The "new body" who can create "new forms of art" for that "new hour" is not the progeny of the intellectual and the proletariat but is instead the intellectual himself, born anew and whole out of this "darkness." Ultimately, what the passage reveals, then, is not the inscription of female desire but the more problematic articulation of an artistic sensibility retrofitted for the new dawn.

The trope of rape, it is worth noting here, appears frequently in proletarian texts. As one might expect, writers most often used it to express the persistence of male dominance within working-class communities (as in Tillie Olsen's *Yonnondio*), the perversity of bourgeois sexuality (as in James T. Farrell's *The Young Manhood of Studs Lonigan*), or the violence inherent in capitalism and the commodity form (as in Richard Wright's "Long Black Song"). Sometimes, however, writers, such as Le Sueur, reproduced this trope in an attempt to convey the intensity of the bodily effects of cross-class contact, even if, paradoxically, it figures the autogenesis of the radical writer as he moves through the body of the sleeping proletariat. The actors can also be reversed, with the proletariat, rendered very abstractly, playing the aggressor who forces himself on the sensitive writer. Melvin P. Levy, a leftist playwright and later the author of many notable screenplays, describes this process in some detail.

> The literature of the proletariat develops from two sources. First, of course, there is that which comes from the militant worker himself or from the intellectual who has cast his lot with him and bends his talent to the conscious expression of working-class problems and aims. But perhaps equally as important—is that writing which deals with the worker, and as a class; not because the writer *intends* it to, but because the powerful stirring of the proletariat has forced itself upon him without his will, impregnated him with the knowledge as a fact of that which he might not be willing to admit even to himself.[35]

Levy's description puts Dos Passos's trope of inspiration in more rapine terms, with the wind now materialized as the proletariat, who overwhelms and impregnates the writer with political knowledge. Unlike Dos Passos's lyric, however, there does not seem to be a precipitating event, no act of state violence or militant strike to initiate such bodily affect. This absence is telling, since it helps reveal that the violent propensity of the state (or elsewhere, of capital) has been relocated to the proletariat, who is the agent in this rape fantasy. The precipitating event, consequently, is the writer's own repressed knowledge of the class struggle. His guilt over this repression (which is also repressed) is displaced onto the proletariat, who becomes its agent of revenge, thus fulfilling the writer's fantasy of being swept into the sphere of political action "without his will." This is actually a passive-aggressive fantasy of volunterism, where desire is all that is needed to make a revolution, but where that desire is displaced onto the reified body of the working class, who acts on behalf of the writer's guilty conscience. In short, this is Dos Passos's revolutionary song without all the singing.

Readers of proletarian literature had fantasies of rape and sexual supplication as well, using them to order their emotional responses to the affective demands of literature that were meant to call them to action. One reader, Zelda Leknorf, wrote to the *New Masses* to describe her response to Le Sueur's 1934 piece of reportage "I Was Marching," a text that, in Leknorf's view, conveys "the futile role the intellectual plays in a vital crisis." To illustrate the psychological effects of Le Sueur's piece and Leknorf's new understanding of her own futility, Leknorf describes a recent encounter she had with workers as she "passed through" New Bedford during a strike.

> I started to walk among them but a self-consciousness about my clothes made me ashamed. The workers wore shabby clothes and their faces were pale and drawn. . . . The workers stared at my finely tailored suit and silk blouse and I was overcome with embarrassment. I ached eagerly to talk with them and be one of them but the resentment and suspicion expressed on their faces caused me to alienate myself. I walked back to the car slowly and a sense of dismal futility gnawed at me. I visualized myself melodramatically tearing off my clothes and offering myself to them to do with as they will.

This is less a fantasy of activation (inspiration) than a substitute for it. Whatever Leknorf imagines would happen once she "offered herself to them," it is not that the workers would hand her some old clothes and a placard and then make her march in their picket. She fantasizes a grand act of mortification for the sin of exploitation, for living in "flabby indolence" while workers are "pale and drawn." She imagines herself as a sacrifice on the altar of her own guilt. Within this fantasy, there is no God and thus no possibility for redemption and forgiveness. There is also, on a more terrestrial level, little possibility of moving forward from this fantasy of corporeal class-crossing to an actual relationship with demystified workers. Leknorf ends, thus, where she began: "The ghastly futility of our [intellectuals'] plight is overwhelming."[36]

The editors of the *New Masses* appended a response to Leknorf's letter, criticizing her for "indulg[ing] in hysterical self-flagellation." She "miss[ed] the whole point" of "I Was Marching," they continued, which "reflects very clearly the psychological transmutation of an isolated, self-enclosed, self-adulating ego, into a living throbbing, and, at least momentarily, integral part of a vast fighting revolutionary mass."[37] Their implication is that Leknorf should have gone through with her fantasy or at least with some less obviously libidinal version of it, that the proletariat is a living, throbbing mass and that one should transmute oneself into it. This is, admittedly, a fair gloss of Le Sueur's piece, which does, as the editors note, advocate integration—instead of flagellation—as an answer to intellectual alienation. But they miss the undercurrents of the text that Leknorf's fantasy makes apparent: integration can only be achieved through flagellation, through violence enacted on the body by the throbbing mass; and though the endpoint is explicitly integration, it is implicitly and more centrally self-realization.

Le Sueur begins "I Was Marching" much as she does "The Fetish of Being Outside," with a critique of the middle-class point of view.

> I have never been in a strike before. It is like looking at something that is happening for the first time and there are no thoughts and no words yet accrued to it. If you come from the middle class, words are likely to mean more than an event. You are likely to think about a thing, and the happening will be the size of a pin-point and the words around the happening very large, distorting it queerly. It's a case of "Remembrance of Things Past." . . . That is why it is hard for a person like myself and others to be in a strike.[38]

In this confessional opening, Le Sueur introduces the text's main theme: the need for a new mode of comprehension. If there are no words yet accrued to the strike (a cut against mainstream news coverage) and if words mean more than an event (if middle-class language is dematerialized and signifiers sit a long way from their referents), then this particular event is both invisible and incomprehensible to the middle-class writer. Bereft of communal knowledge, the intellectual searches for words but gains only distortion. Le Sueur's linkage of this verbal distortion to Proust is not incidental; the story is as much about writing as it is about striking. A favorite touchstone for proletarian writers as they debated the relative merits of the bourgeois tradition, Proust frequently stands for a generalized middle-class literary response to modernity. In this case, "remembrance" signals the twin sins of bourgeois nostalgia and intellectual inaction. Attempting a cognitive wholeness by retrospectively re-membering an event prevents the writer from attaining the revolutionary wholeness of the present collective action. What we might otherwise call internality is, in effect, a defense mechanism that keeps the writer from adequately attending to the experience at hand. According to Le Sueur, such a tactic is now bound to fail, since "in a crisis the word falls away and the skeleton of the action shows in terrific movement" (159). The only way to represent movement is to be inside of it, writing actively, subjectively, and from the "body."

Le Sueur's narrator is, however, initially apprehensive about being inside of the crisis, hesitating repeatedly at the door of the strike head-quarters. "The truth is I was afraid. Not of the physical danger at all, but an awful fright of mixing, of losing myself, of being unknown and lost" (160). Yet the process of being born anew requires just such a loss of self and just such an act of personal dis-integration. When she does eventually enter the strike headquarters, "with sweat breaking out on my body," she experiences a series of mortifications that disas-sociate her identity from her individuality. A woman who "didn't pay any special attention to me as an individual" leads her into a "kitchen organized like a factory," where she is "put to pouring coffee." "At first I look at the men's faces, and then I don't look any more. It seems I am pouring coffee for the same tense dirty sweating face, the same body, the same blue shirt and overalls. Hours go by, the heat is terrific. I am not tired. I am not hot. I am pouring coffee. I am swung into the most intense and natural organization I have ever felt. I know every-thing that is going on. These things become of great matter to me" (164).

Le Sueur's language in this passage is as precise as Ernest Heming-way's, one of her most obvious influences. Like him, she writes against the Proustian disassociation of sensibility that uses language as a mere bridge between cognition and action, two realms that it finds inescapably distant. Like Hemingway, she sees this gap but tries to make language a more active, connecting device. Hence, when she writes, "These things become of great matter to me," she invokes a materialization of experi-ence that should be transferable to the reader. This also lies behind her use of parataxis, the repetition in the phrase "the same tense dirty sweat-ing face, the same body, the same blue shirt and overalls." These repeti-tions not only represent the factorylike process of the cafeteria, they present this process as one that inheres in the cafeteria's linguistic after-life.

This method is also close to T. S. Eliot's objective correlative, an affiliation between proletarian literature and modernism that was recog-nized (and indeed applauded), though Eliot's name was tactfully omit-ted from the discussion. Compare, for example, Joseph Freeman's definition of what is best about proletarian literature: "The best art deals with specific experience which arouses specific emotion in specific peo-ple at a specific moment in a specific locale, in such a way that other

people who have had similar experiences in other places and times recognize it as their own."³⁹ Freeman's most significant revisions to Eliot's
objective correlative entail his radical narrowing of its efficacy from the
universal to the specific and his substitution of experience for Eliot's
objects, situations, and events. Freeman's reiteration of the word *specific*
is, I think, code for class specificity, just as his use of experience seems
aimed at refashioning the correlative into a tool for the creation of class
consciousness. Presumably, what one recognizes through what we might
now call the "subjective correlative" is one's similar exploitation under
the regime of capitalism, a recognition that puts Eliot's emphasis on sensory experience on more collective somatic terrain.

But Freeman's adaptation of Eliot's objective correlative only begins
to describe Le Sueur's efforts to radicalize this principle. Both Eliot and
Freeman presumed that the functionality of the correlative depends on
some preexisting characteristic in the reader. Eliot, as I argued in chapter 5, believed that people have an inherent set of sensory responses to
stimuli. This makes emotion manageable. Freemen's translation of this
precept from biological essentialism to the subjective realm of "similar
experiences" was motivated by other reasons—among which was probably his desire not to stray from the economic essentialism of the Communist Party's platform in this period. In other words, for Freeman, the
correlative functions to connect specific experience to specific experience only because these experiences share a common point of origin in
the meta-experience of exploitation.

But what about literature that describes an experience a reader has
not had, Le Sueur's stated goal? As she explains in her preface (included
only with the original *New Masses* publication of "I Was Marching"), she
begins by addressing "the reaction of many artists, writers and middle
class to the strike here": "they felt frightened, timid, inferior."⁴⁰ Thus she
assumes a narrative persona who is far more politically naive than Le
Sueur could have been in 1934. But after addressing this common experience, she moves to a more exemplative and pedagogical stance, using
language to make the sensibility it affects. The text becomes the shared
experience, which obviates the need to rely on a revolutionary proletariat—or even a revolutionary intelligentsia—that, in contrast, needs to
be summoned. That is why, to return to "I Was Marching," the narrator's
brief experience of anonymity, of being unknown and of serving "the
same body," is an essential prerequisite to her insertion in that body. The
expectation of Le Sueur's contemporary reader, given the eighty-year
history of the social exposé, is that these "sweaty faces" will either be indi-

vidualized or fetishized. But the experiences of the factory, the mass strike, and this text are subjected to neither of these methods. For Le Sueur, the experience is one of collectivism.

But crucially—and this is where Leknorf's hysteria proves insightful—the experience of collectivity requires not only the initiating experience of anonymity but the shared experience of violence enacted on the body. Swept into action after a group of strikers are killed or wounded by the police, the narrator recounts:

> At first I felt frightened, the close black area of the barn, the blood, the heavy moment, the sense of myself lost, gone. But I couldn't have turned away now. A woman clung to my hand. I was pressed against the body of another. If you are to understand anything you must understand it in the muscular event, in actions we have not been trained for. Something broke all my surfaces in something that was beyond horror and I was dabbing alcohol on the gaping wounds that buckshot makes, hanging open like crying mouths. Buckshot wounds splay in the body and then swell like a blow. Ness, who died, had thirty-eight slugs in his body, in the chest and in the back. (166)

This is a fantasy neither of rape nor of sexual supplication, and it would be a mistake to conflate the narrator's earnest participation with Leknorf's defeatism. Still, Leknorf's fantasy of self-immolation is not altogether different from Le Sueur's assertion that "something"—the press of bodies and wounds experienced by others—broke all her surfaces. In both cases, the writers posit a system of corporeality that allows them to repudiate their class complicity by vicariously experiencing proletarian pain. In Le Sueur's case, of course, the participation is not vicarious, even if the rupture of surfaces is. Because of this difference, the experience of rupture can be described through metaphor rather than fantasy. Also, and this is Le Sueur's central point, the experience is much more productive, aligning the narrator not with middle-class words (or a sense of futility—which, for Le Sueur, is the same thing) but with proletarian "gaping wounds" that hang "open like crying mouths." These mouths are an alternative location for the authorial function, their cries absolutely unmediated by Proustian remembrance or even language in a conventional sense. They communicate (within) the muscular event through what Le Sueur describes in "Fetish" as "communal sensibility."

The question is, can these crying mouths similarly incorporate the reader into this communal sensibility? We are voyeurs as well. Can Le

Sueur's prose break our surfaces? Unless our reactions are as performative as Leknorf's (and I do not discount the possibility), we are liable to remain where Le Sueur found us: on the outside of this text. But just because corporealization has its limits is, of course, no reason not to push the tactic in hope of surpassing them. This is what Le Sueur does in the two concluding paragraphs of "I Was Marching," where she not only revisits the image of crying mouths but also uses a careful manipulation of rhythm and diction to linguistically replicate the feeling of marching—to materialize communal movement.

> I was marching with a million hands, movements, faces, and my own movement was repeating again and again, making a new movement from these many gestures, the walking, falling back, the open mouth crying, the nostrils stretched apart, the raised hand, the blow falling, and the outstretched hand drawing me in.
>
> I felt my legs straighten. I felt my feet join in that strange shuffle of thousands of bodies moving with direction, of thousands of feet, and my own breath with the gigantic breath. As if an electric charge had passed through me, my hair stood on end, I was marching. (171)

Though this ending does achieve what the editors of the *New Masses* claim—showing the narrator as part of a "vast fighting revolutionary mass"—it has not always met with approval, even from readers who share Le Sueur's political affinities. Constance Coiner, for instance, contrasts the proliferation of the narrative "I" in these two paragraphs with Le Sueur's later, more dialogic prose. Coiner observes that whereas the narrative voice in *The Girl* (Le Sueur's 1930s novel extensively revised and published in 1978) disturbs any notion of individual subjectivity, " 'I Was Marching' at once lauds a subsuming of the individual by the collective and affirms individual subjectivity and perception."[41] This is an apt point; it cuts directly to the central contradiction within Le Sueur's early work (and, as I have been suggesting, within the work of others in the proletarian literature movement). But to Le Sueur (or at least to the Le Sueur of 1934), the relation between the individual and the collective was not as contradictory as Coiner's criticism suggests. Indeed, Le Sueur finds the relationship constitutive: the individual can only have perception after he or she has been subsumed by the collective. When Le Sueur reaches past conventional tropes (and past even the use of rhythm and sound) and incorporates the relatively new technique of Eisensteinian montage (giving us disarticulated "gestures" that come together to make "a new movement"), she may well be attempting to craft something like collective perception. The moving, marching, revolutionary body creates its own muscular subjectivity. The continued presence of the "I" as an organizing point of narration is, especially in light of Le Sueur's experimental novel, an Emersonian atavism. But it does not, in and of itself, disable Le Sueur's move toward subsumption.

The more fundamental problem lies not with the "I" but with the surrounding collectivity. Like the sleeping body in "Fetish," the marching workers seem to be oddly unaware of the motive force drawing them forward. Perhaps the problem is that Le Sueur does not know where to locate this awareness. The body parts that work to constellate a collective sensibility do not have a head; their experience must be transduced by the narrator. When Eisenstein presents a raised hand or marching feet, these shots are brought together only proximately by the eye of the camera. The underlying structural synthesis depends on a Marxist dialectic that forms the causal relation within a narrative of historical materialism. This narrative is not altogether missing from "I Was Marching," since we know the workers march in protest and defiance of police brutality. But the class relations of that narrative are too vaguely explored to support the kind of radical textuality Le Sueur wants to employ. When the crying mouths who speak the proletarian body reappear triumphantly at the text's conclusion, they are too disarticulated—from history, from the specific struggle, and even from each other—to communicate their demands. The only message we clearly hear is Le Sueur's celebration of her middle-class defection and the origins of her radical sensibility.

This is not, of course, an inconsequential message. When Klein argues that experience and sensibility are the two organizing themes of proletarian literature, his critique is only halfhearted. It is possible, as Caren Irr has shown, to update Klein's language as a way of valuing the work of Le Sueur and other writers of reportage. In a brief discussion of "I Was Marching," Irr argues that "[r]eportage . . . offered an intermediate zone between the subjective and the objective."[42] It "recaptures the objective"—which is to say, it makes the objective possible within partisan writing—"by making the writer one object among many" and by "making the conditions of writing one of the objects of writing." Reportage produces, then, a "situated subject" whose narration does not reify its working-class objects, since this narration is also understood to be object to economic and social forces. The writer's mode of perception is thus, like any labor process, ultimately determined by the mode of production. However ideal this is in theory, Le Sueur's text underscores several problems facing "situatedness" in practice. The "emphasis on the self-conscious writing subject" that Irr argues "is characteristic of left-wing reportage" often does more to situate its subject than to situate its object.[43] Objectifying writing is not, in other words, the same as subjectifying the working class, who, on the contrary, remain in the object world in part to receive the recently objectified writer. Though writing is work and the conditions of its production are integral to the process of meaning making, writing is not the same kind of work as factory labor or even as marching. The materialization of language in proletarian literature can either foreground this difference or cover for it. If it does the latter, writing tends to allegorize labor, which does indeed situate the writer, but once again at the expense of reifying labor.

COLLECTIVE BODIES

The overlapping strategies of mediation, embodiment, and situatedness that I have thus far explored with regard to proletarian literature do not solve the various problems that trouble representations of the working class under capitalism. These problems are, as I have argued, both persistent and endemic. They influence even the most radical attempts to use culture to remediate the inequities of class. Because of this, these attempts need to be critiqued, particularly from the left. To its credit, the proletarian culture movement began this process itself, as writers and critics explicitly and implicitly evaluated each other's work. Hence the movement's greatest contribution to a left critique of culture lies in its dialectical process of creation and self-criticism, rather than in any one particular tactic it discovered or deployed. The critical battles that raged within and between the *New Masses* and the *Partisan Review*—which often specifically considered the problem of amalgamation and cross-class integration—cannot, therefore, be dismissed as petty power struggles, frantic attempts to follow the Soviet line, or mean-spirited personal attacks (though evidence of all these approaches exists).[44] Taken together, they constitute a consistent attempt to formulate a radical theory of literary praxis that brings the writer and the working class together under the sign of revolutionary struggle.

Freeman, Hicks, Gold, and others well understood that crafting a literature of praxis that avoided reification might well entail developing new literary forms. Formal experimentation, Michael Denning notes, proliferated particularly in 1934–35, with the rise of "'the proletariat avant-garde' as young communist writers and artists produced a wave of little magazines and exhibitions." This avant-garde movement was brought about, in Denning's estimation, by a surge of revolutionary struggle in 1933–34 that "culminated in a wave of strikes following the National Recovery Act, including the left-led general strikes of 1934 in Toledo, Minneapolis, and San Francisco."[45] Le Sueur's "I Was Marching" it is worth noting, emerged from the Minneapolis strike and is just one instance of a writer reaching for the new technique of reportage to capture wide-scale radical actions. Leftist writers also employed formal experimentation in this period because of a shift in Communist Party doctrine. Though the ultraleftist policies of the Soviet Union's "Third Period" did not formally end until the Popular Front of 1935, a series of conferences and theoretical statements in 1932 and 1933 promoted greater literary heterogeneity and broke down some of the implicit barriers to employing modernist formal techniques.[46] From January 1934 until September 1935, the U.S. Communist Party promoted what we might call (following the language circulating in the *New Masses*) a "United Front" policy.[47] Though this terminology was subsequently folded into the lexicon of the Popular Front, the policies of the party during this period were quite different. Within the political sphere, the party persisted in foregrounding a revolutionary socialist critique of capitalism, regularly taking aim at the New Deal as simply capitalism with a kinder face. At the same time, the party began, if not always successfully, to shed some of its most sectarian baggage. On the cultural front, it continued to encourage working-class writers and activists (heavily promoting its John Reed Clubs, where more experienced writers and artists taught methods to working-class students) and began valuing more heterogeneous literary forms. Simultaneously, it remained committed to revolutionary cultural praxis. Though it is impossible to quantify influence, these policies certainly nurtured writers within the proletarian avant-garde as they worked to bring culture into the revolutionary upsurge.

In addition to reportage, which, by any measure, reached its height of influence during this period, writers in the proletarian avant-garde explored and developed the formal possibilities of the "collective novel." As Barbara Foley notes in her chapter on this form (far and away the best analysis of the collective novel in the U.S. context), the collective novel developed from multiple antecedents. It reflected, in part, the influence of Soviet and European attempts to use multiple protagonists, discontinuous plotlines, and the inclusion of historical documents to both embody and rupture the mimetic effect of traditional realism. But it drew most centrally from the work of John Dos Passos. In *Manhattan Transfer* (1925), he first experimented with multiple protagonists, naturalistic settings, and verbal expressionism. In the *U.S.A. Trilogy* (1930–36), he combined these elements with documentary "Newsreels," historical biographies, and the autobiographical "Camera Eye" to multiply reflect class struggle.[48] During the United Front period, a number of other novelists—many of whom were closer to the Communist Party than Dos Passos—turned to the form to escape from the individualism of single protagonist novels and the internality of the psychological focus of bourgeois realism. In April 1934, Granville Hicks included a discussion of the collective novel as one of the four forms available to proletarian writers. Though his structural analysis has now been superseded (by Foley's), the fact of its occurrence in this period testifies to the form's acceptance within the movement. Indeed, Hicks went so far as to wonder whether "the collective novel will be the novel of the future."[49]

According to Foley, the three main features of the collective novel—its "treatment of the group as a phenomena greater than . . . the sum of the individuals who constitute it," its "frequent use of experimental devices to break up the narrative and rupture the illusion of seamless transparency," and its "direct documentary links with the reader"[50]—all work together to move the novel away from the precepts of bourgeois culture. Not only does its focus on the group dispense with the conventional individuation of the traditional novel; its use of multiple plotlines forces the reader to find causal links outside of individual motivation. Foley explains that "[o]nly when the text's protagonist is construed as a trans-individual entity does the trajectory of the narrative gain coherence" (408) and that it gains coherence, moreover, only by virtue of the reader's participation, as a "dialectician," in the meaning-making process (441). Its twin insistences on multiplicity and readerly process suggest that this form would be ideally suited to avoid reifying the proletariat. Unlike reportage, the collective novel imagines a situated reader, rather than a situated writer, as the solution to the problem of class-specific representation. It does not, like Le Sueur, posit one proletarian body to which the writer must find entry. It constellates a group of classed characters whose coherence as the proletariat becomes, in some sense, the plot of the narrative. Foley (402) argues that the reader is brought into this process as an interpretive agent who should duplicate ideationally what the characters do in action—bringing together the strands of the narrative into a vision of social totality.

For the purposes of this discussion, however, it is once again worth investigating the differences between the form's theoretical possibilities and its textual limitations. What, in particular, galvanizes the working-class characters into the proletariat? What tropes tie this process to read-erly investment? In Foley's assessment of the politics of the collective novels she analyzes (as opposed to the politics of the form itself), she is rather critical. Drawing attention to precisely this issue of collective embodiment, she concludes that "Third-Period texts . . . articulate either a productive forces determinism or a romantic workerism that obscures various facets of the political process by which militant workers will con-stitute not simply a collective, but a revolutionary agent."[51] Agency, in other words, is missing from exactly the point—textually and histori-cally—where it should be in evidence: the point of revolutionary action. Foley's diagnosis of this problem relates to her general thesis: that we can trace political and formal textual flaws back to such doctrinal errors as productive forces determinism and workerism. I think these flaws are less localized and more related to overarching problems with class rep-resentation; and once again, I think the mediating entity of the body—here writ collectively—is where these flaws inhere.

William Rollins's *The Shadow Before* can serve as one of a number of possible examples of this. Written in 1934 and received with almost uni-versal praise, it revisits the events of the Gastonia Strike in North Car-olina, which had previously formed the basis of Mary Heaton Vorst's *Strike!* (1930), Fielding Burke's *Call Home the Heart* (1932), Myra Page's *Gathering Storm* (1932), and Grace Lumpkin's *To Make My Bread* (1932). Rollins, however, resituates these actions to a mill town in New England and translates their multiracial dynamics into a multiethnic struggle. Like Vorst, he includes actual characters in a barely fictionalized form. But he also inserts newspaper headlines, actual trial testimony, and other techniques of defamiliarization. These include, most notably, the inter-ruptions of "*THUMP* THROB; *THUMP* THROB" in several key factory scenes, "reminding the reader," Foley observes, "of the industrial process over which bosses and workers are warring."[52] Most important, Rollins widens his fictional lens so that it not only follows the actions and emo-tions of the strikers but includes Communist organizers, mill owners and managers, their disaffected wives and children, scab workers, and cor-rupt police officers and town officials. The combination of these tech-niques and this use of a collective protagonist produces, in Mary Heaton Vorst's estimation, a novel of great power and verisimilitude: "Everyone who is interested in the new forms of writing and the labor movement should read this exciting book and see how much closer to the truth the author has gone than have any of his predecessors."[53] The truth, Vorst indicates, is collective rather than individual, and it inheres not in specific locations or in fealty to particular events but in the novel's ability to grasp the movement of multiple actors as they come together in struggle. "The primary merit of *Parched Earth* and *Shadow Before,*" writes Philip Rahv, "lies in the fact that their authors are actually conscious of the *material* reality of art and character. And it is precisely this consciousness of the economic factor as the leading factor in the determination of life under capitalism that makes it possible for them not merely to state the mounting contradiction between the classes, but also to resolve it."[54]

Yet is this really why these characters come together and behave as they do? Economic forces may prompt the workers to act in unison (though Rollins is not spontanist—his workers need outside organization), but these forces hardly explain why Ramon Vieira, a working-class immigrant, sides with the mill owners while Mickey Bonner, a factory worker and Vieira's sometime girlfriend, sides with the strikers. Economic forces help explain why Mr. Thayer, a plant manager, is so often absent from his home and family, but not why his wife is an alcoholic and a sex addict or why his daughter Marjorie is, in Foley's words, "repressed and paranoid."[55] Similarly, economic forces may set the stage for the mill owner's son, Harry Baumann, to defect to the revolutionary working class, but they hardly begin to explain why his actions—fitful, violent, and self-destructive—take their eventual shape. Perhaps this is to say, merely, that the connections between characters must have motives that include more than class struggle if the novel is to avoid simplistic mechanism. However "experimental," the collective novel still must make recourse to traditional methods of character motivation in order to achieve what Vorst calls its "truth."

In this case, Rollins relies heavily on redundancies (Foley's term) and commonalities within these characters' sexual desires and within the general libidinal landscape of this fictional town. Readers have long noted that Rollins uses sex—Mrs. Thayer's rapacity and Henry Baumann's rape of Marjorie Thayer—to expose what Foley calls the "emotional psychopathology of bourgeois life."[56] If these were the only two instances of sex in *The Shadow Before,* this interpretation might be adequate. But any catalog of sex and sexuality in the novel would surely need to include a discussion of the sexual behaviors of all the main characters and how these behaviors are linked to class politics.

Mickey's couplings, for instance, reflect her changing politics and the different attitudes of the male characters toward sex. When the novel

opens, she is desperate to continue a relationship with Ramon, forthrightly offering to go with him to "the cave" (a symbolic site of libidinal
completion in this novel) or even to meet him in the woods for a briefer
tryst. These offerings do not succeed in securing his long-term affections, as he moves increasingly into the camp of the mill owners. Later,
when Mickey senses that (the now radicalized) Henry is attracted to her,
she waits for this cross-class amalgamation with growing frustration over
his (overtly symbolic) inaction: "[A]fter dinner they sat around talking
about the strike and theory and deviations, Harry eagerly talking; while
Mickey for the most part listened sympathetically. But he hadn't ever
made a pass at her; *not one measly pass*" (317). Harry is all talk, both politically and sexually. When he finally does address Mickey, "with repressed
excitement in his eyes" (321), she mistakes this excitement for sexual
desire and offers to "take a little walk" (322). Yet once in "the cave"
(322), Harry again wants to talk politics. What he confesses, through his
"repressed tone," is his desire to "do something for the strike" (322)
rather than to do something with her (though the latter eventually happens at another point in the narrative). The culmination of this scene
comes when he confesses his desire to burn his father's mill.

> But now he was talking, excited broken phrases, that fell unbearably on
> her in the darkness, sickening her; jabbing senseless words . . . that sud-
> denly became a scene: a great familiar building, black windows glowing,
> living, with fire, fire spurting above the roofs, writing, voluptuously
> blackandyellow, lifting into the night sky, *"making me one with you people,"*
> poor, a criminal like Marvin and maybe me sometime, *"for you,"* for us,
> making him come down to my level, want to—.
> "No, no, Harry!" (323–24; ellipsis in original)

Mickey has good reason for resisting Harry's advance. The sexualized
terms of his political desires—both to violate (with phrases that "fell
unbearably" and "jabbed senseless words") and to amalgamate (*"making
me one with you people"*)—are objectifying, condescending, and politically
egotistic. Mickey recognizes this and decides to tell Ramon of Harry's
plot, both so that Ramon will stop Harry and out of a vague hope that she
and Ramon can resume their relationship. Adapting Harry's conflation
of politics and sex, she asks Ramon to "meet me at the cave tonight"
(344), where they have sex and she reveals Harry's secret plan. After
Harry's plan fails (due as much to his own ineptitude as to Ramon's
intervention), he kills himself in the same cave, either symbolizing the

eventual dissolution of the bourgeoisie or, less telescopically, culminating the theme of his impotence.

Ramon, for his part, serves as an equally unadmirable figure of indiscriminate potency. He begins the novel in a relationship with Mickey; flirts (and perhaps couples) with Miss Waters, Mr. Thayer's secretary; takes up with another factory worker, Maria Diez, after Mickey joins the strikers; and has a brief set of encounters with the sex-starved Mrs. Thayer. Indeed, Ramon is on his way to meet Mrs. Thayer when he is seduced into the cave by Mickey, who then tells him of Harry's plot. He subsequently brushes Mrs. Thayer off, which is part of the reason she commits suicide. Ramon's promiscuity, in brief, far surpasses Mrs. Thayer's. If her desire bespeaks the psychopathology of bourgeois life, his signals something about the psychopathology of (some part of) the proletariat. Though he is virile, takes action, and works hard to gain what he can by playing the capitalist's game, his libido is too diffuse. Unchanneled, unregulated, and undisciplined, he will prove a dead end in the working-class struggle. Even if he achieves the spot in middle management he so anxiously desires, this personal agency does not, Rollins insists, put him in harmony with the historical agency of his class.

Rollins contrasts Harry's impotence and Ramon's promiscuity with the disciplined asceticism of Larry Marvin, the Communist Party organizer. Larry rides into town on a motorcycle, quickly gets a job in the mill, and immediately sets about organizing the workers. What this constitutes, at least at first, is reforming their profligate ways. In addition to the twisted affairs of Ramon, Harry, Mickey, and the Thayers, the town is overrun with liquor, fighting, and bizarre scenes of sexuality. (In the most bizarre, Stella, a young striker, is caught handing out circulars and is punished, corporally and in public, by her father, under the orders of a judge: "And tense, breathless, they all watched the big man sit down and pull the pretty girl across his knees. He drew back his huge paw, brought it down with a thud. . . . Judge Simonski was leaning across his bench, burning eyes on the prostrate girl. 'Harder!' he said. 'She must be taught a lesson,' he added hoarsely" [181].) Larry's solution to these societal ills is to insist that the alcoholics "cut out the liquor" (123) and that the strikers take up arms to guard each other from attack. All the while, Larry remains chaste, dedicated, and often supremely isolated. His role is, as Foley notes, to be a mentoring character and to step offstage before the book's end.[57] But what he must teach the workers is sublimation rather than simply class struggle. They already understand their exploitation, and they are graphic participants in scenes of their victimization. Their response, however, is to get drunk, to get into fights, and to either soothe themselves with casual sex or use sex to enable fantasies of class mobility. They suffer from false consciousness, to be sure; in the more moralistic strike novels of the 1890s, the walking delegate would be preaching sobriety and rectitude in the face of their exploitation. But this is not what Larry teaches them. He teaches them to channel, rather than to disown, their libidinous desires, to channel them into political activity—not impotently, like Harry, but collectively into the union and the revolutionary struggle.

Mickey embodies this lesson at the text's conclusion. The strike has ended (badly for the workers), and Larry and his co-organizers have been sentenced to long jail terms on fabricated charges. In a rambling internal monologue, Mickey reveals that she is pregnant: "She was sure of it, for all the girls said, because she never before had been a day late. It must have been Ramon, too, since Harry took precautions after the first day; but she wasn't thinking of that. She whispered: 'eh, kid?' again, and giggled. She supposed she ought to get herself a husband . . . Alfonso was always after her—" (387; ellipsis in original). Yet after she finds a note from Larry ("keep a stiff upper lip . . . it's always darkest before the dawn" [388]), she decides to name the baby Larry or Nikolai Lenin and to "stick it out and lick them" (389). The narrative ends with Mickey blending into anonymous third-person narration (in all capital letters) as she works in the factory while planning her future: "THE GIRL WITH AUBURN HAIR MOVES FINGERS SNAPPING ONE OFF AND BRUSHING IT BACK" (389).

In Foley's estimation, this last narratological shift is one of the text's political high points, since it testifies to Mickey's emergence as "a strong and determined strike leader" and reminds readers that as part of "the documentary apparatus, . . . Mickey is in some sense a real historical agent."[58] Unlike Harry and Mrs. Thayer's suicides, which reflect productive forces determinism (which is to say, are too optimistic in giving us bourgeois self-destruction), this ending is how the collective novel makes meaning, how it resolves contradiction in favor of collective agency. But what are we to do with Mickey's pregnancy, Ramon's patrimony, and Larry's letter? Rollins's shift to third person, coming after these events, is meaningful in a different manner than Foley imagines, since the real conclusion comes through the triangulation of Mickey, Ramon, and Larry that produces their shared progeny—an imagined American Lenin. This child (a boy, Mickey presumes) will carry forward his biological father's potency and his ideological father's discipline. Mickey drifts into third-person anonymity, then, not because she is now a historical agent but because she has found her clear role as that agent's vessel. She has not become more political, less focused on her sexuality, or even more dedicated to the union (since she was already very dedicated). But her sexuality has finally been channeled into a maternal and hence more productive direction. Given this conclusion and the sexual thematics throughout the narrative, it is clear that this novel does indeed, like other collective novels, suffer from determinism—and it suffers from it throughout. But this determinism does not derive only from productive forces, which alone do not account for the characters' behavior and the novel's plot. It comes also from reproductive forces, whose assertions are equally powerful. Mapping biological processes onto political programs within an overarching heteronormative sexual structure, reproductive forces allow the novel to create a "union" and to augur a revolutionary future.

Such "sexual/textual politics," to borrow Toril Moi's phrase,[59] are evident in another sort of collective narrative, one that has received far less attention than the single-author collective novels. Prompted, perhaps, by the Communist Party's John Reed Clubs, which encouraged workers to write creatively about their labor conditions, "group[s] of anonymous workers and usually one published author . . . met together," explains Paula Rabinowitz, "to create a story or novel."[60] As Rabinowitz notes, these texts were then either shared informally or, like "Stockyard Stella" (the only collectively written narrative from this era that is readily available), serialized in the left press. Hence, unlike collective novels, which achieve their collectivity textually through interactions between multiple protagonists, collectively written texts move from collective authorship to collective readership regardless of their formal attributes. While this collective process does not preclude formal experimentation, collectively written texts do tend to be formally conservative, perhaps because there is no impetus to use form to compensate for the narrative's more typical single authorship and the novel's traditional conditions of isolated readership. In one sense, we might say that the politics of the form lie largely outside of the text itself—in whatever interactions the authors had while writing and in whatever responses readers or groups of readers had while reading and discussing the text. Nevertheless, the material form must—as always—be the vehicle for the text's meaning. Thus the conventionality of this form and the sexual politics of the plot still effect the radicalism of the narrative's message.

In "Stockyard Stella," for instance, the form "relies on the conventions of melodrama," and the plot is heteronormative. This may mean, as Rabinowitz argues, that "the group of women workers who produced 'Stockyard Stella' for *Working Woman* clearly understood that they were writing a 'proletarian love story' because they could not imagine a literature that did not narrate desire." But it does not mean, as Rabinowitz also claims, that this proletarian love story "provided a means for transcending the gender and class divisions within the left."[61] Desire is clearly used as a vehicle to promote collective class actions, but in a manner that not only ascribes to traditional gender relations but reinscribes these relations broadly at the figural level. Such a story could, no doubt, have been written by an individual man or woman, but the gendered and collective conditions of this story's production add weight to the romantic ideology it communicates to its female audience; that is, the fact of its collective authorship invokes a communal authority that lies behind the vision of collective achievement through romantic desire. While Rabinowitz's point throughout her book *Labor and Desire* is that women's revolutionary fiction always uses desire to craft radical unity, "Stockyard Stella" shows that, at least in this case, desire limits the political scope of that unity. Using romantic desire as an entry point for class consciousness, "Stockyard Stella" ends up positing romantic fulfillment as the culmination of collective struggle.

We first meet Stella on her way to the packinghouse where she works canning meat for fourteen dollars a week. Though Stella is not described, the work is described with details that hearken back to Upton Sinclair's *The Jungle* and that immediately establish this text's authority to speak for the working class. Work is tolerable, however, since Stella's fiancé, Eddie, also works there, moving cans from the packing tables to the warehouse. Eddie dreams of getting rich "so he could get [Stella] a car and nice clothes and a home of her own some day," away from "the smell of the yards." But Stella loves Eddie even without these things, since he works hard and is honest. They plan to marry, but "right now he had to support his parents and two young brothers still in school."[62] Matrimony is further deferred after Eddie is fired for telling the "fat, sweaty" foreman to keep his hands off Stella, an act of harassment the foreman repeats every time he yells at the women workers to speed up. Stella insists that the foreman "had no right to fire" Eddie and that there must be some recourse, but Eddie wants to "hop a freighter to South St. Paul" and try his luck in the stockyards there.[63]

Yet if sexual harassment coupled with the economic conditions of exploitation stand in the way of Stella and Eddie's union, we learn in the second installment that they do not have to "take it lying down." The next morning, while Eddie gets nowhere with the company representative (a man "fat enough to give birth to a set of dishes full of roast beef"), Stella goes to work and there discovers a "mysterious pink paper lying on the locker floor." This turns out to be the "Armour Young Worker," a circular put out by the Young Communist League, who, as the title implies, defends young love in the class struggle.[64] Inspired by the pamphlet, Stella invites a group of workers to her house, including "Dick, who was one of the most popular men in the department"—and who, we later learn, is also a Communist. At the meeting, Eddie is initially "lifeless."

> [He] didn't put his arms around [Stella] the way he used to. Could it be that losing his job made him feel beaten? Did he think perhaps she wouldn't like him so much now? Or was her mother frightening him away? Stella slipped her hand into his. He squeezed it so tightly that he hurt her, and then heaved a deep sigh. No words could have expressed more discouragement than this sigh of a discouraged, jobless man who didn't feel he deserved to be loved, because he couldn't support his girl.

Dick, however, manages to buoy Eddie and to inspire him to fight, since Dick "always stood up for the workers."[65] Eddie, too, stands up, at a key moment during the concluding episode, when Stella and a group of workers return from the superintendent's office after having successfully argued for Eddie's job. Stella spoke for the cohort (a materialization of women's voices in the text) and now knows "what it means for us workers to wake up and kick for our rights."[66] Hearing this, Eddie "lifted her from the table. This time his arms were strong as steel around her. In front of the entire department he held her up in the air."[67]

The sexual politics of "Stockyard Stella" are too apparent to require very much interpretation. Aside from the (not inconsequential) fact that Stella (as a cipher for the authors) finds her voice in finding her politics, the story hews closely to the norms of domestic melodrama that fold social and political problems into the overarching libidinal problem of consummation deflected and deferred. This plot has a history in American radical literature, dating back at least as far as 1888, when Edward Bellamy published *Looking Backward*, a utopian novel wherein the narrator, Julian West, drugs himself into a coma out of sexual frustration due to the fact that his fiancée won't marry him until their house is complete, an event continually deferred by labor strikes in the building trades. In the future world of the year 2000, Julian finds and marries the great-granddaughter of his fiancée, which corporealizes the social harmony of that era's socialist society. The plot of "Stockyard Stella" is not altogether different. Although the motivating problem is the foreman's sexual harassment of Stella and the other women workers—that is, their right to work without molestation—the issue quickly becomes Eddie's (phallic) ability to defend his right to Stella. His ability is in some doubt since, after his initial confrontation with management, he is more prone to run (which, not incidentally, would leave Stella to her own defenses) than to struggle. Indeed, it is Stella who must find "Dick" to play Eddie's surrogate and stand up for Eddie's rights. This turn of events positions the Communist Party as Eddie's libido, and it marks romantic/collective "union" as this libido's object. When Stella says her parting line, "All of us together have strength" (5), the phallic significance could not be more clear.[68]

The problem with the plot of "Stockyard Stella" is not simply that it is heteronormative—that Stella's violation becomes Eddie's phallic trauma—but that it is politically conventional in other terms as well. Casting this drama around the problem of individual rights and romantic desire means that the solution comes only in those terms. Even if we push those terms to their limit, the text's politics remains circumscribed. Though Stella's right to work without harassment should, of course, be absolute, so should her "right" to the entire product of her labor. Though Eddie's right to defend another worker (any other worker) from class violence should be absolute, so should his "right" to struggle for possession of the means of production itself. This second set of rights—communist rights, perhaps—lie just outside of the ideological and discursive scope of this story. The fictitious resolution of the romantic drama—that is, the resolution of proletarian desire—simply leaves them there.

FROM WORKERS TO PEOPLE

Barbara Foley ends her examination of the collective novel (which, in turn, ends her study of proletarian novelistic forms) on an ambivalent note. Structurally at least, collective novels present the most radical attempts to deal with class and collectivity in narrative form. They promise to situate and activate the reader, thus avoiding reification and an introspective focus on artistic sensibility. In practice, however, they often fail to live up to their structural promise. The multiple plots can substitute determinism for reification, and the connections between characters can follow regressive and normative political lines. This regressive tendency leaves the form open to political co-optation—or, to put the matter in a less partisan form, to non-Marxist conceptions of the collective. "In Popular Front-era collective novels," Foley concludes diplomatically, "the representation of collectivity can facilitate non-class-specific definitions of social groups, denying the intrinsic and unremitting opposition of labor and capital."[69]

Though Foley stops short of a full examination of the fate of proletarian literature within the Popular Front era, any account that focuses specifically on representations of workers, class, and the collective body must follow this problematic to its conclusion in Popular Front and New Deal textual forms. This is not only because, as Michael Denning has argued, "there is more continuity between the 'proletarian cultural movement' and the 'Popular Front' than appeared to the advocates of one or the other," but because their relationship is more causal than even the term *continuity* implies.[70] The Popular Front constituted, among other things, a response to the aesthetic tactics of the proletarian cultural movement, a recognition of its flaws and points of impasse, and a thorough retheorization of textual collectivity aimed at solving the seemingly intractable problems I have been discussing. This is not to argue, of course, that these problems, or, indeed a recognition of them, played a determinant role in the Communist Party's decision to shift their political doctrine in 1934–35. The rise of fascism in Europe, the continued isolation of the USSR, and the disastrous results of Communist sectarianism in Germany all prompted the Comintern to abandon separatism for a strategic alliance with socialist and liberal political parties. But within the cultural realm in the United States, this shift made other, more specifically aesthetic responses, possible. In the main, it availed a broad tropological shift from "workers" to "the people" as the dramatis personae of left cultural texts. In one sense, this shift merely mirrored the Communist Party's move from sectarianism to popular alliance, broadening the representational lens to foreground subjects and characters that lay outside the proletarian culture movement's focus on workers as privileged agents of change. This broader focus mitigated against the movement's previous tendency to reify and romanticize the working-class body and its (fictive) biological imperatives. Yet as "people" replaced "workers" in the pages of the left press, much of the specific focus on class dissipated into left populism and romantic nationalism. Given the problems endemic to representations of class, this might seem like a good thing. But the proletarian literature movement lost its raison d'être in the middle of its most productive period, when it was still trying to solve the problems of class representation within a Marxist framework. By removing the specific imperatives of class, Popular Front forms diverted what was—all its problems notwithstanding— the most sustained attempt to simultaneously engage class and culture in U.S. literature.

As literary histories have long noted, the shift from "workers" to "people" became apparent as early as April 1935, in Kenneth Burke's address to the American Writers Congress, a meeting of distinguished U.S. leftist writers that was called by the Communist Party. In "Revolutionary Symbolism in America," Burke, a longtime fellow traveler and a talented cultural critic, summarized his theory of symbolic action. "In every social movement, he argued, people responded to a "unifying principle" conveyed to them in the form of "a myth" that makes "various ranges and kinds of social coöperation possible."[71] In a "revolutionary period[,] . . . people drop their allegiance to one myth, or symbol, and shift to another in its place. . . . The symbol of bourgeois nationalism is in such a state of decay to-day, for instance—hence the attempt of Communists to put the symbol of class in its place" (88). But class, or (as he also puts it) "the symbol of the worker" (88), can only act as a "polarizing device," or, in more technical terms, as a "negative symbol" (91). The worker does not "embody an *ideal*" (89).

> [T]here are few people who really want to work, let us say, as a human cog in an automobile factory, or as gatherers of vegetables on a big truck farm. Such vigorous ways of life enlist our *sympathies* but not our *ambitions*. . . . The symbol I should plead for, as more basic, more of an ideal incentive, than the worker, is that of "the people." . . . It contains the *ideal,* the ultimate *classless* feature which revolution would bring about— and for this reason seems richer as a symbol of allegiance. (89–90)

I quote Burke at such length here because his address, although now legend in histories of literary radicalism, is rarely either quoted or discussed in detail. His proposal was roundly denounced at the American Writers Congress, only to be adapted in its entirety some months later, giving historians occasion to applaud Burke's prescience and the Communist Party's fickleness or, less frequently, to see Burke as a liberal harbinger of the Left's doom. The text of the address is, however, more complex than its usage as a historical touchstone will allow. As Denning has recently argued in his own account of Burke at the Congress, the address is best understood as a manifestation of controversies within the Left, not between the Left and an idiosyncratic critic. Burke's promotion of "the people" was not as prophetic as it may seem. He spoke for a shift that was already in motion.[72]

This shift entailed not only a substitution of mythic personae but, more fundamentally, a reorientation of the Left's symbolic focus, from the negative symbolism identified by Burke to positive symbolism. The worker, as Freeman, Hicks, and Gold first hypostasized "him" (always "him"), was an ideal whose ability to evoke symbolic allegiance came specifically from his position outside bourgeois cultural norms. His position, as I have noted, prompted various aesthetic tactics of displacement and compensation, including reification and libidinal projection, but it was never intended, as Burke claims, to act as "propaganda by inclusion" (93). Indeed, the worker was already "included" in the bourgeois nationalist system of myths that the 1930s Left inherited. Such writers as Gold, Freeman, Hicks, Le Sueur, and Rollins went to great lengths to deconstruct the now failed myth of working-class republicanism and to make the worker the standard-bearer of the proletarian revolution. They never intended for this to be inclusive in the manner Burke describes, though their idealization was, as he correctly notes, discordant with "our ambitions."

The positive symbol of "the people" that Burke advocates and that the Popular Front adopted works, in marked contrast, not by sharpening the contradictions of capitalism or even by clarifying the role of class in social struggle. It appeals, rather, to the ideal of classlessness—the ends, rather than the means, of revolutionary change. This lapse into futurity, what Burke surely knew was itself an idealization, was already part of the Left's cultural baggage by 1935. Casting the radical intelligentsia in the role of the still "unconscious" revolutionary proletariat (to use Le Sueur's terminology) was the proletarian literature movement's uneasy solution to the doctrinal demands of workerism in a time before large-scale working-class activism. That said, none of the critics in the era before the Popular Front were as ready as Burke to slide from class struggle to the symbolic ideal of classlessness. Such a leap would have seemed a species of American exceptionalism and, if nothing else, would have erased the very friction that gave proletarian literature its symbolic motive. Indeed, it is unclear what Burke actually means by "the people" and what sort of revolutionary program would be made possible by allegiance to this symbol. Class, Burke tells us, is really only a myth that galvanizes social action. For him, it has none of the specifically materialist

qualities that make it more determining. But even within this dematerialized system of myths, "the people" is inarguably more vacuous than any
conception of class would allow. Since so little lies outside its domain of
specification, there is little it can—or cannot—symbolize. This is, of
course, Burke's point and the argument of others who find the Popular
Front symbolically enabling.[73] But if "the worker" makes a bad symbol
because "there are few people who really want to work," then "the people" makes an even worse symbol because there are no people who are
not already people. On its own, the symbol can only motivate the personification of persons who are not already within the realm of representation—recognizing the invisible, the dispossessed. It cannot move
from this sort of recognition toward anything like the revolution to
which Burke still ascribes. Moreover, since the myth of "the people" was
already so laden with nationalist ideology—a fact Friedrich Wolf pointed
out when he compared Burke's suggestion to Hitler's use of "the
Volk"[74]—its usage could hardly serve to counter the bourgeois cultural
nationalism Burke saw in decay. On the contrary, the Popular Front's
use of "the people" revivified this nationalism, removing the patina of
jingoism that had momentarily obscured its power in the early 1930s.

To rephrase this argument slightly, the shift from "the worker" to
"the people" leaves proletarian literature completely coterminous with
the documentary. When these texts engage "our ambitions," what these
ambitions lead to is self-recognition: we are the people. This does not, in
and of itself, erase class as a material reality that specifies identities or
even processes of exploitation. But it does reconceive of that reality as
something that lies before or beyond textuality. Whereas both reportage
and the collective novel tried, however successfully, to include the writer,
the reader, and the text itself within a process of revolutionary collec-
tivization, the documentary typically had no such pretensions. In its most
radical form in the 1930s, it aimed at remembrance or recognition, a
stance that tries to motivate political action outside the cultural realm.
To note these differences is not, I want to stress, to discount the
efficaciousness of the documentary's symbolic power. Indeed, as most
cultural historians agree, the documentary was an immensely influential
cultural form in the late 1930s. But set beside the aims of the cultural
program of proletarian literature, the documentary's goals seem much
more modest. In the main, the documentary book, the documentary
photography of the Farm Securities Administration, the living newspaper, and even documentary poetry ended the decade within the cultural
milieu of the New Deal, working to buttress Roosevelt's various social

reform programs. These programs were, needless to say, immensely important to their working-class beneficiaries, and as Michael Denning has recently reminded us, they came as close as any institutional reforms to achieving social democracy in the United States.[75] Still, we should also recognize that making capitalism kinder, gentler, and more functional was a goal remarkably at odds with the political imperatives of early 1930s proletarian literature. While the formal continuities between proletarian literature and the Popular Front cannot be denied, these continuities end when we consider their different political goals.

The simultaneous presence of formal continuities and political discontinuities are evident in a number of Popular Front texts and produce, especially in the more overtly political literature, a marked set of antinomies. Perhaps no text better exemplifies these antinomies than Muriel Rukeyser's stunningly affective documentary poem *The Book of the Dead*.[76] Written in the epic tradition of the American long poem but built with stanzas fashioned from congressional hearings, interviews, and stock reports, *The Book of the Dead* takes as its subject Union Carbide's ruthless mining practices in rural West Virginia. Beginning in 1929, the company used a subsidiary to contract with the state to divert river water through a three-mile tunnel from Gauley Junction to Hawk's Nest for a hydroelectric plant. While drilling the tunnel, the company discovered a rich vein of nearly pure silica—a mineral with valuable applications in processing steel. Although the accepted method of mining silica was to use water drills and safety masks, Union Carbide excavated the tunnel without any such equipment. A congressional hearing eventually concluded that as many as two thousand miners subsequently died of silicosis, or "white lung," an easily preventable result of silica inhalation.[77] Though Union Carbide used various tactics to hide the incident from public view and to evade legal penalties, the event became one of the better-known domestic news stories of the late thirties. However, few of these front-page exposés conveyed the miners' struggle and sense of resolve with as much poetic power as Rukeyser's testimonial verse.

Although *The Book of the Dead* now enjoys increasing critical attention and almost unanimous scholarly esteem, when Rukeyser published it in 1938, it was only ambivalently received. The mainstream press found it too anticapitalist and too antipoetic in its use of nonliterary forms.[78] And the left press tempered its praise of Rukeyser's documentary intercutting with criticism of her insufficiently radical politics. Her most ardent leftist critic, John Wheelwright, accused her of writing in a "snob style" and of provoking her readers with the story of "this abomination" only to leave them with reformism as her political message: "The poem attacks the excrescences of capitalism, not the system's inner nature. Like any good capitalist, Rukeyser condemns bad, shockingly bad, working conditions, but makes no root attack on everyday exploitation."[79] While scholars now regularly revisit Wheelwright's criticisms on their way to praising Rukeyser's heteroglossic use of multiple documents and, indeed, to canonizing *The Book of the Dead* within a new lineage of formally experimental political texts, they only engage Wheelwright's admittedly too static differentiation between capitalism's "excrescences" and its "inner nature."[80] None consider the validity of Wheelwright's basic charge: that the poem offers only reformism as a solution to the horrors it so aptly presents. Perhaps this is because reformism is now an attribute the Left aspires to rather than a term of approbation. Be that as it may, Wheelwright was more perceptive than we might want to understand. Though poetically powerful, the poem is politically circumspect.

Both the form and the politics of *The Book of the Dead* were in large part already determined by Rukeyser's choice of protagonists and her choice of the documentary mode. The various sections that make up the poem give us not only miners and their families but a variety of experts—a social worker, congressmen, and doctors—who speak of and for the former in aggregate. The documents Rukeyser includes similarly produce both the intimacy of the lone voice speaking in the vernacular (in the biographic sketches: "The Face of the Dam: Vivian Jones," "Mearl Blankenship," "Absalom," "George Robinson: Blues," and "Juanita Tinsley") and the power of official language to typify the people (as in the social worker's report "Statement: Philipa Allen" and the various sections dealing with medical testimony: "The Disease," "The Doctors," and "The Disease: After Effects"). The subtextual poetic tension, then, is between aggregation and disaggregation, between the document's power to create both typicality and intimacy. Rukeyser negotiates this tension through the central conceit of documentary photography, the privileged documentary medium of the thirties, which makes meaning precisely by composing familiar figures within unfamiliar environments that threaten to cause anonymity (the migrant mother) and by foregrounding the enormous discrepancies in scale between specific human tragedy and vast social and natural forces. Rukeyser is the cinema director as well, replacing the poet's usual emphasis on sensibility and internality with the well-wrought edit, the effectively plotted crosscut. This lends her poem some of the objectivity typically granted the photograph in the late 1930s, though it cannot quite achieve the photograph's task of humanizing its subject. This is because the miners and their families are authenticated by an official discourse that objectifies them inasmuch as it needs their bodies to stand in evidence of the violence perpetrated against them.

There are, to put this interpretation differently, two kinds of representation operating in *The Book of the Dead:* the poet represents "the people" either through description or through quotation, and experts represent "the people" through their greater knowledge (social workers and doctors) or because that is what there were elected to do. "The committee is a true reflection of the will of the people," Rukeyser writes in a section on the congressional investigation, "Praise of the Committee" (20), adding, "These men breathe hard / but the committee has a voice of steel" (23). The miners breathe hard, of course, because their lungs are coated by silica. But their words—and their will—is reflected in the voice of their elected representatives on the committee, a voice Rukeyser allies with steel, the ultimate product that drives silica mining. Poetic representation and legislative representation—that is, the people's representation by the state—are thus two modes (again, intimacy and aggregation) that are significantly allied in this narration of corporate greed. This alliance, which is both political and formal, puts *The Book of the Dead* at some distance from proletarian literature that, as in Dos Passos's poem, used "breath" or "inspiration" to constitute a collective not already instantiated in official institutions. When, in the early thirties, Kenneth Fearing quotes official discourse in his documentary montage poems or when a proletarian novel features the voice of a government official, this is explicitly framed as unrepresentational, as the simulacra of collectivity mimed by a bourgeois state hopelessly obedient to the will of capital. Though *The Book of the Dead* includes criticism of the committee's efficacy ("Investigate. Require. / Can do no more" [64]; "The subcommittee subcommits. / . . . It cannot be enough" [65]), it never questions the committee's ability to speak for the people. Indeed, the people, the country, and the state are figuratively collapsed in images of "the map and x-ray" that "seem resemblent pictures of one living breath one country marked by error and one air" (61).

Rukeyser's Popular Front poetics—the way she balances typicality and aggregation through political representation—also plays a role in dictating the shape of the poem, the way voices are connected in poetic montage. Consider, for instance, the following particularly affective passage of edited medical testimony from the section "The Disease."

This is the X-ray picture taken last April.
I would point out to you : these are the ribs;
this is the region of the breastbone;
this is the heart (a wide white shadow filled with blood).
In here of course is the swallowing tube, esophagus.
The windpipe. Spaces between the lungs.

　　Between the ribs?

Between the ribs. There are the collar bones.
Now, this lung's mottled, beginning, in these areas.
You'd say a snowstorm had struck the fellow's lungs.
About alike, that side and this side, top and bottom.
The first stage in this period in this case.
. . . .
　　What stage?

Third stage. Each time I place my pencil point:
There and there and there, there, there.

　　"It is growing worse every day. At night
　　"I get up to catch my breath. If I remained
　　"flat on my back I would die."

　　It gradually chokes off the air cells in the lungs?
　　I am trying to say it as best I can.
　　That is what happens, isn't it?
　　A choking-off in the air cells?

Yes.
　　There is difficulty in breathing.
Yes.
　　And a painful cough?
Yes.
　　Does silicosis cause death?
Yes, sir.

                                                    (31–32)

As William Carlos Williams wrote in his review, "Rukeyser knows how to use the *language* of an x-ray report. . . . She knows . . . how to select and exhibit her material. She understands what words are for and how important it is not to twist them in order to make 'poetry' of them."[81] Indeed, what is so gripping about this passage is the way that Rukeyser has edited these words to foreground the poetry already inherent in them. Not only do we get the doctor's own recourse to figural language

("You'd say a snowstorm had struck the fellow's lungs"), but we also get the precision of the medical lexicon acting just as words in a good objectivist poem should act: producing, through their materiality, the presence of an object perforce unseen.[82] This is, in other words, exposé taken to its extreme. The exposure of the body to silica, the exposure of the lungs in the X-ray, the exposure of the doctor in testimony, and the expository value of language itself are all aligned to produce truth. The reader is sutured here not with the body or with the doctor but with truth's advocate, the committee whose interrogatory lines ("Between the ribs?" "A choking-off in the air cells?") lead up to the question, "Does silicosis cause death?" Since we already know the answer to this from previous passages, the doctor's deferential reply—"Yes, sir"—serves other than informational purposes. His testimony reinforces the value of testimony itself and solidifies the committee's power to exercise the will of the people (in this case, the readers). The voice of the worker ("It is growing worse every day")—artfully intercut by Rukeyser—serves, then, neither to question nor even to stand in dialectical alterity to this official testimony. Though affective in its own right, its role is to serve as the official discourse's authenticating agent. It is, so framed, almost an echo from the grave.

My intent is not to discount Rukeyser's use of voice, which, as I have noted, is elsewhere dominant and always avoids caricature, fetishism, and pathos. My point is, rather, that this voice is always in harmony with the poem's instantiation of the state in the body of the committee. Even when this committee proves unable to rectify the crimes wrought by Union Carbide and to realize in perpetuity the will of the people, it is never questioned or even replaced by a collective working-class alternative. Indeed, within the poem's political cosmology, such a collective is altogether unnecessary, since the collectivity—the people—is already democratically embodied. What is required is for this force to be ever revivified by an active citizenry, for the reader to follow this closing injunction: "What three things can never be done? / Forget. Keep silent. Stand alone" (66).

The first and second parts of the poem's closing injunction are achieved, in a sense, by the poem itself, which, following the mythic structure of the Egyptian *Book of the Dead*, highlights the resurrectionary power of incantation. As others have noted, this is an adaptation of T. S. Eliot's mythic method.[83] But it is an adaptation that delinks resurrection from phallic power and connects it instead to a matrifocal narrative of remembrance. "He shall not be diminished, never," says Mrs. Jones, the poem's iconic mother, about her dead son. "I shall give a mouth to my son" (30). Inasmuch as the poem gives both Mrs. Jones and her son "a mouth," it succeeds on exactly the terms it sets out for itself: materializing the body in poetry as a way of aligning articulation, documentation, and democratic representation. But as the undertones of the Christic metaphor may suggest, inspiration through annunciation tends to short-circuit the political process of collectivism that such poems typically involve. As in Eliot's *The Waste Land,* the mythic is an alternative, transcendent realm, set apart from mass politics. The mythic method is a way to express a transcendent realm that is not isolated but that is nevertheless at odds with the terrestrial imperatives of the social.

Thus, to achieve the last part of the poem's closing injunction, to not "stand alone," Rukeyser must give us a figure for unity that is labile but that also grounds her use of myth in the literal. She does this by invoking Whitman's democratic vistas in a celebration of the landscape.

> You standing over gorges, surveyors and planners,
> you workers and hope of countries, first among powers;
> you who give peace and bodily repose,
>
> opening landscapes by grace, giving the marvel lowlands
> physical peace, flooding old battlefields
> with general brilliance, who best love your lives;
>
> and you young, you who finishing the poem
> wish new perfection and begin to make;
> you men of fact, measure our times again. (70)

She couples this passage with a recapitulation of the democratic power of the document itself.

> Carry abroad the urgent need, the scene,
> to photograph and to extend the voice,
>   to speak this meaning. (71)

This is where, I think, the poem is least successful. To stand together is, of course, the central lesson of the 1930s Left, a lesson that the proletarian literature movement bequeathed to the Popular Front as its fundamental tool for change. Popular Front texts, however, operate within a tropological realm where such unity—the committee, the people—can be presumed rather than taken as the goal of the artistic endeavor. Inspiration is thus personal, poetic, or mythic, rather than a path to the proletarian revolution. This moves the Popular Front text from agitation to eulogy and testament. The people are a "symbol" (to return to Burke's theory) to which we may aspire. But having achieved personification—even personification of those subjects traditionally absent from the documentary lens—what more is there to do within this symbolic economy? How do we find, in the people, enough revolutionary direction to move beyond remembrance to liberation?

PROLETARIAN BODIES, AMERICAN BODIES, INDIVIDUAL BODIES

When the current revival of scholarship on the thirties reaches its maturity, critics may conclude that texts from the late thirties represent the decade's finest achievements and the culmination of its political and aesthetic goals. This claim is implicit in the revival of Rukeyser's *The Book of the Dead,* and particularly in readings that find her using the documentary mode in ways that look forward to postmodernism. Rita Barnard and Jonathan Veitch applaud Nathaneal West's work in the late thirties in similar terms, explicitly positioning his surrealism and use of irony against the naive earnestness of proletarian realism. Though Michael Denning decenters literature as the privileged form in the Popular Front era and is less interested in finding formal precursors for postmodernism, his magisterial book *The Cultural Front* may well prove the deciding argument in favor of considering the late thirties as the locus classicus of labor culture. While he would be the first to insist on a broad set of continuities tying proletarian and Popular Front forms, his argument for the ultimate efficacy—at least culturally—of the Popular Front's populism all but subsumes the proletarian culture movement as a visionary, though flawed, foreshadowing of what was to come.[84] This renewed interest in the Popular Front is no doubt overdue and, if nothing else, will help us understand how (to paraphrase Denning's argument) broad groups of people came together to use culture to agitate for a more humane society. But in our return to the Popular Front, we should not forget to contextualize our efforts in our own historical moment. Denning's celebration of the strategic alliances within the cultural front gains credence in part because of a large-scale distrust of unitary party politics in the 1990s and 2000s. His positive evaluation of populism and the achievements of the welfare state resonate in part because we have recently seen these achievements taken away. Our recovery of the Popu-

lar Front and our new appreciation for its praise of "the People" measures, in other words, not only its real successes but our real losses.

Even at its inception in the midthirties, the Communist Party's movement into the Popular Front was articulated in defensive terms, as a
strategic alignment with other leftist groups to save the bourgeois democratic state from fascism so that it could be transcended at some more
propitious time. Though the irony of this was not lost on the Popular
Front's Trotskyite critics, the Communist Left, including its cultural
workers, by and large embraced this new defensive tactic. "The chief bat-
tleground in the defense of culture against barbarism," wrote Mike Gold,
"is the question of the national tradition. . . . Walt Whitman, Henry
Thoreau, Mark Twain, Ralph Waldo Emerson, these are the spiritual
forefathers of the proletarian writers of America, and the champions of
the American people. It is time we understood this better and made
them our own."[85] Making them "our own" meant, in this sense, rearticu-
lating them as proponents of democracy against fascism and, in some
obliquely symbolic way, against capitalism's own political tendencies
toward that totalitarian form. The causal tie between capitalism and fascism within Popular Front discourse remained, however, so implicit as to
be regularly ignored.

As I noted, the turn to "the people" and to the "national tradition"
within the literary Left also seemed to resolve some of the problems that
appeared endemic to class representation within the proletarian literature movement. "Quite the most obnoxious of these," according to Alan
Calmer, "was the blind worship of a hypothetical worker" whose tastes
and, indeed, whose very presence as a symbolic center prompted proletarian literature's various methods of collective integration. For Calmer,
who had been one of the editors of *Proletarian Literature in the United
States,* the turn toward "the native quality" in Popular Front literature was
a necessary development past this moment of workerism and vanguardism: "[A] mature literature could not be created solely out of the
immediate plans and activities of a party but must be cut out of the whole
grain and fibre of national existence." The problem, as Calmer likewise
described, was that this whole grain and fiber left little room for the revolutionary focus that gave proletarian literature its raison d'être: "It was
a relief to see the old 'leftist' excesses routed, but these excessive
emphases were wiped out so thoroughly that there remain no (Marxian)
emphasis at all."[86]

Though Calmer's critical history of the proletarian literature movement is perceptive, the movement's dissipation within Popular Front

nationalism was not really a problem of emphasis. Though critics within the movement believed otherwise, populist nationalism was never fully compatible with the movement's earlier investment in revolutionary Marxism. These two "symbolic systems," to echo Burke, were substantially at odds. They both tried to amalgamate the same objects seen differently (workers or people) under the sign of very different collective bodies (communism or Americanism). Despite the Communist Party's attempt to make this equation work by doctoring the outcome through their Popular Front slogan "Communism Is Twentieth-Century Americanism," communism and Americanism were never, even as abstract symbols, coterminous.[87]

The disjuncture between these symbolic systems is apparent even in Langston Hughes's "Let America Be America Again," part of his well-received poetry collection *A New Song*, published in 1938 by the Communist-led International Workers Order.[88] This iconic poem of the Popular Front probably works as hard as any text from that era to make the case for Communist Americanism. Indeed, the poem is in large part a debate between these two positions. The naive patriot idealistically charges:

> Let America be America again
> Let it be the dream it used to be.
> Let it be the pioneer on the plain
> Seeking a home where he himself is free.[89]

This charge is answered by "mumbles in the dark" from a radical dissident: "America was never America to me" (9). This voice—the voice of "the farmer," "the worker," "the Negro," "the red man," and "the immigrant" (9)—articulates a stinging critique of the idealist's belief in freedom. In lines cut by Hughes during the cold war,[90] the dissident complains:

> Who said the free? Not me?
> Surely not me? The millions on relief today?
> The millions shot down when we strike?
> The millions who have nothing for our pay? (10)

But after the voice of radical critique has finally had its say, has symbolically gained a hearing from the idealist, the two harmonize in a conclusion that largely reiterates the idealist's opening position.

Out of the rack and ruin of our gangsters death,
The rape and rot of graft, stealth, and lies,
We, the people, must redeem
The land, the mines, the plants, the rivers,
The mountains and the endless plain—
All, all the stretch of these great green states—
And make America again!

(11)

The problem here is similar (though perhaps more extreme) to the problem in Rukeyser's *The Book of the Dead*. The complaints against America—its falsehood, its exploitation of workers, its oppression of people of color—cannot adequately be answered by a renewed faith in its vision. Exposing nationalism's dependence on a fictitious past does not quite make the case for faith in its future. Thus reformism seemingly has an impossible task, since that which is to be reformed is less a system than a set of signifiers that name "the land that has never been yet" (10). But perhaps, to look at the matter differently, that is what makes this poem function so well and what accounts for its continued popularity. *America* is such an empty term—emptied historically of its "promise" and linguistically of any objective meaning—that it can be reform(ulat)ed merely by emphasis. Indeed, the drama of the poem's final stanza is the drama of the critical voice shedding its particular identities (farmer, worker, Negro, red man, immigrant) in favor of an oath taken on behalf of "we, the people" (11). Nationalism thus stands as an answer to its own deficiencies, just as Burke's people personify themselves in affirmation. However, the concrete steps necessary to achieve redemption (the space for a communist imaginary) are not and cannot be specified within this rhetorical operation. Having unified as a "we" to recover a past that has "never been yet" and to achieve a future whose details are only given shape by the landscape, the voices of Hughes's poem cannot name those who stand outside of its rhetorical scope—the antagonists to freedom whom proletarian literature never hesitated to name capitalists.

However difficult it was to combine Americanism and communism in Popular Front literature, this task became even more problematic as the U.S. Communist Party allied itself not only with America (that is, with nationalism), but with the politics and vision of the New Deal state. Earl Browder, the Communist Party's general secretary, signaled this shift in policy in a number of addresses he delivered in 1937, as Roosevelt was, ironically, trying to defend himself against charges that he was a Communist sympathizer. Thus, while Browder did his best to publicly insulate

Roosevelt from the Communist Party, he nonetheless affirmed the party's support for Roosevelt's political vision. Responding, for instance, to Roosevelt's Constitution Day address, Browder pronounced, "I have no hesitation in declaring for the Communist Party and its followers, that with the central thoughts and the direction of President Roosevelt's speech, we are in practical agreement, and that on such questions with which we disagree these are not questions for immediate practical solution." This rather opaque reference to disagreement referred to the means by which America was to progress toward the egalitarian vision that the Communist Party and the Roosevelt administration now purportedly shared. Browder more than met Roosevelt halfway, by renouncing revolutionary communism several paragraphs later: "The Communist Party repudiates now as in the past, all theories or proposals looking forward to a forcible imposition of Socialism or any utopia upon the majority of the people."[91] Gradualism in defense of the liberal state was now the order of the day.

The effects of this change on left literature were at once subtle and profound. As writers who published through the magazines and presses run by the Communist Party moved increasingly into the sphere of the New Deal, their works came to articulate some of its more important tropes and metaphors. Rukeyser's "The Road" from the opening section of *The Book of the Dead* and that poem's inclusion in a collection entitled *U.S. 1* foregrounded, for instance, the newly nationalized highway system and celebrated it as a harbinger of free movement and social unification. The Farm Securities Administration's focus on the imperiled fertility of the land (graphically illustrated in many of the 164,000 photographs shot under its direction) also made its way into the figural lexicon of leftist writers, running the gamut from Rukeyser, Steinbeck, and Hughes to James Agee and Howard Fast. In the early 1930s, only a few proletarian writers (Ben Fields, Jack Conroy, Don West) used "the land" as their principle metaphor; by the decade's final years, the earth, the landscape, and America's geographic expansiveness became a central—perhaps the central—mode of encapsulating "the people."

As one might expect, writers were more tenuous in their embrace of the state itself as a vehicle for individual and collective fulfillment. They never adopted it with the romantic fervor with which the proletarian movement had adopted the Communist Party. Still, as Michael Szalay has demonstrated in his revisionary account *New Deal Modernism: American Literature and the Invention of the Welfare State,* the New Deal state redefined the terrain on which leftist literature struggled, when writers

in large part adopted its definitions of social progress as their own. Identifying Social Security (in all its institutional and symbolic facets) as the
Roosevelt administration's key ideological statement, Szalay writes:

> At bottom, Social Security made the State not an instrument of coordi-
> nated economic planning but rather a system of exchange essentially
> compensatory for human experience. The New Deal thus embraced
> actuarial models of governance that revolved around the statistical con-
> struction of population groups, and the calculations of probability for
> such groups, and the varied application of these probabilities to individ-
> ual persons. . . . this led to a literature of liberal interdependence, as writ-
> ers looked to reconcile at time conflicting impulses toward individual
> agency and collective affiliation.

This reconciliation was made, as Hughes's poem demonstrates, in favor
of the collective "we" but at the expense of the economic and racial particular, and it was made, in more cases than not, in pursuit of "security"
rather than the "freedom" that still propels Hugh's lyric. Indeed, security
became such a central literary trope because it so neatly connected the
personal emotional drama of life in the Depression with the state's own
struggle for legitimacy. In Szalay's estimation, this led writers to "inter-
nalize the procedures of governance within literature itself": art was no
longer a class weapon, it was a way to legitimate, solidify, and extend the
state's own vision for personal and collective safety.[92]

Of course, in the late 1930s, writers had practical as well as ideo-
logical reasons for defending the state. Many of the writers associated
with the proletarian literature movement—including Floyd Dell, Edward
Dahlberg, Kenneth Patchen, Ralph Ellison, Claude McKay, Philip Rahv,
Nathen Asch, Arna Bontemps, Richard Wright, Jack Conroy, Nelson
Algren, Meridel Le Sueur, Kenneth Rexroth, Tillie Olsen, Kenneth Fearing, and Erskin Caldwell—worked for the government's Federal Writers'
Project (FWP), a unit of the Works Progress Administration (WPA).[93]
Though some of these writers had supervisory positions and others, such
as Wright and Le Sueur, were awarded money to work on individual projects, most did the research and initial drafting for the WPA's vast collection of state and regional guidebooks.[94] These guides are themselves
testimonies to the ideological contradictions of the Roosevelt administration. Jerrold Hirsch notes that the guides use progressive accounts of
local history and regional difference to "reconcile cultural diversity, as a
fact and (in their view) as a positive value, with cultural nationalism."[95]

However, as Christine Bold observes, the guides simultaneously use such accounts to elide the most challenging aspects of this diversity within "a system of social differentiation" that was "considerably less threatening . . . than . . . other discourses of difference . . . , that is, discourses of race and class."[96] Accounts of the FWP's effect on leftist literature are also, not surprisingly, contradictory. On the one hand, some writers, such as Jack Conroy, felt, as his biographer put it, that "the US government filled a vacuum created when the left largely abandoned its sponsorship of worker-writing." Ralph Ellison probably spoke for many others when he recalled, "Actually to be paid for writing . . . why that was a wonderful thing." On the other hand, many blamed the WPA for delivering the final blow to the proletarian literature movement, a position Michael Denning has recently reiterated. Anzia Yezierska quotes an unidentified writer as saying: "Mass bribery, that's what W.P.A. is. Government blackmail. We'd fight, we'd stage riots and revolutions if they didn't hush us up. We're all taking hush money." Malcolm Cowley, the editor of the *New Republic,* agreed: "The New Deal kept the ablest of them [displaced intellectuals] out of revolutionary movements by giving them employment." Even Philip Rahv insisted that the popularity of WPA jobs among leftist writers marked the final step on the Communist Party's chain of errors: "Proletarian fiction cannot *maintain its identity* while following its political leadership into alliance with capitalist democracy."[97]

Both the appreciators and the critics of the WPA fail, however, to describe its full appeal to the leftist writers who worked within its institutional parameters. Certainly these writers were not (or not only) hushed, distracted, and led astray. Something about the FWP fulfilled enough of their aesthetic and ideological desires to win them over in large numbers to its vision. According to Szalay, the FWP not only fulfilled their personal desire for security, in the form of a paycheck, but also fulfilled that desire in a particular way, owing to how and why that paycheck was delivered. As he notes, within early debates about proletarian literature, the nature of the activity of writing was hotly debated. As we saw with Le Sueur, "the radical writer restructured the definition of 'what writing is' such that the 'activity' of writing took precedence over the objects that activity produced."[98] The problem, however, was that the activity closely resembled the activities of bourgeois individualists who wrote to exercise or develop a sensibility. Alternately, writing could seem like a form of capitalist speculation where one exerts one's labor in hopes of one day achieving the payoff of a best seller. The FWP, however, solved that problem by quite literally making writing into proletarian labor.[99] Not only were writers given a regular wage, they were given a production quota of fifteen hundred words a week. And as in any factory, the products of their labor carried no specific marks of their creators. All essays in the guidebooks were issued without bylines.[100] Clearly, this was not what critics and writers had in mind in the early 1930s when they debated the meaning of the term *proletarian literature*. But perversely, the FWP fulfilled some permutation of this definition by making writing work.

Simply put, the proletarian literature movement was neither exactly killed nor died of its own internal contradictions. Its contradictions—its propensity to reify workers and to objectify them in its efforts to achieve collectivity—left it weak and lacking a sophisticated understanding of class. But writers, artists, and critics in the movement were aware of this and were struggling to find other political and aesthetic ways to shape revolutionary culture. The proletarian literature movement was, however, co-opted before these developments could take place—first by the Popular Front and then, more profoundly, by the New Deal. Whereas Diego Rivera's Communist Party–era murals or Clifford Odets's agitational plays used workers' bodies as fervent symbols of a social revolution, the WPA used these same bodies to reinvent a hardy America, resilient and unified in the face of economic hardship. The post-Depression novels of Dos Passos and Steinbeck can equally testify to this phenomenon. These authors did not abandon the aesthetic vision of the thirties; they simply removed all of its class-specific political messages. Such texts from the Popular Front era as Thornton Wilder's *Our Town* (1938), which would, in the 1940s, become a touchstone for "New York Intellectual" Dwight Macdonald's attack on thirties culture, was, as Macdonald charged, ridiculously sentimental and overtly nationalistic. Yet *Our Town*'s cloying overtones of a blandly populist America do not represent the fullness of the political vision of the thirties, however problematically this vision was realized in practice. Rather, they convey the aftereffects of this vision, as it was reinvented for the purposes of cultural Americana.

Dwight Macdonald's reaction to *Our Town* and the other "cultural nightmare[s]" of the late thirties was, in this sense, not unjustified. What Macdonald famously castigated in his essay "Mass Cult and Mid Cult" was not Wilder's populism (which came close to Macdonald's own politics) but the form these politics took. In typically corporeal terms, Macdonald accused the thirties of producing a "hybrid bred . . . culture" that "predigested art for the spectator . . . [by including] the spectator's reactions in the work itself." Shorn of its agitational edge, the "vulgarized" body politics of the New Deal turned the techniques of literary propaganda into the sin of bad culture.[101] A play like *Our Town* did not even promise the new vision or the new art of the proletarian literature movement. Rather, its insistence on inserting its middle-class audience into "the people" only replicated a pastoral nationalism that had been culturally present for at least a century and a half.

Though MacDonald's criticism is accurate, it would be a mistake to conclude (as he did) that literary populism and nationalist visions of "the people" were the proletarian literature movement's sole bequest to the twentieth century. While literary historians in the Cold War period typically found only a devolved mass culture (the "vulgarized" offspring of literature for the masses) and an evolved avant-garde (a reaction to social realism), there were other literary progeny. The literature of labor did not die in the thirties, as revisionist critics are beginning to recognize. It lives on, in different forms, though without as much praise or as much denunciation from the cultural mainstream. While a history of post-Depression labor literature is beyond the scope of this study, such a history would surely need to attend to the number of distinct strands that draw from one or more trends within proletarian literature. The late naturalism of Richard Wright, Nelson Algren, Edward Dahlberg, and Hugh Selby, for instance, initiated a darkly determinist vision that persists, most noticeably, in films such as *Menace II Society* (1993). Another lineage runs from the more domestically focused writing of Tillie Olsen and Meridel Le Sueur (who both continued writing long past the 1930s), through the literature of Paula Marshall and Harriette Arnow, to more contemporary domestic novels, such as Sandra Cisneros's *House on Mango Street* (1989). Finally, such a history would need to attend to a more self-conscious continuation of labor writing in lyric poetry, which has produced not only such exemplative figures as Philip Larkin but movements such as the "New Work Writing" of the 1970s and 1980s.[102]

However, despite their obvious aesthetic and generic differences, all these strands of post-proletarian labor writing share a staunch disinclination to traffic in the tropes of collectivity that formed proletarian literature's conceptual basis and that, in more mediated forms, were present in the long history of labor writing I have been chronicling. Contemporary labor writing backs away from or, at the very least, questions this previously central goal. When we get representations of the collective in contemporary labor writing, these most often are limited to portraits of the family or the neighborhood or are expressed eulogistically, as in Denise Giardina's fine historical novel about the West Virginia coalfield wars, *Storming Heaven,* or in many lamentive poetic tributes to empty factories and mothballed mills. The sites of so much bodily violence have now become the objective correlatives of a collective consciousness seemingly past recuperation.

There is much to be said about this turn toward the individual, the personal, and the nostalgic in labor writing—enough, indeed, to fill the pages of another good-sized book. What should be said here in closing is that this turn was already in process by the early 1940s, marking with clarity the end of the efforts toward cross-class assimilation I have been examining. James Agee and Walker Evans's *Let Us Now Praise Famous Men* (1941) is, for instance, in many ways a reaction against and a rejection of the assimilative discourse of documentary reportage. In the text's lyrical prose, fragmented narrative, and recapitulative plot, Agee repeatedly refuses "to pry intimately into the lives of an undefended and appallingly damaged group of human beings . . . for the purpose of parading the nakedness, disadvantage and humiliation of those lives before another group of human beings." In what may be the first (but not the last) documentary about the impossibility of documentation, Agee and Evans insist on the "obscene and thoroughly terrifying" parallel between the Depression's economic and discursive exploitations of the working class.[103] The only true documentation in this tribute to three southern sharecropping families may be the fifty-thousand-word description of their homes and belongings. This passage is a lesson in literalism. Agee will only objectify those things that are already objects; the animate must be allowed to speak for themselves. The difference between middle-class observer and working-class subject must not be abrogated by the violence of representation.

Though very different in form and purpose, Richard Wright's *Native Son* (1940), shares Agee and Evans's suspicion of discursive assimilation. Though he still traveled in Communist Party circles at the time he wrote this novel, Wright was beginning to lose faith in the ability of discourses of party and class to fully attest to the subjectivity of such characters as Bigger Thomas. Though he is a native son, a product of U.S. racism and exploitation, Bigger forcefully exceeds the comprehension of those who would seek to understand him. Even the novel's voice of social testimony—Bigger's lawyer, Max—insists both that Bigger is a particular "type" and that this type is so marginal to the society that has formed him that he falls outside of society's ability to amalgamate him through operations of sympathy. Indeed, as Wright himself has written, the novel is, in the main, an attack on the sympathetic mode of apprehension, one of the traditional mainstays of labor literature and the social novel up to this point.[104]

But whereas Agee, Evans, and Wright had radical reasons to question the assimilative dictates of literary discourse in the New Deal era, this move away from collectivity took a regressive form during the cold war. What began as a rejection of the amalgamative operations of state nationalism turned, in the 1950s, into a disavowal of the collective itself—in all its embodiments. The fascism of Germany, Italy, and Japan and the state socialism of the USSR served as twin alibis for a renewed faith in what Thomas Hill Schaub has called "the liberal narrative."[105] Thus, in the shadow of totalitarianism abroad, we find critics such as Lionel Trilling arguing for the sanctity of the individual in books like *The Liberal Imagination* (1950), a study that argued for the symbolic importance of Henry James above the authoritarian social reach of Theodore Dreiser. Since the 1950s, critics and writers have rejected most of the political impulses of McCarthyism, yet this one gesture remains intact. The social and the collective seem suspect and are replaced by the individual and the internal. Though the 1960s may have taught us that the personal is political, by privileging the personal as the only domain of politics within cultural texts, we have perpetuated a legacy born of this conservative reaction to communism and its social pretensions. Within this discursive formation, we get class (along with race and gender) as an attribute of the individual, something that shapes people into subjects but that is shorn of the dialectic ability to move them past their individualism into a collective response.

There is hope, however, in the persistence of classed representation itself. As Fredric Jameson has written, Marxism will remain relevant as long as capitalism remains relevant.[106] So, too, will the impulse—undefeatable by amalgamations as well as by more active attempts at silencing—to write about the broad processes and structures of exploitation. Though our continued recourses to class and to the cultural texts that class helps produce mark our continued existence under the regime of exploitation, this continuity, however expressed, also marks our resilient desires to comprehend our misshapen existences and to struggle—collectively—to a postcapitalist future.

Notes

CHAPTER 1

1. Rebecca Harding Davis, *Margret Howth: A Story of To-day* (1862; repr., New York: Feminist, 1990), 152. Future references will be given parenthetically in text.

2. Jane Tompkins, *Sensational Designs: The Cultural Work of American Fiction* (New York: Oxford University Press, 1985), xvii.

3. Michael Zuckerman, "The Dodo and the Phoenix: A Fable of American Exceptionalism," in *American Exceptionalism? US Working-Class Formation in an International Context,* ed. Rick Halpern and Jonathan Morris (New York: St. Martin's, 1997), 30.

4. Deborah L. Madsen, *American Exceptionalism* (Jackson: University Press of Mississippi, 1998), 2.

5. Irving Howe, *Socialism in America* (New York: Harcourt Brace Jovanovich, 1985), 136.

6. Fredric Jameson, *The Political Unconscious: Narrative as a Socially Symbolic Act* (Ithaca, NY: Cornell University Press, 1981), 79.

7. The amount of work on sympathy and sentimentalism that has come out following Tompkins's 1985 publication of *Sensational Designs,* makes any attempt at a bibliographic note provisional at best. Shirley Samuels edited volume *The Culture of Sentiment: Race, Gender, and Sentimentality in Nineteenth-Century America* (New York: Oxford University Press, 1992) is a good starting place. See also Elizabeth Barnes, *States of Sympathy: Seduction and Democracy in the American Novel* (New York: Columbia University Press, 1997); Suzanne Clark, *Sentimental Modernism: Women Writers and the Revolution of the Word* (Bloomington: Indiana University Press, 1991). A few scholars have reacted to Tompkins's optimistic view of sympathy by producing powerful studies that have influenced my critique. Central here are Gillian Brown's *Domestic Individualism: Imagining the Self in Nineteenth-Century America* (Berkeley: University of California Press, 1990) and Amy Schrager Lang's *The Syntax of Class: Writing Inequality in Nineteenth-Century America* (Princeton, NJ: Princeton University Press, 2003).

8. Thomas L. Haskell, "Capitalism and the Origins of the Humanitarian Sensibility," *American Historical Review* 90 (April 1985): 339–61; 90 (June 1985): 547–66. The quote appears on p. 342.

9. Julia Stern, *The Plight of Feeling: Sympathy and Dissent in the Early American Novel* (Chicago: University of Chicago Press, 1997), 24.

10. Ann Cvetkovich, *Mixed Feelings: Feminism, Mass Culture, and Victorian Sensationalism* (New Brunswick, NJ: Rutgers University Press, 1992), 1.

11. For a discussion of this trend, see Eric Schocket, "Revising the 1930s for the 1990s, or The Work of Art in the Age of Diminished Expectations," *American Quarterly* 52 (March 2000): 159–67. Very few scholars have examined the literature of the thirties within the broader context of cross-class labor representation. A notable work of exception is Laura Hapke's *Labor's Text: The Worker in American Fiction* (New Brunswick, NJ: Rutgers University Press, 2001). Hapke's volume is encyclopedic and a wonderful starting place for scholarly research.

12. William Stott, *Documentary Expression and Thirties America* (New York: Oxford University Press, 1973), 216–17.

13. Erskine Caldwell, *Call It Experience: The Years of Learning How to Write* (New York: Duell, Sloan, and Pearce, 1951), 163.

14. Stephen Greenblatt, *Shakespearean Negotiations: The Circulation of Social Energy in Renaissance England* (Berkeley: University of California Press, 1988), 9.

15. Donna Haraway discusses these dioramas in *Primate Visions: Gender, Race, and Nature in the World of Modern Science* (New York: Routledge, 1989), 26–58.

16. Quoted in Stott, *Documentary Expression*, 223.

17. Nancy Fraser, *Justice Interuptus: Critical Reflections on the "Postsocialist" Condition* (New York: Routledge, 1997), 6.

18. Raymond Williams, *Keywords: A Vocabulary of Culture and Society* (New York: Oxford University Press, 1983), 61–62.

19. See Mary Poovey, "The Social Construction of 'Class': Toward a History of Classificatory Thinking," in *Rethinking Class: Literary Studies and Social Formation,* ed. Wai Chee Dimock and Michael T. Gilmore (New York: Columbia University Press, 1994), 15–56; Peter Calvert, *The Concept of Class: An Historical Introduction* (New York: St. Martin's, 1982), 12–25.

20. Max Weber, *Economy and Society: An Outline of Interpretive Sociology,* vol. 2, trans. Ephraim Fischoff (Berkeley: University of California Press, 1978), 928–29. For a cogent explanation of Weber's theory of class, see Calvert, *Concept of Class,* 95–114.

21. Williams, *Keywords,* 61–62.

22. See Martin J. Burke, *The Conundrum of Class: Public Discourse on the Social Order in America* (Chicago: University of Chicago Press, 1995), 22.

23. The term *struggle concept* comes originally from Maria Mies, *Patriarchy and Accumulation on a World Scale* (London: Zed, 1986), 36.

24. Jean L. Cohen's *Class and Civil Society: The Limits of Marxian Critical Theory* (Amherst: University of Massachusetts Press, 1982) provides a useful introduction to Marx's various conceptions of class.

25. Stephen A. Resnick and Richard D. Wolff, *Knowledge and Class: A Marxian Critique of Political Economy* (Chicago: University of Chicago Press, 1987), 110. Resnick and Wolff are quoting Marx's preface to the first German edition of *Capital,* vol. 1, trans. Ben Fowkes (New York: Vintage, 1977), 92.

26. E. P. Thompson, "The Peculiarities of the English," in *Socialist Register 1964,* ed. Ralph Miliband and John Saville (London: Merlin, 1966), 357.

27. Resnick and Wolff, *Knowledge and Class*, 1–37, 109–63. See also Harry Braverman, *Labor and Monopoly Capital: The Degradation of Work in the Twentieth Century* (New York: Monthly Review, 1974), 24: "The term 'working class,' properly understood, never precisely delineated a specific body of people, but was rather an expression for an ongoing social process." For another excellent book applying Resnick and Wolff's paradigm to literature, see Julian Markels, *The Marxian Imagination: Representing Class in Literature* (New York: Monthly Review Press, 2003).

28. Michael Kazin, "A People Not a Class: Rethinking the Political Language of the Modern U.S. Labor Movement," in *Reshaping the U.S. Left: Popular Struggles in the 1980s*, ed. Michael Sprinker and Mike Davis (New York: Verso, 1988), 257.

29. Ibid., 266.

30. Resnick and Wolff, *Knowledge and Class*, 161.

31. Peter Stallybrass, "Marx and Heterogeneity: Thinking the Lumpenproletariat," *Representations* 31 (summer 1990): 83.

32. *The Collected Works of Abraham Lincoln*, ed. Roy Bastler et al., 9 vols. (New Brunswick, NJ: Rutgers University Press, 1953–55), 2:364.

33. Erik Olin Wright, *Classes* (New York: Verso, 1985), 17.

34. Burke, *Conundrum of Class*, 124.

35. Fredric Jameson, "Actually Existing Marxism," in *Marxism beyond Marxism*, ed. Saree Makdisi, Cesare Casarino, and Rebecca E. Karl (New York: Routledge, 1996), 40.

36. Henry Louis Gates. ed., *"Race," Writing, and Difference* (Chicago: University of Chicago Press, 1986). On this paradigm shift, see also Judith Butler, *Bodies That Matter: On the Discursive Limits of "Sex"* (New York: Routledge, 1993), 247 n. 15.

37. See Resnick and Wolff, *Knowledge and Class*, 161; J. K. Gibson-Graham, Stephen A. Resnick, and Richard D. Wolff, eds., *Class and Its Others* (Minneapolis: University of Minnesota Press, 2000), 21 n. 17: "We are not arguing for the abandonment of terms such as 'working class' but for an approach to their use that does not know in advance what they mean."

38. Jameson, *Political Unconscious*, 80–81.

39. "Will the Working Class Be Invited to the Diversity Banquet?" was the title of the grant application that the Center for Working-Class Studies at Youngstown State University submitted to the Association of American Colleges and Universities. See Jeff Sharlet, "Seeking Solidarity in the Culture of the Working Class," *Chronicle of Higher Education,* July 23, 1999, A9.

40. John Guillory, *Cultural Capital: The Problem of Literary Canon Formation* (Chicago: University of Chicago Press, 1993), 13. See also Rita Felski, "Nothing to Declare: Identity, Shame, and the Lower Middle Class," *PMLA* 115, no. 1 (2000): 33–45.

41. These arguments are most apparent in the edited collections put together by Janet Zandy. See particularly *Liberating Memory: Our Work and Our Working-Class Consciousness* (New Brunswick, NJ: Rutgers University Press, 1995) and *What We Hold in Common: An Introduction to Working-Class Studies* (New York: Feminist, 2001).

42. Vivian Gornick, *The Romance of American Communism* (New York: Basic, 1977).

43. Louis Althusser and Étienne Balibar, *Reading Capital*, trans. Ben Brewster (New York: Verso, 1997), 87.

44. Dimock and Gilmore, *Rethinking Class*, 2. Future references will be given parenthetically in text.

45. Ernesto Laclau and Chantal Mouffe, *Hegemony and Socialist Strategy: Towards a Radical Democratic Politics* (New York: Verso, 1985).

46. Althusser and Balibar, *Reading Capital*, 87. They are quoting Karl Marx, *Grundrisse der Kritik der Politischen Ökonomie* (Berlin: Dietz Vertag, 1953), 22.

47. Resnick and Wolff, *Knowledge and Class*, 130

48. Butler, *Bodies That Matter*, 10.

49. Jameson, *Political Unconsciousness*, 88–89.

50. Butler, *Bodies That Matter*, 2.

51. Georg Lukács, *Essays on Realism*, ed. Rodney Livingstone, trans. David Fernbach (Cambridge, MA: MIT Press, 1981); Ian Watt, *The Rise of the Novel: Studies in Defoe, Richardson, and Fielding* (Berkeley: University of California Press, 1959); Nancy Armstrong, *Desire and Domestic Fiction: A Political History of the Novel* (New York: Oxford University Press, 1987).

52. See Philip Fisher, *Hard Facts: Setting and Form in the American Novel* (New York: Oxford University Press, 1985).

53. Jameson, *Political Unconscious*, 89.

54. Marx, *Capital*, 1:164–65, 164.

55. Carolyn Porter, *Seeing and Being: The Plight of the Participant Observer in Emerson, James, Adams, and Faulkner* (Middletown, CT: Wesleyan University Press, 1981), xi.

56. Cvetkovich, *Mixed Feelings*, 182.

57. Henry Krips, *Fetish: An Erotics of Culture* (Ithaca, NY: Cornell University Press, 1999), 7.

58. Laura Kipnis, "'Refunctioning' Reconsidered: Towards a Left Popular Culture," in *High Theory/Low Culture: Analyzing Popular Television and Film*, ed. Colin MacCabe (New York: St. Martin's, 1986), 28.

59. Bill Readings, *The University in Ruins* (Cambridge, MA: Harvard University Press, 1996), 80.

60. Ibid., 95.

61. Matthew Arnold, *Culture and Anarchy*, ed. Seymour Lipkman (1861; repr., New Haven, CT: Yale University Press, 1994), 5.

62. See particularly Richard Hoggart, *The Uses of Literacy; Aspects of Working Class Life with Special Reference to Publications and Entertainments* (London: Chatto and Windus, 1957); Raymond Williams, *The Long Revolution* (London: Chatto and Windus, 1961); E. P. Thompson, *The Making of the English Working Class* (1963; repr., New York: Vintage, 1966).

63. Thompson, *Making of the English Working Class*, 9.

64. Readings, *University in Ruins*, 94.

65. Perry Anderson, *Considerations on Western Marxism* (London: New Left, 1976), 92.

66. John Fiske, *Understanding Popular Culture* (Boston: Unwin Hyman, 1989); John Fiske, *Reading the Popular* (Boston: Unwin Hyman, 1989); Lawrence Grossberg, Cary Nelson, and Paula A. Treichler, eds., *Cultural Studies* (New York: Routledge, 1992).

67. Jameson, *Political Unconscious*, 81, 291.

68. Ibid., 63.

69. Ibid., 291.

70. Ibid., 296.

71. Walter Benjamin, "Theses on the Philosophy of History," in *Illuminations: Essays and Reflections*, ed. Hannah Arendt (New York: Schocken, 1969), 256; Jameson, *Political Unconscious*, 19.

72. Peter Hitchcock, *Working-Class Fiction in Theory and Practice: A Reading of Alan Sillitoe* (Ann Arbor, MI: UMI Research Press, 1989), 38.

73. Walter Benjamin, "The Storyteller" in Arendt, *Illuminations*, 101.

74. Lauren Berlant, "'68, or Something," *Critical Inquiry* 21, no. 1 (1994): 137–38.

CHAPTER 2

1. Rebecca Harding Davis to James Fields, January 26, 1861, Richard Harding Davis Collection, no. 6109, Clifton Waller Barrett Library, Manuscript Division, Special Collection Department, University of Virginia Library.

2. See Sharon M. Harris, *Rebecca Harding Davis and American Realism* (Philadelphia: University of Pennsylvania Press, 1991), 57; Tillie Olsen, biographical interpretation in *Life in the Iron Mills, and Other Stories*, by Rebecca Harding Davis (New York: Feminist, 1985), 69–174; Jane Atterbridge Rose, *Rebecca Harding Davis* (New York: Twayne, 1993); Jean Pfaelzer, *Parlor Radical: Rebecca Harding Davis and the Origins of American Social Realism* (Pittsburgh: University of Pittsburgh Press, 1996).

While I have no wish to discount the valuable work and numerous insights of the feminist critics who have succeeded in canonizing "Life in the Iron Mills," I want to suggest that when class and race are used as points of entry into the text, other, more troubling readings of it appear. The value of this approach is confirmed not only in my own scholarship but in the arrestingly keen readings of this text that have been produced by Amy Schrager Lang. In both a landmark essay ("Class and the Strategies of Sympathy," in *The Culture of Sentiment: Race, Gender, and Sentimentality in Nineteenth-Century America*, ed. Shirley Samuels [New York: Oxford University Press, 1992], 128–42) and in her 2003 study of nineteenth-century representations of class (*The Syntax of Class: Writing Inequality in Nineteenth-Century America* [Princeton, NJ: Princeton University Press, 2003], 71–86), Lang compares Davis's representations of mill workers to Harriet Beecher Stowe's near-contemporaneous representations of African Americans. Lang argues that whereas Stowe finds Uncle Tom completely legible, Davis finds mill workers resistant to representation. Davis's sense of her own "complicity, as a member of the possessing class, in the system of oppression . . . [she] described" made "sentimental narrative impossible," claims Lang, and led to a nearly unbridgeable "literary impasse" (*Syntax of Class*, 71).

Although I share Lang's apprehension of this impasse—and was indeed very influenced by her initial work on this subject—my own conclusions are quite different. I do not find Davis as cognizant of her complicity, and thus I find her epistemological problems to be more fundamentally grounded in the lack of an adequate analytic language of class. Further, while Lang argues that, under the pressure of complicity, "the story offers us no alternative position [than compla-cent indifference] in which to locate ourselves" (ibid., 75), I argue that white-ness—what readers presumably share with mill workers—is precisely this posi-tion.

3. Eric Lott, *Love and Theft: Blackface Minstrelsy and the American Working Class* (New York: Oxford University Press, 1993), 136.

4. Sander L. Gilman, *Difference and Pathology: Stereotypes of Sexuality, Race, and Madness* (Ithaca, NY: Cornell University Press, 1985), 85.

5. Rebecca Harding Davis, *Life in the Iron Mills, and Other Stories* (New York: Feminist, 1985), 11. Future references will be given parenthetically in text.

6. Rebecca Harding Davis, *Margret Howth: A Story of To-day* (1862; repr., New York: Feminist, 1990), 6.

7. Lang, *Syntax of Class*, 20.

8. George Taylor, *The Transportation Revolution, 1815–1860* (New York: Rinehart, 1957), 270–300. See also Susan Hirsh, *The Roots of the American Working Class: The Industrialization of Crafts in Newark, 1800–1860* (Philadelphia: Univer-sity of Pennsylvania Press, 1978), 79; *The United States on the Eve of the Civil War, as Described in the 1860 Census* (Washington: U.S. Civil War Centennial Commission, 1963), 61–64; Anne Norton, "The Meaning of Slavery in Antebellum American Culture," in *Alternative Americas: A Reading of Antebellum Political Culture* (Chicago: University of Chicago Press, 1986), 221–39.

9. Eric Foner, *Politics and Ideology in the Age of the Civil War* (New York: Oxford University Press, 1980), 24.

10. Although some critics have argued for a distinction between the terms *work* and *labor*—most famously Hannah Arendt in *The Human Condition* (Chicago: University of Chicago Press, 1958)—I have not been able to discern any clear difference between the way each term is used in the American lexicon during the nineteenth and twentieth centuries. Therefore, I use the terms inter-changeably.

11. Anson Rabinbach, *The Human Motor: Energy, Fatigue, and the Origins of Modernity* (New York: Basic, 1990), 4.

12. Daniel T. Rogers, *The Work Ethic in Industrial America, 1850–1920* (Chicago: University of Chicago Press, 1974), xi, 8.

13. Perry Miller, *The New England Mind: From Colony to Province* (Boston: Bea-con, 1953), 40.

14. Max Weber, *The Protestant Ethic and the Spirit of Capitalism* (London: Unwin Hyman, 1989), 159, 62.

15. William Evarts, *New York Tribune*, November 11, 1857, quoted in Eric Foner, *Free Soil, Free Labor, Free Men: The Ideology of the Republican Party before the Civil War* (New York: Oxford University Press, 1970), 12; Daniel Webster, speech at Saratoga, NY, August 19, 1840, in *The Writings and Speeches of Daniel Webster*, vol. 3, *Speeches on Various Occasions* (New York: Little, Brown, 1903), 24.

16. See Edward Pessen, *Most Uncommon Jacksonians: The Radical Leaders of the Early Labor Movement* (Albany: State University of New York Press, 1967).

17. Thomas Lovell, "Separate Spheres and Extensive Circles: Sarah Savage's *The Factory Girl* and the Celebration of Industry in Early America," *Early American Literature* 31, no. 1 (1996): 4. See also Cathy Davidson, *Revolution and the Word:*

The Rise of the Novel in America (New York: Oxford University Press, 1986), 28.

18. Sarah Savage, *The Factory Girl* (Boston: Munroe, Francis, and Parker, 1814), 22. Future references will be given parenthetically in text.

19. Lovell, "Separate Spheres," 10, 1.

20. Rogers, *Work Ethic,* 28.

21. Jonathan A. Glickstein, *Concepts of Free Labor in Antebellum America* (New Haven, CT: Yale University Press, 1991), 258.

22. Karl Marx, *Capital,* vol. 1, trans. Ben Fowkes (New York: Vintage, 1977), 272.

23. Lovell, "Separate Spheres," 1.

24. Throughout Davis's time in Wheeling, Virginia (now West Virginia), the iron mills employed African American slaves along with white, predominantly immigrant, laborers. This aspect of ironwork is, for reasons that will become clear, explicitly absent from Davis's portrait. See Kathleen Bruce, *Virginia Iron Manufacture in the Slave Era* (New York: Century, 1930). The best source on Davis's early life is Helen Woodward Shaeffer's unpublished PhD dissertation, "Rebecca Harding Davis: Pioneer Realist" (University of Pennsylvania, 1947).

25. Rebecca Harding Davis, *Bits of Gossip* (Boston: Houghton Mifflin, 1904) 3, 3–4, 109.

26. Leo Marx, *The Machine in the Garden: Technology and the Pastoral Ideal in America* (New York: Oxford University Press, 1964), 18.

27. Charles Dickens, *Hard Times* (1854; repr., New York: Penguin, 1985), 65.

28. Pfaelzer, *Parlor Radical,* 50.

29. William Jay, "Immediate Emancipation or Continued Slavery," in *The Reform Impulse, 1825–1850,* ed. Walter Hugins (New York: Harper and Row, 1972), 168.

30. Frederick Douglass, *My Bondage and My Freedom* (1855; repr., Urbana: University of Illinois Press, 1987), 207; Harriet Wilson, *Our Nig, or Sketches from the Life of a Free Black* (1859; repr., New York: Random House, 1983), 65.

31. William Grayson, *The Hireling and the Slave, Chicora, and Other Poems* (Charleston: McCarter, 1856), 51.

32. Lang, "Strategies of Sympathy," 138.

33. Barbara Fields, "Ideology and Race in American History," in *Region, Race, and Reconstruction,* ed. J. Morgan Kousser and James M. McPherson (New York: Oxford University Press, 1982), 152.

34. W. E. B. DuBois, *The Souls of Black Folk* (1903; repr., Mineola, NY: Dover, 1994), 2.

35. Douglass, *My Bondage and My Freedom,* 188.

36. David Roediger, *The Wages of Whiteness: Race and the Making of the Working Class* (New York: Verso, 1991), 46, 66, 87.

37. Ibid., 20.

38. Lang, "Strategies of Sympathy,"128.

39. See Nina Baym, *Novels, Readers, and Reviewers: Responses to Fiction in Antebellum America* (Ithaca, NY: Cornell University Press, 1984), 219.

40. Henry James, *Hawthorne* (1879; repr., New York: St. Martin's, 1967), 61.

41. Newton Arvin, *Herman Melville* (New York: William Sloan, 1950), 238.

42. Herman Melville, "The Tartarus of Maids," in *The Piazza Tales, and Other*

Prose Pieces, 1839–1860 (Evanston: Northwestern University Press and the New-
berry Library, 1987), 327–28. Future references will be given parenthetically in
text.

43. Michael Newbury, *Figuring Authorship in Antebellum America* (Stanford:
Stanford University Press, 1997), 19–78.

44. Marvin Fisher, "Melville's 'Tartarus': The Deflowering of New England,"
American Quarterly 23 (spring 1971): 87.

45. Robyn Wiegman, "Melville's Geography of Gender," *American Literary
History* 1, no. 4 (1989): 743.

46. See Lise Vogel, "Hearts to Feel and Tongues to Speak: New England Mill
Women in the Early Nineteenth Century," in *Class, Sex, and the Woman Worker,* ed.
Bruce Laurie and Milton Cantor (Westport, CT: Greenwood, 1977), 73; Philip
Foner, ed., introduction to *The Factory Girls,* ed. Philip Foner (Chicago: Univer-
sity of Illinois Press, 1977), xvi.

47. Eric Foner, *Politics and Ideology,* 57.

48. James Hammond, speech before the U.S. Senate, March 4, 1858, *Congressional Globe,* 35th Cong., 1st sess., 962.

49. George Fitzhugh, *Cannibals All! or Slaves without Masters* (1857; repr.,
Cambridge, MA: Harvard University Press, 1960), 17.

50. William Harper, "Harper's Memoir on Slavery," in *The Pro-Slavery Argument* (1852; repr., New York: Negro University Press, 1968), 53.

51. Eugene D. Genovese, *The World the Slaveholders Made* (New York: Pantheon, 1969); Larry E. Tise, *Proslavery: A History of the Defense of Slavery in America,
1701–1840* (Athens: University of Georgia Press, 1987). Although Walter Benn
Michaels's *Our America: Nativism, Modernism, and Pluralism* (Durham, NC: Duke
University Press, 1995) suggestively reads the postbellum plantation novel as a
pro-slavery anti-imperialist genre, it does not examine these works' antebellum
predecessors. For one of the only recent examinations of antebellum, pro-slavery
literature, see Susan Tracy, *In the Master's Eye: Representations of Women, Blacks, and
Poor Whites in Antebellum Southern Literature* (Amherst: University of Massachusetts
Press, 1995); unfortunately, Tracy's book concludes without a consideration of
the 1850s.

52. George Fredrick Holmes, review of *Uncle Tom's Cabin,* by Harriet Beecher
Stowe, *Southern Messenger* 18 (1852): 742, quoted in Thomas F. Gosset, *Uncle
Tom's Cabin and American Culture* (Dallas, TX: Southern Methodist University
Press, 1985), 213. Gossett (431–32) helpfully lists a number of novels written in
debate with *Uncle Tom's Cabin.*

53. Mary H. Eastman, *Aunt Phillis's Cabin, or Southern Life as It Is* (Philadelphia: Lippincott, Grandbo, 1852), 73, 74.

54. John W. Page, *Uncle Robin in His Cabin in Virginia and Tom without One in
Boston* (Richmond, VA: J. W. Randolph, 1853), 30–31, 22, 34.

55. J. Thornton Randolph [Charles Jacobs Peterson], *The Cabin and Parlor, or
Slaves and Masters* (Philadelphia: T. B. Peterson, 1852), 152.

56. [Matthew Estes], *Tit for Tat: A Novel by a Lady of New Orleans* (New York:
Garret, 1856), 179, 60–61.

57. Catherine Gallagher, *The Industrial Reformation of English Fiction: Social
Discourse and Narrative Form, 1832–1867* (Chicago: University of Chicago Press,

1985), 6. Gallagher is referring to British industrial writers, but I think her assessment applies equally to American writers and texts.

58. The various epistemological difficulties of this novella have engendered a surprisingly enduring debate over its use of sentimentalism and romantic tropes. Walter Hesford ("Literary Contexts of 'Life in the Iron Mills,'" *American Literature* 49 [1977]: 70–85) argues, for instance, that the novella clearly arises out of and is hampered by the sentimental romance genre. More recent studies by Harris and Pfaelzer recognize this influence but argue that Davis's text, for the most part, surpasses its literary contexts.

59. Rosemarie Garland Thomson, "Benevolent Maternalism and Physically Disabled Figures: Dilemmas of Female Embodiment in Stowe, Davis, and Phelps," *American Literature* 68 (1996): 572.

60. Wai Chee Dimock, "Class, Gender, and a History of Metonymy," in *Rethinking Class: Literary Studies and Social Formation*, ed. Wai Chee Dimock and Michael T. Gilmore (New York: Columbia University Press, 1994), 94–95.

61. Amy Schrager Lang (*Syntax of Class*, 25) makes a similar point with regard to Gerty, a character in Maria Cummins's *The Lamplighter* (1854).

62. Toni Morrison, *Playing in the Dark: Whiteness and the Literary Imagination* (New York: Vintage, 1992), 59, 32–33, 37, 33, 32.

63. Elizabeth Stuart Phelps, *The Silent Partner* (1871; repr., New York: Feminist, 1983), 48, 54, 189, 394, 295, 300. Amy Schrager Lang cites these and other incidents of racial discourse in her excellent essay "The Syntax of Class in Elizabeth Stuart Phelps's *The Silent Partner*," in Dimock and Gilmore, *Rethinking Class*, 267–85.

64. Hamlin Garland, *Main-Travelled Roads* (1891; repr., New York: Penguin, 1962), 97. I am grateful to Carrie Tirado Bramen for pointing out the racial implications of this passage. See her discussion of this passage in *The Uses of Variety: Modern Americanism and the Quest for National Distinctiveness* (Cambridge, MA: Harvard University Press, 2000), 145.

65. The racial politics of class were also (though differently) important to African American novelists during the middle and late nineteenth century. For instance, in an attempt to solidify a romance and an opportunity for class ascendancy, an African American character in Harriet Wilson's *Our Nig* argues, "I's black outside, I know, but I's got a white heart inside. Which you rather have, a black heart in a white skin, or a white heart in a black one?" (12).

66. Stuart Hall, *Sociological Theories: Race and Colonialism* (Paris: UNESCO Press, 1980), 341.

CHAPTER 3

1. Jacob A. Riis, *How the Other Half Lives: Studies among the Tenements of New York* (1890; repr., Mineola, NY: Dover, 1971), 207.

2. I am grateful to Jeffory Clymer for his generous assistance with my research for this chapter. For a different approach to insurgency in literature, see his *America's Culture of Terrorism: Violence, Capitalism, and the Written Word* (Chapel Hill: University of North Carolina Press, 2003).

3. On realism's moral economy, see Wai Chee Dimock, "The Economy of

Pain: Capitalism, Humanitarianism, and the Realistic Novel," in *New Essays on the Rise of Silas Lapham,* ed. Donald Pease (New York: Cambridge University Press, 1991), 67–90; *Residues of Justice: Literature, Law, Philosophy* (Berkeley: University of California Press, 1996), 140–81.

4. Gayatri Chakravorty Spivak, "Can the Subaltern Speak?" in *Marxism and the Interpretation of Culture,* ed. Cary Nelson and Lawrence Grossberg (Urbana: University of Illinois Press, 1988), 287.

5. Fay M. Blake, *The Strike in the American Novel* (Metuchen, NJ: Scarecrow, 1972), 3. Though Blake's work is relatively unknown, its sixty-eight-page annotated bibliography of strike novels is an invaluable resource.

6. See ibid., 18–54. On Martha Tyler's self-published autobiographical novel, see Judith A. Ranta, *Women and Children of the Mills: An Annotated Guide to Nineteenth-Century American Textile Factory Literature* (Westport, CT: Greenwood, 1999), 239–40.

7. David Montgomery, "Strikes in Nineteenth-Century America," *Social Science History* 4, no. 1 (1980): 86–87.

8. U.S. Commissioner of Labor, *Twenty-First Annual Report* (Washington, DC: Government Printing Office, 1906), 15.

9. See John R. Commons et al., *History of Labour in the United States,* 4 vols. (New York: Macmillan, 1918–35); J. H. Griffin, *Strikes: A Study in Quantitative Economics* (New York: Columbia University Press, 1939).

10. "The Last Street Railroad Strike," *Harper's Weekly,* June 19, 1886, 386.

11. *Independent,* August 2, 1877, 16, quoted in Henry F. May, *Protestant Churches and Industrial America* (1949; repr., New York: Octagon, 1963), 92–93.

12. Gustave Le Bon, *The Crowd: A Study of the Popular Mind* (New York: Macmillan, 1896), 6, xxii.

13. Although Le Bon never achieved the same notoriety in the United States that he did in France and Germany, his work was widely read and reviewed in American popular magazines and scholarly journals. See, for instance, Arthur F. Benley, review of *The Crowd: A Study of the Popular Mind,* by Gustave Le Bon, *American Journal of Sociology* 2, no. 4 (1897): 612–14; unsigned review of *The Crowd: A Study of the Popular Mind,* by Gustave Le Bon, *Nation,* February 18, 1897, 131–32. Serge Moscovici discusses the broad reception of *The Crowd* in *The Age of the Crowd: A Historical Treatise on Mass Psychology* (Cambridge: Cambridge University Press, 1985).

14. Fredric Jameson, "Actually Existing Marxism," in *Marxism beyond Marxism,* ed. Saree Makdisi, Cesare Casarino, and Rebecca E. Karl (New York: Routledge, 1996), 35.

15. Montgomery, "Strikes in Nineteenth-Century America," 85.

16. Alan Trachtenberg, *The Incorporation of America: Culture and Society in the Gilded Age* (New York: Hill and Wang, 1982), 89.

17. Rachel Bowlby, *Just Looking: Consumer Culture in Dreiser, Gissing, and Zola* (New York: Methuen, 1985).

18. Spivak, "Can the Subaltern Speak?" 287.

19. The poem "Eight Hours" was written in 1866 by I. G. Blanchard and later set to music. See, Herbert Gutman et al., *Who Built America?* vol. 2 (New York: Pantheon, 1992), 119. See also Roy Rosenzweig, *Eight Hours for What We Will:*

Workers and Leisure in an Industrial City, 1870–1920 (New York: Cambridge University Press, 1985).

20. Karl Marx, "On the Realm of Necessity and the Realm of Freedom," from *Capital*, vol. 3, in *The Marx-Engels Reader*, 2nd ed., ed. Robert C. Tucker (New York: W. W. Norton, 1978), 441.

21. A number of these sociologists have published seminal essays in *Social Science History*. See especially vol. 17, nos. 2–3 (1994). Working from a different angle in cultural sociology, Ann Swidler has also developed a theory of "cultural repertoires." See her "Culture in Action: Symbols and Strategies," *American Sociological Review* 51 (1986): 273–86. I am grateful to Marc Steinberg for his assistance on this question.

22. Charles Tilly, "Contentious Repertoires in Great Britain, 1758–1834," in *Repertoires and Cycles of Collective Action*, ed. Mark Traugott (Durham, NC: Duke University Press, 1995), 26–27.

23. Ibid., 30.

24. M. M. Bakhtin, *Rabelais and His Own World* (Bloomington: Indiana University Press, 1984), 145–95.

25. Trachtenberg, *Incorporation of America*, 74.

26. Montgomery, "Strikes in Nineteenth-Century America," 97.

27. *The Collected Works of Abraham Lincoln*, ed. Roy Bastler et al., 9 vols. (New Brunswick, NJ: Rutgers University Press, 1953–55), 3:478.

28. The classic study on labor and the Republican Party is David Montgomery's *Beyond Equality: Labor and the Radical Republicans, 1862–1872* (1967; repr., Chicago: University of Illinois Press, 1981).

29. Quoted in Robert Bruce, *1877: Year of Violence* (New York: Bobbs-Merrill, 1959), 90.

30. Quoted in ibid., 229.

31. Eric Foner, *Reconstruction: America's Unfinished Revolution, 1863–1877* (New York: Harper and Row, 1988), 584.

32. Quoted in Bruce, *1877: Year of Violence*, 135–36.

33. Leon Fink, "Class Conflict in the Gilded Age: The Figure and the Phantom," *Radical History Review* 2 (fall–winter 1975): 60.

34. Quoted in Bruce, *1877: Year of Violence*, 243.

35. Tilly, "Contentious Repertoires," 34.

36. Amy Kaplan, *The Social Construction of American Realism* (Chicago: University of Chicago Press, 1988), 7.

37. Dimock, "Economy of Pain," 69–70.

38. William Dean Howells, *A Hazard of New Fortunes* (1890; repr., New York: New American Library, 1965), 380. Future references will be given parenthetically in text.

39. Daniel Aaron, *The Unwritten War* (New York: Knopf, 1973); Edwin H. Cady, *The Realist at War: The Mature Years, 1885–1920, of William Dean Howells* (Syracuse, NY: Syracuse University Press, 1958); Walter Benn Michaels, *The Gold Standard and the Logic of Naturalism* (Berkeley: University of California Press, 1987), 35–41.

40. William Dean Howells, "Editor's Easy Chair," *Harpers Monthly*, March 1912, 636.

41. The most recent analysis of *The Stillwater Tragedy* can be found in Laura Hapke's *Labor's Text: The Worker in American Fiction* (New Brunswick, NJ: Rutgers University Press, 2001), 49–50. For a more extended analysis of Aldrich's career, see Charles E. Samuels, *Thomas Bailey Aldrich* (New York: Twayne, 1965); Ferris Greenslet, *The Life of Thomas Bailey Aldrich* (Boston: Houghton Mifflin, 1908).

42. Thomas Bailey Aldrich to E. C. Stedman, November 18, 1878, box 1492, Widener Library, Yale University.

43. Blake, *Strike in the American Novel*, 22.

44. Thomas Bailey Aldrich, *The Stillwater Tragedy* (1880; repr., Boston: Jefferson, 1908), 167. Future references will be given parenthetically in text.

45. For two recent attempts to read literary realism in conjunction with legal formalism and the rise of liberal capitalism, see Howard Horowitz, *By the Law of Nature* (New York: Oxford University Press, 1991); Brook Thomas, *American Literary Realism and the Failed Promise of Contract* (Berkeley: University of California Press, 1997).

46. Of interest mostly to intellectual and political historians who track his political career and his effect on U.S. foreign policy, John Hay has received relatively little attention from literary scholars. Robert L. Gale gives a readable overview of Hay's literary career in *John Hay* (Boston: Twayne, 1978). Laura Hapke discusses *The Bread-Winners* briefly in *Labor's Text*, 50–52. Brook Thomas (*Failed Promise of Contract*, 88–121) argues unconvincingly for Hay's commitment to the ideals of equity expressed in republican ideology.

47. John Hay, unsigned letter, *Century* 27 (1883–84): 795.

48. John Hay, *The Bread-Winners: A Social Study* (New York: Harper and Brothers, 1884), 7. Future references will be given parenthetically in text.

49. John Hay, unsigned letter, *Century* 27 (1883–84): 158.

50. Unlike analyses of his literary output, information on Hay's political career is widely available. I have consulted Kenton Clymer's *John Hay: The Gentleman as Diplomat* (Ann Arbor: University of Michigan Press, 1975) and Robert L. Gayle's *John Hay*. The quote in text is from a letter cited in Clymer, *John Hay*, 45.

51. Thomas, *Failed Promise of Contract*, 99.

52. Hay, *Century* 27 (1883–84): 795.

53. Hay, *Century* 27 (1883–84): 157.

54. Cady, *Realist at War*, 56.

55. William Dean Howells, *Life in Letters of William Dean Howells*, ed. Mildred Howells, 2 vols. (Garden City, NY: Doubleday, Doran, 1928),1:419.

56. Howells noted the influence of the Haymarket incident on *Hazard* in a retrospective preface. See William Dean Howells, biographical in *A Hazard of New Fortunes*, ed. David Nordloh et al. (Bloomington: Indiana University Press, 1976), 4. A number of excellent biographical studies of Howells focus on this period. I have used Cady, *Realist at War*, 56–138; Kenneth Lynn, *William Dean Howells, an American Life* (New York: Harcourt Brace Jovanovich, 1970), 282–304; and William Alexander, *William Dean Howells: The Realist as Humanist* (New York: Burt Franklin, 1981), 61–139.

57. Carl Smith, *Urban Disorder and the Shape of Belief: The Great Chicago Fire, the Haymarket Bomb, and the Model Town of Pullman* (Chicago: University of Chicago Press, 1995), 3.

58. On the judicial and legislative responses to Haymarket and other labor insurrections of the period, see Fink, "Class Conflict," 69; Michael T. Gibson, "The Supreme Court and Freedom of Expression from 1791 to 1917," *Fordham Law Review* (December 1986): 263–333, especially 321; Andrew Sachs, "Silencing the Union Movement," in *Silencing the Opposition: Government Strategies of Suppression of Freedom of Expression,* ed. Craig R. Smith (Albany: State University of New York Press, 1996); David M. Rabban, *Free Speech in Its Forgotten Years* (New York: Cambridge University Press, 1997).

59. Dyer D. Lum, *A Concise History of the Great Trial of the Chicago Anarchist in 1886* (Chicago: Socialistic, 1887), 93–94.

60. Paul Avrich, *The Haymarket Tragedy* (Princeton, NJ: Princeton University Press, 1984), 205–11.

61. *In the Supreme Court of Illinois, Northern Grand Division. March Term, A.D. 1997. August Spies et al., vs. The People of the State of Illinois. Abstract of Record,* 2 vols. (Chicago: Barnard and Gunthrope, 1887), 2:266, quoted in Avrich, *Haymarket Tragedy,* 211.

62. See Avrich, *Haymarket Tragedy,* 213–39.

63. See ibid., 213–39, 272, 277; Sender Garlin, *William Dean Howells and the Haymarket Era* (New York: American Institute for Marxist Studies, 1979), 6.

64. Quoted in Michael J. Schaack, *Anarchy and Anarchists* (Chicago: F. J. Schulte, 1889), 403.

65. William Dean Howells, *Selected Letters of W. D. Howells,* ed. Robert C. Leitz, 5 vols. (Boston: Twayne, 1980), 3:194, 193.

66. On the court's "bad tendency" test, see Rabban, *Free Speech,* 1–21.

67. See, for example, Alexander, *Realist as Humanist,* 134–35.

68. Dimock, *Residues of Justice,* 163–64.

69. Kaplan, *Social Construction,* 56–57.

70. *Gompers v. Buck's Stove & Range Co.,* 221 U.S. 436–37 (1911). On the case, see Rabban, *Free Speech,* 171.

CHAPTER 4

1. From the original text of Stephen Crane, "An Experiment in Misery," printed in the *New York Press,* April 22, 1894, 2. A copy of this opening is reprinted in *Stephen Crane: Tales, Sketches, and Reports,* ed. Fredson Bowers (Charlottesville: University of Virginia Press, 1973), 862. Future references refer to the 1973 edition and will be given parenthetically in the text.

2. Parts of this chapter have appeared previously as "Undercover Explorations of the 'Other Half,' or The Writer as Class Transvestite," *Representations* 64 (fall 1998): 109–33. See also "Poor Like Me," *Cabinet* 11 (summer 2003): 47–53, for my discussion of Barbara Ehrenreich's *Nickel and Dimed* (2001), a more recent experiment in class transvestism.

3. Jack London, *People of the Abyss* (1903; repr., Oakland, CA: Star Rover House, 1982), 5. Mark Pittenger has located forty-nine published descriptions of such journeys between 1880 and 1920: see his "A World of Difference: Constructing the 'Underclass' in Progressive America," *American Quarterly* 49 (March 1997): 55. I have located several additional sources as well as more than a dozen

fictional accounts of class passing. There are numerous instances of cross-racial passing and a few examples of nonwhite undercover reportage in the United States, but for clarity and precision, I here focus exclusively on white class transvestites. Cross-racial passing is obviously motivated by different social forces, and I have found no instances of nonwhite class transvestism during the period in question. Middle-class African Americans, Latinos, Asian Americans, and Native Americans would have had little motivation to cross class lines given the prevalence of legal and extralegal efforts to enforce an already marginal social status.

4. William James, "What Makes Life Significant," in *The Writings of William James,* ed. John J. McDermott (Chicago: University of Chicago Press, 1977), 649. James's essay (originally published in 1899) is itself an interesting addition to this paradigm. For James, the "blindness" and "mediocrity" of "middle-class paradise" (647) can only be punctured by the heroic "daily lives of the laboring classes." Such heroism is, of course, not allowed to stand unaltered but must be recapitulated within the middle-class "ideal" of "depth . . . of character" (657).

5. Giorgio Mariani, *Spectacular Narratives : Representations of Class and War in Stephen Crane and the American 1890s* (New York: Peter Lang, 1992), 8. See also June Howard, *Form and History in American Literary Naturalism* (Chapel Hill: University of North Carolina, 1985); Keith Gandal, *The Virtues of the Vicious : Jacob Riis, Stephen Crane, and the Spectacle of the Slum* (New York: Oxford University Press, 1997); Rachael Bowlby, *Just Looking: Consumer Culture in Dreiser, Gissing, and Zola* (New York: Methuen, 1985).

6. Howard, *Form and History,* 95.

7. Ibid., 79.

8. Peter Hitchcock, "Slumming," in *Passing: Identity and Interpretation in Sexuality, Race, and Religion,* ed. María Carla Sánchez and Linda Schlossberg (New York: New York University Press, 2001), 162.

9. T. J. Jackson Lears, *No Place of Grace: Antimodernism and the Transformation of American Culture* (Chicago: University of Chicago Press, 1981), 5.

10. See Pittenger, "World of Difference," 30–31.

11. I am grateful to Laura Hapke for first alerting me to the tradition of women's class transvestism.

12. Whiting Williams published a number of works that draw on his early proletarian journeys, including *What's On the Worker's Mind* (New York: Charles Scribner's Sons, 1920) and *America's Mainspring and the Great Society* (New York: F. Fell, 1967).

13. The account is published by Gregory R. Woirol as *In the Floating Army: F. C. Mills on Itinerant Life in California, 1914* (Urbana: University of Illinois Press, 1992), 1, 3.

14. Paul Boyer, *Urban Masses and Moral Order in America, 1820–1920* (Cambridge, MA: Harvard University Press, 1978), 278–79, 287. See also Carrie Tirado Bramen, *The Uses of Variety: Modern Americanism and the Quest for National Distinctiveness* (Cambridge, MA: Harvard University Press, 2000).

15. Agee and Evans's text is, I trust, well enough known. The following is Paramount's summary of *Sullivan's Travels* (written without irony): "A successful Hollywood director disguises himself as a bum and sets off to see America from the bottom up. In the midst of the brutality and despair, he makes a valuable discovery—that what the downtrodden need most is laughter."

16. The recent phenomenon of Barbara Ehrenreich's immensely successful tale of class passing, *Nickel and Dimed: On (Not) Getting By in America* (New York: Henry Holt, 2001), and its theatrical adaptation suggest that the recent boom and subsequent bust in technology stock may produce another wave of class-transvestite reportage. See also Benjamin Cheever, *Selling Ben Cheever: Back to Square One in a Service Economy* (New York: St. Martin's, 2001).

17. Paul T. Ringenbach, *Tramps and Reformers, 1873–1916: The Discovery of Unemployment in New York* (Westport, CT: Greenwood, 1973), 39–81.

18. Robert Bremner, *From the Depths: The Discovery of Poverty in the United States* (New York: New York University Press, 1956), 142.

19. Francis Wayland, "A Paper on Tramps" (paper presented at the American Social Science Association, Saratoga, NY, September 6, 1877).

20. See Ringenbach, *Tramps and Reformers,* 43–47; Carlos A. Schwantes, *Coxey's Army: An American Odyssey* (Lincoln: University of Nebraska Press, 1985).

21. C. S. Denny, "The Whipping-Post for Tramps," *Century* 49 (1895): 794. On the legal rights of tramps, see Amy Dru Stanley, "Beggars Can't Be Choosers: Compulsion and Contract in Postbellum America," *Journal of American History* 78 (1992): 1265–93.

22. There is little specific information on Jack London's time in Coxey's "army." See Joan London, *Jack London and His Times: An Unconventional Biography* (New York: Book League of America, 1939), 71–72; Richard Etulain, introduction to *Jack London on the Road: The Tramp Diary and Other Hobo Writings* (Logan: Utah State University Press, 1979), 1–27.

23. "The Road" appears in Etulain, *Jack London on the Road,* 69–79. Future references will be given parenthetically in text.

24. Josiah Flynt, *Tramping with the Tramps* (New York: Century, 1993), ix. Future references will be given parenthetically in text.

25. See Boyer, *Urban Masses,* 159.

26. Ruth Hutchinson Crocker, *Social Work and Social Order: The Settlement Movement in Two Industrial Cities, 1889–1930* (Chicago: University of Illinois Press, 1992), 2.

27. Alvan Francis Sanborn, *Moody's Lodging House and Other Tenement Sketches* (Boston, 1895), 8. Future references will be given parenthetically in text.

28. Gandal, *Virtues of the Vicious,* 64–65.

29. Jacob Riis, *How the Other Half Lives: Studies among the Tenements of New York* (1896; Repr., Mineola, NY: Dover, 1971), 233.

30. London, *People of the Abyss,* 28.

31. Walter Wyckoff, *The West,* vol. 2 of *The Workers: An Experiment in Reality,* 2 vols. (New York: Charles Scribner's Sons, 1897–98), 4; Walter Wyckoff, *The East,* vol. 1 of *The Workers,* 181.

32. London, *People of the Abyss,* 8, 13–14.

33. Wyckoff, *The East,* 124.

34. Claudia B. Kidwell and Margaret C. Christman, *Suiting Everyone: The Democratization of Clothing in America* (Washington, DC: Smithsonian Institution Press, 1974), 115.

35. Marjorie Garber, *Vested Interests: Cross-Dressing and Cultural Anxiety* (New York: Routledge, 1992), 16.

36. Bessie Van Vorst and Marie, *The Woman Who Toils: Being the Experiences of Two Gentlewomen as Factory Girls* (New York: Doubleday, Page, 1903), 5, 19–20.

37. Wyckoff, *The East*, 61.

38. See Stuart Blumin, *The Emergence of the Middle Class* (New York: Cambridge University Press, 1989), 1–16, 258–97.

39. Karen Halttunen, *Confidence Men and Painted Women: A Study of Middle-Class Culture in America, 1830–1870* (New Haven, CT: Yale University Press, 1982), xvi, xvii. See also John F. Kasson, *Rudeness and Civility: Manners in Nineteenth-Century Urban America* (New York: Hill and Wang, 1990).

40. Lears, *No Place of Grace*, 5.

41. Frederick Jackson Turner, *The Frontier in American History,* with a foreword by Wilbur Jacobs (Tucson: University of Arizona Press, 1994), 4.

42. Melissa Dabakis, "Douglas Tilden's *Mechanics Fountain:* Labor and the 'Crisis of Masculinity' in the 1890s," *American Quarterly* 47 (June 1995): 219. See also Mark C. Carnes and Clyde Griffen, eds., *Meanings for Manhood: Constructions of Masculinity in Victorian America* (Chicago: University of Chicago Press, 1990); Gail Bederman, *Manliness and Civilization: A Cultural History of Gender and Race in the United States, 1880–1917* (Chicago: University of Chicago Press, 1995).

43. For an arresting discussion of a number of these movements, see Mark Seltzer, *Bodies and Machines* (New York: Routledge, 1992), 147–72. Lears (*No Place of Grace,* 59–96) discusses the craft revival as, in part, a masculinist response to industrialism.

44. S. Weir Mitchell, *Wear and Tear, or Hints for the Overworked* (1871; repr., Philadelphia: Lippincott, 1887).

45. For more on the work cure, see Gail Pike Hercher, "The Work Cure at Devereux Mansion," *Essex Institute Historical Collections* 116, no. 2 (1980): 101–10; Edward Van Every, *Muldoon, the Solid Man of Sport* (New York: Frederick A. Stokes, 1929). Edwin Lassetter Bymner satirically responds to Charlotte Perkins Gilman's "The Yellow Wallpaper" and to the ongoing debate about the rest cure, in his celebration of the work cure, "Diary of a Nervous Invalid," *Atlantic Monthly,* January 1893, 33–46.

46. See Richard W. Dowell, introduction to *An Amateur Laborer,* by Theodore Dreiser (Philadelphia: University of Pennsylvania Press, 1983), xii–lv. Though Dreiser published a number of autobiographical and fictional pieces that drew on his time in poverty, in the sanitarium, and as a laborer, the manuscript that would become *An Amateur Laborer* remained unpublished in his lifetime.

47. Ibid., 46.

48. Theodore Dreiser, "Scared Back to Nature," *Harper's Weekly,* May 16, 1903, 816.

49. Dreiser, *Amateur Laborer,* 163.

50. Ibid., 146.

51. Though written soon after his period of unemployment, "On Being Poor" was not published until 1923, in *The Color of a Great City* (New York: Mobi and Liveright). "The Toil of the Laborer" was rejected by all the leading periodicals for being too "dark" (Dowell, introduction to *Amateur Laborer,* xxxi). It was finally published in the *New York Call,* July 13, 1913, 11.

52. Wyckoff, *The East,* vii, 47, 49.

53. Ibid., 216, 218–19.

54. Ibid., 220.

55. Though slightly different in intent, Mark Twain's *The Prince and the Pauper* (1882) precedes *Murvale Eastman* by seven years. The idea of a disguised journey across class boundaries may have first been introduced into U.S. fiction by the penny press and the dime novel industry. For a discussion of a group of dime novels of the 1870s that use the figures of the undercover Pinkerton detective and the agent provocateur, see Michael Denning, *Mechanic Accents: Dime Novels and Working-Class Culture in America* (New York: Verso, 1987), 118–48.

56. Otto Olsen, *Carpetbagger's Crusade: The Life of Albion Winegar Tourgée* (Baltimore: Johns Hopkins Press, 1965).

57. Albion Tourgée, *Murvale Eastman, Christian Socialist* (1889; repr., Upper Saddle River, NJ: Gregg, 1968). Future references will be given parenthetically in text.

58. Jonathan Auerbach, *Male Call: Becoming Jack London* (Durham, NC: Duke University Press, 1996).

59. John Sutherland, introduction to *The Sea-Wolf,* by Jack London (1904; repr., New York: Oxford University Press, 1992), xii. Future references will be given parenthetically in text.

60. Jack London, "South of the Slot," in *The Social Writings of Jack London,* ed. Philip Foner (Secaucus, NJ: Citadel, 1966), 260. Future references will be given parenthetically in text.

61. London, *People of the Abyss,* 32, 55, 39.

62. See C. F. G. Masterman, ed., *The Heart of the Empire: Discussions of Problems of Modern City in England* (1901; repr., New York: Harper and Row, 1973).

63. London, *People of the Abyss,* 221; Robert Peluso, "Gazing at Royalty: Jack London's *The People of the Abyss* and the Emergence of American Imperialism," in *Rereading Jack London,* ed. Leonard Cassuto and Jeanne Reesman (Stanford, CA: Stanford University Press, 1996), 55–74. Although Peluso argues that London's racism clearly allies him with the colonizing dictates of the American imperialist, such racism was just as apparent within the anti-imperialist movement, which feared the effects of cross-racial amalgamation.

64. Jane Addams, *Twenty Years at Hull-House* (1910; repr., New York: Penguin, 1998), 83, 51.

65. Jane Addams, "The Subjective Necessity for Social Settlements," in *Philanthropy and Social Progress* (New York: Tomas Crowell, 1893), 11. *Philanthropy and Social Progress* collects seven essays by various authors and also includes Addams's "The Objective Value of Social Settlement."

66. Laura Hapke, *Tales of the Working Girl: Wage-Earning Women in American Literature, 1890–1925* (New York: Twayne, 1992), 49.

67. Van Vorst and Marie, *Woman Who Toils,* 4.

68. Carroll Smith-Rosenberg, *Disorderly Conduct: Visions of Gender in Victorian America* (New York: Knopf, 1985), 252, 263.

69. Van Vorst and Marie, *Woman Who Toils,* 80–81.

70. Rheta Childe Dorr and William Hard's "The Woman's Invasion" ran serially in *Everybody's Magazine* from November 1908 to April 1909. The quotes in

text are from, respectively, part 4, "The Long March Up and Around," February 1909, 238; part 1, "Fall River, an Outpost on the Edge of the Future," November 1908, 591, 585; part 5, "Humanizing Industry," March 1909, 373; and part 1, 587.

71. Allison Berg, *Mothering the Race: Women's Narratives of Reproduction, 1890–1930* (Urbana: University of Illinois Press, 2002), 4.

72. Burt Bender, *The Descent of Love: Darwin and the Theory of Sexual Selection in American Fiction, 1871–1926* (Philadelphia: University of Pennsylvania Press, 1996), 1.

73. Ann Schofield examines *Sealskin and Shoddy* in "From 'Sealskin and Shoddy' to 'The Pig-Headed Girl': Patriarchal Fables for Workers," in *"To Toil the Livelong Day": America's Women at Work, 1780–1980*, ed. Carol Groneman and Mary Beth Norton (Ithaca, NY: Cornell University Press, 1987), 112–24. Schofield also uses it to begin her collection *Sealskin and Shoddy: Working Women in American Labor Press Fiction, 1870–1920* (New York: Greenwood, 1988). In both cases, she bases her assessment of the text's status as a piece of "labor press fiction" on its serialization in the Knights of Labor's *Journal of United Labor* (July 19, 1888–November 1, 1888). *Sealskin and Shoddy* was, however, previously serialized in the *Detroit Evening News* (February 13, 1888–March 19, 1888), a liberal paper with a heterogeneous audience.

74. Schofield, *Sealskin and Shoddy: Working Women in American Labor Press Fiction*, 115.

75. Ibid., 148.

76. Denning, *Mechanic Accents*, 185–200.

77. Margaret Sherwood, *Henry Worthington, Idealist* (New York: Macmillan, 1899), 15, 53. Future references will be given parenthetically in text.

78. Charlotte Perkins Gilman discusses the industrialization of housework and child care more fully in *Women and Economics: The Economic Factor between Men and Women as a Factor in Social Evolution* (Boston: Small, Maynard, 1898).

79. Charlotte Perkins Gilman, *What Diantha Did* (New York: Charlton, 1910), 239–40.

80. Ibid., *What Diantha Did*, 249, 250.

81. Cornelia Stratton Parker, *Working with the Working Woman* (New York: Harper and Brothers, 1922), ix.

82. Leon Fink, *In Search of the Working Class: Essays in American Labor History* (Urbana: University of Illinois Press, 1994), 219–20. See also Christopher Lasch's "The Moral and Intellectual Rehabilitation of the Ruling Class," in *The World of Nations: Reflections on American History, Politics, and Culture* (New York: Knopf, 1973), 80–99; David Montgomery, *The Fall of the House of Labor: The Workplace, the State, and American Labor Activism, 1865–1925* (New York: Cambridge University Press, 1987), 171–213.

83. Martha Banta, *Taylored Lives: Narrative Productions in the Age of Taylor, Veblen, and Ford* (Chicago: University of Chicago Press, 1993).

84. Herbert Gutman, "Work, Culture, and Society in Industrializing America," *American Historical Review* 78 (June 1973): 531–88.

85. Frederick Winslow Taylor, *The Principals of Scientific Management* (New York: W. W. Norton, 1967), 32.

CHAPTER 5

1. J. M. Mancini, "'One Term Is as Fatuous as Another': Responses to the Armory Show Reconsidered," *American Quarterly* 51 (December 1999): 834.

2. These reactions are quoted in Milton Brown, *The Story of the Armory Show* (New York: Abbeville, 1988), 110. Jerrold Seigel comments on these reactions in his valuable study *The Private Worlds of Marcel Duchamp: Desire, Liberation, and the Self in Modern Culture* (Berkeley: University of California Press, 1995), 7.

3. Kenyon Cox, "The 'Modern' Spirit in Art: Some Reflections Inspired by the Recent International Exhibition," *Harper's Weekly*, March 15, 1913, 10.

4. Mancini, "'One Term,'" 835.

5. Martin Green, *New York 1913: The Armory Show and the Paterson Strike Pageant* (New York: Charles Scribner's Sons, 1988), 4, 7.

6. Ibid., 6.

7. Louis Fraina, *New Review*, December 1913, 964, 965.

8. This pairing is not as random as it may seem. After the Industrial Workers of the World lost the Paterson strike, it moved to Detroit to organize workers in the nascent auto industry. See Stephen Meyer III, *The Five Dollar Day: Labor Management and Social Control in the Ford Motor Company, 1908–1921* (Albany: State University of New York Press, 1981), 89–92.

9. Ibid., 11.

10. Harry Braverman, *Labor and Monopoly Capital: The Degradation of Work in the Twentieth Century* (New York: Monthly Review, 1974), 171.

11. Frank Gilbreth and Lillian Gilbreth, *Fatigue Study: The Elimination of Humanity's Greatest Unnecessary Waste* (New York: Routledge, 1919), 121.

12. Anson Rabinbach, *The Human Motor: Energy, Fatigue, and the Origins of Modernity* (New York: Basic, 1990), 93.

13. Frederick Winslow Taylor, *The Principles of Scientific Management* (New York: W. W. Norton, 1967), 142–43.

14. T. S. Eliot, *Notes toward the Definition of Culture* (London: Faber and Faber, 1948), 45.

15. See particularly Cary Nelson, *Repression and Recovery: Modern American Poetry and the Politics of Cultural Memory, 1910–1945* (Madison: University of Wisconsin Press, 1989).

16. Perry Anderson, "Modernity and Revolution," in *Marxism and the Interpretation of Culture*, ed. Cary Nelson and Lawrence Grossberg (Urbana: University of Illinois Press, 1988), 324.

17. Anthony Giddens, "Modernism and Postmodernism," *New German Critique* 22 (winter 1981): 16.

18. Carl Sandburg, *Chicago Poems* (1915; repr., Mineola, NY: Dover, 1994), 1.

19. Walter Benjamin, "On Some Motifs in Baudelaire," in *Illuminations: Essays and Reflections*, ed. Hannah Arendt (New York: Schocken, 1969), 174, 176, 162.

20. Elsa Nettels, *Language, Race, and Social Class in Howells's America* (Lexington: University Press of Kentucky, 1988), 62–71 and passim.

21. Michael North, *The Dialect of Modernism: Race, Language, and Twentieth-Century Literature* (New York: Oxford University Press, 1994), [v].

22. Walter Benn Michaels, *Our America: Nativism, Modernism, and Pluralism* (Durham, NC: Duke University Press, 1995), 2.

23. J. C. C. Mays, "Early Poems: From 'Prufrock' to 'Gerontion,'" in *The Cambridge Companion to T. S. Eliot*, ed. A. David Moody (Cambridge: Cambridge University Press, 1994), 110.

24. On the scandal caused by the publication of Eliot's early verse, especially the pornographic and racist poems he sent to Ezra Pound, see Vince Passaro, "A Flapping of the Scolds: The Literary Establishment Descends on T. S. Eliot," *Harper's Monthly*, January 1997, 62–68; Richard Poirier, review of *Inventions of the March Hare: Poems, 1909–1917*, ed. Christopher Ricks, *New Republic*, April 28, 1997, 36–45.

25. Mays, "Early Poems," 110.

26. Though Terry Eagleton apparently had no access to the notebook poems, he has also argued that Eliot's early poetry (in this case, his early published poetry) is a search for the objective correlative. See Eagleton's *Exiles and Émigrés: Studies in Modern Literature* (New York: Schocken, 1970), 138–78.

27. Gregory Jay, "Postmodernism in *The Waste Land:* Women, Mass Culture, and Others," in *Rereading the New: A Backward Glance at Modernism*, ed. Kevin Dettmar (Ann Arbor: University of Michigan Press, 1992), 237. Eliot's musical titles in the notebook include "First Caprice," "Second Caprice," "Fourth Caprice," "Interlude in London," "Opera," "Suite Clownesque," "Interlude: In a Bar," "The Little Passion," and "Airs of Palestine, No. 2." Christopher Ricks discusses this in his excellent notes to T. S. Eliot, *Inventions of the March Hare*, ed. Christopher Ricks (New York: Harcourt Brace, 1996), 107. Future references to notebook poems refer to this edition and will be given parenthetically in text.

28. T. S. Eliot, "Dante," in *The Sacred Wood: Essays on Poetry and Criticism* (London: Methuen, 1920), 169.

29. James Buzard, "Eliot, Pound, and Expatriate Authority," *Raritan* 13, no. 3 (1994): 114.

30. Charles Baudelaire, *The Poems in Prose*, trans. Francis Scarfe (London: Anvil, 1989), 197.

31. David Chinitz, "T. S. Eliot and the Cultural Divide," *PMLA* 110, no. 2 (1995): 239, 245.

32. Ibid., 239.

33. Peter Nicholls, *Modernisms: A Literary Guide* (Berkeley: University of California Press, 1995), 115. Though Nicholls makes this observation in a discussion of Baudelaire's "Carion," his point has wider applicability.

34. Feminist Eliot scholars have made this point in a different context. See M. Teresa Gilbert-Maceda, "T. S. Eliot on Women: Women on T. S. Eliot," in *T. S. Eliot at the Turn of the Century*, ed. Marianne Thormählen (Lund, Sweden: Lund University Press, 1994), 105–19; Carol Christ, "Gender, Voice, and Figuration in Eliot's Early Poetry," in *T. S. Eliot: The Modernist in History*, ed. Ronald Bush (Cambridge: Cambridge University Press, 1991), 23–37.

35. Eliot, "Tradition and Individual Talent," in *Sacred Wood*, 53.

36. T. S. Eliot, "Hamlet and His Problems," in *The Selected Prose of T. S. Eliot*, ed. Frank Kermode (New York: Harcourt Brace Jovanovich, 1975), 48.

37. Eagleton, *Exiles and Émigrés*, 139.

38. Ricks provides this date in Eliot, *Inventions*, xv.

39. T. S. Eliot, *The Waste Land, and Other Poems*, selected and introduced by Helen Vendler (New York: Signet, 1998), 6.

40. Ibid., 8–9; ellipsis in original.

41. Ricks notes this in Eliot, *Inventions*, 177.

42. Eliot, *Waste Land*, 9; ellipsis in original.

43. Helen Vendler, introduction to Eliot, *Waste Land*, xviii. The quoted passage from "The Love Song of J. Alfred Prufrock" occurs in Eliot, *Waste Land*, 11.

44. Gertrude Stein, *Three Lives*, ed. Linda Wagner-Martin (1909; repr., Boston: Bedford/St. Martin's, 2000), 87. Future references will be given parenthetically in text.

45. See Wendy Steiner, *Exact Resemblance to Exact Resemblance: The Literary Portraiture of Gertrude Stein* (New Haven, CT: Yale University Press, 1978), 54.

46. Ibid., 24.

47. Lisa Ruddick, *Reading Gertrude Stein: Body, Text, Gnosis* (Ithaca, NY: Cornell University Press, 1990), 14

48. See ibid., 14.

49. William James, *Psychology: The Briefer Course* (1892; repr., New York: Harper and Row, 1961), 44. Unless noted, further quotes from James are from this edition and will be given parenthetically in text.

50. In *The Autobiography of Alice B. Toklas*, Stein has Toklas remark: "The three geniuses of whom I wish to speak are Gertrude Stein, Pablo Picasso and Alfred Whitehead. . . . I have known only three first class geniuses and in each case on sight within me something rang" (Gertrude Stein, *The Autobiography of Alice B. Toklas*, in *Selected Writings of Gertrude Stein*, ed. Carl Van Vechten [New York: Vintage, 1990], 5).

51. For an extremely cogent reading of the relationship between Stein's writing and science, see Steven Meyer, *Irresistible Dictation: Gertrude Stein and the Correlations of Writing and Science* (Stanford, CA: Stanford University Press, 2001). Unfortunately, Meyer's book mentions Stein's *Three Lives* only in passing.

52. Leon M. Solomons and Gertrude Stein, "Normal Motor Automatism," *Psychological Review* 3 (1896): 493. Future references will be given parenthetically in text.

53. Eliot, "Hamlet and His Problems," 48.

54. Gertrude Stein, "The Gradual Making of *The Making of the Americans*," in *Lectures in America* (1935; repr., New York: Random House, 1975), 138.

55. Gertrude Stein, "Cultivated Motor Automatism; A Study of Character in Its Relation to Attention," *Psychological Review* 5 (1898): 295. Future references will be given parenthetically in text.

56. Steiner, *Exact Resemblance*, 33.

57. Priscilla Wald, *Constituting Americans: Cultural Anxiety and Narrative Form* (Durham, NC: Duke University Press, 1995), 271.

58. Steiner, *Exact Resemblance*, 40.

59. Edmund Wilson, *Axel's Castle* (New York: Charles Scribner's Sons, 1959), 253.

60. B. L. Reid, *Art by Subtraction: A Dissenting Opinion of Gertrude Stein* (Norman: University of Oklahoma Press, 1958), 182–83.

61. Stein, *Autobiography of Alice B. Toklas,* 50.

62. Gertrude Stein, "A Transatlantic Interview," in *A Primer for the Gradual Understanding of Gertrude Stein,* ed. Robert Haas (Los Angeles: Black Sparrow, 1971), 15.

63. North, *Dialect of Modernism,* 59–76.

64. Gertrude Stein, the *Making of Americans* notebooks, Gertrude Stein Collection, Yale Collection of American Literature, Beinecke Rare Book and Manuscript Library, Yale University, p. 47 of Leon Katz's transcription of notebook DB, quoted in Ruddick, *Reading Gertrude Stein,* 33.

65. Gertrude Stein, "Composition as Explanation," in *Selected Writings,* 514, 513, 516.

66. Gertrude Stein, "How Writing Is Written" (lecture delivered to the Choate School, Wallingford, CT, 1935), transcribed in William Rose Benét and Norman Holmes Pearson, eds., *The Oxford Anthology of American Literature* (New York: Oxford University Press, 1938), 1446–51; the quoted passage occurs on p. 1449.

67. Stein, "Composition as Explanation," 513.

68. Stein, "How Writing Is Written," 1447.

69. Stein, "Composition as Explanation," 522.

70. Gertrude Stein to Mabel Weeks, 1906, the *Making of Americans* notebooks, Gertrude Stein collection, Yale Collection of American Literature, Beinecke Rare Book and Manuscript Library, Yale University.

71. Quoted in Wald, *Constituting Americans,* 239–40. Though Wald's reading of this letter is different from mine, I find her argument very valuable.

72. See ibid., 241.

73. Graeme Tytler, *Physiognomy in the European Novel: Faces and Fortunes* (Princeton, NJ: Princeton University Press, 1982), 68.

74. Ibid., 5.

75. Henry James, *Great Short Works of Henry James* (New York: Harper and Row, 1966), 7–8.

76. Peter Brooks, *The Melodramatic Imagination: Balzac, Henry James, Melodrama, and the Mode of Excess* (New Haven, CT: Yale University Press, 1976), 126. See also Christopher Rivers, *Face Value: Physiognomical Thought and the Legible Body in Marivaux, Lavater, Balzac, Gautier, and Zola* (Madison: University of Wisconsin Press, 1994), 6.

77. Donald Sutherland, *Gertrude Stein: A Biography of Her Work* (New Haven, CT: Yale University Press, 1951), 50.

78. Ruddick, *Reading Gertrude Stein,* 33–54; Marianne DeKoven, *A Different Language: Gertrude Stein's Experimental Writing* (Madison: University of Wisconsin Press, 1983), 27–45.

79. DeKoven, *Different Language,* 41.

80. Donald Sutherland, "Gertrude Stein and the Twentieth Century," in Haas, *A Primer for the Gradual Understanding of Gertrude Stein,* 147–48, 148.

81. Sutherland, *Gertrude Stein: A Biography,* 34.

82. Gertrude Stein, "A Transatlantic Interview," 26–27.

83. I have already cited both Sutherland and Simpson. Richard Bridgeman's still very useful study is *Gertrude Stein in Pieces* (New York: Oxford University Press, 1970).

84. Jayne L. Walker, *The Making of a Modernist: Gertrude Stein from "Three Lives" to "Tender Buttons"* (Amherst: University of Massachusetts Press, 1984) 23.

85. Sutherland, *Gertrude Stein: A Biography,* 37.

86. Walker, *Making of a Modernist,* 24, 24–25, 27.

87. Ibid., 31.

88. Ruddick, *Reading Gertrude Stein,* 18.

89. William James, *The Principles of Psychology* (Cambridge, MA: Harvard University Press), 285.

90. Ruddick, *Reading Gertrude Stein,* 53.

91. DeKoven, *Different Language,* xix.

CHAPTER 6

1. Philip Rahv, "Proletarian Literature: A Political Autopsy," *Southern Review* 4 (winter 1939): 624, 623.

2. Barbara Foley charts this journey in detail in *Radical Representations: Politics and Form in U.S. Proletarian Fiction, 1929–1941* (Durham, NC: Duke University Press, 1993), 15–29, as does James Murphy in *The Proletarian Moment: The Controversy over Leftism in Literature* (Urbana: University of Illinois Press, 1991), 1–18.

3. While a complete set of *The New Masses* (May 1926 to January 1948) exists on microfilm in NYU's Tamiment library, I have found it incomplete insofar as its issues are frequently missing their mastheads and do not always supply page/issue/volume number. For my purposes, I have decided to be as complete as possible with supplying this information when it is available, and therefore often inconsistent with my citations. "Lenin on Working Class Literature," trans. Anna Rochester, *New Masses* 5 (October 1929): 7.

4. Granville Hicks, *The Great Tradition: An Interpretation of American Literature since the Civil War,* 2nd ed. (New York: Macmillan, 1935); V. F. Calverton, *The Liberation of American Literature* (New York: Charles Scribner's Sons, 1932).

5. On the modernism/antimodernism debate, see Alan Wald, *Exiles from a Future Time: Forging the Mid-Twentieth-Century Literary Left* (Chapel Hill: University of North Carolina Press, 2002), 309–25; Michael Denning, *The Cultural Front: The Laboring of American Culture in the Twentieth Century* (New York: Verso, 1996), 64–67; Foley, *Radical Representations,* 54–63; Marcus Klein, "The Roots of Radicals: Experience in the Thirties," in *Proletarian Writers of the Thirties,* ed. David Madden (Carbondale: Southern Illinois University Press, 1968), 134–57.

6. Stephen Crane, "An Experiment in Misery," *New York Press* April 22, 1894, 2, reprinted in *Stephen Crane: Tales, Sketches, and Reports,* ed. Fredson Bowers (Charlottesville: University of Virginia Press, 1973), 862.

7. Joseph Freeman, introduction to *Proletarian Literature in the United States: An Anthology,* ed. Granville Hicks et al. (New York: International, 1935), 13.

8. Granville Hicks, "The Crisis in American Criticism," *New Masses* 8 (February 1933): 5.

9. Mike Gold, "A New Program for Writers," *New Masses* 5 (January 1930): 21.

10. Bessie Van Vorst and Marie, *The Woman Who Toils: Being the Experiences of Two Gentlewomen as Factory Girls* (New York: Doubleday, Page, 1903), 5.

11. Wallace Phelps and Philip Rahv, "Problems and Perspectives in Revolu-

tionary Literature," *Partisan Review* 1 (June–July 1934): 8. At the time in which Phelps and Rahv wrote this piece, they were still sympathetic to the Communist Party, and the *Partisan Review* was the official organ of the New York City branch of the party's John Reed Club, an organization that instructed working-class writers in literature and art.

12. Georg Lukács, "Propaganda or Partisanship?" abridged and translated by Leonard F. Mins, *Partisan Review* 11 (April–May 1934): 43.

13. See particularly Warren Susman, "The Culture of the Thirties," in *Culture as History: The Transformation of American Society in the Twentieth Century* (New York: Pantheon, 1983), 150–83; Richard Pells, *Radical Visions and American Dreams: Culture and Social Thought in the Depression Years* (Middletown, CT: Wesleyan University Press, 1973).

14. Daniel Aaron's *Writers on the Left: Odysseys in American Literary Communism* (1961; repr., New York: Avon, 1964) was the "big book" on leftist writing in the 1930s until Foley published her revisionist *Radical Representations* (1993). The quotations are from pp. 169 and 261 in the respective works.

15. Karl Marx, *Capital,* vol. 1, trans. Ben Fowkes (New York: Vintage, 1977), 342.

16. Richard Dyer, *Heavenly Bodies: Film Stars and Society* (New York: St. Martin's, 1986), 138.

17. Michael Staub, *Voices of Persuasion: Politics of Representation in 1930s America* (New York: Cambridge University Press, 1994), 20–21. See also Wald, *Exiles,* 17.

18. Malcolm Cowley, "Echoes of a Crime," *New Republic,* August 28, 1935, 79.

19. Mike Gold, "Lynchers in Frockcoats," *New Masses* 3 (September 1927): 6.

20. John Dos Passos, "Sacco and Vanzetti," review of *Life and Death of Sacco and Vanzetti,* by Eugene Lyons, *New Masses* 3 (November 1927): 25.

21. John Dos Passos, "They Are Dead Now—" *New Masses* 3 (October 1927): 7.

22. I am grateful to Cary Nelson for confirming this suspicion of mine. Michael Thurston discusses "They Are Dead Now—" in his *Making Something Happen: American Political Poetry between the World Wars* (Chapel Hill: University of North Carolina Press, 2001), 25.

23. Dos Passos, "They Are Dead Now—" 7.

24. James Boylan, "Publicity for the Great Depression: Newspaper Default and Literary Reportage," in *Mass Media between the Wars: Perceptions of Cultural Tension, 1918–1941,* ed. Catherine Covert and John Stevens (Syracuse, NY: Syracuse University Press, 1984), 159–75.

25. Edward Dahlberg, *Can These Bones Live* (1941; repr., New York: New Directions, 1960), 72.

26. Marcus Klein, "The Roots of Radicals: Experience in the Thirties," in Madden, *Proletarian Writers of the Thirties,* 148.

27. Meridel Le Sueur, "The Fetish of Being Outside," *New Masses* 10 (February 26, 1935): 22–23 (future references will be given parenthetically in text); Horace Gregory, "One Writer's Position," *New Masses* 10 (February 12, 1935): 20, 21. "I Was Marching" is cited in full in nn. 38 and 40.

28. The critical literature on Le Sueur is still small, but the following studies

provide a valuable starting point: Constance Coiner, *Better Red: The Writing and Resistance of Tillie Olsen and Meridel Le Sueur* (New York: Oxford University Press, 1995); Paula Rabinowitz, *Labor and Desire: Women's Revolutionary Fiction in Depression America* (Chapel Hill: University of North Carolina Press, 1991), 114–25; Robert Shulman, *The Power of Poltical Art: The 1930s Literary Left Reconsidered* (Chapel Hill: University of North Carolina Press, 2000), 41–85.

29. The quote is part of Lenin's very corporeal "A Letter to American Workingmen," *Liberator* 50 (January 1919): 10.

30. Vivian Gornick, *The Romance of American Communism* (New York: Basic, 1977), 9.

31. "Head boys" is Josephine Herbst's phrase for the male "entrepreneurs" of proletarian writing. In her reminiscences of the thirties, she indicts both the sexism of the period and the sexism of Daniel Aaron's literary history. Her private correspondence to David Madden is excerpted in the introduction to Madden, *Proletarian Writers of the Thirties*, xxi. Mike Gold's oft-cited passage is from "Go Left, Young Writers!" *New Masses* 4 (January 1929).

32. Coiner, *Better Red*, 6.

33. Rabinowitz, *Labor and Desire*, 31.

34. Ibid., 97.

35. Melvin P. Levy, "Stories of Workers," *New Masses* 6 (May 1931): 19.

36. Zelda Leknorf, letter, *New Masses* 13 (October 2, 1934): 40.

37. Editors' response to Leknorf, *New Masses* 13 (October 2, 1934): 40.

38. Meridel Le Sueur, "I Was Marching," in *Salute to Spring* (1934; repr., New York: International, 1979), 159. Future references will be given parenthetically in text.

39. Freeman, introduction to *Proletarian Literature*, 13.

40. Meridel Le Sueur, "I Was Marching," *New Masses* 12 (September 18, 1934): 16.

41. Coiner, *Better Red*, 39.

42. Caren Irr, *The Suburb of Dissent: Cultural Politics in the United States and Canada during the 1930s* (Durham, NC: Duke University Press, 1998), 181.

43. Ibid., 180.

44. Foley's *Radical Representations* (86–169) contains the best and most sympathetic account of these arguments.

45. Denning, *Cultural Front*, 23, 22.

46. Murphy's *Proletarian Moment* (particularly 1–81) provides the best guide through the various debates within the U.S. Communist Party as well as the best introduction to these debates internationally.

47. My dating as well as my use of the phrase "United Front" derives from an analysis of the *New Masses* during this period. See, for example, "Red Cards for Yellow," *New Masses* 10 (January 30, 1934): 9; "For a Literary United Front," *New Masses* 11 (April 30, 1935): 22–23. See also Murphy, *Proletarian Moment*, 55–81, 105–48.

48. Foley, *Radical Representations*, 425.

49. Granville Hicks, "Revolution and the Novel, Part 2: Complex and Collective Novels," *New Masses* 11 (April 16, 1934): 23.

50. Foley, *Radical Representations*, 400–402.

51. Ibid., 438.

52. Ibid., 414. The quote from William Rollins's *The Shadow Before* (New York: Robert McBride, 1934) occurs on Rollins's p. 47. Future references to *The Shadow Before* will be given parenthetically in text.

53. Mary Heaton Vorst, review of *The Shadow Before*, by William Rollins, *New Masses* 11 (April 17, 1934): 6.

54. Philip Rahv, "The Novelist as Partisan," *Partisan Review* 1 (April–May 1934): 50.

55. Foley, *Radical Representations*, 403.

56. Ibid., 403.

57. Ibid., 409.

58. Ibid., 422–23.

59. Toril Moi, *Sexual/Textual Politics: Feminist Literary Theory* (New York: Routledge, 1985).

60. Rabinowitz, *Labor and Desire*, 26.

61. Ibid., 27, 29, 27.

62. "Stockyard Stella—Serial Love Story—by a Group of Workers and Jane Benton," *Working Woman* 6 (January 1935): 4. Future references will be given parenthetically in text.

63. Ibid., 5.

64. "Stockyard Stella" (February 1935): 4, 5, 4, 5.

65. "Stockyard Stella" (March 1935): 5, 5, 6.

66. "Stockyard Stella" (April 1935): 5.

67. "Stockyard Stella" (March 1935): 5.

68. "Stockyard Stella" (March 1935): 5.

69. Foley, *Radical Representations*, 440.

70. Denning, *Cultural Front*, 25.

71. Kenneth Burke, "Revolutionary Symbolism in America," in *American Writers Congress*, ed. Henry Hart (New York: International, 1935), 87, 87, 88. Future references will be given parenthetically in text.

72. Denning, *Cultural Front*, 444. See also Frank Lentricchia, *Criticism and Social Change* (Chicago: University of Chicago Press, 1983), 86–112.

73. Michael Denning, for instance, roots his own celebration of the heterogeneity of culture in the 1930s in the symbolic plasticity of Popular Front populism and its symbolic reliance on "the people." See particularly his section "The People, Yes?" in *Cultural Front*, 123–36.

74. Friedrich Wolf, "Thirty Years Later: Memories of the First American Writers' Congress," *American Scholar* 35, no. 3 (summer 1966): 506.

75. Denning, *Cultural Front*, 4–21, 77–83.

76. Michael Thurston first analyzed Muriel Rukeyser's affinities with the Popular Front in his important essay "Documentary Modernism as Popular Front Poetic: Muriel Rukeyser's *Book of the Dead*," *Modern Language Quarterly* 60 (1999): 59–84. See also Thurston's chapter on *The Book of the Dead* in *Making Something Happen*, 169–210.

77. Rukeyser conveys most of these facts in the poem's segment entitled "Statement: Philippa Allen," which is on pp. 13–15 in Muriel Rukeyser, *U.S. 1* (New York: Covici Friede, 1938). Future references will be given parenthetically

in text. For a more complete history of these events, see Martin Cherniack, *The Hawk's Nest Incident: America's Worst Industrial Disaster* (New Haven, CT: Yale University Press, 1986).

78. Thurston, *Making Something Happen*, 174.

79. John Wheelwright, review of *U.S. 1*, by Muriel Rukeyser, *Partisan Review* 4 (March 1938): 55.

80. In addition to Thurston's article and book, other recent accounts of literary leftism that prominently feature Rukeyser's *The Book of the Dead* include Michael Davidson's *Ghostlier Demarcations: Modern Poetry and the Material Word* (Berkeley: University of California Press, 1997); Shulman's *Power of Poltical Art*, and Walter Kalaidjian's *American Culture between the Wars: Revisionary Modernism and Postmodern Critique* (New York: Columbia University Press, 1993).

81. William Carlos William, review of *U.S. 1*, by Muriel Rukeyser, *New Republic*, March 9, 1938, 141.

82. David Kadlec makes a similar point (though he draws very different conclusions) in "X-Ray Testimonials in Muriel Rukeyser," *Modernism/Modernity* 4, no. 1 (1998): 29.

83. See Thurston, *Making Something Happen*, 202; Shulman, *Power of Political Art*, 182, 197, 210, 214; Davidson, *Ghostlier Demarcations*, 141.

84. Denning, *Cultural Front*, 65–114.

85. Mike Gold, "Change the World!" *Daily Worker*, October 17, 1935, 5.

86. Alan Calmer, "Portrait of the Artist as a Proletarian," *Saturday Review of Literature*, July 31, 1937, 13, 14, 14.

87. On "Communism is Twentieth-Century Americanism," see Earl Browder, *The People's Front* (New York: International, 1938), 235–48. Browder was the general secretary of the Communist Party during the Popular Front era.

88. See Wald, *Exiles*, 89–90.

89. Langston Hughes, "Let America Be America Again," in *A New Song* (New York: International Workers Order, 1938), 9. Future references are to this edition and will be given parenthetically in text.

90. See Shulman, *Power of Political Art*, 302–3.

91. Browder, *People's Front*, 237, 239.

92. Michael Szalay, *New Deal Modernism: American Literature and the Invention of the Welfare State* (Durham, NC: Duke University Press, 2000), 2–3.

93. Monty Noam Penkower discusses many of these writers in *The Federal Writers' Project: A Study in Government Patronage of the Arts* (Urbana: University of Illinois Press, 1977), 160 and passim. See also Jerry Mangione, *The Dream and the Deal: The Federal Writers' Project, 1935–1943* (Philadelphia: University of Pennsylvania Press, 1983).

94. On Wright and Le Sueur's arrangements with the FWP, see Penkower, *Federal Writers' Project*, 166, 163.

95. Jerrold Hirsch, *Portrait of America: A Cultural History of the Federal Writers' Project* (Chapel Hill: University of North Carolina Press, 2003), 4.

96. Christine Bold, *The WPA Guides: Mapping America* (Jackson: University Press of Mississippi, 1999), 10.

97. Douglas Wixson, *Worker-Writer in America: Jack Conroy and the Tradition of Midwestern Literary Radicalism, 1898–1990* (Urbana: University of Illinois Press,

1994), 421. Ralph Ellison is quoted in Robert S. McElvaine's *The Great Depression: America, 1929–1941* (New York: Times, 1984), 270. Anzia Yezierska, *Red Ribbon on a White Horse* (1950; repr., New York: Persea, 1987), 162. Malcolm Cowley, *The Dream of the Golden Mountains: Remembering the 1930s* (New York: Penguin, 1980), 180. Rahv, "Autopsy," 627.

98. Szalay, *New Deal Modernism*, 46–47.

99. See ibid., 55.

100. See Penkower, *Federal Writers' Project*, 32, 104.

101. Dwight Macdonald, "Mass Cult and Mid Cult," in *Against the American Grain* (London: Faber and Faber, 1979), 34, 37, 28–29, 34.

102. The term "new work writing" is explained in Tom Wayman's *Inside Job: Essays on the New Work Writing* (Madera Park, BC: Harbour, 1986).

103. James Agee and Walker Evans, *Let Us Now Praise Famous Men* (1941; repr., Boston: Houghton Mifflin, 1988), 7.

104. Richard Wright, "How 'Bigger' Was Born," in *Native Son* (1940; repr., New York: HarperPerennial, 1992), xxvii.

105. Thomas Hill Schaub, *American Fiction in the Cold War* (Madison: University of Wisconsin Press, 1991), 3–24.

106. Fredric Jameson, "Actually Existing Marxism," in *Marxism beyond Marxism,* ed. Saree Makdisi, Cesare Casarino, and Rebecca E. Karl (New York: Routledge, 1996), 21.

Index